The Essential Emma

Emma Curtis Hopkins' texts

Scientific Christian Mental Practice

High Mysticism

Resumé

from the original booklets

WISEWOMAN PRESS

An Imprint of

www.portalcenterpress.com

The Essential Emma; Emma Curtis Hopkins' texts: Scientific Christian Mental Practice, High Mysticism, and Resumé, from the original booklets.

Published 2024 by WiseWoman Press, an imprint of Portal Center Press:
www.portalcenterpress.com

ISBN: 978-1-936902-55-2

Publisher's Note:

Emma Curtis Hopkins taught formal classes in her seminaries between 1886 and 1906, after which she traveled, lecturing to large audiences and treating individuals, until her passing in 1925. Her students were enthralled by both her content and delivery, and many took verbatim records of the lectures she delivered, leading to many versions of her lessons being published over the past century.

Of the many versions of the lessons that Hopkins taught to thousands of people over the 40 years of her ministry, the 3 texts in this volume stand out as being the most authentically hers.

The set of little books that comprise the 12 lessons of Scientific Christian Mental Practice were published by her closest associates between 1927 and 1929, soon after her passing, in 1925.

At nearly the same time, the set of little books that lay out her final thoughts on the subject, High Mysticism, were published by that same group of devoted women who were there in her final days.

Then, in 1930, they published her study guide for High Mysticism, which she called Resumé.

The booklets were found in the International New Thought Alliance archives, and lovingly transcribed into the pages that make up this volume by the Rev. Michael Terranova, of WiseWoman Press, whose mission is to make all of Hopkins' materials available in print and ebook form.

A list of the published books may be found in the back pages of this volume.

Contents

Scientific Christian Mental Practice	1
High Mysticism	245
Resumé	545
Afterword	613
Bibliography of Emma Curtis Hopkins materials	615

Scientific Christian Mental Practice

Individual booklets from her lectures and notes, published in the mid-1930s by Hi Watch Fellowship members

Contents of
Scientific Christian Mental Practice

Lesson One The Statement of Being	5
Lesson Two Denials of Science	23
Lesson Three Affirmations of Science	41
Lesson Four Foundation of Faith	63
Lesson Five The Word of Faith	85
Lesson Six The Secret of the Lord	103
Lesson Seven Spring of Life	120
Lesson Eight Rending the Veil	138
Lesson Nine Righteous Judgment	159
Lesson Ten Fearlessness	181
Lesson Eleven The Way of Wisdom	202
Lesson Twelve The Crown of Glory	220

Lesson One

The Statement of Being

THERE are twelve doctrines of Jesus Christ presented in a multitude of statements. It is better to say they are the one method of Jesus Christ put in twelve settings. A diamond has many polished facets. It takes them all to make it shine. The truth has many ways in which it can be expressed. It takes all ways to make some people believe in its beauty and brightness. Each lesson will be the whole doctrine in a new way.

We will consider the first lesson. It is the first idea which mind, everywhere, in all ages, has commenced with when proclaiming that outside of and greater than any power exhibited by anything in nature, or man, is a being called God.

The first lesson in Truth is the word "God." Have you ever heard that there is a marvelous power in every word? Mary Howitt, the English poetess, tells us that there is a magical power in every word. It contains its own potentiality. You can see that if every word contains its own potentiality, then that word, which all the world agrees contains the greatest power, must be the greatest word. Plotinus (A.D. 250) lost himself seven times in a trance of ecstasy by thinking over the word "God" in his mind. God was the beginning of all. God is the presence of all. The use of the word by Plotinus, Porphyry and Spinoza, did not solve the mystery of existence for them, however. They yielded to death and feebleness, even falling into sickness sometimes, like other men and women. There was something lacking in their teaching. There was something lacking in their understanding of God, for the ideal of God is told as "My words are life to them that find them and health to all their flesh."

Jesus Christ had quite a different idea from these men, even though they loved the name of God so devotedly. "In my name preach the gospel, in my name heal the sick." "If a man keep my sayings he will never see death." What name is that which Jesus Christ used, which had such potent energy that, even when it was spoken, it would heal the sick and raise the dead? The Name is within every mind. If it is spoken it will be like letting the electricity loose which the physicist has stored in batteries.

It has been taught from the remotest times that we have the Name stored within us as concealed energy. It can perform twelve great works, by our words, whenever we use it, even without very close relation to it. If we were to use that Name directly, it would instantly work all the miracles recorded of all the mighty men of old. The speaking of words for performing cures is an ancient custom. The Zend-Avesta tells us that it is by the Divine Word that the sick are most surely cured. Sometimes the word is thought in the silent mind. It is not always by the repetition of our words that the cures are wrought. It is by the whole lines of reasoning. The study of the lines of reasoning which bring out your healing power is called the study of Metaphysics. The word Metaphysics means, above and away from the physical.

Thoughts are ideas. We study ideas. But ideas bear an important relation to each other. They make a course of reasoning. Some people study mathematics to train their minds to logical processes. But the study of mathematics does not make the thoughts and words powerful to heal the sick. Some people have believed there is a magical power in numbers just as there is great potency in words. Cornelius Agrippa of Cologne (1486), ascribed to numbers an efficacy. But no mathematician is a healer because of his mathematics. He must use the Healing Word, or the reasoning which brings down somewhat of the power of the Healing Word.

You may be filled with wonder as to what the Healing Word or Name can be. It certainly is not the word "God," for these men, who used that word continually, were not mighty healers. Spiritual Science does tell you the Name. It gives you the most direct reasoning which the word "God" brings out, and consequently gives the best healing power of any line of reasoning in the world.

There are twelve points of doctrine put forth in these lessons in plain terms. All the time you can trace other points of the same doctrine, finer and more subtle, streaming under them like fires from purer altars of meaning than words can kindle. The very finest fires of meaning I cannot tell you in words; you must be of an esoteric or spiritual nature, to read them while I am talking.

We call Metaphysics the Science of Life, because to know pure Metaphysics is to renew the life and make death and accident impossible.

We call Metaphysics the Science of Health, because to know Metaphysics is to be perfectly well and free from liability to sickness or disease of any kind.

We call Metaphysics the Science of Strength, because to know Metaphysics is to be strong beyond any strength you have ever dreamed of. Nothing is too hard for those who are strong with the strength of Metaphysics.

We call Metaphysics the Science of Support, because whoever studies the Science finds his support coming to him in a new way, and he cannot come to actual want, no matter who would have failed if they had been put in his place. The prophecy of Jeremiah and Isaiah comes to pass to whoever studies Metaphysics without blundering in his reasonings. "Bread shall be given him, his water shall be sure."

We call Metaphysics the Science of Defense and Protection, for no ill can come nigh the dwelling of one who puts his trust in the Principle taught by this Science. "His place of defense shall be the munitions of rocks."

This Science of Life, Truth, Love, Substance and Intelligence, is for all who look into it profoundly. Outside of Metaphysics the world is trying for its life by physical performances; working at machinery, books, commerce, cooking, washing, eating, governing each other, employing each other, killing and using animals, wearing fingers and bones into the grave to make a living. But the whole system of living by material efforts is wrong. "Turn unto me, for why will ye die?" saith the Spirit. Death is the reward of hard effort to live by material actions. If you will look into the Science of Spirit you will see that your life is meant to be sustained by the Science of God and not by the science of matter.

God is Spirit, therefore it is the Science of Spirit which we are to study when we open the reasoning with the word "God." God is the name for that Intelligence which out of its own substance bestowed upon you that intelligence you now have. Intelligence is Mind. Thus it is plain that by opening our study with the word "God" we are beginning the study of Mind.

By Mind alone we are taught we are to live and be strong. By Mind alone we are supported and defended. The further on we get in the Science, the more confident we become that it is by words that proceed from the mouth of God that we are to live. Jesus Christ taught this. He was ministered unto by angels, and said: "Man shall not live by bread alone, but by every word that proceedeth out of the mouth of God." This means that God has a way of giving freely from His Mind words that will make alive. He spoke of the manna, which the Jews had eaten while wandering 40 years in the wilderness, as so far from the real bread that the Jews all died. He showed over and over again that the Word is a bread that will keep the life in the body forever. "If a man will eat of the bread that I will give him, he shall never die."

As nearly as possible, the twelve lessons which we now begin will take the absolute meanings of the words of Jesus Christ. If we take the absolute meanings, dear friends, we are obliged to say that our life needs no material or physical effort to keep it forever. It needs only the true Word of God. It is not profitable to say that our life needs no material support. It is only profitable to say that our life does need the Word of God. The Word of God IS Truth.

God works only in Truth.

We may throw true words down into the arena of human life and their power will be God. The power of God is freedom. Jesus Christ said that all who knew Truth would be free. What do you want to be free from? Sin, sickness, death. From these the Word of God sets absolutely free. Miracles of healing have been worked by thousands of men and women, who taught true words concerning God in some of the statements we find set forth in order by Spiritual Science.

Any lesson has the healing strength. Keep your mind open and free to receive that lesson which fits your own disposition best. No matter what type or character or disposition of mind you are, I tell you that one of these lessons strikes your key, and by speaking over and over the words which that one lesson explains, you will let the fire of your own native healing gift from Jehovah kindle health within your own body and in all your neighbors.

Elisha cured a terrible case of leprosy by one of these lessons. It was probably the second lesson. He raised the Shunammite woman's child to life by one of these lessons. It was probably the third lesson. He increased the loaves of bread to feed a hundred men. This was the fourth lesson. He would not have called it the fourth lesson, but he would have felt in his mind all the strength of the fourth lesson as we have it.

The first lesson finds out what your mind is seeking and names it. Can you name now just exactly what your mind is seeking? You would soon be set on the right track to find what you are seeking if you could name what you want. The naming of what the mind of the whole world is seeking is the first statement of Jesus Christ, and is the first lesson of Moses. It is the foundation of thought, even in the minds of the insects, It is the GOOD.

Are you not seeking Good? Why do you move your right hand? You move it to get your Good. Why do you breathe? You breathe to get your Good. Why do the stones lie still and wait? They are waiting for their Good. Why does the bird fly? It flies for its Good. Everything moves and waits for its Good. Do you see that the Good draws everything? The Good which you and I want governs everything we do. Therefore the Good which you are seeking is your God.

Spinoza was called the God-intoxicated man, because he spoke the word God so much. I am convinced that if he had spoken the word Good, instead of the word God, he would have come into a nearer relation to his God.

Moses says that Good created. The Good which you are seeking created you. Just that Good which you want is the combination of words which brought you forth. The honest statement that *"My Good is my God"* has the power to set the mind to a key which is nearer to its normal tone than it is now thinking. John said that in the beginning was the Word, and the Word was God. He also said that out of the Word were all things made and without the Word was nothing made. Paul said that a veil is forever over the face when the Word is read, because so many things have been spoken of God which are not true.

If you take the word God for your starting point, you will not start so near the foundation feeling of your mind as you will if you take the word GOOD. "I am seeking my Good, therefore I am seeking my God." The devout poet who wrote, "I was athirst for thee, the living God," would have found his healing power beginning to stream forth into his life like a fire if he had struck his lyre to the chord, "I seek my Good. My Good is my God." Therefore in the Science of Mind you may take for your first idea one word. It is the word Good. In the science of words you may take the word Good and let it lie before you like a great white stone. It has a revealing power which the word God has not.

John, the Revelator, speaks of the white stone. The white stone is a word. The word is Good. It is the name of what you want. It is the nearest approach to expressing what is in our mind that Science has thus far given us. It is evident that Science will give us the inner stone if we use the outer stone wisely. As we acknowledge that the Good we are seeking must be our God, because it pulls and pushes us all the time to see if we cannot come nearer to it, we must find ourselves better and better satisfied.

The acknowledgement that "I am seeking my Good, and my Good is my God," is telling a simple truth. It is so simple that the tiniest child can say, "I am seeking my Good, and my Good is my God, because it draws and pushes me and moves me." The child who tells this simple truth is telling aloud what the little stones are whispering without words, and the little baby who lisps this simple truth will be fed and clothed by the coming closer and closer to him of his Good.

If I should take the unspoken sentence, which lies like a hidden jewel under the jagged covering of your thoughts about the things you do not like, I would read it, *"There is Good for me and I ought to have it."* There is nothing but has in itself the conviction that there is Good belonging to it that it ought to have.

The Prince reels from the banquet hall, seeking the Good he believes he ought to have. The thief runs from the daylight seeking the Good he thinks he ought to have. But none of them speaks the simple truth about his movements. If any one of them did he would come nearer to finding his good. God, the Omnipotent Good, works through the word of Truth. Get to speaking the word of Truth, from the first to the last statement, and God will be found working for you, and through you, with almighty power.

The first name of God is Good, and the first name of the Good is God. "There is Good for me and I ought to have it," says the unconscious instinct of the worm crawling at your feet. When you look at the worm and tell the truth about it, why it moves and why it keeps still, you will be in league with its life. It will feel your unity with it. When you look at a drunkard, or miser, you will say he his seeking his Good. His heart will be better satisfied the instant you speak out what his unspoken instinct is feeling. He does not say so. If he should say so his life would come nearer being satisfying. The moment anybody speaks out the Truth of his life he has spoken the Omnipotent Principle.

The unconscious Truth is that *there is Good for me and I ought to have it*. Nothing can kill that unconscious feeling. It is indestructible. It is omnipotent. Thus the Omnipotent Truth is kept hidden in the stillness of the mind of man and the mind of the rocks. The Omnipotent Truth shall not be hidden in the stillness any longer, and the satisfaction of the living things will come when they are told that the reason they move, or do not move, is for one Good.

In the Scripture we have read, "Acknowledge me and I will pour out a blessing." "In all thy ways acknowledge Him and He will direct thy paths." To acknowledge God is to admit we are seeking our Good. It is well to give one day a week to acknowledging that we are seeking for our Good. We tell what our Good is. Is not our Good the free life we want? Do we want a burdened, obstructed hampered life? Out of the word Good name a Good which is Good to you.

The free life of the lily is the name of its Good. As the lily works out its life problem, it is telling as plainly as it can speak that its Good is its free life. You may name your Good as your free life. When you speak for yourself you speak for the world. It is the one chord to which, if you speak it, all nature will spring free. There will be no opposition to that Truth when you speak it. You can name your Good as free health. All nature will say "Amen!" if you proclaim that the Good you are seeking is free health. Nothing wants its health interfered with; it wants unlimited health.

There is a unity of feeling between you and the stones and the thief, when you tell aloud, or consciously, what they feel unconsciously about their health. The moment you feel this Truth, and speak it, the chord between yourself and your neighbor catches a new breath of health. Sometimes when you say to the sick man, mentally, that the Good he is seeking is his God, and God is free health, he will get well in five minutes. His mind was unconsciously groping around for the Divine Word that could heal him, and you spoke for him.

The prophet who felt there was something lacking in his life said: "We grope for the wall as the blind." It is better for us to speak our own words, but if somebody opens the door for us it will teach us to open the door ourselves. That is, if we do not speak our words, and so are not satisfied with Good, another may speak, and our satisfaction will come.

When we say that the Good we are seeking is our free life, we certainly do feel the breath of new life blow through us. When we tell the lifeless plant that the Good it is seeking is its free life, and its Good is God, for God is its free life, we shall see the plant revive. Everything rises to acknowledge Truth. You see that it is God, for Good is God. Sometimes you will feel the reviving life stream so hot, like a fine oil, throughout your being, while you are naming God as free life, that whatever you touch will feel thrilled with a quick sense of pleasure.

God works in Truth. Tell the Truth of God and the Omnipotent God is moving.

Nothing can resist the very first proclamation of Truth, if we let it be spoken through us. There are many names of our Good. They are all names to which all the universe will respond. The irresistible name of God is Good. It is an idea which is in everything, everywhere, and therefore you speak an omnipresent idea when you say; "I seek my Good; my Good is my God. My God is my free life. My God is my free health."

Another name of the Good we are seeking is strength. All things look for strength. They love strength. The baby laughs at every waft of strength through its little frame. The insect runs and rolls with speechless delight at every quiver of new strength. The Good it seeks is strength unlimited. It wants free, boundless strength. So do you. If you name your Good as unlimited strength, you will feel free and strong at once. As you look at some feeble woman, and think for her that the Good she is seeking is unlimited strength, she will let her mind shine with yours. She has felt that unconsciously. She will feel strength consciously. Everything you tell the Omnipotent Truth to, that its strength is God and God is its strength, will rise and be strong; and you will be stronger the more you proclaim the irresistible idea which all creation feels. It is only naming God.

Among the names of Good which we name, surely our heart strings will chord with one which will bring satisfaction into your life. So hungry is the world for satisfaction that it has been set down that the problem of life is to live and think so as to get satisfaction.

The sciences of man have not started their reasonings near enough to the foundation idea of mankind to obtain this end. At the word "God," many a mind rebels, because it has become bruised by trouble and disappointment. At the word that there is *Good for everything and it ought to have its Good*, each thing agrees.

The principle point of Truth is that satisfaction comes through mind. Mind speaking Truth through the lips, or thinking Truth consciously, can bring all the satisfaction to the world which the world is seeking.

No material process can bring health. By a Metaphysical process health will quicken and thrill mankind. Nothing material can strengthen mankind, but the Omnipotent Truth can strengthen mankind with all the power of Truth.

Another name for God is support. God is your support. As you turn to the right or the left, you turn for sustaining. You breathe for support. You hope for support, Thus one name for your Good is support. To tell any man who is poor that the Good which he is seeking is support, is to tell him a truth which his mind has held unconsciously always. The chords of his mind chime when you speak the Truth that God is his support, and his support is his God, because it is Good.

God works in Truth.

That is Truth, therefore God works for that word. It is not Truth to say that man depends upon any kind of work for his support. His work is not the Good he is seeking. God does not work in the lie which a man tells when he says he is seeking work. He must tell the Truth and God will work for him.

Support is another name for substance. Plato and Spinoza both called God the substance of the universe. All metaphysicians have called it the One Substance. The one support that man is looking for, that will absolutely satisfy him, is that kind of support which will not fail him. Let him sit down alone and tell the truth about what kind of support he is seeking. God works in Truth.

Everybody, nearly, tries to cover up the main purpose of his life. He tells all kinds of stories to himself, and others, about what he is seeking. Often he tells that all he asks is just enough to feed and clothe and house his family. Let him tell the honest Truth — *that he seeks for unlimited bounty*. Nothing can possibly satisfy anybody short of unlimited supply. God is the idea of unlimited supply which men keep covered so deeply within their minds. If you name your Good, do not fail to say: "My Good is my unlimited support, my unfailing support." The Good will soon bring you marvelous support. New provisions will be made for you. There is no limit to the bounty of Truth. The substance of Truth is shown by the happy prosperity which can come to you, and is sure to come, when you speak Truth.

Jesus Christ said that all who learned his doctrine would have a hundred-fold more possessions in this life. Tolstoy, the Russian writer, says that Christians do not have a hundredfold more than they would have if they were not Christians. (This is because they are not really Christians.)

In order to be a Christian one must tell the Truth of God. One Truth is that God the Good careth for us. We are told by Christ to take no care for ourselves. To sit down and proclaim to the universe that "My support is my Good, my Good is my God, thus God is my support," is to stir the air to work with the mountains and seas to bring me my new provisions.

Jesus Christ said we would have tribulations while getting our Good support by telling the Truth, but he said: "Be not afraid, I have overcome." He meant He had come over all the worldly way of being supported by telling the Truth, and that it would surely come out right with us.

Tribulations are the oppositions which we meet by telling the world that we get our support by thinking and speaking the Truth. Tribulations are the feelings we have when we first set forth as grown men and women into the way which is exactly opposite to our former way of thinking. It is a tribulation to attempt to cast away all anxiety. It is a tribulation to give up trying to get our living by our old mind. After practicing saying that your Good is your support, your old business will not be interesting to you. It will leave you, yet you will have your living. By and by you will have great and wonderful miracles of support come to you. Yet, for a long time, some of those who have told the Truth about their Good being unlimited supply do not have the faintest idea where their supplies are coming from. They need to say that their God is Intelligence. This is a truth that will work out soon. There will come a time when you will all know that your unlimited supplies are in certain places, and you need have no fear of ever losing sight of the rich provision of the Good.

Good is God. God is Substance. God is Spirit. Therefore your supplies are to come from Spirit. Your supplies, coming from Spirit, are Spirit. It will not be a tribulation to practice providing for yourself by telling the Truth after a little while.

Another Good you are seeking is defense, protection. Another name of Good is defense. The movements of our bodies are all with the hope of being protected from evil. To be explicit in naming our Good, which we feel is for us, we do not forget to name the Good as defense. To every living creature we say, "God is your defense." It is another chord which the unconscious mind is glad to agree with. There is a bond of unity between us and all things. Fear leaves us. Fear leaves us by telling the Truth.

Metaphysicians, in tracing the cause of evil conditions, have all agreed that fear of evil is the only evil. So, by telling the Truth, that our Good is our defense, we see that in every place where we proclaim that defense, is the Good we are seeking. That Good is our God, thus God is our defense.

Love, Life, Truth, Substance, Intelligence, are names of our Good. We may tell that our Good is Truth. This will cause our lips to speak Truth. Pilate asked, "What is Truth?" The Egyptians of the unhistorical past said, "Truth is God." The continual speaking for several years, by the Christian Scientists, that "Truth is God" finally brought them to where they could see exactly how Truth is God. It is because telling the exact Truth about what Good is, is an irresistible energy for bringing Good to pass.

Men formerly supposed it was truth to say sickness was good for them. They thought it was something sent of God. But God is Truth. Truth is a healing principle and not a sickening principle. They found much sickness following them up all the time. As soon as we say "God is not the author of sickness, God is Good, Good is Truth, Truth is God," we are brought to where we cannot tell that sickness is Good. Good is God, therefore God is health.

Love is the Good we are seeking. Love is the highest name of God, Love is the fulfilling of the law. At the height of our spiritual teachings we find God covering us with love. We find ourselves loving all things and all people. Edward Irving put his hand on a dying boy's head and said, "God loves you." The boy lived.

It is well to say that God is unbounded unlimited love. God is our love. There is an instinctive moving of all things for love. Love is another name for life. Many a dying man has been saved by feeling his mother's soft kisses on his forehead. Many a woman has lifted her dying face and lived when the sound of her son's voice was heard calling her name. Love is God. Do not forget to say 'The Good I am seeking is Love."

The heights and depths and splendors of Love have not been told. It is the name of God which Jesus Christ used. He said it so much that little children came close to his knees. Poor neglected women followed him. Blind old beggars clung to his clothes. I do not suppose it would be possible to name the Good by the magic word Love too often. Love is not something which comes to us in any one man, woman or child, and then goes away. That is only the sign of Love. Love, that is God, is eternal, infinite.

The first lesson of the Science of Mind tells the foundation idea of Mind. It has been called the Statement of Being. Being is that which is. It is certain that the Good that is for us is the Good we ought to have. How shall we arrive at our Good? How shall we get hold of our Good? Not by working with our hands, for countless ages of labor have failed. It is by the Jesus Christ method only. The Jesus Christ method is the Truth method. Jesus Christ means Truth. The Jesus Christ method brings the fulfillment of all our expectations. "I know the thoughts that I think toward you, to bring you an expected end." This expectation of Good has been a long time waiting for us to declare what our expectations are. To expect Good and to be very definite in the Mind that it IS coming, *is* to see it coming.

Many people would have their Good come instantly if they could name it, and have a clear idea of how it ought to be. A little dumb, paralyzed girl, heard the Paris doctor, Bouchert, praised so highly for his healing power, that she went to see him, and by seeing him she was cured. A blind woman heard a shoemaker praised so highly for his power in prayer that she went to him, and she felt Jesus Christ's teachings so plainly that soon her eyes burst open. Both cases had a strong and clear idea of how it would seem to be well. They felt that those men could heal them.

If you have a clear idea of how sweet life, free and unburdened, must be, look to this Science to bring you this life. And tell very plainly that sweet, free life is your Good, It will come streaming through you like the elixir vitae of the ancients. Maxwell, the Scotch doctor, caught sight of this fine, fleeting, life-fire that streams through all the world.

If you think that health is Good, have a clear idea of how sweet, joyous health would feel. Name it as the name of Good. Have a clear idea of what is your Good. It will come and settle upon you. It will sift itself through you. It can be lapped up by all the little tongues of your system.

The word Good is the only word that can make all things. Good with its descriptions is as high as our mind and speech has ascended. There is no spot or place where the idea of Good as ours cannot come. It is the one conviction of animate and inanimate things. It has never been beaten out of anything. Being undefeated and never to be defeated, it is omnipotent. It always knows that it is right. It is omniscience, Know it, and it knows all things. Let the magic name Good be the name of all names in your mind. It is the name that Jesus Christ comes to be understood by. After speaking over the names of the Good, let your mind add the name of Jesus Christ.

Another thing which the name of Jesus Christ teaches is humility and willingness. It is the meekness of character he manifested which brings us the victory over evil. He said, "The meek shall inherit the earth."

Once a man, who had become completely discouraged, determined to let his dog lead him around, for he felt that his dog was more like God than he was. He went following the dog until he led him to a wise and good woman, who led him to be a follower of Jesus Christ.

There was never any other character of history who gave orders to keep repeating his name. A large number of people will testify how wonderfully they have been led by repeating this name.

The meekness of obedience is the mystery of Godliness.

The Statement of Being was continually in the mouth of Jesus Christ. Let it be in your mouth also. Be definite when you give this statement of Good, which is the Statement of Being. Expect to see it work quickly. Truth is not slow. Truth is quick. With Truth, all is NOW. Jesus Christ said: Now is the accepted time.

Truth does not have to make things new for you. In Truth it was so from the beginning, as the first verse of Moses reads. All Truth is waiting for you to say plainly what is your Good. The speaking out continuously what we have felt and thought intuitively, is the first movement toward demonstration, toward manifestation, toward satisfaction.

Make now the statement of Good:

>*The Good I am seeking is my God—*
>*My God is my Life.*
>*The Good I am seeking is my health—*
>*God is my health.*
>*The Good I am seeking is my strength—*
>*God is my strength*
>*The Good I am seeking is my support—*
>*God is my support.*
>*The Good I am seeking is my defense—*
>*God is my defense.*
>*Life is God—*
>>*Truth is God—*
>>>*Love is God—*

Substance is God.
God is Intelligence,
    omnipresent, omnipotent, omniscient.
God is Life,
    omnipresent, omnipotent, omniscient.
God is Truth.
    omnipresent, omnipotent, omniscient.
God is Love,
    omnipresent, omnipotent, omniscient.
God is Spirit,
    omnipresent, omnipotent, omniscient.

The name "OM" was a name of God which the ancient people of Asia used to repeat, and do even repeat it now. They hold their breath while speaking it. It means: Good beyond Good. Far beyond even our ideas of Good, there is Infinite Good, waiting our words.

The people said, "Let us take with us words and go unto our God." The first words we will take with which to go unto our God are statements of our Good. That is as high as we can think or speak.

Have some special time to make the Statement of Being. This will make you a great thinker. The Mind of God will think through you. The words of God will sing through you. The skill of Spirit will work miracles through you. The judgment and beauty of God will inspire you. You will be so one with your words that you will be able to say with Jesus Christ, "I and the Father are one." You will drop off the garments of flesh. You will see that by Speaking Truth you are Spirit, and that by speaking Truth you are Omnipotent.

God works through Truth.

If you give up your mind to Truth you are all God. Your substance being the Mind of God, by speaking Truth, you can see there cannot be any disease or death or sin touch you any more than disease or sin or death can touch God. It is through realizing this that so many strong, young students have said that God had set his own name in their foreheads. They read where Moses was told to tell the Israelites that the name of the Good which was working for them was "*I that I am.*" If ever the name of this Good, which is your God, comes to you, do not hesitate to speak it. All the names of your Good which you can name are right names. Write down the names of your good which you are seeking. That will be naming God. And such a practice will be manifested in your life. God is not slow to come into the life of him who acknowledges the Good.

God works only in Truth. All Truth is all God.

There are students arising who give all their mind, might and strength to Truth.

"*If a man keeps these sayings, he shall live forever.*"

Lesson Two

Denials of Science

IF the statement of what is true from the very nature of our own mind is called to our attention then we are able to see at once what is not true.

Is there a conviction of Good belonging to you now in your own mind? That is an omnipresent conviction. Everything and everybody believes the same way.

You will notice that the moment you will acknowledge that there is Good for you which you ought to have, it arises within your mind that you do not have the Good that belongs to you. You feel that your Good is absent from you. This is also a universal feeling. Every man, woman, child, stone, stick and snail feels that its Good is somewhere else than in it or with it, This is known as the conviction of absence. The conviction of presence is not uttered. That is, we feel the idea of the Good being for us, but we do not say so, and we feel the idea of the Good being absent and we keep saying so. We think that our Good is absent. We say aloud that our Good is absent.

Do you see any possibility of entering upon your own beautiful inheritance of satisfying Good by looking this strong fact in the face? Does it not remind you that John, the wise disciple of Jesus Christ, said that without the word nothing is made? How plain it is that you have been ready with the rest of the world to say that your Good is absent from you. How plain it is that you have been silent on the main idea that there is Good for you which you ought to have. Thus it seems that the silence of your mind with respect to Good is accountable for all the appearances of what is not good.

Moses said the Spirit moved upon the face of the waters and said, "Let there be light." Moses and John were lovers of God. They felt great laws and principles moving through the universe and tried to express them. Moses did not always speak in symbols. He said to the people that the "I am that I am" spoke through him. He felt the Good within himself speak.

The moment that the idea which has always lain so silently in the mind is uttered it begins to tell great things with respect to itself. This is why it is called the Stone of Revelation — because it reveals. It brings a feeling of light and hope to the mind, and this is why Moses said, "Let there be light." He felt the strange darkness of the talk around him concerning the absence of Good, and instinctively understood the gloom of the silence as to Good. Good is the name of God. The Good that is for you is your God. Do you not move towards your Good? If you wish, is it not for your Good? Thus you are governed by your Good.

The metaphysical teaching calls attention to the law that if you tell the truth about your Good it will appear in your life. It is like speaking of the relation of numbers in arithmetic until you see exactly how they work. Repeat the multiplication tables, and sometime along the way, if you have taken the steps before multiplication, you will see that it is quick counting. If you simply repeat the tables at the dictation of another mind you may have to work a long time to find how to add by the tables of multiplication. But taking the adding and multiplication together it dawns upon you what the after process means.

The Science of Mind always runs by orderly steps in the same way. The first chapter of Genesis is the Science of Mind stated in the exact order of coming forth as power, as intelligence, as substance.

The idea of the absence of Good is plainly spoken enough. The idea of where the Good must be, and is, we are not talking about as a race. It is to the race mind that Moses addresses himself. John also speaks to the universal conviction of absence. I will tell you that between you and your

Good which belongs to you, and which you ought to have, is your idea of the absence of Good.

The second movement of your mind, after telling what truly is, you will find to be putting away your ideas that interfere with the substance of what you are seeking. You put away the absence idea the first time you speak of your idea of Good. Tell the absolute truth about your idea. Is there any absence of it? Is there any mixture of evil with your highest idea of Good? Where do you keep your idea of Good? Do you hide it in your mind and never express it? How do you know how much light might break over you and brighten your life if you would let it come up from the hidden place in your mind — your perfect idea of Good.

It is like every other mind's ideal of Good. Thus we deal with the universal Mind when we tell that in our highest ideal of Good there is no evil. We say that in our idea of Good there is no absence. The Good that we are all seeking is our Substance. It must be substantial to us. It must be present with us or it is illusion — it deludes. Here then you see why metaphysicians of all ages have made two great denials:

First — There is no evil.

Second — There is no matter.

This is because they looked so steadfastly at the word God, or Good, in their mind that its Native action began in them. The stone of revealing makes you say that there is no evil and no matter.

St. Augustine said, "There is no evil." Jehosephat said, "There is no iniquity in God." Emerson said, "Evil is negation." They did not explain that it was their idea of Good that it should have no evil mixed with it. If every man, woman and child expressed his idea of Good it would be found to be like every other person's idea of Good.

Spinoza said, "I choose to know Spirit rather than to imagine matter." Channing says that since the beginning of time, in philosophical study, men have held that all is Spirit, and that matter is but an appearance, a delusion, having no reality. Thales, the Greek, thought so. Empedocles thought so. They did not explain that it was because their idea of Good was an enduring and substantial presence that could not fail and could not disappoint. They could not tell that matter is the result of thinking that Good is absent. Matter is that appearance which results from steady silence as to what and where our Good is; we might say as to where and what the Good is upon which subject all mankind are so silent. We may say "Our Good" or you may always say "My Good," for each one of you is the unit of his own life, and all his conditions swing around himself.

Demonstration of mental science means the making visible our ideas. We must make it visible that there is no evil if the idea is true. The Truth makes free. The perfect goodness of the Good that is for me is that all I am expected to do in the case is to tell the truth about what and where Good is. Good is God. Thus the making good demonstrations will come as surely out into our life as we live, if we tell the truth about God.

Jesus Christ said, "The Truth shall make you free." Let us tell the truth. To say, "In my idea of Good there is no mixture of evil," is to tell the truth. It is a truth which will work freedom from evil. It will show that all evil is delusion. Here is where the denial of matter hurries in. Say that in your idea of Good there is no delusion. Very soon all matter will appear as delusion. You cannot say that in your idea of Good there is no mixture of evil without coming straight to the realization that all matter is delusion, built by the belief in the absence of Good, which is evil.

Carlyle speaks of the everlasting NO of this world, whereby the world seemed to be a charnel house and demoniacal, till he faced it with the stupendous "NO" of his Soul, and said to all evil "I am free." In the *Book of the Dead* we find how the Soul talks after it is not afraid of the body any more. It, the Soul, says, "I never committed adultery. I never stole from my neighbor, I never told a lie. I was never intoxicated." Every known sin is pronounced NOTHING. Formerly it was not thought safe for men to speak these ideas while walking about on this plane of existence.

Jesus Christ said that if any man would come after him he must deny himself while dealing with the world. He knew the mystic relation of boldly spoken Truth to the redemption of man from the conditions of matter. "If a man eat of the bread which I will give him, he will never die." "The flesh profiteth nothing." "The words I speak unto you, they are life."

The second lesson of his life was denial, exactly as the second lesson of Moses was denial, and exactly as all profound thinkers have given denials to all claims of mortality. It all comes of putting down the idea of Good in the mind and looking at it as to a white substance with power of revealment in it. The highest word that we know how to express is "Good." It is certain that for a progressed realization there must be another word to express what we seek, but "Good" is found to bring us out the most safely thus far.

If we put down the idea "first cause" as a foundation word to watch, it will not be long before we find ourselves knowing all about the causes of all things, whether good, bad or indifferent. Gautama Buddha thought "first cause" till he found out the causes of evil, and spent all his years seeking to combat and destroy evil.

Put down the word "satisfaction" in the mind, and it will tell you what will satisfy everybody. The idea "first cause" is very enlightening. It will take the mind back to the cause of anarchy. We can soon see that it is caused by the idea religion has given to man that we all owe so much to God. This is the wrong way to look at God, the Good. The Good owes itself to us. We have only to tell the Truth. If the Truth makes free when it is told, and we are not free, then the Truth has not been told. The Truth that the Good belongs to us, is greater than the idea we might give our time, our labor, our life, and all we are to the Good, and still never satisfy it. To tell how impossible it is for us to give enough to God broods rebellion at existing orders. To tell that the Good asks nothing of us but to receive its substance, will rest and comfort the people. The word "satisfaction" is a great word to use, but does not show forth as quickly as the word Good. Good is the universal name of God. Satisfaction is not the universal name of God.

In all sciences we deal first with general principles, applicable to all races and conditions alike, and then later we deal with particulars as applicable to special individuals. Thus we hit upon the foundation rock of our convictions when we say, "The Good that is for me is my God."

The denial of matter has never been made satisfactorily. Notice that all the metaphysicians have concluded that there is no reality in it. They have said that it is all the imagination of our mind; but what imagination it is they have not concluded. To persistently declare that there is no matter will dissolve material conditions. It will cause a swelling to disappear if you look at it and say that there is no matter. Whatever of matter seems most real to us is the first to disappear when we deny matter.

If money is something that you cling to, and you say that there is no matter, it will begin to disappear. If friends in the body of flesh are your idols they will get out of sight swiftly upon your putting forth the denial into your atmosphere. Such is the power of an idea held as truth. The denial of matter is the same as if you said that your omnipresent idea of God is that God is Spirit. Thus your God is Spirit.

Your idea of God must not be burdened with the transient and unreliable. Matter is transient and unreliable, because the idea of Good as absent is transient and unreliable. Sometimes the mind feels that its Good is near, and sometimes that it is far off. So, matter, which is the representation of the idea of absence, must sometimes bring you great darkness or void, because of loss, or bring something that pleases, you very near. The regularity of the seasons results from the periodic habit that all the race mind has of sometimes feeling that its happiness or Good is interfered with, and then feeling that its Good is near and free again.

Some people keep on the mental strain of feeling that they do not have anything that they want at all. They feel neglected, unloved, burdened nearly all the time. They are the cold, barren Northern regions. Indeed it is such types of mind that make an external region of barrenness and cold. Let every such mind rise and refuse to hold the absence idea as part of the way its Good deals with it, and the cold regions would soon disappear.

The statement that in my idea of Good there is no absence of Good, compels me to say that in my idea of Good there is no evil. The statement that there is no delay in my idea of the way Good comes to me, compels me to say that there is no matter. Matter is all the hindrance we know. Spirit is free, untrammeled, unhindered, irresistible. Matter is burdened, trammeled, limited, inert. The best way is to make the two denials of unreality boldly. If you wish to help yourself you can say, "In my idea of Good there is no mixture of evil, therefore there is no evil."

How dare you say this? Because everybody and everything feels the same about his idea of Good but never tells it. Sit down at a certain time every day and write down on paper what your idea of Good is. Write the highest ideal of Good you have. You cannot write a stroke higher than the slave's idea of Good, but you will find that such a practice will pin you down to the Truth, and it is in Truth that there is power. All the sacred books of the earth tell that God is Truth, and that Truth is God.

The bold second denial is that "There is no matter, all is Spirit." If you notice that you are opposed to any interference with your Good you can write it down that in your idea of Good there is no interference and therefore there is no matter.

If you will speak boldly that there is no matter, it will handle all your affairs on a new basis. If you say "All is Spirit, nothing is matter," that is making a denial of matter. Every time you refuse to believe any statement you are making a denial. Every time you say that a thing is not so you are making a denial. Negativing what is told you, or what seems to be real, but is not real, is a denial.

Looking up suddenly from their deep thoughts, metaphysicians have declared that "there is no life, substance or intelligence in matter." They have affirmed that all life, all substance, all intelligence is Spirit; and therefore there is no life in matter, no substance in matter, no intelligence in matter. Spirit occupies the place that matter claims to occupy, therefore life occupies the place matter claims to occupy. In the spot where matter even seems to be a dead substance the life of the Spirit is moving. Spirit is the substance where even the stones seem to be.

Spirit is the pure Intelligence. There is no place where matter seems to be intelligent, is there? Yet, *"there is no absence of life, substance or intelligence."* If the metaphysicians had said, *"There is no absence of life, substance or intelligence,"* they would have demonstrated life better than they have. For if life is Spirit, never absent, why speak of no life? And if Spirit is substance omnipotent, why speak of substance as no substance anywhere, and the same of intelligence.

It was subtle agreement with the absence on the part of the metaphysicians to speak of Intelligence as absent from anywhere. One reason why the substance of the metaphysicians has so often failed is because of saying: "There is no substance in matter." Yet, that denial in particular cases is a very healing one. As for instance: if a tumor claims to absorb the life of the body, it will disintegrate it to tell that there is no life in matter, as well as to tell that there is no matter. If darkness seems to act with an intelligence of its own or if insanity carries on as if it has shrewdness, it is a claim of

Scientific Christian Mental Practice

matter to be something, and to have an intelligence of its own opposed to Spirit. In such cases you can see that it is wise to say that there is no life, substance or intelligence in matter, as well as that there is no matter whatsoever. The metaphysicians who have had their minds set upon healing disease, insanity, deformity, etc., have been successful in their work by using this denial.

In the second lesson on general principles we are speaking entirely of certain revelations of our own mind, of the Truth, as they come forth from laying down the word Good in the mind, and making it express what controls us, moves us, and what we seek.

Therefore, the third denial is: *"There is no absence of life, substance or intelligence in my idea of Good."* Life will thrill along through every pore and cell and fibre of your being if you declare this. It will soon seem thrilling and vibrating every particle of your environment. Nothing can seem to you to be dead. If you speak often, *"There is no absence of substance,"* it will not be long till you feel how unmixed with the miseries around you is your free Spirit. No matter what people seem to be doing they cannot draw you into their network. You live your free life in Spirit as a substance of reality, quite separate from their delusions. All things take on an enduring substance in your sight. You feel supremely real. Life seems real.

If you should be in great trouble you could not get help from God by begging for help. You would get help at once if you would stand aside from your trouble, as above and greater than it. Then you would feel the help of the omnipotent God, Reality is the strength of your free Spirit which refuses to be mixed with evil.

The only cause for evil is the idea of absence. That is all the evil there is. The belief of apartness from Good is the foundation of the word evil. The idea of absence of Good had to be called something, so it was called evil. Ideas always make conditions. Thus the idea of absence, being named evil, finally made a host of phantoms of appearances called evils.

Ancient metaphysicians taught in their practice "There is no apartness." They hit upon the most perfect denial that could be spoken. It covers all the ground of evil. It touches the course of evil at its root. If this idea is persistently adhered to it cannot fail to make a vacuum around you into which all Good must come streaming to fill you with delight. The Truth is that Good is God, and God is omnipresent and omnipotent, thus the Good is omnipresent. If the Good is omnipresent the evil is nowhere present, and there is no apartness. This is the reasoning. All reasoning has the effect of controlling the environment. Your whole life conditions change if you change your modes of reasoning.

Having been trained for years to reason your life out on the basis of Good being absent from you, you now begin to reason from an entirely different basis. You judge not by appearances, but by righteousness. Many conditions slip away almost instantaneously. They were built up by your false general reasonings, and with these gone they have no props. As for instance; you have poor eyesight. It became so because of some little notion you persistently held. You now give up that notion. You cannot help giving up that notion, because the new reasoning makes it impossible to think that way any more. The poor eyesight must fall away for the good eyesight to show up. Some changes occur instantly and some are more slow.

You take an entirely new basis when you say that if God is Intelligence, then Intelligence is omnipresent, for God is omnipresent. Here then you must say that there is no absence of Intelligence. Your mind may suddenly feel very clear and intelligent, or it may be startled. If there is no absence of Intelligence you are now rich with the Intelligence of God. You know all things. There, where the idiot seems to be, you must see that the Intelligence of God is present.

Why does a man not seem to be intelligent? It is because of the belief the race keeps shedding over the planet that Intelligence is absent from some spots of God, or some places in God.

When the metaphysicians say there is no life, substance or intelligence in matter, they unconsciously intimate that there is matter, but it is empty. They do not mean this, and therefore have done some very good healing and restoration of judgment by using this denial. Others have become tangled in the subtle statement and have never been able to do a single bit of healing by saying there is no life, substance or intelligence in matter. They believed in matter so strongly that the mention of the name made it seem present. At once it seemed to have no life, and somebody they loved caught the effect of their saying there is no life in matter, and gave up the appearance of life. So with substance and so with intelligence. Yet, that third denial of metaphysics is perfectly correct, and in your use of it may do great works. If it tangles you at all make the third denial in a simple speech as *"There is no absence of life, substance or intelligence in omnipresent Good."*

Carlyle felt poor and lonely and incompetent. Hardly one on the face of the earth has not had these feelings. They come from the belief of being apart from God — apart from our Good. Those who have met the feeling with a strong "NO" have routed it out of their premises. Such feelings are the NO to Good. We meet them with the NO to evil. Carlyle calls the meeting of the NO to Good with the NO to evil "Everlasting NO." He was met so strongly that it seemed as if all nature told him that the universe was void of life, of purpose, of volition. It was one huge, dead, immeasurable steam engine, rolling on its dead indifference to grind him limb from limb.

All at once he entered his protest. His whole God-created nature rose and said "I am not thine, but free, and forever hate thee," He felt that when he entered his protest against the power he began his spiritual birth. He then began to be a man.

"All evil is negation," says Emerson. Negation is nothingness. The reality of being is Truth. With the Truth we set ourselves free from negations. Does it not seem as if matter were reality? Yet it is nothing. We speak the Truth, and the spiritual power we have rises in its divine substantiality and every material thing becomes subject to it. Does it not seem as if there were absence of life in some things? Yet life is omnipresent. Does it not often seem as if Intelligence were lacking? Yet perfect Intelligence is omnipresent. Marked and wonderful changes in your life begin with your reasoning along this line.

The fourth protest we make against the claims of matter is to deny that sensation is a physical or material experience. Sensation is a faculty of Soul. Soul is God. God is Spirit, Mind. Thus sensation is a mental process. As God is omnipresent, sensation is omnipresent Good. For ages metaphysicians have called the fourth denial of metaphysics the denial of sensation. But sensation is sight, hearing, tasting, smelling, touching. God is your sight, therefore you cannot lose your sight, God is your hearing, therefore you cannot lose your hearing. God is your skill in every faculty, therefore you cannot lose any faculty or the skill of any faculty.

The main idea of denying sensation was to get rid of the sensations of pain to which mankind are subject. Grief, pain, horror, indignation, are hateful sensations. Had life been all delight, all pleasure, nobody would have chosen to deny sensation. Many, with their minds set upon sensation as painful, or ending in pain, have cured pain in patients by repeating over and over the statement: "There is no sensation in matter."

If they had trained their mind to the high Truth that there is nothing to hate, they would never have come to the position where they met pain or grief or indignation, or any of the hateful sensations which all stand for the universal claim that Good in the way of sensation is absent. If Good is not absent, then the sensation of Good is never absent. "At thy right hand are pleasures forevermore." "With thee is fullness of joy." Thus the protests against the absence of God as joy should not be that there is no sensation but that *there is nothing to hate.*

The race mind is exactly like your mind in its willingness to make all the protests of metaphysics. It is ready to see that a course of good reasoning will bring out a happy life if a course of wrong reasoning will bring out misery.

Claudius, the fourth Roman Emperor, kept exclaiming continually "What do you take me for, a fool?" The idea that others were not regarding him well finally effected him so that he lost his memory, and did indeed appear foolish. People often speak of how little they know, and finally others think so too.

Socrates said that men act wrongly because they form erroneous judgments. When they learn right judgments they will act wisely and well. Nothing straightens out the mind like looking all the claims of evil boldly in the face with the uplifted conviction that there is nothing but Good; telling all things that there is one substance, and that is Spirit; only one life and that is God; only one Mind and that is God.

There are five denials, corresponding to the five senses. Then there are two particular denials corresponding to the sentiments and moral sense. All five might be used faithfully and not bring to pass the right state of mind. The five which belong to the race open up great avenues of reasoning which delight the Mind, the Soul and the Spirit. The two which delight the life and love of the heart are the two which relate to your own disposition and will.

Plato's five denials did not touch his character. He rejected matter. He rejected evil. He rejected all that we reason against, very nearly on our own basis, but he did not refuse his own prejudices. He had spoken of One Life, One Mind, One Good, then spoke of woman as the failure of blind nature. He could not seem to catch the principle that there is no failure in One Life, One Mind, One Good, therefore there is no distinction of sex in God, He could not rid his mind of some special characteristics. He did not seem to know that it was as necessary to rid himself of prejudice as the belief in matter. So he was always speaking of failure. Failure on his own part. He worked over the ellipse to discover its significance and confessed himself baffled.

Socrates told his pupil, Alcebiades "It is therefore necessary to wait until someone may teach us how it behooves us to conduct ourselves, both toward the gods and men." And Alcebiades asked, "When shall that time arrive, O Socrates, and who shall that teacher be, for most eagerly, do I wish to see such a man?"

Jesus Christ had no prejudices, He condemned nobody and nothing. He felt that all things were under the care and protection of the loving Father. This made his life easy for him to handle. He could lay it down and take it up at will.

There were two schools of theology in Elisha's time. At one of them he found the water very brackish, so much so that the students, who were all men, complained. He put into the water some salt, and the water was instantly healed. Many a student of the highest theology, even on to the five denials of metaphysics, has failed to drink of the healing waters of the Science of Christ, because his moral sentiments were subject to what he believed to be his physical senses. There is no moral chord which must lie mute in the nature. If you are careless about paying your debts your moral chord is not vibrating to some word which you ought to hear. If you use other people's property roughly you do not catch the word which vibrates the chord of honor. If you do the things which inconvenience or weary others your sentiment of justice is not salted.

A man in Paris was accustomed to slay little girls, as he said, for Christ's sake. He passed on in calm hope of reward for his goodness. All his religious speeches had shot wide of the mark of the moral chord. The honorable feeling of kindness, justice and mercy was not quickened. It would take an Elisha, or a Jesus, to find the salt for his brackish character.

Often we see people who yield to some trivial temptation while thinking and talking high Science. It is plain that the water of their character is brackish. Hence, like Plato, we all need to meet some special claim of the absence of Good in our life; some claim so subtle that we may not appreciate its presence. A habit of running people down will run some healthy part of our body down into disease. We must indeed think of, and speak of all people, from the standpoint of their God in them as life and substance, instead of from the standpoint of their appearance to us, before our sickness will be cured.

The two denials we ourselves need are often very subtle, as I say, but the fifth regular denial suited to the race often leads one into his own needed cleanings. Notice the fifth regular denial. It is this: *"There is no sin, sickness or death."* Where is there no sin, sickness or death? In God of course. Where is God? Everywhere. This removes the sins out of our sight, which were put there by our belief in the absence of Goodness in people. We shall certainly see people more honorable and chaste for being where we are, when we have spoken of sin, sickness and death as not possible in a world occupied by Goodness. We shall certainly see less sickness if the idea of the people, and undivided wholeness of Spirit is real to our mind. We shall be utterly free from seeing death in any form, or under any circumstance, if we appreciate that in omnipresent Life there is no death. If we are not set free from ever coming in contact with sin, sickness and death by these five denials we may be sure we have some special prejudices of mind to get rid of. Hence it is well to devote one morning every week to reasoning out why we are, in Spirit and Truth, free from these errors.

Carlyle dates his new birth from such a denial of all that held him in bondage. You must know that after all, sin, sickness and death were very real to him, so he went through all these pains of consequences of believing that the Good that belonged to him was absent from him. We can generally point to the very strong ideas of men that certain Good is very absent from them, when we see how miserably sick or poor they are. It is the same with ourselves.

Let us reason with the Almighty as Job did. He was accused of wickedness as the reason for his bodily ills. He made the grandest protest that had ever been made in the world — "Thou knowest that I am not wicked, for thy hands fashioned me." This healed him. It restored his goods.

Paul said that we should have a reason for the hope that is in us. There is a reason why we ought to be well, intelligent, blessedly happy always. Using that reasoning we come into close touch with our health, wisdom and prosperity.

John, the Revelator, saw the second stone of the Temple as Sapphire. This is wisdom. It is peace and health. Moses saw the second state of Mind as light, brought to us by the Spirit of God. The Spirit of God is the Word of Truth. We are building the Temple of our own character. If we take the first lesson of Truth according to Spirit, we lay in Zion the foundation of Jasper, which is the diamond, irresistible in beauty and brightness of purity. If we take the second lesson of spiritual Truth we lay the Sapphire stone of our character. Our peace and wisdom are set free.

The second lesson of Truth gives the reasons why:
1. There is no evil.
2. There is no matter.
3. There is no absence of life, substance, or intelligence.
4. There is nothing to hate.
5. There is no sin, sickness, or death.

The reasonings of Job cover all the ground of why we may declare against those personal characteristics which make up our hardships in life — "Thou knowest that I am not wicked for thy hands fashioned me."

Because of this, you may take your habit of scolding at people in a way that is far worse than their offenses, and proclaim that as a son or daughter of Spirit, you do not chide or condemn anybody. On this plan of reasoning you may set yourself free from the poverty that troubles you, or the sickness that discourages you. On this plan of reasoning also take up the other traits you are willing to name. As a child of God you cannot have a habit of hurting or torturing people by your speeches or actions. You cannot have a habit of being jealous. You cannot feel easily offended. You cannot resent the way people act with you. You are not envious of anybody. You are not filled with eagerness to be praised. You are not cowardly about being blamed. You are not penurious. You are not glad to know that your enemies are unfortunate, You do not feel discouraged when you have tried and do not succeed.

Take some two evil tendencies you have, as a consequence of believing in the absence of Good, and tell God that they are in Truth no part of you, because God himself fashioned you in the Spirit of his own nature. These are all simple negations to your Good, which, like Carlyle, you must face with a bolder negation to their evil.

It is one duty we seem to have laid out before us as a race, viz., to reject the idea of the absence of Good by the word of Truth boldly spoken concerning Good as omnipresent. This teaching goes forth from the Mind in a mysterious influence. Sickness falls away from the people we meet. Death comes and looks into our homes, but hurries away like a dream. Sin falls from the character of our neighbors and they do not seem the same to us any more. Our own sickness soon sinks into the sands of nowhere.

Try the denials of metaphysical reasoning and see if you do not feel a new freedom. Light on your pathway will break the deepest gloom. You will find something to live for. You can take these denials and dissolve your hardest trial. Take one of your own trials and say that in Truth it has no reality whatsoever. Say that as God fashioned you out of his own Goodness you have never had any trait of character which could result in absence of Good. Tell now that you reject the common feeling of the absence of Good. As God is not absent Good must be here.

We do not need to wait to be free. As God is free now, so we are free now.

Lesson Three

Affirmations Of Science

THE text of the third lesson of Spiritual Science is "God saw the light that it was Good." God is Mind. Light is Wisdom. Mind perceives that Wisdom is Good. Mind understands the Good.

You will perceive, as you go on thinking of first principles, that it is your nature to be happy and powerful in proportion to your ability to appreciate what is Good.

If a beggar child, looking through an open gateway into a beautiful garden, is filled with pleasure at the sight, forgetting his misery for a moment, he has given his own character a new vigor of goodness, and has increased the strength of his life in some metaphysical relation of mind to life. He has unwittingly given himself a treatment for prosperity.

You will note that, for the most part, the heart dwells with grief upon the contrast between its own lot in life and the bounty and happiness it realizes to be near it, and yet far from it. The heart may still cling to its misery while it is observing happiness. Here is where the office of denial comes in. Denial is elimination. In Science we are taught the value of elimination.

Between *om* and *presence* is the little syllable "ni." *Ni* means nigellum. Nigellum means nothing. *Ni* means nihil (L). Nihil means nothing. So, between Om, the Mind, and its rightful possessions of power, place and Science, or Wisdom, is the claim of darkness, or nigellum, which is negation, standing as if it were something, while it is nothing.

Thus, between your mind and the attainment of its supreme bliss, is the everlasting "ni," or the very bold assumption of nothing, that it is something. By dropping the claims of misery, you step through the valley of the shadow of the apparent reality of misery, into the reality of blessedness divine.

Now this "ni," which lies between you and the presence of your Good, is as apt to be one of your virtues as one of your vices. If you are one who takes pride in never speaking or acting from impulse, and feel a sort of contempt for people who act impulsively, your virtue is the claim to be something when it is nothing.

Does God take pride in never speaking nor acting from impulse? Let that pride in your virtue be eliminated from your character. Hear the apostle Paul on the subject "Though I should bestow all my goods to feed the poor, and though I should give my body to be burned, and have not charity, it is as sounding brass or a tinkling cymbal." It is well to act with discretion, but sounding brass to take pride in your discretion.

Suppose you are very prompt in paying your debts, and take pride in it, speaking scornfully of people who do not pay promptly, this pride in your virtue hides the virtue. One good day you may believe yourself unable to pay your debts, and if it causes you to be more lenient with people who are careless you will pass the shadow "ni" that stands between your mind and its satisfaction, present, so near, yet with the distance of a personal trait between.

In our last lesson we named these "ideas of absence." We called our protests against them "denials." We spoke of the two particular traits: in the science of numbers you subtract what is not wanted from what is wanted. In the science of geology you say "This is not aqueous rock, this is igneous rock." You show as much wisdom by negation as by your affirmations. One tells you that this is a picture of Napoleon and a dear friend wounded in battle. You say "No, it is Aeneas bearing away his father Anchises." One tells you that sin is a terrible evil which God permits. You say "No, God is the only presence, and tolerates no other nature in his realm but his own nature." If you protest, all sin will seem like a dream of the night, not worth rehearsing. There are five affirmations belonging to the negations we make, to which I will now call your attention.

These are the five Wise Virgins of the object lesson of Jesus. They are called virgins because they are the most simple and reasonable statements the mind can make when telling why the negations of its Good are not reasonable. The two affirmations that belong to you each in particular we will describe under the miscellaneous affirmations. These affirmations are all mentioned in the Book of the Dead.

Your two special affirmations are not virgins. They are strong defenders and providers. They are the strength and wisdom of your own life, in its unique relation to all life. As your mother cannot do your eating for you, nor your breathing, so no one can charge you with the strength of your own denials and affirmations.

John, the Revelator, said that the third foundation stone of the Temple was Chalcedony. Our character is the Temple, or the Holy City. The Chalcedony is the love stone, translucent like the opal, always gleaming with the purity of the diamond, and the heavenly blue of the sapphire, shone upon by the hot sunshine of a light that never fails. There is upon the earth no Chalcedony stone like that one John saw, gleaming with the white light of primal Truth, of the omnipresent, omnipotent, omniscient goodness of God with blue flashes of wisdom and unchallenged peace, and the red gold of love of Truth and goodness, set on fire by challenging negations. Without this stone, character is not glad and strong and fixed and secure.

There is no use making the affirmations until we have made the denials. You will see people affirming that they are God, who are quite willing to do ungodly deeds. This is because they have not met the everlasting 'ni' of Carlyle with the irresistible NO! They have not taken their unreasonable prejudices by name and told the reasons why they are free from such claims against them. The strange part about the claims of negation is that, whatever they are, everybody seems to see them.

So the two mighty appearances of evil in man, not being met by denials, or bold reasons why they are not realities, leave the character making great religious professions, but badly inconsistent therewith, and they fill their neighbors with disgust. When the right denials are made, the affirmations will be exceedingly hot and effective. James, the half-brother of Jesus Christ, said, "The effectual, fervent prayer of the righteous man availeth much."

The photographer, in a yellow glass room, has light and heat enough for fixing beautiful pictures upon his cards, but still there is a mysterious something lacking, and he cannot take the photograph in such light. Thus, in bringing out the answers to our prayers, the actinic ray, which is the cutting, pungent ray of denial, is as necessary as the sun-ray is necessary in bringing out the images in photography.

The day set aside for denials leaves the mind a clear draught for the finest affirmations to blaze hot on the firmament of our daily life. If a great fire is smoldering under a house, it will never make a bon-fire of the house until an opening is made somewhere for a draught. If a powerful steam pressure is set against the machinery of an engine, it will not move a wheel until a valve is opened for a vent for the steam. So the mighty Truth, filling every mind with its energy, waits to move through the sluice-like ways made by scientific protests, like Carlyle's energetic "I am free."

"Let your light shine," said Jesus Christ. He would not have the great Mind, with which we are all stored, hidden under a bushel. He would have our Mind free. It is a good denial of evil to reason out, as Carlyle did, why we are free. We must then affirm our nature, and hold on steadfastly to our affirmations.

The race religions have talked about one Word, somewhere in the universe, which contains all the potency of all denials and all affirmations. Jesus Christ used that Word, evidently, but only to the ears attuned to it was its tone clear enough to be heard by man. So, as nobody received it, he told them to repeat His name. If you will repeat the name of Jesus Christ you will, step by step, come into his quality of mind. Then you will, step by step, become cognizant of the divine nature charging your being. You will feel a delight in your substance. You will see how the wisdom of God is your wisdom. You will see that your wisdom is God. But you will never realize this till you have given a free vent, or clear passage, through your mind, for the powerful pressure of the God Mind to speak and think through.

The syllable "ni," which stands between *om* and *presence*, is the thick wall of belief in the absence of Good. It is sometimes called the dark river. It is often called a veil of flesh. It is sometimes called a bridge, over whose mysterious claims we are to walk into the presence of our Good, or over which our Good comes to us. Many men who have accidentally, as it were, stumbled upon the denials of Science, have made some of the affirmations with good effect. They did not make the personal denials. You have seen that personal cleansing is as important as general doctrine.

David cried out, "Cleanse thou me from secret faults." You would, like Carlyle, give a reason why there is no reality to the appearance of faults. To the great Om, which is the pressing intelligence and wisdom of your own mind, you would say, "Thou knowest that I am not wicked, for thy hands fashioned me." You would take your selfish disposition, and to the great Om, or Om Mind, you would say, "Thou knowest that in Spirit and in Truth I am not selfish, for thy thought sent me forth, thy mind thinketh my life, thy hands fashioned me."

It would not be long, after wise and earnest denials, before you would be uttering mighty affirmations of Science, and your life would be consistent with them. Pythagoras, a Greek philosopher, born 570 B.C., made certain of the denials of Science. Especially he saw that sensation is mental, not a physical exercise. After determining thus, he found himself affirming that our Soul is an emanation from the universal Soul, and partakes of the divine nature. The Soul in man is the self-moving principle.

Anaxagoras, 500 B.C., said that matter is only the result of ideas. Soon after this he had to make an affirmation on the subject of matter as being absent, and Spirit as present. He said the force which shapes the world is not in the nature of matter. It is not impersonal force. It is Mind. This Supreme Mind is distinguished from matter by simplicity, independence, knowledge and supreme power. Plato found that evil is a way of believing, and not omnipotent. This denial opened the way for him to affirm "God is Goodness." A denial and an affirmation always seem to match each other.

When Jesus sent his messengers forth, he sent them in pairs. You will see, by reading over the characteristics of the men, that one was positive while the other was negative and receptive. As for instance, Peter and John. Peter is impulsive and positive. John is trusting and yielding. He therefore coincided with all the eloquent impulses of Peter.

Jesus Christ spoke his sentences with negation and affirmation, as, "Call no man your father upon earth, for one is your father, even God." "Come unto me all ye that labor and are heavy laden, and I will give you rest." He put his negations sometimes as if they were realities, as for instance, he seems to be admitting the reality of labor and weariness in this quotation, but he called flesh nothingness, so he was not making a reality of its operations.

A young man, who was seemingly very sick indeed, said suddenly, "Satan, get out of the way! God Almighty do your work!" Now the young man had been brought up without any belief in satan, so he was only meeting a condition of unreality by a name applied to the whole "ni" of the whole world, to the whole run of evil in creation. Jesus often called our belief in the absence of Good by the name satan. Job called it satan.

A strong Scientist said he had to meet all his prosperity by a strong negative statement, or form of expression, or his mind would not work it out into view quickly. If he was requiring money he never said, "I am supplied with all I can use." He said, "I do not need money." And thus he made a clear way for his bounty to come to him. Some people, who cannot sleep, will fall into peaceful sleep by saying, "I do not need sleep." For, you see, they made the word "need" a great reality. It is the name of their belief in the absence of Good.

The belief in absence takes many ways of exhibiting itself, and clothes itself in many words. Some of you may have the belief in the absence of Good take the form of being grateful that you are so much blessed, more than others. There is no point where one is blessed more than another. It sometimes flatters our vanity to have people tell us how much more of Science we know than they know. Be not deceived into admitting it for an instant. All are partakers of the Divine Mind in equal potency and might. If people cling to us it is because they have not learned to appreciate themselves. When they realize that their understanding, or their wisdom, is good, they will not depend upon you for anything. It is evident, if they do lean upon you, that you ought to think towards them, and for them, in a way to turn them toward their own relation with their own divine nature. If you watch yourself, you are very likely to discover that you lean upon some- one for companionship or strength or sympathy.

Emerson prophesied that the high laws to be taught in the future would teach mankind to find themselves self-companioning and self-strengthen-ing. This is discovery. It comes with the affirmations of Science. It is evident that you must see, as Divine Mind that your own nature is self-companioning.

Successful men and women, along any line, have borne about within their own minds strong, native affirmations. Sometimes they took them as children. They are hardly aware how important a part in their lives their positive conclusions have played. High resolves made in intense feeling have been like oak trees.

One of the Popes told how, as a boy in the field, he decided to be Pope of Rome. Euripides, the son of a fruit dealer in Greece, took some lofty resolve, as a boy, and rose to be the friend of Socrates. With him the glory of the Athenian stage descended into the tomb, says the historian. Virgil, the baker's son, lifted his thoughts on high, and they took him to the plane of such ideal concepts that, when he had written his poems, the Roman people would rise in the theatres to show him the reverence they paid their Emperors. Epictitus, a Greek slave, put up the thoughts of his young mind to noble principles of life, and though he was deformed and sickly, his noble affirmations lifted him free from being the slave of a cruel master to being the honored companion of lords and princes. The young man's ideals wait for demonstration on the heights of affirmation.

The mother, whose tired feet touch the hills of light, shall say, "My God is rest.'" She shall see that her thoughts are good. The care-burdened father shall sight the port of the heavenly city of "Well Done," and God, his God, shall take away his care. "And they shall be mine, saith the Lord, in that day when I make up my jewels, and I will spare them as a man spareth his own son in whom he delighteth."

The hilltops of delight are the true meanings of affirmations. They cannot be reached except by clean feet and pure hearts. All the way of life with beautiful health, beautiful judgment and happy success, through spiritual doctrine, lies open to him who, commencing with the Jasper stone, feels the love gleam of the Chalcedony, the third message of Jesus: "God is Love."

The first universal affirmations are:

1. My Good is my God. My God is Life, Truth, Love, Substance, Intelligence; omniscient, omnipotent, omnipresent.
2. In God I live, move and have my being.
3. I am Spirit, Mind, Wisdom, Strength, Wholeness.
4. The I AM works inevitably through me to will and to do that which ought to be done by me.
5. I am governed by the law of God and cannot sin, fear sin, sickness or death.

Set apart a morning each week to making your mind touch the mountain peaks of the most noble thoughts. They have many ways of being expressed, but these have the substance of them all.

Your own two affirmations, which, if you would use them, would lift your life out of bondage, must be sought out and spoken by yourself. If your life seems turbulent, you had better speak of peace. If your life seems defenseless and unprotected, tell the defense and protection of the Most High God. If you seem to fail in everything you undertake, tell how your God can take the small and insignificant things of human seeming and glorify His own name and nature thereby. It is not in the seeming failures of your life you must look for your reputation among the angels of light, but in the purpose you have held.

> "What matter smile or frown, if angels looking down
>
> Shall each to other speak of thee in tones of love continually,
>
> Until the name on earth but seldom heard,
>
> Hath come to be in heaven a household word."

There is no storm of adversity that can shake your name through the ages, if your affirmations are lofty enough concerning the dealings of your God with you.

There once was a woman who held on and held out that she must cast all her care on God. She would never admit that she got her support from any other source than Almighty God. She would not admit that her life was assisted, or kept, by any other means than straight from Divine Mind. She feared nothing and nobody, because the everlasting God was her rock and fortress. From being the child of adversity and misfortune, in the seeming all the conditions of her life grew easy and bright. She took, as a principle to hold in her mind, that the yoke of Jesus Christ is easy and his burden is light. You may take any position you like, and hold onto it, until it makes your life demonstrate it. It will be your own affirmation.

Many people change their affirmations. You can add to your affirmations, but you should not change them. You may explain your affirmations, then the repetition of them will help you.

Let us explain the first affirmation that makes the first denial. You remember it, do you not? "My Good is my God. My God is Life, Truth, Love, Substance, Intelligence, omnipresent, omnipotent, omniscient." Why do we each say, "My Good?" Because we are each the unit around which our Good swings. If we are right, entirely right, in our relation to our Good, and we can explain how we secured our Good, we can tell the world how to attain its Good.

Jonathan Edwards made a noble discovery under this point. He said he found the supreme plan to be that he should attend to the salvation of his own Soul. He put the idea crudely, and spoke in the language of his time, which called the exhibition of our divine nature the "salvation of the soul." You can see for yourself that your Soul does need saving; it needs to be made visible. The power of your Soul shows itself upon the least little exhibition of determination not to believe in the reality or power of evil. On any plane of thought you will find that the resolve to be on the side of good and right will win victories for you. Health will come plainly into sight. Prosperity is certain to come to you. Happy life comes to you.

Why do we say, "My Good is my God?" Can we not see that every move we make is to get some good to ourselves? Do we not breathe because we think it will be better for us? If you wish to stop breathing, even that will be because you think it more comfortable not to breathe. You feel deeply that there is Good for you, so all the time you do your best to get that Good. It makes the Good your governor. It makes it the governor of your life. Thus it is your God. It is your choice to make your God the most high principle Jesus Christ taught, or the incidents and happenings of your everyday lot in life.

Whatever draws you toward it, making you think it can satisfy you, governs you, and is your God. This is the reason so many have stood upright on their feet and said, "I am my own God." They thought it better to be self-ruled, or governed, than to be governed by appetite for food, hunger for praise, search for home, quest for health, hope for friends, etc.

It is very safe to say, "My Good is my God." It is then our privilege to say *what* is our Good, We have a natural tendency to love life itself. We may have been displeased with our conditions in life, but we do not mean Life itself when we are telling how we hate our life, if it is hard and disagreeable. No, we mean we hate the conditions of our life. We do not think that the free elixir of quickening forever, which breathes like a fine wind through the universe, is not Good. So we look straight toward the free, fine elixir that breathes through the universe, and we say, "Life is Good, Good is God, thus Life is God."

It is natural for our mind to love Truth. "What is Truth?" asked Pilate of Jesus. Whether he spoke jestingly or scornfully or sincerely makes no difference; the fact remains that every man, woman and child would like to know what is really true.

There is, even in the mind of the most devoted religionist, always a doubt as to the absolute truth of what he is talking about, when he tells that God was so angry with the world that his only son had to take the part of a scapegoat of the Jews, in order to pacify him for the world he made having turned out so badly. It seems strange to see educated, noble-looking men, standing on high platforms and pro- claiming such a childish acting being as the Jehovah of Goodness. They doubt it in their secret hearts. But nobody doubts that the free, fine Spirit that breathes intelligence through the rocks and through mankind is God. This is Truth.

The speaking of this Truth leads on to other Truth. We seek for absolute Truth; thus our God is Truth. Jesus Christ said, "I am the Truth." He meant that he spoke the Truth. He also said, "I am the Life." He meant that he understood the fine, free, undivided and eternally abiding Life, that fills and swells and breathes, like a wind of delight, through all the universe. Truth is Good. Good is God. Thus God is Truth.

There is an uplifting strength comes with acknowledgment that God is Life and God is Truth, which does not come to the man who says his Good, or his God, is his beer or his horses or his billiards. The face and form show what the thoughts proclaim as your Good. What have you sought after? Was that your acknowledged Good? It has marked your face and form. Take a true thought in your conscious mind, and say it, either silently or audibly. Soon you will mark your face and form with another light.

Moses said that the acknowledgement of the right and true God would be like a wind moving across the face of the water for the light to break over. Waters are conscious thoughts. If we have occupied our thinking mind with what we shall eat, drink, wear and such subjects, we are in a dark state of mind. It is the Egyptian darkness. If then we begin to occupy our thinking mind with the subjects we call divine principles, we feel the glow of On High shining, either suddenly or slowly, over and through the mind.

Again we name our Good. We keep on naming our Good. We say our Good is Love. We do not mean the selfish clutch of some human being upon our time or attention, our body or our thoughts; we do not mean the clutch we sometimes feel upon the time and attention of some human being. We do not mean the clutch we feel toward money, toward food, toward home, toward animals or friends. No, we mean the free, fine life of delight, that streams with kindness and mercy, and gentleness and entrancing beauty, through the universe, and draws, with its irresistible kindness, all things and all people to love it and feel its love.

"I drew them with the bonds of love and they knew not that I healed them," said the goodness of Divine Love that never clutches at us, nor is caught by our hungry clutching. It is the Most High Good, nameless in the life of man while he seeks material good, and nameless in our thoughts while ever we think there is some power operating against us; nameless in our thoughts while we believe there is something good absent from us; nameless in our mind while we think we have inferiority or hardship or suffering or loss. The Most High Good is Life, Truth, Love. There is a wonderfully uplifting energy in the words "Most High Good." The mind is lifted to higher feelings of Truth and Love. The Most High Good is higher than any Good we have yet realized. So we speak on the lofty heights of our highest words. Out of the reach of words we have the Love that draws the universe, and keeps all things seeking and seeking it, but never finding it, until the mind meets the great plane of unreality, and strikes it with the omnipotent NO!

"Yea, I have loved thee with an everlasting love, therefore with loving kindness have I drawn thee." It is the true and eternal substance that wooes us with its everlasting love. To lay hold upon your Good is to be satisfied. Then there will never be any feeling that what we love and are satisfied with will leave us, or fail or disappoint us. God is Love. Love is God. God is eternal. Eternal Love is God. When we love somebody, and then do not love them, it is only that we have a mental feeling of absence. It shows that while we felt the love we gave no word to it—that it was eternal God.

It is by the right word to all things that they show their real character and do not hide from us. The delight that we now feel, in the little glimpse of the feeling called love, is a foretaste of a substance that we have here at hand, hidden only by our feeling that our Good we were to lay hold upon, is absent.

One and another of the world's great thinkers found that there is a shadow system gathered over us that is a great, dark something, hiding us from the Good we are seeking. If you study into the matter you will see that it is all a mental state. Rise, like Carlyle did, and proclaim your freedom from the claims of your incompetency and ignorance. It will vanish, and you can stretch out your hand and lay hold of some new good each moment.

You will first notice your freedom from sickness. Then you will see how much better you get on with people who seemed before to be hard and ugly. You will notice that your own disposition is better. You will soon be more prosperous. Many things will change into your favor that hurt you before. It is the only way offered to mankind to change by a method at all worthy of the idea of the easy yoke and light burden promised, by accomplishing great works through a doctrine.

To some it seems an easy task to sit down alone by themselves and reason out their freedom. To others it seems almost like nonsense. The reasoning seems all right enough, but it takes a basis so different from the world that it seems that there is a fallacy in it somewhere. To such, we recommend the fact that many have stumbled upon the process without knowing they had touched the keynote to the power of God for all men.

For instance: a Russian General said that it would seem as if his body were too sick or weary to undertake the hard tasks of the day. He would say to his body, "You must be strong and able; you cannot be sick or feeble. Do as I wish you to do. Be up and about your business." Soon he got his body trained so it would rise from a great claim of misery.

The father of Henry Ward Beecher would say to his overtaxed mind, "Go out every thought; I will have none of you in my mind; I will shut the doors and lock you all out." After awhile he would shut out every thought. Napoleon Bonaparte could do the same thing. If it is hard for you to fasten your mind to a treatment, such as this, write down just what you would like your body to do and be, and read it over at intervals. Read it aloud. By and by you will accomplish with your body exactly what you wish. We are entirely built up and moved by our thoughts.

In the *Theologia Germanica*, a religious book, written about the time of Martin Luther, by an unknown writer, we read that if any practice in religion seems at first hard and almost impossible, to persevere, in practicing it, until it is easy and natural.

In this statement of what God is, we say, "God is Life, Truth, Love, Substance, Intelligence, Omni-presence, Omnipotence, Omniscience." Everything that is evil seems present enough. That which we call good may seem to fail us easily. Presence which endures is substance. That which we can take hold of, and keep, is the kind of Good we would have. Paul tells us to feel after God. God is substance. God is Good. Our Good is Substance. It is a very good part of the statement of Truth to say that God is Substance, present with us. Our Good is substantial presence. For people who believe that their Good is absent it is a helpful word. There is no poverty, no lack, no loss, no want in this word Substance. Our Good is near as Substance.

If you are one who believes that you are absent from your beloved friends, this part of the statement of Truth will bring you great satisfaction in some marvelous way.

Nothing is out of the reach of the power of these statements. After awhile they come around with their fruit like seeds to fruitage, or like planets to their orbits.

It must not dismay you if you do not work with your mind as quickly as others. There is always one thing in which each one of us is quicker than others. It is a great practice to offer glad praises that God has made the way of the Holy Spirit through you so successfully. There is a self-supporting power in the Holy Spirit which, when you let it operate unhindered through you, leads straight to your substantial support. People will think you fortunate, but it will be simply because you have thought on a high plane of provisions till you have opened a gateway of mind. Support is Substance. Skill in action is Substance. If you can do things skillfully you have the substantial action of the Holy Spirit. The Most High Good lets fall the easy touches of her all-powerful fingers. Give glad, joyous praises every night, before going to sleep, to the Most High Good, that the Holy Spirit fills your thoughts with ardor, and fires your affairs to splendid achievements.

Your Good is practical, substantial satisfaction. You must be satisfied in mind to be utterly satisfied, must you not? If the beggar child, looking through the window, and forgetting her physical misery, because her mind is so happy, can keep that up for five minutes, she can cause her mind to draw someone to feed her body that very day. Suppose you multiply your Soul's delight, in the knowledge that God is the very substance of the things you want, by a number of degrees more than her delight, the arm of the Lord is not shortened that it cannot save you from every want.

God is Spirit. Then you see the Substance you long for is Spirit. Very well, be spiritually happy, and the material shadows, the affairs of your life, must be happy. This is the process of Intelligence. We have to use our intelligence to be acquainted with our Good. God is Intelligence. When we know God we have touched the very Substance which can inform us how to work each minute wisely, so as to be clothed and fed and housed and healed, without any other process than simply *knowing* God.

To know God is to be God. We are exactly like what we know. Does it not take intelligence to know intelligence? The more we can appreciate that the Mind is God, and that it is the only Intelligence there is operating through the universe, the more we know in and of ourselves. It keeps fixing the mind to new intelligence to say, "God is Intelligence." The Psalmist wrote how the mind of God is forever saying, "Acquaint now thyself with me and be at peace." In you is all knowledge. By saying that God is Intelligence, that God within you begins to show forth through yourself great wisdom, along some line. You may be very wise in healing the sick. You may be very wise in speaking in public. You might suddenly be able to speak in many languages, as did the apostles of old.

The words applied to the Most High Good, as Omnipotence, Omnipresence, Omniscience, will enlarge your sphere of action, by lifting your mind away toward the heights and depths which do contain God, the eternal, changeless Principle. You are the mind that stands back and uses great words to express your ideas about the Most High Good. Do not get entangled in your own words. You are greater than any words you ever used. At present you use words to approach unto your own Good. *There will come a time when you will not use words.*

The Eastern mystic repeats the word "Om" by drawing in his breath and speaking the word twelve times. Then he holds his breath and repeats the word twenty-four times. Finally he feels that he himself is "OM." To feel that OM is your substance, your Life, your Mind, is greater than to feel that the words you say are OM.

The only words you can speak and be identified with, wisely, are, "*I am my own understanding of God.*" These words bring you face to face with the highest of yourself. You can be identified with your own understanding of God. Understanding, as far as you have it, is the Mind of God. It is perfect as far as you have it. To speak of it as yourself increases it within yourself. People who speak of God as a wonderful being sending calamities are not exhibiting their understanding of God. They are hiding it. In you is the understanding of God in perfection. Speaking of your understanding intensifies it. So, the second affirmation, which has been, "In God I live and move and have my being," has always meant "in my own understanding of God."

There is a great intensifying of the fine intelligence of the mind that stands up and identifies itself with its own understanding of God. No word can express your understanding of God. You are it. Live in the second affirmation much, "*I am my own understanding of God.*" or this one, "*All that God is, I am.*" It balances the denial, "*There is no matter,*" for understanding is not material, it is spiritual. And what understanding of God you really feel, or really show, is all the substance you show. Your understanding is your substance. This is true of everything. Its only substance is its understanding of God. This leaves Spirit the only substance.

The third affirmation is, "I am Spirit, Mind, identical with God, wisdom, strength, holiness." This is your understanding, which is the same substance that God is. If we have called God Spirit, then we are also Spirit. If we have called God Mind, then we are also Mind. If we have called God the Universal Breath of Life, then we also shed abroad the Universal Breath of Life. It will seem to cause fine, free nature to make itself felt through you in power. Wisdom will beam from your countenance. Did not Aristides tell Socrates that his presence illuminated him with wisdom? So, all who let the Spirit be themselves, as it is God, will show the same Spirit as God. So, all who let the Mind be themselves, as it is God, will speak and think the thoughts of God in wisdom. There will be no loss of mind, no weakness of mind. Thoughts will flow free and strong. Thoughts will shed abroad healing. Thoughts will reflect their thinker. That is, we mean by reflect, that they will shed abroad the Mind of God by wonderful thoughts, which can accomplish great and wonderful things. All power is given unto Mind. All accomplishments are given under the power of thoughts. The world will uncover from its shadows of grief and sin by right thought. The world has covered itself with pain and poverty by wrong thoughts.

The fourth affirmation is, "God works through me to will and to do whatsoever ought to be done by me." That is true. Our understanding does all that is done for us. We are clothed and fed and housed and healed, we have all our blessings by our understanding. This is God. If we would have these marvelous works increased or perfected, we must intensify our understanding. This is being more of God. We may be all of God. We may be as little of God as we please. Being free to speak what we please, and thus free to make our understanding show forth great or small, free to make our word, we therefore make what we now experience by our understanding of God.

If you put up with many small annoyances, thinking that by such conduct you smooth things out, is it not your understanding of Good which causes you to act that way? If you would have your conditions perform to please you better, you must understand a larger Good. Whatever you do, and whichever way you turn, it is certainly by your understanding of Good. The statement, "God works through me to will and to do that which ought to be done by me," can be put in this way, "My understanding makes my world according to itself." Either way of putting the affirmation will perfect your understanding. Yet, when I say, "perfect your understanding," I do not mean that your understanding can be perfected. What I mean is that you have never loved your understanding enough. There is nothing you can be so well pleased with as your understanding. Watch it, and give it credit for all the Good you receive. You will soon love it, and this is loving God. Thus you will be in the same idea with God who saw the light that it was Good. It is the mind seeing that its power of understanding is Good, that brings it all its Good.

The fifth affirmation, which matches the fifth denial is, "I am governed by the law of God, and cannot sin, cannot suffer for sin, fear sin, sickness or death." Do you remember the fifth denial? It was, "There is no sin, sickness or death." Why do we call them regular denials and affirmations? Because they are those reasonings which, step by step, come forth after saying that first foundation sentence, that there is One Power, One Presence and One Mind. That One Mind, which occupies all things, says there is Good. The conviction is understandable, thus all-powerful. The Good is. The Good is God. Thus God is. There is One Mind and that is Good. Thus God is Mind, There is One Power and that is Good. Thus God is Power There is one everywhere present idea that is Good, thus God is omnipresent as the idea of Good. After reasoning this way from your own mind you cannot help making the denials of Science.

Remember, denials mean rejecting the appearances against Good. Appearances against Good are the negative of Good. This we meet by denying the evil and proclaiming the Good, It is as if something denied the Good. We meet the lie with the Truth. We meet the appearance with reality. We meet the claim of absence with the truth of presence. This we have sometimes called the omnipresent "No." We have called it universal negation.

Logic is mental reasoning. We are reasoning out the laws of the action of Mind as it conquers the universe with righteousness when we step along in ideas with Moses and Jesus. All mankind sets out to overcome evil; to overcome ignorance, pain, sickness and grief. But it is by instituting other forms of ignorance, pain, sickness and grief, that all achievements of the earth are wrought. Wars and hardships, and cruelty of man to man mark the great works of the world. By way of Jesus Christ there is peace on earth, good will to all men. It is by taking hold of a doctrine which, by thoughts and words of a certain character, lets all things come to pass as God wills. It is that action of the Mind whereby all mankind would let the reign of God come on earth, and be glad to let it come. Their whole nature is changed by seeing the reasonableness of the reasoning.

The fifth affirmation is the same as saying, "I govern my world by my understanding of Good, without sin, sickness or death. I understand God, therefore I love God." You certainly do govern your world by your understanding of God as Good; and if you have agreed to say that you see how it is possible to get along without sin, sickness or death in your world, it is your privilege to say so. You realize that you are governed by your understanding of Good. This is your understanding of Good. This is your God. It is God. It is all the God there is. It is Principle—high Principle.

He who knows the unreality of sin does not fear it nor grieve about it. He who knows the unreality of death pays no attention to it. To him there is no sin, no sickness, no death, To him there are other affirmations easy to believe. He can say with the Psalmist, "With me is understanding! I am strength!" He can heed the prophet's voice, "Say no longer, 'I am a child' see, this day I have set thee over the nations, over the kingdoms." You will feel that you are a transcendent nature. You cannot help feeling that all power is yours to use. You cannot help using your divine wisdom and power. You cannot help understanding Christ, and as you understand Jesus Christ, you have His Mind. When you have His Mind wholly, you have an understanding of the apostle's injunction to let the same Mind be in you that was in Jesus Christ. Then you will understand how so many Scientists have spoken their Divine nature as God, and you will see that it is through not yet understanding that others have criticized them. Your nature is God. Your possessions are power, wisdom and substance.

Between you and your possessions lies the claim of the absence thereof. You proclaim your right of way, and down falls every evil. Try it, and so prove your divinity. It is written in the Scriptures, "Prove thyself." We prove ourselves. By uniting with our power we are married to God, our Good. We are identified with our understanding. This is marriage. Jesus Christ was married to God in that he was united to his understanding.

All your noblest aspirations are to be fulfilled by being in full understanding of God.

Set apart one hour, or one day, each week, to affirm your divine relation to God — your GOOD.

Lesson Four

Foundation of Faith

THE words *omnipresence, omnipotence, omniscience,* grant revealing. The repetition of the word "Om" by the Brahmins was their name for God. The presence of the word is substance. The dividing syllable between "Om" and "presence" means nothingness or absence.

If a principle is nothing to us until we know it, this principle of the value of words in relation to our lives may seem to be unreal until we watch the difference which knowing the nature of words makes in our lives.

We silently speak the words *omnipresence, omnipotence, omniscience*. Soon we feel larger and more powerful and wiser. Perhaps we do not see that our duties increase. Our power to carry on large affairs enlarges. Our judgment is better. Perhaps we do not see all this quickly.

The Brahmins attained to great power and wisdom by meditating much on "Om." They dealt wisely with the great negation, except that they did not meet the first claim of the negation with the right "No!" For instance, when the claims of the ages met them, saying that Brahm had made woman without a soul, they did not say, "It is not true, the Soul of woman is Brahm as the Soul of man is Brahm, for Brahm knows no partiality." They neglected many negations in the same way. They did not meet them with the rightful reply. In our own time we have such things undone which we need to do.

There is always one perfect way of meeting every situation and every affair so as to adjust it rightly, and see it come out well. Carlyle tells, "The situation that hath not its duty, its ideal, was not ever yet occupied by man." In your life problems every one of them has a way, has exactly one way of dealing with it, so as to have it come right at once.

There is a way to raise the dead instantly. There is a way to heal the sick instantly. There is a way to educate yourself in all art, science and language instantly. In the Science, as far as known, we are conscious of putting in ideas needed and leaving out some non-essentials. We keep our mind's eye fixed on the Science, with our whole mind, that we may drop what we do not need from our statements and bring forward what we do need.

If a Scientist has a sickness which he cannot meet with prompt nullification, he has not touched the keynote to his own power. If he has poverty or grief which he cannot make leave his premises, you may not scorn him, you may simply see that he has not touched that sentence, which, if he would speak it as truth, would heal him of poverty or grief.

The main thing to do in a demonstration of this Science is to notice what sentences work quickly in your behalf, and use them altogether. They have revealing power, and will quickly put you on the track of your right line of thinking. This is wherein the orderly arrangement of the Science is, so far as we have it, of the greatest benefit. It follows the order set out by Moses, and is so arranged that we can tell on what line of thought we are strong, and on what line we must add to our strength.

The first is a statement of foundation principles. The second rejects whatever contradicts those pro- positions. The third rallies every idea that confirms them. The fourth tells our relation to them, as to why and wherefore our lot in life is as it is, and may become what we please.

Jesus Christ called this lesson "Faith." He did not say, according to thy denial nor according to thy affirmation be it unto thee, but "According to thy faith be it unto thee." Moses said, "'Let there be a firmament in the midst of the waters." "Ment" means mind; it is from the Latin word "mens." We call a firm mind "Faith."

If you see a tailor cut up a long strip of broadcloth, you know he will bring forth a beautiful coat from the apparently useless cuttings. This is confidence in the correctness of a process. We see the sick child receiving the right thoughts of a practitioner or healer, and we commence to believe, although there is no sign of healing as yet, that the healing has begun. We have this confidence in our life conditions when our affirmations are working.

Paul noticed that the people who undertook the Christian ideas had moments of great exultation, then they suddenly fell into deep depression. He said, "Call to mind that after ye were illuminated ye endured so great fight of affliction." He saw how often it happened. Moses called it the "trial water." We have it in poetry and song to this day, "When peace like a river flows into my soul, when sorrows like sea billows roll," etc. Again, "The waters of sorrow are drowning my hopes." Here is the time, says Moses, when we must show firmness.

He who shows firmness in the midst of surging miseries solidifies a firm character. He makes a substance of his mind. Faith in the success of Good, when evil seems to be harrowing your life, will act like a gallant ship over the stormy main.

People often know the promising passages of the Bible by heart, but when trouble strikes them they have no confidence in them as absolute Truth. Just once holding onto them when you are in trouble would give you a good start in faith. Holding onto the great principles set forth in scripture, while you are in trouble, will invigorate your character marvelously. It is the very mystery of Godliness. How sure people are to come out right who have a strong, honest confidence that they will come out right! It is perfect proof of the teachings of Jesus Christ, "According to thy faith be it unto thee." As a result of your being certain that the thing which has come surging over your life cannot hurt you at all, soon the perfect condition will show forth, and things will come out right.

Bacon said that he had never made up his mind that a firm conviction that things would turn out right helped them to turn out right. He thought it helped us to bear things cheerfully, but was not certain that it affected conditions. We will not take Bacon's shaky uncertainty of the Omnipotent. Jesus said, "Thy faith hath made thee whole." It is rather strange that Bacon did not have confidence in the wisdom of Jesus, enough to take his teachings for granted, whether he himself had proved them or not.

We must know what we are to have faith in. We are to have faith in God, said Jesus. Thus we have faith in the Good as cutting out our life conditions just right for us, no matter how much evil there seems to be operating with us. God is Life. Thus we are to have confidence in Life as the outcome, no matter how death may seem to act. Life will win. We must be firm on this point, God is Truth. We must believe that the truth about the Good will act anyhow. We must be sure of it. We speak boldly that our patient will live. This is the truth about Good. Moses said, "Be firm." Paul said, "Stand." Jesus said, "Thy faith hath saved thee."

Truth about Good is God. You may go away out of the room from the sight of what death seems to be doing and tell the Truth. Truth is God. God is omnipotent. You will strike the life key of the patient and he will live. Every man, woman and child has a life key. You have the skill to touch it and turn him into free life. So with the truth about any situation. Tell the truth about your child, about its goodness. Its goodness is God. No matter how much water may sweep over that child be firm in saying, "All is well, God reigns, my child is good."

The same truth about health. Be very firm. Tell the air around you that health is God. Sickness is not God. God is all. Sickness is nothing. Then be firm. Say nothing else. Stand to it. Allow no other idea. That is Truth. Why should anything but Truth interest you? Why should what seems to be sickness baffle you and fill your mind, if the Truth is God, and you have the Truth in the possession of your understanding?

Begin today to practice this: Look into your life, look it over and see what you lack. Then tell the truth about it and be firm. See how it will come out. Faith means to be firm. Faith brings things out all right. Firmness on the side of evil is stubbornness. It opposes Good. As evil is not God, there is not a particle of firmness in evil. You may argue that the child will die because death seems to be acting, but the man who sees that Life is Good and is firm, will beat all your ideas of death, even if one hundred thousand doctors are on your side, for death is not God, Life is God. Lies are not God, Truth is God. Stubbornness to bring out death, or keep a person sick, is not God. Firmness to bring out health, because health is Good, is God. That is, Faith itself is God. Hence we have Jesus telling us that Faith is God.

We have a mental quality which can increase faith, so that the whole world does as we say. It shows Good at every turn. It drops its evil appearance at every turn. We become very firm in Good. We do not give a farthing for evil. We laugh at it. We ignore it. It is nothing. We are so firm, so steady, that all things are seen by us as God made them.

There is one thing about your firmness that I wish to speak of. It is this: You need not try any experiments of putting your will on the patient, nor against evil, nor for Good. You may only tell the truth about God. The Truth is its own will. It is the omnipotent will. You might get weary trying to exercise your will, but you would be strong from being firm. The truth that you speak asks only your announcing it and standing by it.

There is a generation of faith, like the generation of electricity. We speak the truth about the Good as sure to come out in our life or in our work. We stand firmly to the Truth. It goes out stronger and stronger as a power to drive back the belief and appearance of evil. We do nothing but speak the Truth and stand to it. If we feel confident one moment that all will come out right, just because a little appearance for the better shows up, and then our heart sinks the next moment because a bad appearance sets in, we are unstable. We are judging by appearances; and Jacob said to his son Ruben, "Unstable as water, thou shalt not excel."

Firmness as to Mind, or Good, being the power, does not make the Good come out right. It makes us see the Good in its true light. All is Good in reality. We have power to see things in reality. We see things in reality by being firm in our minds. The firmness of our minds as to Good is the original substance of all things. Thus substance touches substance when we speak the truth to the sick man. He is drawn out into sight as well. He is exposed as alive.

Firmness to any principle will expose a power. More than that, it will expose the very thing you seek in it. If you have, for instance, set your mind to heal heart disease, and are sure that there must be a remedy, keeping firm to that idea, and seeking for the healing of heart disease in every plant and every stone, your mind will get firmer and firmer, till one day it feels a quickening certainty. At that moment you may be handling clover leaves. You give some clover leaves and the patient gets well. Then you insist that the clover leaves made him well and cured him. But it was the new quality of your own mind.

Firmness developed a new working efficiency. You might have been handling camphor gum at that time and it would have been the same. While you keep your mind and heart intent upon healing heart disease those clover leaves will obey the streams of healing energy that quiver forth from your Soul. When you have withdrawn your thoughts, or the influence of your mighty confidence has passed into another realm, the clover leaves will no longer cure.

Paul's aprons and handkerchiefs served to cure people, because radiating from him went a buoyant confidence in his own principles. Shaky and feeble people felt the confidence of him as a brace. It took hold of that concealed substance within their own natures and it recognized itself.

All great remedies discovered by man have owed their curative energies to the continuous confidence of some firm mind. When that mind left the remedy it would not work. Once there was a man who cured thousands of cases by using the powdered thigh-bone of a criminal. They flocked in hordes to see him. He had assistants who administered it. His confidence passed right through them to the patients and they revived. Finally he passed on, and no longer would the powdered thigh-bone of a criminal work to cure anybody. It is for this reason that the faith should be set on God. God is eternal. Faith in God being generated on the earth, everything and everybody will breathe it, and it will touch the substance of their life and unite them to eternal cure.

Abraham was working for the power of faith and suddenly received it. He had an "H" from Jehovah's name inserted within his own, and he became Abraham, Father of the Faithful. This was the mysterious old-time way of expressing every mental quickening by calling it a direction straight from the Lord. So it was indeed.

All the liberating of the inner fire within us to operate on the world without us, by laying hold of its substance, is the speaking of the God voice within us. This voice may come from the God voice without us, as it did to the prophets. If we feel that around us is God we may hear a voice from the bushes, like Moses. We may hear a voice from the air, as Samuel did. We may hear a voice from the clouds as Jesus Christ did. If we contemplate the God within us we shall feel the voice within us, and it will be as audible as if it were without us. Whichever way we may hear it we seem to turn our faith in that direction, and so our strength comes from that kind of faith. If we are determined that ALL is God we shall not be limited to the voice within nor the voice without. Everything will bear witness that we are in God.

Then there is no seeking, and no command to be firm. We are firm and fixed in our eternal Godhead and power.

Science pursued has four accomplishments to work out. Jesus Christ said it would give you power to preach the gospel, heal the sick, cast out bad tempers, and raise the dead. Every time the waters of opposition float over us we stand firm, and the Good comes into sight.

The fourth idea with which this Science deals is the doubt that the Good is working to prove itself quickly in our behalf. This doubt has a rushing and overturning action with us. You all know what it is to fear that you are not going to have things come out your own good way. This is doubt. It shows that either consciously or unconsciously you have been taking some high thoughts of God. Likely you have thought of God from a much higher standpoint than your minister or preacher or anyone ever spoke to you. It was so much higher than the world that when the trial came you could not reconcile the conditions with the great goodness of God, which you felt to be true. So you doubted that Good was cutting out the pattern of your circumstances to please your heart. Here is where you are to remember your highest thought of God which you have ever held. Hold it firmly. If need be you may speak over your truth rapidly and constantly, so as not to let any other idea, be spoken by you, even in thought.

Nehemiah, the builder of the walls of Jerusalem, would not listen to anything but his own ideas of the presence and power of his God, so he succeeded, to the astonishment of his enemies. Ezra built the temple in conjunction with Zerubbabel, when neither of them would listen to one word against the power of Jehovah to take a feeble and weakly congregation and out of it build a mighty people.

Miracles are nothing to the power of this faith or firmness, when it is once liberated in you by your firm holding out for the omnipotence of Good, for the omnipotence of the truth of Good, for the certain action of the principle of Goodness. This was so plain to Jesus that he said one grain of faith would move a mountain. Faith is a self-increasing property, just as jealousy is said to be. The jealous person, you know, sits down and imagines a whole sequence of actions. He then feels so strongly that he acts upon his feelings and does dreadful things. His jealousy feeds itself by his thoughts until it handles him entirely.

Faith in Goodness will feed itself and increase itself in the same way, till we rise and work miracles by reason of it. We do not seem to handle our faith. It handles us. We become our faith. We always were our faith. It is, in its intrinsic nature, God himself. So, one name for God might be Faith.

In pure spiritual doctrine, we have an axiom for the science of denial in its relation to environments. It is that mind is as free as it has courage to deny. Looking around us we perceive that what our mind determines the environing circumstances demonstrate. We are as free from evil as we refuse to think about it. Whatever of evil we think about, that we are mixed up with. Whatever we positively will not think about we never get hurt by.

There is another very beautiful axiom. It is that mind is as great as it has courage to affirm. This also will demonstrate in the life. "I will be Pope of Rome," said a little boy, and he was. "How did you become so great?" they asked Sir Isaac Newton. "By intending my mind," he replied. An intention is a strong affirmation. "I will be an artist," said a child. He could not even draw a plain picture well. Yet, he became a wonderful artist.

For this fourth lesson there is an axiom which is very true in demonstration. It is that mind will certainly demonstrate as much greatness as it has courage to stand by its intention. It is not so much by what we do as by what we think that we stand by our affirmations or intentions.

For instance, no amount of dosing with drugs, or rubbing, or poulticing, could avail to cure your patients. But your mind holding firmly onto its denials and affirmations is certain to cure them, though you do not lift a finger.

Euripides, a Greek dramatist, was one of those thinkers of the far past whose axioms have come down to us. About 450 B.C., he said, "One right thought is worth a hundred right hands." And so it is. A child's prayer can do more to clothe and feed a family than its father's daily toil; exactly as your treatment in a sick room will do more in curing than a hundred doctors' best prescriptions.

In all great lives you will see that it was what they did when some storm of adversity struck them which made their character count. Nehemiah never flinched when they told him that if he stayed outside the Temple he would be slain. When they threatened him he arose and said, "Should such a man as I flee? I will not go in!"

Paul sang praises to God in prison, Silas joined him, and a great earthquake shook the foundations of the prison at the sound of their singing. Certain tones have power to shake rocks, to crumble walls, to lift weights. Paul and Silas thought only of omnipotent Good, and it shook off their bonds. It opened their prison doors. This way of treating exile was so different from the way Seneca acted, who was exiled about that time, and wailed and lamented so abjectly that his high-sounding phrases seemed a mockery.

There is always once at least when are called to stand steady to our principles. In one of the Brontë novels it is spoken of in beautiful language, that we do not know the value of our high principles and laws until we test them in trial. This night take your hardest trial and put some denial and affirmation before it. Then from that hour stand by your denial and affirmation. Stand firm. This is your faith that builds character. Nothing is sure at all in your life until it has been put through the furnace, which is the meeting of the opposite to it with its noble steadfastness to itself.

"There is a spirit in man, and the inspiration of the Almighty giveth him understanding," says Job. This Spirit in man is his God. The inspiration is his breath of God. The

God within and the God without are united by breathing. But the external breath of air into the lungs is only a symbol, a hint of the true breath which right thoughts can give, if they are put forth and taken in at the moment of intense experience called trouble. It is equally powerful if in a moment of great joy one keeps firm to the same great Truth. Firmness is poise, balance of character. Balance, poise of character, is a great healing quality. We become healers of disease according to our poise of character.

The thoughts of Good within us are opposed to the beliefs of evil that seem to swell and surge without us. This makes an apparent conflict. If the firm will stands by the Good "the middle wall of partition" is broken down. Paul speaks of the thoughts of evil, which make seemingly evil conditions and surroundings, as the "middle wall of partition," because between our good thoughts and the world of reality is our line of false thinking which reports such ugly things to our mind. It is the mystery of the word omnipresence over again. "Ni" is the middle wall of partition, yet it is nothing. It is the "No, you are not good," which faces all people. When met by the NO of your proposition it falls away.

It is the same with many of the words of Scripture, whether we have before observed it or not. Take the word "Ho" in the sentence, "Ho everyone that thirsteth." Students have been surprised to see how appropriate it is to the sentence, outside of a mere exclamation. H-O were the two letters which in ancient alchemy represented water. In modern chemistry they use the formula H_2O. But it was an expression far beyond the simple first sight of the word. It is the same with all scripture language. Take the word "firm-a-ment" — firm to God in all things. It has the full meaning of a mind firm to holiness, firm to goodness, firm to God in all things. Firm to Good when evil appears, firm to life when death seems near, firm to health when sickness seems reigning, and so on. A mind striving to set itself free in steadfastness from the waters of these trials.

The "A" which divides the word "firm" from the word "ment" is the angel in the sun, of whom John the Revelator speaks. When he seems dark he is Abaddon, according to the Hebrew tongue, or Apollyon according to the Greek tongue. When he is the dark angel he is the angel of the bottomless pit. But it is only in misunderstanding that he is darkness. In understanding he is an angel and archangel of light and life and joy. It works out in human character as the forces which are said to follow men as the sun follows them, or as the night follows them.

The first is approbativeness, and is very strong in all mankind from early childhood. The second is amativeness, which comes later. The third is ambition, which comes in its fullness later on. The fourth is acquisitiveness, which is yet later. When the character is in the light, these four are seen to be: First, artlessness, which is innocence; second attractiveness, which is beauty and judgment; the third is aspiration; and the fourth is ascension, or the complete absorption of the mind and life in spiritual themes. The transformation of character I from the first four to the last four comes when we meet temptation with the right spirit.

One may say, "I cannot help being afraid when I see sickness showing its mastery over health." Yes you can. No man was ever tempted beyond what he is able to resist. There is always a way of escape from the greatest or least seeming evil. One may as well say there is no Omnipotence as to say that he cannot help what it is his very omnipotent nature to throw off easily.

One may say the drunkard cannot help drinking any more than a child can help crying. This is an insult to the omnipotent Spirit resting within him. It places a man where he is not divine in nature, but satan. It puts him in mind of where he must be restrained. It is siding with the great "nihil" claim against him, which comes as, "You are a weak-willed fool," You must not side with the claim that man is too weak to resist drinking. You are the weak fool you say he is, for we are what we accuse our neighbors of being.

Some say the sharp-tongued scold can no more help her hateful words than a child can help breathing, because it is her nature born with her. Who told you that anybody had a mean, wicked nature? Did Jesus say so? No, he said all came forth from God. Stand firmly to your Jesus Christ principle that ALL are strong, that ALL are well. Stand in the waters of seeming and see the real nature come smiling up.

Some say, "I cannot help crying when I see my best feelings, my generosity, my kindest efforts insulted." What is that omnipotent spark within you for, if it is not the Principle to be agreed with when the waters of grief come rolling toward you? That is the way to talk.

There is no seeming temptation that is too great to be met with the Good and put down into the nowhere and nothing. The woman who speaks sentimentally of how the poor drunkard cannot help his drinking, and with condoning smoothness puts up with him as a weak thing, will be severe enough with her own children. The man who sentimentalizes over his drunken partner will vent his rage on his wife and daughter. It is because they themselves do not resist. Hence it is part of the action of mind in its relation to environment that we take one half day to changing that old angel of accusation of weakness into the angel of ascension, by saying, "*I do not believe in a mixture of good and evil in the world, or in myself; all is Good.*"

There are no two sides to this question. There is only one side. There is only one Being to make your covenant with, and that is Omnipotence. To make a covenant with, is to agree with. We agree with Principle by declaring that we believe in it.

Did you ever say that it was your feeling that justice and right would sometime be done in the world? Did you say that the time seemed very long? Did you think that it would be far ahead in the millennium time of the poets and prophets? Tell me why you thought the time for the triumph of Good to be far ahead? I am sure you are judging by appearances. Why do you do so? Can you see that when making a choice as to whom to believe you chose the poets and the prophets rather than Jesus Christ? He said, "This generation shall not pass away until all be fulfilled." If he was speaking to the people, can you not see that he meant that if they took this doctrine they would see the fulfillment of their words in their own day? He said, "This day is salvation come."

It is certain that when you put out great words of Truth into the air you may expect to see them come to pass any moment. Notice the way these texts read: "Immediately his leprosy was cleansed." "Immediately he received his sight." "He lifted her up and immediately the fever left her." "Immediately she was made straight and glorified God." "And immediately he was made whole." "And immediately I was in the Spirit." The idea of Spiritual Science seems to be entirely of instantaneous demonstration, if the words of Jesus are believed, rather than the ideas of the poets and the prophets.

The whole fact of demonstration rests upon wise choice. Today, if you will choose the teaching of Jesus Christ, you will be based in mind, you will know where you stand. A good base of mind is a good healing power. It is a better policy to either believe in something entirely or disbelieve entirely than to be up and down in changes of feeling about matters.

A business man who believes in nobody is a certain man to deal with. You are sure he will show no favors so you do not whine and shake around where he is. You stand up and keep your eyes on your own affairs. A business man who believes in everybody has exactly the same effect, only that he braces you to believe in yourself, because he believes in you. Then agree with some principle. Stand to it. Here is a commandment of Solomon: "Keep sound wisdom and discretion, so shall they be life to thee."

Hear this idea of the power of faith: "The Lord is your confidence, and shall keep thy foot from being taken." When the Lord is your confidence you will never find yourself at all deceived by the ways and speech of men and women, though they be very brilliant, if they speak outside of the Principle that demonstrates healing and goodness and life.

Do you remember two pieces of statuary by Thorwaldson, the Danish sculptor, which he called Day and Night? On the breast of the woman, who symbolizes Night, repose twin babes, death and sleep. So limp and terrible looks the little figure of "death," so absent from life looks the little baby "sleep." On the shoulders of "Day" smiles the child of quickening life. Life and joy and vigor laugh in every curve. One is the symbol of unreality and the other is the symbol of reality. In Truth there is no sleep and there is no death. All is life. Life at its joyous height is the rest of God, which sleep tries to symbolize. Life at its sweetest charm is the peace which night tries to typify. The promise is that there shall be no night there in that life of Truth we are told to live. Neither shall there be any death.

There is no fate that can come up to face you with defeat. You were not made for failure, no matter who you are, nor how much you know, nor what anyone has told you. God is your prosperity. God, the Most High, is your defense. God, the absolute Good, is your friend. Do not heed that high sounding poetry which reads that — "on two days it is useless to run from thy grave, the appointed and the unappointed day. On the first neither balm nor physicians can save, nor thee on the second the universe slay." It is good poetry but it is not the Truth.

Error is put in very bright packages of beautiful words, but it is better to have a mind of your own. Do not covenant with the principle of limitation to believe in it. It is the teaching of Jesus Christ that he has, by his doctrine, set before us an open door which no man can shut. We have unlimited power.

If we do not use that power it does not alter the fact of its being our inheritance. We have a store of unlimited wisdom. If we do not draw upon it, that does not alter the fact of its being ours. We may tell how little we know. We may complain of our feebleness, but that touches not our strength. We have exactly what we say we have, so far as appearances go, but appearances are nothing.

Principle is so generous and full of faith that it takes it for granted if you say you are ignorant you surely must want to be ignorant, for man's word is his own to do with as he pleases. And a man's word is the weapon with which he cuts out his destiny. Or it is the stuff out of which he builds his life. If you have the use of all wisdom by saying, "I am wise," and the use of all ignorance by saying, "I don't know anything," you are rather ungrateful if you choose to complain. In the years of travel through the wilderness the Israelites provoked the Lord with their complainings. Complaints increase the conditions.

You may hear people who profess to have confidence in the Holy Spirit, telling how badly their stomach feels, how weak their limbs feel, how heavy their head is, how blue they feel. They do not show any signs, by such drafts on the orders of blankness, that they have any communion whatsoever with the Spirit. Do not take your ways of thinking or acting from them. Look to your own relation to the Spirit. When anyone speaks on the side of evil you will say, within your own mind, "I do not believe a word of it." Thus you will be on the reality side, and will call them out of their sleepiness, for all talk on the side of death or weakness is sleep. There is no life in it. It is even worse than talk about the weather, or gas pipes, or statuary. The subjects which interest the mind are the stuff out of which happiness is made or not made. Only one theme is full of life and beauty and increasing strength.

Let me tell you the twelve effects of thinking of the Spirit: You will have life, health, strength, support, defense, thinking faculty, wise speech, ability to record well your ideas, joyous song, skill in carrying out your principles, beauty of judgment and great love.

The musician thinks he is skilled at the piano because he practices hard. Not so. It is because he has in some moment covenanted with the spiritual feeling or ideal that stirred him, and it has come forth so far as to lead him to be willing to practice to give it more freedom. It is certain that if he really knew that it was the Holy Spirit expressing itself through him, he would see that it is not his practice but his free mind that enables him to be a good musician.

It is the Spirit that doeth all things. It is never anything else but Spirit that does all the good that is done. All the beauty of life, all the love of life, all the kindness of life, is of the Spirit. The Spirit is God. David says that God proclaims, "I have made a covenant with my chosen." The chosen are those who speak in the Spirit. They have chosen to speak on that side, and that covenant God will not annul. He will not break it. It is His promise that, "Thy seed will I establish forever, and thy throne to all generations."

It is ours to choose our principle. It is the way of the principle we have chosen to deal with us according to itself. Jesus Christ said, "His ye are to whom ye have yielded yourselves servants to obey." He also said, "No man can serve two masters."

John, the Revelator, called the fourth step of Science the fourth foundation stone of the City of Peace. We have great peace in the Spirit; there is no turmoil whatever in the Spirit. If there is turmoil it is a signal that we have tried to believe in both evil and good at the same time. It cannot be done. When turmoil comes before you make haste to say, *"I do not believe in a mixture of good and evil, I believe only in Good."* If the turmoil is within your own mind, you will make haste to say, "I believe that my God is now working with me to make me omnipresent, omnipotent and omniscient. I believe only in the Good as ruling in and with my life. I have faith in God. I have the faith of God."

It shows that you have to make some decided choice in and with your mind. It is the experience which comes after realizing some great ideal in spiritual life, which your human lot seems to be far from carrying out. Its symbol is the emerald stone, symbolizing that the choice on the side of Good is made.

Joel, the prophet, was looking over the people of the earth, and when he realized how we see principles and how we judge of life, he cried out, "Multitudes, multitudes, in the valley of decision." That is, not yet decided. Goethe, the German writer, wrote, "Choose! choose well! Your choice is brief and yet endless." The choice is ever before us, for evil always seems very real and very powerful, until met with the Truth.

Our way of believing deep down in our convinced mind is our faith. We are sure to speak out from that faith. If we talk against our faith, that is, we do not quite believe that the health principle is most powerful, and yet we keep on talking health, for health, and will not admit that we are afraid of the sickness, we surely will find our faith coming around to the side of omnipotent health. This is the way of entering into faith by a straight line of procedure. If, when we are trying to talk for health, and talk for prosperity, and talk for wisdom, everything seems against us and everything hurts us greatly, we must put great vehemence into our saying, "I do not believe in sickness, I believe in health. I do not believe, or think, that misfortune has any power whatsoever. I believe in prosperity and success."

God is working, as we put deep feeling into the circumstance. For instance, if you feel grieved, you must put as much feeling into your declaration of faith as you have grief in your mind. The two states of grief and vehement words will act together to form a new base in your character. They are like silver in solution, which a certain kind of acid can precipitate into fine flakes of silver again. So the right circumstances are hidden in the solution of your grief. You put strong words into your feelings, and a new state of mind comes forth, which is a great power. In the even daily life you can prepare the soil of your mind with a certain set of ideas which will go beforehand like a King's Guard and cut out or down all the trials in your way.

Your own radiance of mind, engendered by your noble thoughts, will go like protecting fire before you and stop calamities, stop sickness, stop the tongues of your seeming enemies, and do all things for you. It is the Spirit that goeth before to guide, as it is written, "I will guide thee with mine eye." All your days of ease from sickness and calamity should be filled with words and thoughts which have this protecting power.

Divide your days into statements that can accomplish miracles. Take Monday for one kind of thought, Tuesday for another, and so on. And when Thursday comes around, why not take that day for discussing or meditating upon the fourth lesson in Science, since Thursday is the fourth day of the week's activities.

This law of thought concerning spiritual doctrine is the law Jesus Christ taught. That is why it has been called *Christian* Science. If you will look up the history of art and science, especially chemistry and physics, you will see how often practical usages of great principles are named after the men who first used the principles.

Jesus Christ taught that we may uplift our life by uplifting our thoughts. Jesus Christ taught that the only uplifting thoughts are the thoughts of God. The true thoughts of God were given to us by him. We now take them and resolve them into twelve definite propositions, which are not only in the same order in which he expressed himself on spiritual matters, but are the actual processes of our own mind, as soon as we give it freedom. The statements usher us into a new realm of life.

We find that it is not spiritual nobility to be brave in warfare, nor to be able to cure the sick, nor to be able to rise above temptation to do wrong. By thinking wisely ahead of these circumstances we never come into them. If you say in a moment of anger that you are unlucky, and that brings you a stroke of hard luck, can you not see that it is no special credit to you to get bravely out of the mess into which you have deliberately plunged yourself by your words? Can you not see that you would be far more noble to do the right thing beforehand? Getting bravely out of a scrape is just like putting your hand into live coals then asking us to praise you because you are a good surgeon in cutting it off, and so patient in bearing the deprivation or loss of your hand.

We make our own conditions. And this brings us to the preparation of our feet with the Gospel .so perfect that if we choose we never enter the seas of misery. Paul said, "Have your feet shod with the preparation of the Gospel." The new covenant which is prophesied in the Scripture the Lord will make with his people, means this agreement with the Spirit, Spirit is to do all things for us, and we do nothing for ourselves. Our only relation to the perfect way being that we agree to leave ourselves entirely in its keeping. On this account, if you will make your covenant with the omnipotent, external Spirit, to do all things, and you will do nothing but trust it entirely, you also will be that people with whom the prophesied covenant is made. You will find it mentioned by Jeremiah: "Behold the days come," saith the Lord, "that I will make a new covenant with the house of Israel, and the whole valley of dead bodies shall be holy unto the Lord. It shall not be plucked up nor thrown down any more forever."

Paul writes of this new covenant in the eighth chapter of Hebrews. Here he shows how wise the covenant will make mankind, and how happy and free. It is heaven here and now without fighting or waiting any more for it.

Jesus Christ is called the Mediator of the New Covenant, because he teaches that by his principle we have an easy yoke and a light burden. He does not praise hardship or suffering. He praises faith and freedom. It will help you into a mighty understanding of Spirit to covenant with Spirit for the action of the Holy Spirit with you in this perfect fashion.

Do not covenant with the Spirit for pain or suffering. In Spirit there is no such manner of dealing. The Pietists (1700 A. D.) told the Spirit they were willing to suffer. The Spirit never asked them nor anyone to suffer, but, as they covenanted for suffering, they got it. A certain pastor of an English mission was very much pleased that he got his expenses paid by praying for them, and had about $14.00 left over. As all the wealth of the earth was offered him you can see that he was not especially honoring God by having such a little bit at his disposal.

Sit down by yourself, and honestly and lovingly say:

"I hereby covenant with the Holy Spirit for my life, and I will do nothing to preserve my life; my life is the life of the Spirit.

I covenant with the Holy Spirit for my health; and I will do nothing to preserve my health; my health is the health of the Spirit.

I covenant with the Spirit for my strength, and I will do nothing for my strength; my strength is the strength of the Spirit.

I covenant with the Spirit for my support, and I will do nothing for my support; my support is the providence of the Spirit.

I covenant with the Spirit for my defense, and I will do nothing for my defense; my defense is the protection of the Holy Spirit.

I covenant with the Spirit for my mind in its perfect thinking, and I will do nothing for my thoughts; my mind is the mind of the Spirit.

I covenant with the Spirit for my right speech, and I will do nothing for my speech; speech is the voice of the Spirit.

I will do nothing to fix, or record, or write my Truth unto the earth, for my record is the record of the Holy Spirit.

I say, as Job said, My witness is in the heavens and my record is on high.

I covenant for my joyous song of life, and will do nothing to be joyful; my joy is the joy of the Spirit.

I covenant with the Spirit for my demonstrations of efficiency and skill in rightly doing all things, and I will do nothing to perfect myself.

My efficiency is the working skill of the Holy Spirit, according to the words of Jesus Christ, who said, 'The words that I speak unto you, it is not I that speak, but the Father within; he doeth the works.'

I covenant for my judgment in its beauty, and the beauty of judgment; for the Spirit is my judgment.

I covenant with the Holy Spirit for my love, and will do nothing to make myself loving or beloved, for all is the Holy Spirit now acting with irresistible goodness through me."

This will make it easy for you then to say, from the depths of your heart, "I do believe that my God is now working with me and through me and by me, to make me omnipotent, omnipresent, and omniscient. I have faith in God. I have the faith of God."

This is the fourth lesson in Science. We are hereby taught about being fixed in an eternal choice. This a lesson in faith, with an explanation of why we have a reason for the faith that is in us. It is a lesson in the covenants. Look up all you can and about the covenants of the people with God, and how much more beautiful the covenants of Jesus Christ are than any of them. "I come not to do my own will, but the will of him that sent me."

Our own will says; "Believe with the world." But God's will says: "Believe in Me."

Lesson Five

The Word of Faith

THERE are three ways of dealing with the principles announced in Truth. There is the deep thinking which the mind exercises respecting them. There is the speaking them forth which we do not hesitate to do. There is the careful recording of them, which is writing down what we know of them. The next is living them, which we are sure to do, if we think, speak and write them. It is by faithfully doing all these ways with Spiritual doctrine that we accomplish the works of the Spirit in us.

Sometimes a practitioner of healing is astonished to find that he has cured a half dozen people of very miserable conditions, and yet those cured patients will not speak of their cures nor urge other people to be cured by the same means. It is because the practitioner has not recorded the miracle on paper and caught the principle as it were; to abide in his house so firmly that when a patient is cured it is a fact so present in his consciousness that he cannot forget it and has to speak of it.

Cures are the works of Truth. Cures or works are wrought by faith. That which we have faith or confidence in is our mental character quality, and goes through our thoughts, through our writings, through our speech, to others. If we do not write down our thoughts we leave out an important part of our way of shedding abroad our healing quality. There are certain writers who have not yet come into their stream of consecutive, careful, thinking power, but they can write the truths of the Science, and through their writings they convey a sweet healing. After a while the writing of their thoughts leads them out into consecutive thinking. Then they heal by mental reasonings.

Peter told the Christians, to whom he wrote letters, that they ought to have a reason for the hope that was in them, and be able to tell that reason. The telling of that reason has been the means many times of healing those who told it, as well as those who heard it. To say to a man with a lame foot that he is a spiritual being entirely, and that as Spirit it is not possible to be lame, is to touch perhaps the only chord in his mind which could influence the foot to be well.

There is always one chord in every mind which is capable of responding promptly in the cure of the one ill that threatens you or anybody. It is when this healing chord is not struck that people continue in their old sickness.

There are twelve ideas with healing power in them. There are thousands of ways of presenting those twelve ideas. Sometimes a practitioner of healing will find that he cannot make his thoughts train his body by positive or direct statements, he has to come to his nature by negative or indirect processes. For instance he cannot make his thoughts work out his affairs right by saying: "My prosperity is satisfactory to me." He has to say, "I do not need prosperity. I do not need anything." It is all a matter of belief. Thus we often hear people telling about having a "belief" of this or that malady. It sounds strange and affected, but quite expresses the state of affairs. If they are strictly in the faith; of Jesus Christ they do not believe at all in sickness. They do not permit themselves to believe in any doctrine which makes sickness.

It is not yet known very widely that certain religious beliefs make sickness. For instance, a belief in satan makes some people ill. The belief in an end of the world by fire and brimstone makes others sick. A belief of a personal God on a great throne in the skies makes people sick. If one has a great belief in inheriting conditions from his ancestors, it may be the whole mental cause of his physical disorder. Thus thoughts which move in the mind make the body, as waters moving upon the land change and form the land.

It is this Moses refers to in his statement of the principle that thoughts arrange and formulate outward conditions. Notice that he says, after having your mind firm in Truth, "Let the waters be gathered together in one place, and let the dry land appear." Let it be plainly seen what you believe. It cannot be hidden out of sight, really. It is a certain law that, "According to thy faith be it unto thee." What we believe is written out on our bodies, and we cannot hide the handwriting.

What the waters do is plainly seen by the land. It is not specially interesting to symbolize spiritual thoughts and their results by land and water, and stars and stones, but it is record of one thing surely and that is that as the stars and the earth act they each and all act, and each and everything symbolizes the mind.

The great minds of the world have felt that the study of matter has not done them any good, only to teach them that such knowledge profiteth nothing. They are convinced that all things have an inner significance, and it is that inner significance which it is worth while to know. The things themselves have no value apart from their divine meanings.

A celebrated physician was once speaking to a thoughtful woman about the influence of faith in the cure of disease. He said that he believed greatly in the effect of a powerful faith, it had often accomplished what regular prescriptions had failed to do, but he did not believe that faith itself could be studied and understood, because of the prejudices of mankind, which would interfere with such studies.

"I feel that Jesus meant we have a right to freedom from prejudice with all the rest of our liberations, when he said, the Truth shall make you free," said the lady. This unconvinced doctor shook his head.

Here is where our fifth step in mental action, our fifth lesson in life Science, finds us. Do we believe Power operates through all things? Yes. Do we believe that Power can be understood by us? If we can honestly answer that we do believe the Omnipotent Power can be understood, do we believe it is worth our while to give all our mind and all our strength, and all our life to finding out how to deal, with it?

It is certainly the Jesus Christ doctrine that we take no thought about what we shall eat, how it shall be prepared, where it comes from, what it costs, what we drink and wear, where they come from, how they are made, along with other subjects which interest the people who look to the phenomena or the material things. He would have us know all things, have all things, without trying to have them, and be filled with power without long practice in science or art, and so on through the list of worldly ways. It lies often to our choice how far we will undertake to follow Christ.

The choice sets our mind to a key note. This key note we always strike when we meet people. They feel our mental tone. They feel it with their mind. If they have thought along our lines they respond gladly. If they have thought quite differently they feel mentally opposed to us. But if we do not change our base, do not falter in our faith, there will be a constant sounding of our tone that will break down their opposition. They will come to respond with their own tone which is like ours. They will be healed. They will be uplifted. Our mental conviction that evil is nothing real, causes evil to falter in their feelings. Our mental conviction that Spirit is the only substance will spiritualize them. The more firmly we hold to our own thoughts, the more the conscious reasoning, which we keep thinking, will change and alter their conditions. Our own conditions will change for the better, and still on for the better, world without end.

Our words along the nature of our faith, make our faith a working principle. The waters of a river might be walled up into a great basin, but if a channel is made for that water, it flows down over the lands and makes them fruitful. Thus our words are the outlet of our faith. Our words in the silence of our mind are as potent for good as our spoken audible words.

If our faith were small, and we should keep talking, keep thinking, keep writing ideas absolutely true, our faith in those words, which lies hidden in our natures would finally come forward. If we did not greatly believe something, but should keep speaking it, or thinking about it, we would construct an artificial faith in our words, and make conditions like our persistent ideas. You will remember that Napoleon talked much of what he would do in case of defeat. So his defeat came at Waterloo.

Jesus Christ taught the importance of the word. "By thy word, thou art justified and by thy word thou art condemned." "If a man keep my sayings he shall never see death."

Two ministers of the old school of theology were accustomed to call themselves miserable sinners, and also to tell that there is a dreadful place prepared for sinners. One of the ministers came back, after he had passed through what is called death, and communed face to face with the other. He said, "I am condemned to a place of burning, and justly too." He tried to say more but could not. We know why. It was the justice of the law, that if it is as we speak that we are condemned, he who had said miserable sinners, of whom he was one, must all be burned, must honorably share the fate of the rest of the sinners. He had not really had faith that he should burn, but the waters of conscious speech fixed the lands or settled the places of his lot. So we are told to guard our heart's thought. So we are told to watch our tongues.

Some minds quickly translate their thoughts into actions. You, yourself, may have a habit of fearing some little thing and it keeps coming up till it finally begins to seem real. For instance, you fear that the old pain in your head may trouble you if the car is warm, so you open the window and yet your head aches. Looking at the window you find you did not open the window leading out doors, but one leading into another carriage. There is such a subtle connection between the thoughts of your mind and all your affairs that the affairs can report themselves to your unconsciousness.

Now suppose you had risen in mind with calm self-poise and said, "I am not a victim of headaches, I do not believe in them; neither do I believe in material causation." You would have, by your very words, compelled things to be as you said. You would have been free from pain.

You, yourself, are the arbiter of your own destiny. Why give in to the old ideas? Old ideas are old beliefs. You are not obliged to believe that you are a being liable to misery.

This changing of all events by thoughts is called works. If the faith is good we do not have to take many conditions in hand specially. They take care of themselves and let us deal with the principles. As for instance, if your faith is established in Truth, you will probably find people will be well and easily recover from their maladies from association with you, while you keep on thinking the twelve propositions of Mind Science. On that day which you devote to the fifth proposition you ought to see people very well, without especially thinking for their particular health. If they are not well you must speak specially to them.

Do you remember the fourth statement? The fifth is like unto it in showing how we make our own happiness or unhappiness so far as this phenomenal world is concerned. The spiritual, or Real World is not changed by our words. It is the same changeless good yesterday, today and forever. All our faith, all our reasonings, are to open our eyes to see the Real World. From the standpoint of Truth it is thus with us always. From the phenomenal standpoint we have chance and change and unhappiness. The fifth statement is,

"As Divine Mind, which I am, I preach the gospel heal the sick, cast out passions, raise the dead. I work the works of God who works through me to will and to do that which ought to be done by me, according to the doctrine of Jesus Christ. The words that I speak unto you, it is not I that speak, but the Father that dwelleth in me, he doeth the works."

Such an affirmation makes you realize that you have nothing whatsoever to do, for do you not see that if the spiritual world is already perfect, if that is the Real World, you do not really have anything whatsoever to do? *Thus the highest working power is the power to see that we have nothing to do.*

Our demonstration of this will come out in many unexpected ways. For instance, we are in hard straits with our business affairs, and we insist that it makes no difference to us in reality. This may show out in our power at healing, or in our bodily health, before it shows in our affairs. Even at their best what are our affairs? They are symbols of our real life. If they please us they are pleasing symbols, but nothing is real except Spirit. So this idea will come step by step to make our environments right. We cannot fail while we are daily speaking the lofty principles of that Kingdom on the earth, though not of it, which will come up before our vision more and more.

We were not made to fail. We were not made to be burdened. Probably you will notice that the fifth lesson seems to take away our own management of things. It is therefore the great lesson in meekness. It touches most nearly that word of Jesus Christ, "Not my will but thine be done." We are willing to submit to the law of our words. We are willing to give up old words to let the Word of God be spoken in us and through us.

God hath given the Holy Spirit the speech and thought of the universe. In us is the Holy Spirit. We let it speak and think through us, then we are like John on the Isle of Patmos. We cannot realize time or people or events. They come and go as we hasten nearer and nearer to our sight of the Heavenly City. If we speak of preaching the gospel, we mean telling the world of the spiritual Kingdom — speaking from the absolute standpoint, "if we tell of healing the sick, we do not mean that there are sick people, we mean that we see people more nearly as they are. If we speak of casting out passions, which are called demons and devils in scripture, we do not mean that there are devils or demons. We mean that we see the Holy Spirit in mankind instead of passions and tempers.

We mean the same by raising the dead. There is no death, yet we speak of raising the dead as a work of Science. How is this? We mean that we see life where we have believed in death. If we should say all the time, "I see life; I see health; I see strength; I see prosperity, and so on," we should mean exactly what we do by saying that as Divine Mind we heal the sick, cast out demons, raise the dead.

There is only One Mind. That Mind is the source of all thoughts. We think the first thoughts of that Mind when we think according to Jesus Christ. All other thoughts are no thoughts. All other words are no words. Thoughts and words not in Science make thicker and thicker fictitious conditions. They are all subject unto us.

Do not fail to keep some of the words of Truth running in your mind continually. It is well to have the Truth ideas running because they lead the mind out into the events of the day.

If we were involved deeply in thinking mathematical problems we would not carry a healing presence. If we were the greatest musician that ever lived we would not carry healing power by our scales and chords; but at the first trump of the doctrine of Jesus Christ within our mind we are filled with healing presence. It works through us like a fine fire of sweetness.

There will come a moment when we appreciate how closely related our thoughts are to our world. We will see that our reasonings based on the premise of matter being real, are not enduring, as to the conditions they have made. If we have spoken of riches as being the possession of material things, and then reason why we should have riches, we are talking entirely of nothing. Riches are the presence of the Holy Spirit in us. All reasoning based on that premise is solid reasoning and will demonstrate in good symbols.

Swedenborg thought so much upon God that his face shone so that sometimes his servants were afraid of him. Do you suppose he asked that his face might shine? No, he was thinking beyond faces. Mme. Guyon, the French Pietist, could heal the sick wonderfully. Do you suppose she asked to heal the sick? No, she asked to be married to God. This means to give up her will entirely to the Divine Will.

She had a few wrong notions of what the will of God is. She said God's will is that we suffer great tortures of mind and body to discipline us. She thought it was through suffering that God perfected his people. If all miserable conditions result from miserable ideas of God, it is no wonder she had miserable conditions. Other religious people had miserable conditions. They had them as the outcome of their mistaken ideas of God.

Job's friends tried to persuade him that it was God who had afflicted him. He denied it. That is our duty also. We deny the being of a God capable of afflicting people.

Guyon, Fenelon, à Kempis, Luther himself, all ignored the doctrine that according to thy faith so be it unto thee, as related to human experiences, and accepted what others taught them. Luther never seemed to apply it to the persecutions he received from mankind. You remember Luther was so unhappy by reason of the ill-treatment and maligning he received from people that he was in the depths of despair a great deal of the time. Now and then Luther agreed that faith could heal the sick. He himself healed the sick sometimes by the prayer of faith. He had the same privilege in the matter of stopping persecutions. Faith in Good, as God, will stop persecutions, poverty, sickness, sin and death.

The greatest mystery about the goodness and intelligence of the ancient Pietists was their ignoring the Jesus Christ idea of God, already implanted within their own good intelligent minds, and taking the teachings of other men about the ways of God. After having announced and intensified the idea of faith as the keynote to demonstration, they believed the most outrageous things. They are our examples. By their lives we see how faith in evil operates as well as how faith in good operates.

An accepted writer on the dominant theology of today, says to the world that the sufferings of good men are not explainable. He thinks some might be called discipline, some just chastisement, but the rest are out of the reach of reasoning. Yet he well knows the principle that according to what we believe so it all happeneth unto us.

Environments are works. Our works are the activity of our faith. There is one state of mind which indicates no settled conviction. It is called in the Scripture, "The fearful mind." John, the Revelator, said the fearful mind would enter the lake of fire. He means by 'the lake of fire,' the troubles of this human experience, and the experiences that follow on after the human, called the astral, or after-death state. This again signifies that as long as our confidence in Spirit is not yet fixed we must suffer. Yet suffering is still no part of God's plan with us. It will still be our own state of mind.

Is it any part of the principle of mathematics that we should get off the track at five and three are ten? Yet it is the way mathematics acts every time. God is the life principle. Go contrary to it and off the track we get. Yet in the pathway of our easiest mental powers is our fearless confidence. This fearless confidence we must enter into. If at first it requires what seems to be an effort, what of that?

There was a book written in Luther's time in which we are told that in the practice of trusting that only the good could happen unto us, we might find it almost impossible, but if we would persevere therein we should find finally it would be the easiest thing for us.

A Frenchman of long ago took up the idea of being married to God. He became so unified that all things he asked for he got. He did not ask for persecutions, so he never got them. He asked for death and he got it. There was nothing wanting. What we ask for in faith believing we shall surely get. Jesus taught this. But Jesus would not have us ask for death. "My words are life," he said.

Because the world works out its homes, its health, its friendships, its prosperities, on the plane of believing in evil need not make you work out your home, your health, your friends on that basis. This is the only point in Christian doctrine wherein strict reasoning compels us to sever from the best religious ideas of even the professing Christians of all ages. We do not believe in trouble. We do not believe in pains. We do not believe in poverty. We do not believe in sickness. We do not believe in our fears. Only joyous prosperity can come to us. Only plenty and abundance can come to us. Only health can come to us. Only safety can come to us.

Algazali, a Mohammedan, said that faith is the point of contact between God and man. Abraham joined himself to God by faith. Faith is God, Our substance is our faith. We have only so much substance in us as we have faith in the Good. We can control our destiny only so much as we have faith. We have the use of all faith. We can lay hold upon all the faith of God if we please. The disciples cried unto Jesus, "Lord, increase our faith." He said unto them, "Why are ye fearful? Be not faithless, but believing." If this great confidence were not something we could easily secure, His orders would make the Christian way just as hard as the preachers have made it. He never called His way hard. He even made healing the sick easy for us all. "All things are possible to them that believe," he said.

Very soon his disciples got so strong in faith that they wrought miracles. Those to whom they preached wrought great miracles also. For three hundred years there were great works of healing brought to pass by the Christians, then slowly the ministry of healing ceased. It came to be a sign of power in Spirit, and sometimes people not high in church office could heal better than the high officers. This aroused jealousy. Jealousy is not a healing quality, so they entirely stopped healing ministries, first in the high church dignitaries through feeling jealous, and second in laymen through being forbidden to heal. The true faith gives freedom to all men exactly as to ourselves. You can tell when you have true faith by the pleasure you take in seeing others successful and prosperous in their own ways.

It is human nature to wish to compel others to do as we think they ought to do. It is divine to see that their own way is their true way. One man thinks he ought to be allowed to have plenty of air in his office. So he has it. He thinks his clerk ought to keep his office full of fresh air, simply because he thinks it is best, while the clerk's mind is inwardly rebelling that he cannot have his own way about his own office. Now that employer might be wondering and mourning over his not working out one of his hard places right. He cannot bring it around. He has not the slightest idea that he is a slaveholder on a small scale.

Slaveholders have always one hard and undemonstrated proposition of their own religion. They cannot for the life of them see why, when they try so hard to be Christians, it happens so miserably with them. People who hold tight rein over children often wonder why they are held from prosperity and good health. Some cannot heal well because of it. "You must not drink water now! You must not eat so much!"

We hold tight rein over our friends. We do not like them if they go out or come in, when we wish they would do differently. If they associate with people we do not like, we drop their acquaintance and grieve them. Then we wonder why our health is poor. We wonder why we do not get good healing. Give all people absolute freedom in your own mind. This will cause them to do right exactly.

In Norway the merchants leave their wares in booths and write on cards that people who wish the articles may leave the price in the box and the merchant will come and get the money at the end of the week. This freedom from suspicion causes the buyers to leave the right change. They do not steal. There is no question that giving our neighbors freedom from our ideas of them, that they need our counsel or need to do our way, will cause them to do right. Right, which is Good, which is God, acts only through freedom.

If I am a mournful type of mind, I am thinking that the Divine Mind has disappointed me in some way. This suspicion is a kind of blot between me and the sight of good health in my patients.

If I hate tobacco, or hate rum, or hate any man or woman, I put up a dark steel-like screen between myself and the sight of good health in that patient I am trying to cure. If I think the doctors of medicine are in great error because they think that healing is possible by the use of drugs, I stop some energy of the Spirit from being free through me. I am the one to tell the Spirit how free it may be, but the Spirit never acts through accusation. Doctors think the healing power acts through drugs, and you think the healing power acts through words. All the time that healing power is operating through that one who has confidence in the Good as health.

God acts through confidence in Good. God acts through freedom, because the feeling of freedom is one form of confidence in Good. God acts through our toleration of doctors, because toleration of the rights of others is a sign of confidence in Good. Any act and thought, any feeling which evidences confidence in Good, will have the power of God acting through it at once. This compels us finally to have our confidence in the law of the Good itself, not in the drugs themselves, not in words themselves, but in God, the Good. "I take my refuge in thy order, Om," said the Brahmin. So we take refuge in the way God works.

It is customary for us to say that we wonder why people do not accomplish more with their religion. We speak sharply of our clergymen because they do not go down out of their pulpits into the hospitals and prisons. It is a belief in respect of persons. It is a sign we believe God has given the ministers more power than he has given us. If we feel there is a work to do, we may be certain we are the very ones to do it. We see that crime increases and we want it cured. We say so. That very speech or thought is the signal for us to cure the crime of the world in the thoughts of our own mind.

We may be keeping books, or keeping store, or keeping house, with our hands, but our thoughts are free to go and take down the hand of the man who is going to strike. We may go on the free thought to the hungry child, and lead him straight to the house, or place, where he will get all he wants. We have no time to waste condemning people for not doing great works. We must get on about our own business.

"All crimes shall cease
And ancient wrongs shall fail;
Justice returning, lifts aloft her want,
And white-robed innocence from heaven
descends."

says Milton, He put this blessed state of affairs afar off into the future. Why did he do this do you think? He did not know the law of speaking from what is *now* in Spirit. He did not know affirmations.

We may keep the health we would like still ahead of us, by thinking we are going to be well sometime. Aeneas of Lydda was always expecting to be cured sometime. Peter came near him. Peter never believed in waiting for anything. It would do you great good, if you have always been thinking in the future, if someone who believes in doing everything NOW, should speak scientifically to you. You would spring at once to a sight of your benefits. Also you would yourself, all alone, catch hold quickly, if you would put the word "Now," into your affirmations and denials, into your statement of faith and into your working affirmations. The Truth is NOW.

Scientific Christian Mental Practice

People often wonder, while looking at the phenomenal world, after speaking scientifically, why things do not change for the absolute better immediately. What is the phenomenal world? It is the unconscious mind of the world. What is the unconscious mind of world? That which the conscious mind has made. What is the conscious mind? The thoughts we are aware of, while we are speaking them. Our bodies are the register of past thoughts consciously thought. Bodies are machines which are going around with the affairs of our life mechanically. If we set them to the conscious tones of our true words, they are quickly respondent.

When people's bodies do not quickly respond to their scientific statements, we may know that they have set their bodies hard to great positive and determined errors. Their bodies will not quickly respond to the touch of their spoken words, though these words are very earnestly spoken. It seems as if they must actually begin to make new bodies. It is the same with affairs. They are machines which register our past ideas. We speak Truth once or twice and then wonder why the affairs do not change at once.

When we speak Truth and feel thrilled to our very feet by a cool fire of feeling, we may know that from zone to zone of our being our unconscious mind is shaped toward Truth. We shall not fail to see our bodies and affairs exhibit the thrill. There is the order, according to Christian Truth, to transform our bodies by renewing our conscious thoughts on the plane of Truth. Truth will utterly build over the brain. Some begin to build at the brain first. Some begin at the bones. Some have actually begun with their hair. That is, they changed its color or nature.

It is told of a lady whose ancestors were colored, that when one of her children had the kinky hair of her race, she spoke to the hair and it became straight at once. Some touch their environments first. Even the winds obey their words.

Some tell coffee and tea that they cannot make them nervous, and the coffee and tea become harmless.

The best way to fasten our scientific statements into our conditions is to give a reason why the scientific statements are true. Tell that in reality your body is Spirit, the coffee is Spirit, and therefore all it can do is to inform you of some new and sweet law of God.

Some of the very first Scientists gave for their reasons why material food could not hurt them, that matter could not hurt Spirit. They being Spirit, the material food could not possibly affect them, and so on. The later students would not accept that way of reasoning, because it implies more than one substance. The first Scientists did do beautiful healing however by such ideas. They would look at a man who thought his food hurt and mentally tell him that being Spirit nothing he could do could hurt him. Food was harmless. Then aloud they would tell him to eat his dinner without fear. The food never hurt him after that. He was utterly cured of indigestion.

In their class rooms they were told that their physical bodies were nothing at all — pure unreality. Matter in every form was unreality. This is true. We are Spirit. We do not need to show material bodies at all. We may show only our spiritual body, which is our true nature. We may see all things as Spirit. This is our privilege now, As Spirit, which is Mind, we think what we please. In the Absolute we do not think anything about bodies, or matter, or affairs of earth. You can see that all conscious thinking about such things is no thinking at all. The affairs of earth, as they show up materially, are nothing. The conscious thought that made them is nothing. Only by so much as we realize Spirit is there any substance to our thinking. Only by so much as we realize Spirit are all things real. Every realization of Spirit brings our bodies out from their unconscious machinery into their glorious reality and freedom.

Jesus Christ could manage matter in all its forms instantaneously, but he did not teach anybody else to do so. He taught what to think that would eventually result in instantaneous demonstrations. The disciples could do everything but save themselves from persecutions. We take the conscious teachings and train ourselves till our machine-like bodies spring to as quick intelligence as our consciousness itself.

People were perfectly astonished when they first found that there is as great intelligence in the feet as in the brain. There being no material brain, no material feet, all being the Spirit of God, who is this that dares say that one part of Omnipotent God is more intelligent than another? It is "no-mind" which is called the conscious mind. What is wrought out by thinking of material things as reality? Your bodies, of course, with their troubles and pains. But as it was "no-mind" that thought these things, they are nothing. They must disappear. They disappear for the true conditions to show out.

Even thinking the truth about numbers will change the shape of the head. The mathematician will keep thinking and thinking about numbers till he seems almost discouraged, he is so far away from his right answer. He keeps on calculating, however, and some day his mind is capable and strong in numbers. His very head has changed its shape. His face looks different. He did not ask to change the shape of his head. He did not expect it would happen so, but it did.

So you, by repeating the twelve propositions of Life Science, will change your entire life conditions. You must consciously think what is true. This is what Moses called the waters of being. You will soon be what is true in all your looks and actions. These are your fixed estates. These are your mechanical tablets, your records. If you can set the red blood coloring your face by a thought, you can also straighten your crooked bones by your thought. When you rise into the highest thoughts you can write, or think, or speak, you see your body as a white glory of beauty, as transfigured by your thoughts as Jesus was transfigured by his thoughts.

Yet, he was not really changed. Peter and John and James had been saying the words he had told them, and suddenly their eyes were opened to see him as He is. So your eyes will be opened. So your mind will perceive things in their reality. So your own body will show forth its hidden beauty like unto the transfigured Jesus. John called this accomplishment of the mind, the Sardonyx stone of our Temple of Life.

Every stage of this manner of reasoning has power to heal. From the ways of the first Scientists in their earnestness, to the ways of the new Christian Truth healers with their determination, there is healing power in the Truth, whether you ask to be healed or not. There is power, and there is beautiful prosperity in the Truth, whether you ask for them or not.

Keep one early morning every week for the fifth word of the Truth of Life. Let us close our lesson with it. You will find your thoughts going out to their works with obedient kindness if you keep this saying faithfully.

As Divine Mind, which I am, I can preach the Gospel, I can heal the sick, I can cast out demons, I can raise the dead. I work the works of God, who works through me to will and to do that which ought to be done by me, according to the doctrine of Jesus Christ. The words that I speak unto you, it is not I that speak, but the Father that dwelleth in me; He doeth the works.

Lesson Six

Secret of The Lord

IT is said of a Western physician that he always spoke so encouragingly to his patients, that every family liked to have him enter their house, because he radiated courage and buoyancy. He always told people nearest death that there was no reason why they should not get well right away. He lost some of those cases, speaking from the standpoint of appearances, but their loss did not seem to affect his practice at all, because other physicians who looked melancholy and hopeless lost more than he. He had no high standing as a school man, but drugs administered by him had more healing qualities than the same drugs given out by studious book doctors.

The constant affirmation to his patients, "You will get well; you are better off than you have been imagining," finally became his whole mental state, and his presence radiated it like sunshine. It was his independent mind, shining by its own convictions, which shed healing. Had he been swayed from idea to idea by his fellow physicians, learned in the shadow system of drugging, he would have been sometimes like what he read in books and very seldom like himself.

We are told of General Ben Butler that when he entered a room, or restaurant, though nobody knew who he was, there was about his presence that which finally attracted attention, and a certainty that he was a strong and great man.

There are people who do not strike us as beautiful to look at, who uplift us, and command our admiration, even while they are doing or saying very little. There is something about some people which wins their way everywhere. What is it? It is their way of thinking.

There are ways of handling your thoughts quite independent of what seems to be going on, and quite independent of the opinions of others, which will make you a lofty soul in the feelings of people. It is not too late to begin that way of handling your thoughts, even if you are now seventy or eighty years in the world's belief. You should have a systematic mode of reasoning with power in itself to quicken you into a bright understanding of Principle.

You will not start out with your noble ideas for the sake of the respect and attention of mankind. You will start out with the noble ideas for their own sake. It is the nature of every man, woman and child to choose great themes for the mind, if those themes are started within them. This, the twelve stones of the temple of Divine Science, or the twelve lessons of Jesus Christ, are sure to accomplish. Nothing like their marvelous potency was ever discovered in the line of reasoning. By some of them we find ourselves enabled to quickly distinguish right from wrong, in places where once we would not have detected differences.

Paul said, "I had not known sin but by the law," when he found how quickly his mind detected error. Your judgment of affairs will be quick and accurate. But this you will notice, that while you can instantly separate chaff from wheat in affairs, the evil, or imperfect, does not hurt or disturb or anger you, as it did formerly.

The denials of Science have the double effect of dividing off the erroneous promptly and making it harmless instantly.

The fifth lesson showed the law of the word — showed how essential it is that even after faith is established the speech and thought should express the faith constantly.

Many seem to think that they should keep faith so secret that it does not work outwardly. Emerson spoke of the unreality of evil. He spoke of the omnipresence of God as his faith. But he said that the gods overload with great disadvantages those whom they would compel to do mighty tasks. He said this so powerfully that it effected his human lot powerfully. He lost his family. He had great opposition to meet. He had softening of the brain, or a strange loss of mental faculties. This was his overloading to keep pace with his words, for he was great and must therefore take his own drugs for greatness.

It is this law of the word which carries the faith into quick and irresistible action. Moses told his people, after they had been wandering forty years in the wilderness, to keep all of the words of the covenant with God, and do them, that they might be prospered in all their undertakings. Notice how like our lesson it runs — the covenant first — then keep the words thereof, then prosperity. Jesus called prosperity the Kingdom of Heaven.

"God saw that it was good." God is Mind. Mind sees that all is Good. What it sees and smells and tastes is Good. Nothing hurts. Nothing offends. This is the power of the covenant kept with God. We covenant with death and receive death. Isaiah prophesies that there shall be an action of Spirit with men sometime whereby their covenant with death shall be annulled and the agreement with hell shall not stand. All the refuge of lies shall be broken. Then comes prosperity.

"Judgment also will I lay to the line and righteousness to the plummet." "Behold, I lay in Zion, for a foundation, a stone, a precious comer stone, a sure foundation; he that believeth shall not make haste." Read the twenty-eighth chapter of Isaiah and see how it fits the lesson of Science in the best way Isaiah could interpret his own prophetic feelings. Nobody need strive or haste for his prosperity if his faith is fixed, and his words keep repeating his covenant.

There surely comes a moment when the full power of the words comes surging through us. The power comes through the words. The power is the Kingdom of God. You remember Paul said, "The Kingdom of God is not in word but in power." So we really do not see and hear and smell and taste and feel that all is Good until the sixth lesson of Science has come with its meaning and potency.

It is not until the power of the word has come that the word is worth while. The word is a pathway to the power of God. The great interpreter of the Bhagavad Gita is Mohine M. Chatterji. He says, "The powers of Deity are beyond description and enumeration, yet both description and enumeration are needed for the benefit of the devoted."

Hosea said to his people, "Take with you words and return unto the Lord." We hear people telling how useless words are, because it is the power of God that accomplishes all. Yes, that is true. But it is the revelation of mind, and the experience of mind that it is over the pathway of right words that the devoted come into their demonstration of power. You will notice a great difference in your power if you say that everything good that happens in your life is a demonstration of the presence of the Holy Spirit.

Your acknowledgment of it will affect you mysteriously. It will not alter the fact that every good and perfect gift cometh from God, as James told his friends, but it will alter your relation to the good in appearance. I do not tell you that in reality anything is altered, but in appearance everything is altered.

Maybe you think you have such a miserable life that you cannot be thankful. That cannot be true under any circumstance. Paul said, "Every man has his proper gift of God." He told Timothy to stir up the gift that was in him. So there is some special gift native to you alone. The thought engendered by the repetition of the twelve statements of Science will stir up your own gift. They will open up a way for you to exercise that gift. Everything will yield to that gift.

The third lesson, you remember, was full of praises and thanksgiving. Such an attitude of mind is very clarifying. Jesus always gave thanks before he wrought a miracle. He never attempted to raise Lazarus to life till he had given thanks. So far as externals went, he had nothing to be thankful for, except that he had the gift of God in him stirred up, with all this gift roused to its highest power.

Yet he let himself be used exactly as if he had no power, in order to show each man what to do under all circumstances. He said, "My God, my God, how Thou hast glorified me!" when he was being crucified on a cross of shame. People looking on said that he cried out that God had forsaken him. That was the human or natural way of looking at the glory of the presence of God. There was the same misunderstanding of his glory when the voice from heaven spoke of glorifying itself through him, and called him the beloved Son. People said it thundered.

It is evident that the power of God is exhibited only over the highway of righteousness, over the highway of a true premise with its irresistible sequences. What premise is nobler than, "God is all?" What is nearer irresistible sequence than to proclaim that if God is all, then that which is not God is nothing?

If I am, what must I be? Must I not be God in substance, nature and office? And if the I AM of me is God, then that of me which is not God is not the I AM of me. It is nothing. Then as flesh I am nothing, and as Spirit I am substance. The rest of the reasoning based on the first premise is exactly as righteous. If this is true, then I must believe it. If I am the Truth in my substance, I must believe in myself. I must have faith in my own Truth. I must be the word of Truth, or my words are nothing. By the utterance of this reasoning the power of God is expressed. It is by the word of the Lord that the heavens were formed and all the hosts of them. This is prosperity when we speak the word in power.

It is time when we, as Mind, put forth our perfect senses. The senses of Spirit are called seeing, hearing, smelling, tasting, feeling, exactly as we speak of senses. "Thou, God, seest." "Thou hearest." "God saw that it was Good." "Taste and see that the Lord is Good." The character which thinks strongly in the right way will feel a pleasure in life entirely unknown to one whose ideas are wrong.

And this sight of things by reason of true premises is something all can learn. On a desert island, a man kept saying, "Living water!" while his companions were mourning about their thirst. There was no water there, but still he kept saying the words, "Living water." Finally he felt that he must dig for water. The rest laughed at him, but he was persistent in spite of their jeers, and he struck a spring of water so powerful that they had to pull him out suddenly or he would have been drowned. It was the same with the fishermen who obeyed Jesus Christ and cast their nets on the right side of the boat. It will be the same with us if we persist in the high true way of thinking; keep speaking high and noble Truth.

A Japanese youth suddenly found himself gifted with miraculous healing power through constant praise of Deity for all his blessings. It took several years to accomplish it, but he did it. He was cured of consumption in its worst form by that one practice. The power of God came to him. It is sometimes called the Holy Spirit, and sometimes understanding. Its symbol in the life temple we are building is the Sardius stone, which is the glittering or shining stone.

Understanding is a clear seeing of how works are performed. If you were found to be full of healing power and should know how to use it, you would be pleased. You would see that the healing power was good. If you were found to be full of genius for writing books and should understand how to write them, you would see that your genius was Good. So God sees all things in the universe as things he understands how to use for His own glory and satisfaction. It is all Good in His eyes.

Swedenborg says that the angels looking at us see only our good; our evil they behold not. It is to this absent evil and present Good the study of the Divine Mind leads us. We become like what we study. The sight of our mind is the girth of our powers. While we see Good, we are powerful.

The instant we see evil we are paralyzed, for the darkness of our mind is come. Half the globe sees the sun and half sees the shadow. It is the prophesy that all shall be light some time. This is the external appearance of the state of mind which is to prevail through seeing all things Good.

There are two standpoints to look at in the propositions of this Science before the demonstrations are achieved. One is the material or human, and the other is the spiritual. While one is studying the Science for the sake of the body, his business, or intellect, his words are like shells filled only with desire. He will strike a moment when be will see that the Science is to be studied for its own sake, that its ministry may bring him its gifts in its own order at its own judgment. The Science is not a new enterprise to make money by, nor a new patent medicine, nor a new phosphorous for increasing brain forces. It is for its own sake. It is for the expression of the Soul.

The Soul is careless of money, careless of business, careless of bodily conditions though it shines over these with beneficent prosperity to them. The doctrine of the Soul is that while knowing all things, and doing all things, it is identified with nothing; it is absolutely free. To the Soul there are no works to be done. Yet all works are done by the presence of the Soul. The Soul, as it is called, is the Divine "I" of each man, woman and child. When it is prominent there is a radiation of power from the mind and character. The mind that best causes the Soul to shed abroad its power is the mind that is absorbed in the study of Principle.

The mathematician who studies mathematics for the sake of a seat in the university is not a successful mathematician; he is superficial and external. D'Alembert, the French mathematician, looked with great coldness on a young man who solved some abstract proposition with a view to a seat in the academy. "You will never secure it with that motive in mind," he said. The young man was not making mathematics his goal, but a seat of honor.

Shall the Science of Spirit be less jealous? It is to be studied for itself, not for its external performances, for in keeping your eye on external works you can see that the works are your goal, while the goal ought to be the Spirit itself. The Spirit being looked at will give us its substance. This is the meekness of Spirit, that while knowing it does no works, it kindly overshines the operations we call works.

The earliest teachings of Buddhism show that it is our part in life to stand aside and let the Spirit within fight for us. Yet we fight the battles of life as though we ourselves, external as we seem, were fighting them. He who best stands aside for the Soul to do his work, while yet he does all, is as though himself were doing all, and is most powerful in overcoming and outdoing natural defects and unkind destiny.

There are certain practical ways by which we are to read the Science of Mind. For instance, we do not fast in order to become spiritual, but often fast because we are spiritual. One does not speak true words in order to become spiritual, but because he is spiritual. If he were not already spiritual, it would be false to say, "I am Spirit." It is because I am Spirit that I say so. The appearance may be that I become more and more spiritual, but it is only that I more and more show forth my real nature.

I do not say I am health in order to become healthy, but because I, in my Divine Truth, am Health itself. I tell the Truth about it. I do not say I am wise in order to become wise, but I tell the Truth, I am already wisdom itself.

I do not say I am owner of the universe in order to get hold of great possessions, but because it is true that as Spirit I am the possessor of all.

In the Scripture we read of the angel of life and death, time and eternity, spirit and matter, who is the angel of mystery, crying with the roar of a lion. Then the seven thunders uttered their voices. The lion always typifies the strength of purity. Pure Truth is spoken. It touches the mystery of life and death, time and eternity, Spirit and matter, and immediately all materiality thinks itself is to be advantaged because health, strength, support, defense are named as the result of Truth. But this is its bitterness for the words of pure Truth cause materiality to disappear.

The pure Truth is spoken like itself, not like what it is commanded to do. Thus the premise being utterly independent in Spirit will rouse the native energy to express itself, and we have a great and mighty character evolved.

We do not take the premise that there are any sick to cure or any sinners to reform. But as Spirit our energy makes nihil of sin and sickness. We do not take the premise that our brother needs to be cured of swearing or stealing. We say he is free to do as he pleases. This takes off the burden of our heavy supposition, and he feels free to cease swearing and stealing. This is more like the way of the Spirit than if we were to take the solid seeming premise that our brothers needs reforming, and cure him of his habits by treating him.

Do you catch the strong metaphysics of this idea? It shows that cures are often the result of a strong will coming against a weaker will and overpowering it. Thus it is that it is more like Spirit to cure sickness, ignorance and death by being in the Spirit where there is no sin, ignorance or death, than to rise in the power of an antagonistic feeling and overcoming. "My Spirit shall not strive and cry."

To the Holy Spirit, all the life of the universe, all the joy and skill of the universe, is given, and one does not have to beg for it or work for it. It is so. That is all. This stately standing place is ours. The greatest miracles may be wrought out under the most unpropitious circumstances by holding to the loftiest ideal you can conceive of faithfully.

Miracles are prosperity. They come for every type and kind of religious feeling which is addressing itself to its highest. Luther begged the God he described to have the men at the Diet of Nuremberg grant toleration to Protestantism. Suddenly he ceased praying as a beggar and shouted, "We have won the victory." He was many miles away from Nuremberg, but his words burst over the situation with their power.

Right in the place where we now stand we may work miracles. There is nothing in Scripture about running away from duties that lie nearest to hand. Shakespeare, the student of phenomena, noting how certain types of mind act with environments they have wound themselves up in, makes one of his characters obey the fiend within him, advising him to run away from his obvious duty. But Scripture says, "Stand thou in thy lot to the end of thy days. Stand and see the salvation."

There are two standpoints then from which to view all things, to ask questions, to talk. One real, the other unreal. There are two kinds of faith. Take the faith of the two ministers believing in the burning lake for sinners, and believing themselves sinners; that was expressed faith. Believing not that they themselves ought to go into that lake, yet never saying so; that was unexpressed faith. We ought to trace our logic to its deepest practical outcome. This we ought to do by definite speech or thought. It will bring us up from the deeps further and further till the push of the springs of truth within us is externalized. Jesus called it, "A well of water springing up into eternal life."

At each purer realization the world takes a different turn in our feelings. It shows its best to us step by step. The lily in the night looks a different object from the same lily in the sunlight, yet it is the same lily. So this world in which we walk looks so different by this night time of thought. It will be the same world when the sunshine of pure Truth strikes through our minds in its glory.

Here in our midst abides the glory of God. Here all is Good. There is a state of mind in which, if we get into it, we shall see what Jesus Christ called, "The Kingdom of Heaven." There has always been a teaching in the world that there is a Kingdom of beauty and goodness near at hand. How to enter it, or how to see it, was the mystery. The people of the past fasted and prayed and limited themselves every day in order to see it. Still it seemed afar off. Stephen saw it, just as he was breathing his last breath upon earth. Jesus walked therein always.

Moses took the Israelites through the wilderness with such thoughts in his mind as the Kingdom near him gave him. Their shoes and clothes lasted forty years to symbolize the enduring Kingdom of the Good.

Now and then in the wilderness spots of this earth, there are sights and sounds vouchsafed to the simple of heart, which show that the less our mind with its earthly descriptions of life and love, touches anybody or anything, the more we may see of heavenly things.

A young man of seventeen or eighteen years of age went from Germany to seek his fortune in Africa. He used often to wander in the sands alone, hiding himself behind clumps of bushes when the Kaffirs came toward him. He says he used often to see on the sands ahead of him, beautiful cities with mosques and minarets and towers and wonderful homes. Going on and on he never found these cities. They are not in Africa. He has traveled over many countries but has never seen any cities like them. No picture of spots on earth represents such scenes as he saw when, as a simple youth, he wandered alone to make his fortune.

The same kind of untouched cities may have been seen in the untrod fields of the far North. Many a long-neglected spot of earth, not touched by the thoughts of man as he now thinks, has suddenly exposed some scene to the traveler in the early morning. It is promised that cities shall spring up in the deserts, and roses of tropical clime blow where not even a grass seems to thrive. This will be the new way of thinking which now comes with Science. It opens our eyes to see things as they are.

Intellect and matter call this idealism. It is pronounced transcendentalism. But under the reign of intellect and matter limitation is continually put upon even the power of God himself.

Have you ever heard of learned men saying that a sick child must die? Did you ever hear of Jesus saying that a child must die? And he who feels most of the Mind of Jesus thinks most of life. He goes to the child and cures him. He does not agree with intellect or matter. He is practicing transcendent teachings. They are all of unlimited, unhindered, untrammeled spiritual vitality, force, health, protection, provision, here and now, by the union of the mind of man with the Mind that is God.

    The Mind of man is the Mind of God.
    The Life of man is the Life of God.
    The Soul of man is the Soul of God.
    The Spirit of man is the Spirit of God.

Mind, Life, Soul, Spirit are names of God. They are the Substance of God. They may represent to our way of thinking very different things, but being all names of God, they are one.

The Science of Mind must be the Science of Life. The Science of Soul must be the Science of Spirit. There is no matter, so there can be no science of matter. Therefore, he who studies, trying to establish a science of things material, must be forever baffled.

There is a call in every heart for something that will endure. Only Spirit is eternal. All the study of snails and asteroids in which you can spend your time must cease with extreme age. The brain fails, whose cells have been the dry and dusty storehouse of material facts; but there is no old age in Spirit. The brain that is cleared to its tiniest cell of the facts about comets and earthquakes, gleaned from observations and histories of matter will revive and renew strength and buoyancy, till there is no sign of a material brain in sight. The clear light of Mind, shining with the understanding of eternal Truth, glows like the aureole of the supernal visions of John and Jacob.

Though this has been proved only a little way, it is strong enough when once begun, to lead those who are ready to risk all to the marriage of their life with the life that is God, to persevere.

"He who hath led thee to this way,
 Still on the way will show;
He who hath taught us of this way
 Still more will make us know."

Jesus Christ took the premise that from God, the Father, he could call all power unto himself to use at a moment. He did not use all that power. He used as little as he could help. When he used very little power against the soldiers they fell on their faces. He needed no guns or swords or bows or arrows to fight for him. He needed not to answer their taunts or questions. He stood aside from the ways of matter and intellect. David stood aside from the ways of warfare when he slew Goliath of Gath. He was the forerunner of Jesus. We will stand aside from the methods of the world in every particular, and thus be forerunners of those who will come after us.

How far have I gotten on by standing aside from the ways of the earth? We will ask ourselves. No man shall ever hear our answer to him from his own standpoint when he speaks of evil. No day shall hear our complaint when it shows us death or foolishness or evil or sickness and tells us these are our lot. We will look up. We will think on high. We will trust to the Spirit of God.

David spoke to the Philistine giant of his age as we are expected, in the Science of Spirit, to speak to the giant-like apparitions of poverty, failure, sin, sickness, death, old age and weakness. He said to the Philistine, "Thou comest to me with a sword and with a spear and with a shield, but I come to thee in the name of the Lord of hosts, the God of the armies of Israel, whom thou hast defied."

Does not the shadow system of pain and discouragement, from the study of matter, face us with defiance of the teachings of Jesus Christ concerning eternal life, eternal health, eternal intelligence here and now?

There is a heart, a quickening secret to the teachings of Jesus Christ, which few have touched as yet. It is called in Scripture, "The Secret of the Lord." Note that he ascended and descended at will. With the air spheres for stepping stones he arose into heaven and came again and again to the sight of his people. We read that he appeared thus to them. He was seen of Mary Magdalene and Mary the mother of James with other women, and unto the two on their way to Emmaus. He was seen of the twelve disciples. He was seen of about five hundred at once. Then James saw him. Then again all the apostles. And Paul testifies that he too saw him. He came through the walls to greet his beloved people. He was the irresistible Spirit. It is worthwhile to obey his directions insofar as we can find them recorded.

This Science is the nearest primitive Christian doctrine of any being spoken on earth now, but there are some words yet to be spoken. There is a secret not yet revealed to mankind, even in this Science thus far. How can we tell? We know by the signs. "By these signs shall ye know when ye are my disciples." Though these signs are partially manifested they are far from His demonstration. Therefore, as Spirit, we must rouse our whole being to proclaim that we do understand the Secret of the Lord concerning life, health, strength, support and defense, without material means.

By the utterance of this word of the Inner Spirit, breathed deep into us all by the Spirit of God, we shall catch these thoughts beyond our thoughts, which whisper the secret of healing of the world. We shall speak those words beyond our words which tell the secret of Divine Love that can raise the dead.

The sixth lesson deals with the Secret. Its message is all about the quickening power of the Spirit in understanding. We tell of a mathematician that he understands numbers. We praise Euclid and d'Alembert for their splendid understanding. But theirs was not the understanding that makes and keeps alive. It was their manna in the wilderness, but it was not the bread of the true Science. We praise the musician who startles the world with his sounds of glory, but one by one they drop into the grave and only the echoes of their songs are left. Theirs was not the Secret of the Lord. They knew not music in understanding. Like the manna the Jews ate, it fed their minds with what promised to be life, but it lasted only a season. The bread that Jesus gave is so alive that if a man eat thereof he shall never die. This Secret He gave to the world, and He said, "Abide in me." "Keep my words." "The Holy Ghost will come in my name."

Sometimes to repeat the name of Jesus Christ takes us closer and closer into His Mind, where the living Secret rested. We speak of that Spirit within ourselves which is exactly like His Spirit, and of It we say, "I understand the Secret of Jesus Christ." It is not in order that we may understand His secret that we speak, but because, as Spirit, we do understand. It is the Truth of Spirit we speak — Spirit works only in Truth. It comes forth in freedom over the highways of Truth.

If you watch all the writings of the devoted and spiritually minded of all the ages, you will find them speaking sometimes of Spirit as the reality and sometimes of matter as the reality. That was because they had not their revelations or thoughts in perfect understanding.

In Genesis we find the first chapter telling how perfect are all the creations of God. They are Good. Perfection cannot fall. Can God fall? Can goodness become badness? Can strength become weakness? Yet Moses tells in the second chapter how the perfect son of God fell from his high estate of goodness into the dusty sinfulness of Adam. He is speaking in these two chapters from two standpoints, one is Reality and the other is unreality. Christ, the Spirit, is Reality.

Both these natures come calling our attention, even within ourselves. One is pure Adam nature, with its erroneous ideas of God and Life. The other is our Christ nature, with its faithful ideas of God and Life. One is our substance, the other is our shadow. One is our real and the other is our unreal. We abide in the Light by acknowledging only our Christ nature. We are torn in the conflict of change, and ups and downs, by acknowledging two natures. We abide in the darkness by yielding to the idea that we are matter and intellect. Intellect is the Adam intelligence, naming all things by material names, telling of them as matter. Intellect will subside in meekness when we give utterance to Spirit—when we admit that the Spirit is all in all and the only Reality.

Understanding this we put ourselves in the ranks of spiritual being: fearless, satisfied and powerful. We understand the way of our life. We understand God. There is no study that can bring forth this fearless, capable mind, except the study of the fearless Spirit.

By the study of Spirit we become acquainted with Spirit and realize that the trees are in reality Spirit, whispering great secrets of how to be happy and free. We realize that the men and women on the streets of restlessness are Spirit. In Truth they are walking secrets of the splendor of God. We know that all that is real is Mind thinking such thoughts as demonstrate goodness and health.

All that is really thought demonstrates health, goodness and peace. That which demonstrates otherwise is the shadow of thought—the Adam claiming to be real but never real at all. True thought demonstrates intelligence and somebody is wiser when we think a true thought. True thoughts demonstrate in peace, and somebody is at peace when we think Truth. "Acquaint now thyself with Him and be at peace." "Taste and see that the Lord is good."

"Perceive in thine heart that there is only God. Thus shall thine eyes see thine own kingdom." Every sense faculty shall be quickened, intensified, extended out from the Central Fire which burns within us, till we perceive as the Divine Mind wholly. To God all is Good. To Mind all is Mind. To Spirit all is Spirit. To Soul all is Soul.

"As God I perceive that all is Good," says the Divine One within us. "As Mind I perceive that all is Mind," says the Divine Mind. "As Spirit I perceive that all is Good," says the Holy Spirit within us.

John, the Revelator, could only see this sixth movement of Science through our thought as a shining stone in a foundation. It is indeed a foundation principle, which, being understood, makes life another thing quite from what it was when we had not the doctrine of Spirit in understanding.

Take now a right premise and reason on with it until the light of understanding breaks over and through you. With the sixth light of Science we are prepared to meet the world with our own free independence of thought, able to make nothing of its worst appearances.

Lesson Seven

Spring of Life

THE seventh separate statement of Moses is, "Let the earth bring forth." Earth here means mind. Let the mind bring forth. What can mind bring forth except thoughts? But Moses is talking entirely of the Divine Mind in man. It is not acknowledged by us as the only Mind and thus is hidden entirely. Hide it not. That is letting it bring forth.

Immediately we uncover the Divine Mind in man, it shows its action in making fresh life in everybody and everything we meet. It brings out their original health. It strengthens them wonderfully. It brings provisions and bounty to them. It brings them defense and protection from accidents, from trouble, from afflictions. But all its ministry is only showing more and more nearly what is already worked out in Spirit. Remember this: even healing is not healing, because Mind needs no healing. Our saying that Mind is given its freedom is also a statement of appearance only. For as God is free, so Mind is free.

Moses is using a figure of speech entirely by saying, "Let mind do thus and so" — for the Spirit, which is God, which is Mind, has its own way entirely. We are to see Spirit. We can see Spirit. And the more of Spirit we see the more perfectly we see things.

The man appears sick to you because you see him that way. If you let your Spirit tell what it sees there will be no talk about sickness, no discussion of what is distressing anybody. Really all things are waiting to be looked upon by us as they really are. Did you ever notice how you feel that the one who feels your worthiness seems to understand you best?

Take the old Lord Fauntleroy as an example. Little Lord Fauntleroy thought he was generous and good. He really believed it. He praised his old grandfather. Everybody else condemned him. Consequently the grandfather would say, "Ask Little Lord Fauntleroy; he knows me, he will tell you what I will do." Now, even if the old Lord Fauntleroy had appeared to all other people to be savage and ugly, his Soul was generous and good. The little child saw the Soul. He could see nothing else. This is true of everybody and everything. They feel that in Truth they are Good. So they who see them as Good please them best. Here is where it probably seems impossible to you. You think that the beastly characters we read of must not be called good. You see very plainly the faults of those you meet every day, and it is impossible for you to call them good.

Moses and Jesus teach the same story. Let it be of the Soul you speak. Let Spirit utter herself. The evil disposition, the greed, the appetite of mankind, is all unreality. It signifies how far we are from seeing spiritual Truth when we see evil. You can see for yourself that if God the Good is omnipresent, then that which is not good is not present.

It is a tenet of the most ancient religions that what seems external exists not at all. And wherever we find profound thought and feeling, we find men thinking the same way of outward and external things. Nothing exists outside ourselves, as to what seems outside. When we realize God we are sure to say we feel God. The realization is within ourselves. We have supreme power over and with our realizations.

All realizations of Good externalize in good. We train our realizations first. Then, as phenomena or the world that folds us round comes second, we deal with our world secondly. In this Science, there are six lessons devoted to the Self Mind alone, that is, devoted to the realization of God in the Soul. And there are six lessons devoted to our relations to the world.

There is no religion which has not, in one way or another, taught that "As a man thinketh in his heart, so is he," and, "By thy words thou art justified." The words we speak and the thoughts we think constitute our breath of mind, as the air constitutes the breath of nostrils and lungs. There are words which exhilarate the mind, as there are airs which exhilarate the body.

The Japanese believe that praise of all things will exhilarate first the mind and then the body. A young man in Japan, named Kurozumi Saki, in 1814, became very gloomy through complaining. Complaining and praising are two separate processes. They bring very different results. He had breathed in the spirit of gloom till he was in deep-seated consumption. Their theological term for gloom is "inki." He suddenly resolved to cease mourning. It was hard for him not to complain at first, but he was one who could hold to whatever he had made up his mind to do, and he began to praise everything and everybody. He went on for some years, breathing into himself an entirely different set of words. He began to be very cheerful. His consumption kept growing worse, but he did not heed it. He kept on praising everything he thought of. One night, just as he supposed he was breathing his last, but while he was praising the early rising sun, a sort of buoyant ecstasy seized him. His breath grew deep and electrifying. He straightened himself up from the ground, where he was prostrated on his face, and found that he had breathed into himself the elixir vitae, the vital breath of health. The Japanese call it "yoki," the spirit of cheer. He was more than well. He was buoyantly quickened. His very breath was a healing vitality, if he breathed on deformed or dying people. His fame spread abroad into all lands. He was a miracle worker.

There is an elixir in the words of Truth. Keep them going continually. They will change your entire life and change your powers. You are a miracle worker by inherent right. Give your Soul the chance to do all your thinking, all your speaking.

A young man had a cancer in his nose, which had gone so far that there was no material remedy. He betook himself to prayer. There is always God waiting for us to depend upon when we come to where we find that nobody and nothing else can help us. He had prayed and prayed and still no signs of healing, when he suddenly felt the cheerful elixir of his Spirit breaking through him, and he was healed.

In the Bible we read, "In the morning sow thy seed, and in the evening withold not thy hand, for thou knowest not what a day may bring forth.'" Again we read, "Be not weary in well doing, for in due season ye shall reap if ye faint not."

Agassiz was a great student of nature. He felt that there were secret springs within all forms which he would like to understand. When he did, it would seem miraculous how some other new points of interest would come up to lead him on. A poet expressed it beautifully, for it is the very way the Spirit of God works with us, if we set out to make ourselves one with it.

"When the way seemed long,
   Or his heart was beginning to fail,
She would sing a more wonderful song,
   Or tell a more wonderful tale."

A young Catholic priest in Germany, about two hundred years ago, was so buoyant and cheerful in Spirit that when he spoke in a loud and authoritative tone of voice to a sick man's disorder to disappear, and commanded health to appear, they obeyed him almost instantaneously. He would wet his finger on his tongue and make the sign of the cross over the sickness. The saliva on his finger was a symbol of ease. The up and down stroke of the cross means that nothing has any evil power. The right and left stroke of the cross symbolizes that the Good now reigns. If they did not get cured at his first order, they did at the second or third. He was persistent to his own ideas. The howlings of the people did not disturb him. He lived his own life alone with the Spirit.

Why should you say that God has afflicted you, if saying such a thing makes your breath a disease breeder? Why should you say that you feel unhappy, if saying this shuts up a gate against the breath of the spirit of the morning of joy? Are you not a chooser of the thoughts you shall think? Have an hour in the morning for some special message to the world, or about yourself. Have an hour in the afternoon for some words of Truth to the world. These words will come to fruitage. No matter if you have a special tendency to some grief, or your way is lonely and hard, tell the way of the Spirit so often that she comes stealing through you and you become a health giver and a cheer bringer.

Sometimes you may find yourself seeming to be sick. Nothing has happened to you, yet you are sick. You have caught some of the world's false beliefs in your thought. Maybe they are old notions you used to think which are just showing themselves. No disease comes from material causes, although we say so when we talk as the world talks. All is in thought first. This Science deals with the thoughts, just as Jesus did, and then it speaks of externals.

Learn to get exactly right ideas, and you will afterwhile educate the world by just thinking Science. You do not have to tell a man that he has no disease, that he never took a chill, etc., when every bit of him is sure that he had been in a draft and that he has influenza. You treat him silently. You need not talk all the time about any point in Science, but you may know the Truth. Jesus said, "Ye shall know the Truth, and the Truth shall set you free."

A very strong mental healer was afraid of damp drafts before she was in the Science. She was already past sixty years of age, according to symbolic reckoning, and she kept taking apparent colds whenever a damp draft struck her. She was sensible enough not to say a word in the presence of a draft, except in her mind, for her words had not power apparently to annul drafts. After a while her mental feeling got so strong that drafts never affected her.

Do you think that it was primarily the draft which gave her the sign of hoarseness so often? No, it was the fear of certain people. She had always been the kind of mind that has someone it fears all the time. Certain people always have something that they are fearful of. Look them squarely in the eye of their mental face and you can trace it every time to the fear of some person.

It is well, said Jesus, to agree with your adversary quickly. That is, while you are alone with yourself, take up that man or woman and settle the question decidedly that you are not afraid of them. They cannot enter the sphere of life where you dwell. Your thoughts push their evil down and leave the Holy Spirit of them free to do you great good. Much of material misfortune can be traced to dread or fear of people's influence or opposition. You may lead your own free life in mind, and it will unconsciously rebuff every hurt. The hurts may at first seem real, but as the mind puts out its wings stronger and stronger it blows even the memory of evil away as a chaff. You rise out of the reach of the things that frighten you. You forget the feeling of repugnance. You drop even the memory of the things that brought it on.

Sometimes the way to meet hardships that have clung to us for years is not, by saying that they are nothing at all. It is by stopping and finding the Holy Spirit of them. A young Scientist had a bronchial affliction which never yielded at all to calling it nothing, though other parts of her body had quickly healed through telling them that nothing could ail them. One night she faced up the hoarseness which had kept her whispering instead of speaking for about three months. She said, "You seem to stay around me as if you had nowhere else to go and belonged here. Now I feel that you have some good mission to me. God sends me a message by you, and I have been snubbing you and treating you badly. I will do so no more. As God, with good for me in your presence, I bid you welcome in love. You may stay with me as long as you please." In the morning the cure was wrought. She found out that it was true that it was a message of goodness for her, for her gloom of mind had left her. She touched the same principle which the Japanese worked upon so many years, viz., rejoicing in the things instead of mourning about them.

If I were to be asked directly as to the quickest way for a Scientist to get his healing power going, I would probably say, "Praise everything and everyone in your mind, and as far as your mental convictions will demonstrate promptly, speak these praises aloud." If it should be through fear that you did not speak audibly about things, you must redouble your thoughts, and speak a few times to your seeming discredit. If you are timid about telling people that they are well NOW, I would advise you to run the risk of your pride of name a few times, and say, like a Denver doctor, "I do not care if you do seem to be sick, I don't believe in sickness, and I think this is all imagination. You must be sitting up by the end of an hour and well by tomorrow." It is different with different states of mind however.

Your timidity is often because you are afraid it won't come out right, and people will think you are foolish, and tell others so. Can you not trust your reputation in the hands of Truth? Which do you suppose had the larger practice, the cheerful, buoyant doctor who always told everybody they would get well, or those who tried to be sensible and judge by appearances? Why, it was the one who told everybody that they would get well, whether or no and laughed cheerfully. His presence to cheer was an elixir for the family, and they sent out their cheerful feelings and buoyed up the sick man's mind, and he caught the vitalizing sparks of electric cheerfulness. You must break over the bounds you have put upon yourself sometimes.

But again, so much of denial of the patient's seeming malady is talked out like an intellectual problem that patients do not catch healing, they catch fear. Perfect love of your Science takes away your fear, and after a while you do not talk Science much, you heal by some hearty, simple, cheerful word, that bubbles over from constant thoughts of health and life, irresistible spiritual vigor, and unhidden goodness in everyone.

There was one doctor who, it was reported, laughed his patients well. Everything they said and did amused him so that he laughed uproariously. Patients would get to laughing in spite of themselves. He would sit and roll up bread pills, or anything else that came handy, and tell the patient that he was more scared than hurt, that he was resting up a little and would be all right soon. He took many a seemingly dying man and laughed him back to life. Change the groove of the patient's mind.

Doctor Abercrombie went to visit an old schoolmate, and found her seemingly breathing her last. "Do you remember the crow's nest?" he asked her, in his buoyant, boyish tone of voice. She smiled, He said something more, Not as if he were urging or coaxing her to think of old school days, but as if they were something to remember. It brought back to her fainting mind the memory of her springing, happy girlhood, when the birds sang in the Summer trees, and the boys and girls played and laughed in the orchards. That change of mind cured her.

A great healer once said that he always kept his mind dwelling on the enchanting airs of Summer time. He remembered how the chirp of grass hoppers and the far away song of birds and brooks sounded. Then he would feel the soft flakes of health. There is a faculty of your health whereby it loves to drop down into your mind and distill like the dew through your flesh.

Thus God has chosen the weak things of this world to confound the mighty. But you do not have to watch anything or anyone for your health. God is health. Ever present with us is God the health of the universe. You need not depend upon any physician or friend for your strength and courage. God is strength.

"Though all around thee courage fail,
   Do thou be strong.
Though all around thee doubt prevail,
   In faith move on."

It is the dependence upon outside help, or even what seems to be outside help, which the Truth takes away. We learn to see God in the sick man as health, because we know that as health God is there. We learn to see strength in the feeble man because God as strength is there. Our strength rises and goes forward to mankind, because we know that our strength is God. It goes forth just by our knowing that it is so. Tremendous strength is tremendous health. Thus John, the Revelator, calls the effect of certain denials "beasts" which is a word for strength. There is an atmosphere of uplifting about one who knows he is strong in Spirit. He realizes that his Soul is always rising on the wings of aspiration above the conditions of his lot. You may breathe strength itself by talking to strength itself. The Holy Spirit is strength. God has given to the Holy Spirit all the strength of the universe. If you praise the Holy Spirit for this strength you will be surprised how it will take hold of you. Some morning or some eventime its energy will thrill you.

You will not find any timidity about telling patients how the snow flakes of healing are falling around them all the time, if your heart is sure of it; but you will be wise enough not to speak of such seemingly impossible process if your heart is full of certainty, for you will see that your presence is all the speech they need.

Do you think you must say something audibly or mentally to sick people? Bind no burdens of necessity around your neck. If you have awakened in the early morning with right thoughts for the day, just keep still when your first case comes in, or when you see her or him. "Wait on the Lord." "Stand still and see the salvation of the Lord." "Stand aside in the battle, and let the warrior within thee fight." "Wait I say, on the Lord."

There was a young practitioner who had spoken mighty praises in the morning of the way God, as the health and salvation of the people, would work through her to will and to do. She was not as yet a successful healer and it troubled her. She meekly acknowledged that God was doing great things for her and through her and by her, even though she had not seen it so. Her first case that morning was a lame man. She felt divine compassion for him, but had no thoughts, for she felt that if God did not manifest through her she could not make him do so. And this held her silent, almost helpless, as if she were nothing at all and God were all. All at once, quite unexpectedly to herself, she told him to throw down his crutch and try to walk across the room. He obeyed at once. He found that he could limp without his crutch very well. She had him try two or three times more and he was cured. It seemed as if his flesh and muscles drank in the elixir of a new mental atmosphere. Very likely he was thirsty for the waters of the refreshing God presence, with nobody's thought to interfere with him. (Lameness is a pretty sure sign of a mind interfered with.) This little woman made herself so silent that the voice of the Spirit could speak to the waiting Soul of the man.

There are ways of thinking about your environment which will make you like a harp in the fingers of love, so enchanting will be your silent mind to the world-hurt traveler, so blessed will sound your voice to the bruised child of human hardships. You need not worry about whether you shall speak or not. You will have your feet shod with the preparation of the gospel if you take the fresh morning for giving thanks and glad praises unto the Spirit, and speak forth with freedom some lesson of Science.

In this Science there is really no need of studying the symbolic language of Moses, as we have done. We know these great principles without going back over the ages to past men's thoughts. But we are inclined to look through the files of thoughts which have run through men's minds and made them famous or made them miracle workers. Moses was a miracle worker. What idea did he hold which made him work miracles? The mind of the man is expressed in his writings. This is true of all miracle workers. If they spoke loud words what did they say? Their healing power was God. God with them, in them, through them, is the same God of whom we seek to get the high healing knowledge. There is a secret of healing. The method of it is nothing.

The Japanese breathed upon his patients and they were healed. The German priest made the sign of the cross and cried with a loud voice, "In the name of the Father and of the Son and of the Holy Ghost let the devil appear." He meant the disease. It was his expression for evil. He wished the evil to show itself plainly that it might get out of the way entirely at his order. Then he made the sign of the cross in the air, and again he cried with a loud voice, "In the name of the Father and of the Son and of the Holy Ghost let the disease be gone." Then to the patient he would say, "From this time forth be healed." In our time we find some people healing by one means and some by another. Whenever they begin to acknowledge that God is the health of the people you will find them using less and less material helps toward healing each other. Yet you must be sure that whatever health is brought to mankind it all comes from God. Material methods are apt to turn the mind away from remembering that it is from God that all health comes. So, practitioners have resorted to thinking out great reasonings about God's presence as a healing presence, and the results have gone out in good health and invigorated life with as sure certainty as by any other method. The more spiritual the feeling the practitioner has while healing the patient, the more certain is permanent cure.

There is something about reasoning about the presence of God, and telling about the character of God, which makes the cure effect other needs of the patients besides bodily disease. They are often turned from their old habits. Very often they become attentive to divine ideas and entirely change their tastes.

Scientists become very particular about leaning on the word of God alone in curing sick people. Zoroastrianism, a religion older than Brahmanism or Buddhism, has for one of its principles that one may heal by herbs, another by the will, but it is by the divine word that the sick are most surely healed. The practice of healing by the word lets us most quickly into the secret of healing. But, it is no more the words that heal than it is the herbs, for if it were the words themselves one would heal by using them as well as another. We all know that one may use the words faithfully and not cure the case, while another may use the same words and cure the case in a few minutes.

This has led students to talk of faith in words as the healing power of mind. But if words do not cure unless we have faith in them, faith is the curative principle and words are nothing. It is the same as urging us to have confidence in nothing at all to tell us we must have faith in words to make them work, for words without faith are nothing at all. That is no way to instruct mind. It is running it around in the same circle with herbs for its weapons or words for its weapons. Either one must have faith in them to accomplish anything. If you examine it closely you will see that healing is brought to pass by faith in health. The good practitioner has his mind fixed definitely on something which to him is Good. It comes right through the appearance of evil by his mind being fixed on it. All his words about health just express his feelings as nearly as possible. The more perfectly his words express his feelings, though he is only thinking silently, the more real the health of his patient seems to him.

Thus you see it is not words that heal, yet it is while words are being spoken that the feelings go forth as on highways and touch the sick. Yet it is not feelings that heal for people often feel strongly that their patients are cured and they are not cured.

There is a secret spring to the healing practice that has never been taught, except this Science by its reasoning will keep touching it with each one of its lessons. By going over and over the lessons we come nearer the healing feeling. There is not a practitioner of the Science cure who has struck the spring with the touch of such perfect understanding that he works out his cures as accurately and surely as a mathematician works out his problems. Old age, palsy, rheumatism, grief, poverty, overtake them, and they have their match, for they have not beaten their own particular adversary.

The healing Science is like an unexplored and undescribed territory. Columbus discovered America and brought it to the notice of the civilized world so practically that others coming after him could describe it exactly. The healing lands have been discovered for ages but there are only twelve pieces of information given concerning them.

Nobody could tell what was to be the secret of prosperity in the new world discovered by Columbus. But today we know the secret of American prosperity is its plenteous gold, coal-beds, gas wells, timberlands, grain lands, reliable climate, its river courses, its building stone, silver deposits, pasturage, salt wells — all on a material basis, but the foundation for material opportunities. The enterprise and efforts of men in Europe and Africa had nothing to encourage them, but in America all. Yet for ages America lay unknown, though possibilities were within her borders. Norway keeps her records of one who discovered America long before Columbus, but he made no lasting impression in the minds of his contemporaries. He brought home no marvelous products to substantiate his reports.

So in this healing practice we have had many a thinker touching, on its enchanting borders, but only Jesus who could prove his words. We need therefore to believe most in him who proved most. Wherever we are found disagreeing with him we will simply take his word on the subject and keep it as Truth.

If we are inclined to speak slightingly of any practice of healing, we will remember that he condemned none, because the secret of healing was known to him. His coat would heal whoever touched it. But do you think the coat, before he charged it with healing, had any curative energy in it? His words would heal the instant he sent them out, but those who knew him best used those words and failed. The word he consecrated to healing must even now be charged with the same Spirit he felt. How shall we get his Spirit? How shall we use the omnipotent Principle he set before us? How shall we absolutely understand how to heal the sick? Paul said that by letting the same Mind be in you that was in Christ Jesus. He exactly agrees with Moses. Let the Christ Mind speak its way through us.

Now the Christ Mind thinketh no evil, is not puffed up, is not angry, is not vain, is not critical, is full of praise. Here again we come by another line of thinking right upon the same idea of praise which has made so many healers successful. Also I will call your attention to the fact that after a short time vain or critical or proud thoughts seem to stop the healing power of those who at one time were quite strong workers. The vain mind does not feel praiseful toward others. The proud mind does not feel praiseful toward others. This state of mind has no praiseful feeling toward even God. So we make a practice of praising everybody and everything, and above all giving daily thanks that God has done such wonderful things for us in Spirit. We take the twelve statements of Science and sanctify the day with two of them particularly each day. Through such practice the secret of healing is coming to be an open secret. We feel it becoming more and more the inheritance of the world.

Once, a practitioner who had a woman come asking to be cured of catarrh, put down her head, and silently let the Spirit speak through her as I just told you. Then she waited a moment, and to the woman she said, "I pronounce you free from the thoughts of other people. You think your own noble thoughts. You are free, whole, cleansed and good. You are healed! In the name of the Father and of the Son and of the Holy Spirit, I pronounce you well and strong and at peace through and through." The woman was instantly healed when these words were silently spoken.

As we all have a right to be free within our own Spirit, and as we all are indeed free within our own Spirit, it is a truth that everyone who has gotten into the habit of unconsciously yielding to the race belief of one thing and another, is eager to receive. He will be healed at once. If not, you must treat him over again in the same way, the same hour he is with you. If not then, give him the same treatment again. Three times are not too many to give one message. If he comes another day complaining of the same thing, you must change your treatment, but I will speak of that in the next lesson.

If you have a practice of saying, every Monday afternoon, "I as Spirit do not accuse the world or myself of lustful passions or sensual desires. All is good in living demonstration before me," you will heal people before they come to you, and after awhile you will never see any sick people. But you are to handle each case faithfully which does come to you.

There are moments when your healing power will be wonderful. When those moments are gone you may feel mournful, but you must not mourn even about that, for you are to be cheerful under all circumstances. Cheerfulness is a praiseful feeling. It always indicates that the healing power is acting through you. The cheerfulness may rise into ecstasy, then it is instantaneous healing.

Will you now, each one of you, if you can think of someone you believe has a chronic ailment like deafness, or blindness, or curvature, call their name now. Then put down your head with me, and let the Spirit within you say now,

"It was not I that accused the world or myself of lustful passions or sensual appetites. I do not believe in the chronic ailments you say you are afflicted with. I do not believe in sickness, because I have never accused the race of living a life outside of Spirit, or different from Spirit. I believe in health in and for and through everybody now and forever. I believe in you as the perfect man of God."

Now speak again the name of the person you are thinking about, then speak it again, for there is something in a name that strikes down into the very soul of the Spirit, the deep mind and heart. This is the way of a regular formula which we will now use:

You are not afflicted with any kind of disease.
You are Spirit.
The Spirit knows nothing of imperfection.
The Spirit shines through all your being with its clear, holy light.
From first to last, in your real life, no error has fastened upon you, and therefore there is no disease or imperfection in you.
You are Spirit.
The Spirit knows nothing of imperfection.
The Spirit shines through all your being with its clear holy light.
From first to last, in your real life, no error has fastened upon you, and therefore there is no disease or imperfection in you.
You were not born of flesh, according to the law of the flesh, but of Spirit, according to the law of the Spirit.
The lustful passions and sensual appetites of the generations back of you have not descended upon you in disease.
God is your Father and Mother.
You have not inherited disease.

The race mind has not touched you with thoughts of lustful passions and sensual appetites, therefore disease does not touch you.

God enfolds you round about.

People with whom you are associated do not burden you with their thoughts of the senses.

You are not subject to the thoughts or feelings of others, therefore you cannot have disease in your mind.

Your own thoughts of things of matter, as to lustful passions and sensual appetites, have no power in them to give you disease.

You are free from your own passions and appetites in the Spirit, therefore you are cleansed by spiritual thoughts now and are well.

My thoughts do not burden you.

You are free of my error.

You are free in the Spirit.

You are free from all thoughts of disease.

God is your life. You cannot be threatened with death of any part of your life, nor fear death, nor yield to death of any part of your life forever.

God is your health. You cannot be threatened with disease in any part of your health, nor fear disease, nor yield to disease in any part of your body forever.

God is your strength. You cannot be threatened with weakness, nor fear weakness, nor yield to weakness in your strength forever.

God is your substance.

Your health is God in every part of your body.

You are ready to acknowledge to all and to yourself that you are healed.

You are in harmony with your life in every way.

I now realize that you are healed.

I praise you for your life in the Spirit.

I praise you for your strength in the Spirit.

I praise you for your perfect manifestation of God NOW! Amen.

There is in reality no disease or imperfection whatever. When you realize this strongly I hope you will not treat anyone, for this realization is itself a treatment. We will give a treatment to this same case after the next lesson. And so much as you remember you can give twice before the next lesson.

You will notice that we have made one denial. It is the first to be made against disease. We do not deny to destroy anything, but because denial of evil is omnipotent Truth.

Lesson Eight

Rending The Veil

THE eighth lesson in Science is: "Be not deceived." These are the words of Jesus. Spirit never deceives. Matter is the only deceiver. Matter makes up all appearances. Matter is formulated, as you know, by thoughts concerning a God who never existed.

The two friends of Job described one kind of God, and Job described another. Their kind of God was full of punishments for exactly the kind of character they described Job to be. Therefore, in the fullness of time, they reaped the fruits of their ideas; for Job insisted that he was not that character, and they must have imagined it in the peculiar wisdom of their hearts.

Thus it is with all of us. We look upon others in the red, or green, or blue tints of our own ideas, and see them quite entirely different from what they are in reality. Then exactly what we describe as their character, which is not the truth about them, must be our own type of mind in some of its ways. Then when we get the punishments we have felt honestly belonged to them, we are utterly astonished and grieved, and feel much abused. This explains why the righteous are strangely afflicted. They see more faults in mankind than any other class of people. Thus the eighth lesson is, "Be not deceived," either in man or God, for man and God in truth are Good. In appearance they may seem evil. In the Bhagavad Gita, the sacred book of Buddhism, we are told that the Spirit of God sayeth, "Whoever undeluded knows me as the Supreme Spirit, worships me in all forms," in other words, "letting forms remain, opposing nothing, but nowise deceived, recognizes me in all people and in all things." This is another way of saying that Spirit is the only substance.

Thus man is Spirit. If man, or all, is Spirit, then I am Spirit. If Spirit cannot be in poverty, I cannot be in poverty. If Spirit cannot be burdened, I cannot be burdened. If Spirit cannot be sick, I cannot be sick. All these are nothing to Spirit, therefore they are nothing to me. I am not deceived by any of them. This is the only religion which will work practically (with the mind) and bring out the external forms in new combinations. It is a religion which teaches us to be grateful to Spirit for all the good that comes to us, and appreciates that all the evil that comes is by reason of our having imagined something against man or God, or the universe, which could not be possible at all. We worship Spirit in all forms, and let forms alone. We do not try to change them; they change themselves by our thoughts of Spirit. There is a law of setting aside appearances by Truth. We learn Truth, and we are masters of the law.

Moses said the same thing in more symbolic language: "Let there be light in the firmament." He not only means the sun, moon and stars of the skies, but he means the thoughts that made them.

Do not be deceived by your imaginations. Live by Principle. The reasoning based upon pure Principle is like sunlight to the mind and life. We soon learn to know the meaning of all things. We know exactly what to do. So, let the reasoning, based upon a good true premise, guide your life.

As imaginations arise let them alone. The simple knowledge that they are imaginations is sufficient to make them null and void. Imaginations deal with evil, matter, death, sickness, poverty, old age, pain, failure, and other burdens and bondages of the race. Truth does not deal with them; it leaves them alone. We, being in Truth, also leave imaginations alone. By this lesson you will see that you do not have to try to make your Truth work. You know it. You speak it, and it is in its own working principle.

John, the Revelator, says the eighth is the beryl stone in the foundation of Mind as it fixes itself from the first to the word Good. The beryl is the stone which stands for a written record. When a form changes, by reason of our Truth, we have written a record in it. All who see it will see that we have put our seal there. Many a case of sickness would come out for more enduring health if we would write out our treatments and read them over and over by ourselves. One man, who could not feel any illumination from spiritual teachings, became highly inspired after he began to write down the Science. It will be well for you to write out the treatments as much as you can. If new ideas come to you, put them down. They show that your mind is brightening by its own light.

There is nothing so gratifying to a teacher of Science as to see the radiance of his students' minds breaking forth. When they seize the truth for themselves, love it, and reason out each item of their lives by it, and see that no other reasoning has illuminating power, they are the true light in the firmament. When many such minds are utterly wedded to pure doctrine, it is promised that there shall be neither moon nor sun in any material heavens.

When we love our reasonings we are in the light. When we listen to the opinions of man, or side with our imaginations, we strike our darkness at once. Then our intellect is our light. It takes its premise; those are its stars. If intellect believes God is far off, then the stars, which are suns, will be far away. Of course there are other meanings to this text, but I will give you one which is good to remember: "Let there be light," means, let reasoning, based on Truth, be your light of the sun. Let imaginations stand where your right reasonings put them. Eternal reasoning is eternal day. Night with its stars symbolizes the rest which mind takes at certain stages of its reasonings. There are halting places in mental action. Then we speak nothing, think nothing, do nothing. We have spoken.

We have many symbols of these halting places of the mind. There is the Sabbath. There is the halting place between childhood and youth; between middle age and old age. All these are to cease when we understand that they are symbols. Their substance is to be plain to us. We see now how a sick, deformed body will change its looks to robust beauty. But even in robust beauty, as we now see it, we are not beholding the possibilities of beauty and health at their fullest. People have as much more beauty and health and vigor belonging to them as the difference between deformity and the marvelous beauty of Hypatia. For between the night, with its moons, and the day, with its sunshine, is the difference between what we now see, and the real beauty of people and things. "Eye hath not seen, nor ear heard, neither hath it entered into the heart of man to conceive what God hath prepared for them that love him."

To love is to see God in all. This sight, or this love, puts out evil. So of intelligence. Even the greatest minds tell how limited they feel their knowledge to be. They also tell how ignorant and incompetent they feel to solve the problem of life. But such is not the way those feel who are in the light of reasoning, based upon the first principle that God is Wisdom, and Understanding Absolute is in them, and is also in all things, informing them of high Truth. Whenever man tells of his ignorance he is speaking of the formulations of his imagination. This lesson would say, "Let that which is light indeed be your light, or, let Truth be your words. Truth of Spirit, and truth of matter." It is true that matter is ignorant; it knows nothing. Are you Spirit or matter? Tell the truth about it. Reason it out well.

People have gotten mixed up with old delusions. They think they must look forward to old age. This is getting crystallized into the future. They think of a history in matter. This is getting crystallized into the past. This lesson is about the light. It is about freedom. On the material plane light is the freest process of nature. You cannot bottle it up. It will shed itself to the farthest that its nature tells it to. If you hide it under a bushel, it burns the bushel and makes a greater light than ever. If you hide it in iron vaults, it heats things red hot and melts and destroys them. While it lasts you may hide it behind some screen, but you cannot quench it by confinement. So of the eternal, unquenchable light of the reasoning, based on the Truth that there is one God, above you all, and through you all, and in you all. It cannot be spoken without shedding its light through the next and the next statement of Science. And once it is set streaming through the mind, we must speak and think and write and live the doctrine.

The doctrine is a fire—an unquenchable light. It is not like the symbol, which can be put out. It is like the Truth itself, eternal, indestructible. It is along the way somewhere that you get on fire with the Holy Spirit, so that you live the doctrine. If you do not catch the fire the first time along the pathway of the Science, go over the statements again and again. The race is not always to the swift. "Come and let us reason together," saith the Lord. "The righteous shall shine like the sun." "Be not deceived."

Great doctrines have been looked into by thoughtful men, and they have turned about and seen how differently appearances work from principles first uttered. This has caused them to be silent concerning Truth, and much exercised about the effects of Truth which they have called laws. As for instance: If one becomes spiritually minded he loses his taste for certain kinds of food. Seeing this, the Zoroastrians proclaimed that all men should abstain from those foods. They mistook an effect for a cause. They tried a long age of time to prove that fasting from food would make people spiritual. It never did, for material actions are not the cause of Spirit. The reverse is the way of the law. That is, according to the way of the Spirit in man, so will his outer actions be. Men banded themselves together saying that they would neither eat nor drink until they had killed Paul. Such was the outcome of the teachings of fasting.

There is the same idea in the use of words. We speak certain words after we become spiritual. Therefore we have said that speaking those words would make us spiritual. The effect is confounded with the cause again. In the case of words which the Spirit uses, we have no suffering to call more and more attention to the physical body. Fasters are very exercised over their physical feelings, and thus are as materially minded as gluttons. The same with people who beat their bodies, or freeze them, or otherwise abuse them. Their whole mind being given to their bodies, they are even more materially occupied than people who please their bodies with warm clothing, fresh and beautiful adornings, and have freedom from pain of all kinds.

In the case of using words, we find there is nothing at all in great truths to call attention to material things. The words, as we speak them, are given forth as the utterance of the Spirit of Life within us. All point to the Spirit, and go forth from the Spirit. We see them, by their mysterious ways, attending to the externals. So we obey both the Bhagavad Gita and Jesus, and take no thought about what we eat, drink or wear, as to whether it is wise to wear more or less.

Paul became much exercised in his mind over material things very often. At one moment it was meat, and at another it was the length of man's hair and woman's hair. Those subjects are not in the mind of a spiritually minded man. He lets them alone. The man who is thinking righteously will be immaculately neat in his dress and about his person, but it will be the natural, unpremeditated movement of that immaculate Spirit he is thinking about. He will be very honorable in his dealings with men and women, but it will not be because of his thinking all the time about his duties to them. He will perform his duties because his mind is set on right principles.

These are the lights of Moses: the works of a man and the thoughts of a man. Jesus Christ called works signs, which is the same as lights. They tell where a man stands in spirituality, he said. Working to bring to pass anything is evidence of mind being on material things, for, when we are spiritual, we are not trying to bring great things to pass, yet they come to pass.

The lofty reasonings of Science are the sunshine of the Spirit. They are the works of Truth. Truth is in us. Let it shine. Truth performs great tasks. Let it shine on miracles of health, cheering, enlightening the nations.

Discussing symbols is getting mixed up in and identified with what we think and talk about. A young man was treating a lady against coughing so much. While he was treating her he told her a great many good reasons why her cough was not real, but all the time her cough troubled him. He was eager to help her. She kept on coughing for six weeks, to his dismay. One day he said the cough was nothing to him, she might cough all she liked. From that day she never coughed again. He had struck the eighth lesson: "Let forms remain, they are nothing to us."

Such an attitude toward the world of matter is the quickest way to get rid of its abnormal and ugly appearances. Those appearances feed and grow fat on our feeling badly about them, and talking and thinking about them as something that can hurt or disturb us. Notice that the cough was not cured until he gave up thinking it was his burden to cure her. He let the Spirit tell the Truth about it. Then both himself and the woman were free.

Spirit never mourns over robberies nor over deaths, nor over pain and crying. They are nothing to Spirit. He who suddenly realizes any sort or kind of evil as nothing at all, has touched the second treatment of environing conditions, whether people or things are his burden. This feeling in its genuineness comes generally by denying the seeming and affirming the real. It opens the eyes to see purely from a spiritual standpoint. There is a great power of clear sight that comes by setting yourself free from thoughts about lustful passions and sensual appetites. Next you feel that evil is nothing whatever to you; and even if you do not feel that it is nothing to you, the way of the Spirit is your way of meeting appearances. By this I mean that Spirit or Divine Intelligence has one way of looking at the universe and all things in it. That way is to know the Good only. There is nothing else to Intelligence. That which sees evil is no intelligence at all. If we would let Intelligence speak, we must speak as Intelligence does.

If our patient, with any kind of a malady, comes the second time to us, we have received statements of evil against somebody or something, as to their not seeming to be bad but hiding badness. This is a question of deception. If anybody or anything appears good it is our pleasure to believe it is genuine goodness. Do not allow yourself to believe that a man or woman, a child, or an object, hides evil but appears good, for, if you do, they will not come the second time saying in joyful affirmation: "I am entirely cured." You are being deceived by thinking either things or people are deceptive.

Whether it is affairs of business or in sickness, do not believe that there are lustful passions and sensual appetites lurking back of appearances, or that good appearances are hiding bad conditions. And do not believe that there is something wrong with your business, even though it appears to be successful and flourishing. All that looks well is making a heroic fight to be God's good way in your eyes. Believe in it. Speak kindly of it.

The first strength of mind is the strength to endure. This is purity, which is long life. A good man may seem to be very frail, but he will live on and on where others, more robust looking, would falter, because goodness is a substance in man which endures. We get this by never accusing of unclean or sensual nature.

The second strength is the strength of youth, the strength of fearlessness. It comes to you by always believing everything is good which seems good, and that everyone is good who seems good. Do not think tobacco hides a poison; do not think rum hides a sting. Do not think that anyone who is kind to you, or whom you love or respect or enjoy the society of, or who looks kind or good, is bad, no matter who tells you so, or what interior feeling you have that they are. Let your conscious thoughts and words be according to the Good. This will give you a young and fearless look in the face, and keep your vigor. Childhood and youth never believe in bad where good seems to be.

A very childlike man in Massachusetts was told by some men, who were making fun of him, but seemed kind and wise, to send warming pans to the torrid zone. He did so and made a fortune. His simple acceptance of their kindness was a success to him. He could not have been made to believe that such kindly seeming men were trying to deceive him. You will find that anyone who is full of certainty that what seems good is good, has a young look. Old age comes from not refusing to be deceived. Youth is kept by refusing to believe evil of people or things. Not believing evil takes out the sting of what seemed to be evil.

The character which holds its own steadily is a successful character. A certain lawyer wanted to take a boy to train who would succeed him in his law practice. He took a way to test the tenacity of the assembled boys in holding a point until it was brought out satisfactorily. He told a thrilling story of a prize rabbit, which was in a barn which caught fire. Many and varied incidents took place at the fire. Amusing speeches were made, and every boy forgot the rabbit except one keen eyed boy over in the corner. "What became of the rabbit?" he asked. Nothing diverted his mind from the main idea of the story. "You are my boy," said the lawyer, and dismissed the others.

Scientific Christian Mental Practice

In healing your patients your mind must be kept to its first intentions. Whatever comes up to divert your thoughts, go back again and again to your purpose. If you have determined to set anything right by mental action, let nothing turn you from it. You can train your mind so that even while you chat and laugh about various matters, it is running along like a mighty river within you, singing great truths of Science. If you are, by seeming accident of circumstances, put where it seems impossible to carry out your honorable duties, by keeping your mind on them, without saying much, but not diverted from your original intention, all will be fulfilled.

Fretting is being diverted. Crying is being diverted. Where there's a will there's a way to cure your cases, and to straighten out your affairs in the Science of Mind. Even your dreams tell you the state of your mind. Everything that happens tells you how you stand toward your premise. Being diverted from a purpose is being deceived. It is getting mixed with things and people, when you ought to be clear and light.

A certain lady always cures her patients by looking steadfastly at a beautiful Madonna which hangs in her room. She talks to it as if it were the living patient, all in that buoyant young womanhood. Nothing turns her mind away. If it seems to do so, she talks very fast, as thinking quickly compels her to be attentive.

Jonah kept his mind on the memory of how Jerusalem looked, while he was shut up in the whale. It acted as a rope to draw him out into freedom. Greatrakes, the Irishman, never let his popularity at houses of great people make him forget to attend to his healing. He finally was turned out of favor because he would cure animals as well as people by his healing powers and out of loving kindness. In shutting him away they shut away their own health, but he did what he felt was his duty before God, regardless of the favor of the rich or great. This steadfastness is being true to Principle.

Pericles would walk on only one street in Athens. He never dined out socially. He gave his time, his life, his attention to his study of right government. Therefore, he is handed down as the wise governor of Athens. Michelangelo said, "Art is a jealous God. It requires the whole and entire time." He shut himself away from everybody while painting the Sistine Chapel. Newton was no marvelous mind, and one of those who had been his early companion, asked him how he succeeded so astonishingly. "By intending my mind," he said. Upon entering the land of true thinking I call your attention to this high principle of action.

Nothing will return satisfaction like the knowledge of God. Nothing widens and beautifies character like a trained mind. Nothing trains the mind like the daily reiteration of noble propositions of Good and Truth. Mind is not quickened and satisfied by the study of music or mathematics. It is apt to give way under the pressure of years. But the study of Spirit brightens the mind as the years roll on.

Healing by pure reasoning is healing by an ever increasing energy. Healing by pure reasoning is far better than healing by keeping in mind the face of the Madonna. Is not that a material picture? Still, we are not to condemn any practice, you must remember. We are not to speak ill of any thing which has brought ease from pain or weariness to mankind. It is good. It is good to show us its best side.

In the Catholic Church, about fifteen or sixteen hundred years ago, it was said that nothing is evil which brings forth good, but that led to their doing very cruel things, hoping to bring about good results. In Science there is no cruel pathway to some future good. There is no real advantage in surgery. Nobody ever gets wounded to help someone else. The angels of mercy and goodness fly ahead of the true Scientist and keep his pathway free from hurts. In Science there is no call to be brave, because there is nothing to fear. It is a sign of having stood true to Principle if we come out of the lion's jaws safely. It is a sign that we have been steadily true if we never get into the lion's jaws or sore afflictions.

So, it is not a signal that we have been absolutely true to our Principle if our patient comes to us a second time without the perfect cure. It is a sign that we can cure him, however. For, if we had entirely yielded to being deceived, he could not have come. Keep on with your reasonable doctrine in his presence; if he tells of evil symptoms, like pain, or if he tells of what happened to him, like restlessness or unhappiness do not think you need to believe it. Many a case has been cured by mentally saying "No" while people were talking of ills. At any rate, it is nothing from beginning to end. As it is to Spirit, so it should be to you. It is nothing.

One practitioner who caught this idea of persistence to the true idea, being not diverted at all, takes only one case of healing at a time and practices for that one constantly until he heals him. You sometimes hear practitioners telling of having nothing to do. Ask them if they have one case on hand. Oh yes, they tell you. And I tell them that it is the call of the Spirit for them to attend to the duty they have in hand, and the next duty will be attracted as to a magnet. If you do the best you can think of with such material as you have at hand, you will be sowing a principle as great in bringing you out successfully as if you had repeated the multiplication table by putting five more to each statement.

So with healing. Tell off each bead; it is a living blood drop. It will stir your pulses faster; it will throw out the fires of your Soul. They will warm the cold blood of your patient. They will warm your affairs. They will make you a healer whose power will increase and increase.

Each man, each woman, each event that comes to you, will be to you the signal that you are to think a certain way. There are cases that touch your mind like electric batteries, and suddenly you think with vehemence. Sometimes you think so rapidly that it seems more like feeling than thinking. Many people will say that they did not utter any words, and yet their cases were cured, because they felt such a strange hot rush pass through them. This rush of feeling came because the words they had been speaking were just ready to work, and they worked fast. This is a cheering and delightful principle of the right thoughts. They strike you in their strength at such unexpected times. If you devote most of your time to healing, you will most likely heal many cases suddenly. You must know it is because of the ideas you have been holding. Do you suppose that if some great good thought had not been started in you once such fruits could have come to you?

This Truth has ideas which are going forth and changing the mind of the entire race. It is the subtlest doctrine ever sprung upon the race. You are at home and maybe bruise your foot. You immediately say, "It is nothing; there is nothing to fear; there is no pain; I cannot be hurt. I am Spirit." Maybe you just put out your hand with a motion that means "No." The whole pain is gone immediately. Do you suppose that those words ever stop going? No, they are still traveling around in the air, and wherever they drop down upon a mind that thinks its foot or its head is hurt, involuntarily that mind repeats some part of your idea.

The poem, "Beautiful Snow," was thought of by two people simultaneously. As one thought it out, the other caught it flying. It is the same with inventions. There is no knowing which man really thought out any of the great inventions. Many times it is the second thinker who gets the name for the invention, or discovery, as America was named for Americus instead of Columbus.

The main principles of this Truth are old and have long been in the world, but some years ago there were a great many invalids suddenly inspired with the idea of Christ's everlasting healing presence, and thought the same treatments that we now use. They did not think them all; they felt them, and used such ones as came first to mind. For instance, about thirty-five years ago a lady was sitting by her friend, who was very ill. Suddenly she said, "You are healed by the power of God." And it was true. The friend arose at once, entirely well. When asked what she said mentally, before she spoke aloud she answered, "I thought, ''You are well now, not sick, only you don't know you are well; you must know it." You see, to her, the acute illness was nothing. It was not there. If she had held onto that principle as the truth of every seemingly sick one, she would have made a great healer.

Many people feel the idea of health so thoroughly that they cannot feel anything else, even if a man seems to be very ill. Their touch is full of their feeling of health. The touch of Jesus was full of healing. If you put your hand on your patients they are apt to think that it is your hand and not the idea that heals them. This new presentation of Truth is the information to the world that all healing is done by ideas and by nothing else. Therefore, ideas might just as well be given without symbols or carriages, as with them. The good religious man of old times kissed the cross and thought the cross would save him. He ate bread and thought it would make him spiritual. It was the meaning of the cross and the bread which helped him. They meant, "Nothing is evil where Christ is. All is good where Christ is, and he is here now." If he had held to these ideas and left out the cross and bread, it would have been all the same.

You do not need carriages in order to carry your ideas to people. Ideas will go and light wherever you send them. If you call the name, James Brown, he will hear you, even if he is one hundred miles away and you only call mentally. Then if you tell him over and over exactly what you want him to know, he will catch the whole purport of your ideas. If your ideas are the Truth about his health and his life, he will brighten up and get well. Maybe he does not know you are speaking to him. He simply thinks as you think, and feels that he has gotten well without a doctor. He has caught what you said, as the inventor catches the idea of a machine.

The whole race is feeling very differently about religion. They deny the existence of satan. They deny that God made any devil. They deny that God put Bunyan in jail through wicked men, in order to make him write *Pilgrim's Progress*. They deny that God puts us through great afflictions to see what stuff we are made of, to test our character. They deny that children are born with wicked or naughty tempers. They deny everything that the world used to believe. It has a very strange effect upon mankind. They get up strange inventions, because their minds get so clear after feeling those denials blowing in the air about them. In many new and unexpected places gold suddenly appears. It came because somebody said, "There is plenty of gold for everyone." He did not think that the plenty was right in his own hands. He thought it was afar off somewhere. So, afar off, in some remote spot, the gold was born.

What is wanted is a doctrine of now and here. You must take up this Truth in a stronger fashion than it has ever been taken up before, with the idea of Now and Here.

If the man one thousand miles off from you gets well when you tell him his pains are gone, why should not the poor man over there in that place five hundred miles away from you get hold of some money to meet his obligations when you tell him that he has not lost his property, and that he is supplied bountifully. God is just as much the Provider of his children as he is the Healer. "The Lord will provide," is as much Scripture teaching as, "The Lord is thy healer." While healing is very well demonstrated now, supporting is not so well demonstrated, apparently. You will have to see that poverty is no reality. You must not get mixed up with the idea of poverty any more than with the idea of sickness. They all belong alike to the realms of nothingness. You must not be deceived by your seeming to be ignorant or unhappy. Ignorance and unhappiness are as much negation as sickness. Let us altogether say to all the poverty of the world,

"Poverty is unreality; there is no such thing as poverty; it is nothing to Spirit. Spirit owns all things." Let us say to unhappiness, "There is no unhappiness in Spirit. All is joyous peace." And let us say within our own minds, "Now! now!"

All things evil in seeming, that come to us at first for healing, come as the formulations of our talks and thoughts about other people, or ourselves, being in the flesh senses. We say we do not, as Spirit, believe in sensual formulations. This is our first treatment. All things evil which come to us the second time, come as the formulations held there by our talk or thoughts, since we first saw them, about how hard things are to bear, and what poisons and stings and hurts the world has in it. We may have accused our friends of being deceitful or dissimulating or hypocritical. Maybe we have thought that we ourselves are not truthful. Whatever we have agreed with as being an evil, which was not evil, we may be sure something or someone will come the second time for help.

We have a law of morning statements of Truth which we might call prayer. These treatments are all prayers. Our afternoon statements are prayers. The only difference between our prayers in the Truth and the old orthodox prayers is that we pray as if we had already received the blessings instead of begging for them. We say the man is healed. We do not beg for the man to be healed.

In the Buddhist temples they have been striking on the sounding rims of great bells for generations, crying, "O, let the good come." There is such a pathetic intimation in that prayer that the Good is not already here that it is no wonder the Good has never appeared in the way they wish. They ought to name in certainty what Good is already here. That will cause the Good to appear, for indeed health is already in our midst, so we may say it is well. The Good is in our affairs, and if we tell the truth about them, it will exhibit. We make nothing of our words; we only exhibit what is already made. Therefore Jesus said, "Pray as if ye had already received." Of course we have already received, and why should we not be truthful and say so? Through Truth the Good is visible. Good waits for Truth. Good will not show you good health, good strength, good provisions, good life, except through the glass of Truth. Do not expect answers to begging prayers.

Look over all the answered prayers you ever heard of and see how suddenly the beseeching hearts stopped and said, "Thy will be done." The will of God is for health, for life, for prosperity, for peace, for friends, and peace in the home. So, when they ceased begging they were one with the divine will and it was so their will that their prayer that moment was the kind of which Jesus spoke.

In Truth we begin at once to acknowledge the will of God about all things. We become aware that what is not well with us is not the will of God. Through the ages there has been an unprincipled laying of sickness, pain, deformity, and poverty to the will of God.

Persistent thought about the laws of physical force has given man an extraordinary energy of body and mind. He has not yet learned how to use the force intelligently. If he keeps on thinking of how to use the force he had stored himself with, he certainly must come to the knowledge that he needs to use the force.

Persistent thought about healing general sickness, or, as it was said of Jesus, "He healed all manner of diseases," will give you so much healing force you will draw multitudes of sick people to you to be healed. Persistent thought that there is no sickness, will put sickness away from people before you can see them. Persistent thought about prosperity, and how prosperity is brought to us, will make you a magnet for prosperity. Your prosperity will not be the highest prosperity, it will not be useful prosperity, unless you know how to teach others to be prosperous. The pressure of your great riches upon you will make you stiff and sickly unless you can make the spiritual Principle flow freely through yourself to others. There must be a draft or the fire will not burn. There must be a valve or a piston and wheel will wait forever before pulling the cars. There must be a free giving of your Truth, or the world may wait another million years for the wretched poverty of its people to be gone.

So you are to think your Truth and not be diverted from speaking what you know. You are to write your Truth and not be diverted from writing what you know. The beryl stone signifies the need of putting your Truth into everyday tasks. While you are at work, say some mighty word into the fabric of being, as a ventriloquist throws his voice into his wax figures. In your case you are only speaking aloud what the spirit of the fabric is now saying; it is the great I AM.

Do you remember the promise of David that even the night shall be light about thee? And of Eliphaz in Job, that the stones of the field shall teach thee? This is because it is written in them what you ought to say.

It is the province of the pen and paper to hold in eternal place certain things. You cannot afford to write very far off from what the Spirit is whispering through the white sheets of paper. And whatever subjects are touched by the writing you make shall have fastened into them native tongues of Truth, and nobody can handle them without wondering how he came by such unexpected ideas. What you set your pen to tell is the beryl stone. Not until you have written the absolute Truth have you gotten past the beryl stone. If you have written only a little you have not even begun to polish that stone. Maybe it is still covered within the earthiness of long years of thinking the first error concerning the I AM, and also the first error concerning environments.

The more truly you speak of things, the more clearly stands out the meaning of each one. Its countenance gives you its light. Jesus, stooping down, wrote in the sand, and now everything has felt the handwriting he sent under the waters to be sung to the ends of the earth, for all things are to be ready to say, "Amen," when we also shall write down what he said of them. Make your record in all things. Bring out the record in all things. Thus shall all things shine. The night shall be light. The moon is to have the light of the sun, and the sun is to be seven times brighter than it is now.

All things are truly written full of such deep and wonderful messages, let us not be deceived by what is said against them. The air is filled, packed solid with everlasting record of what we ought to have demonstrated. This is the unchangeable handwriting of God. Here is the science of music waiting in the silence for someone to express it. Ages have gone by and still this silent music is waiting for someone to read it. Mankind has never gotten beyond Handel, Hayden, Mozart, Beethoven, in music. Why not, when there is music beyond their highest and noblest?

Here is the science of mathematics packed into the airs, with computations beyond Euclid, LeGendre and d'Alembert. Why does no one read the marvelous handwriting on the solid air walls, and teach us the science of numbers aright? Here is the science of happiness and bliss. Its truth is written in beautiful letters, clear and bright, and legible like the angles and facets of the beryl stone of Revelation. Why does no one read off its easy, easy directions, so that "there shall be no more pain, neither sorrow nor crying, neither shall there be any more death"?

Right here is our Truth whispering in our ears. That is our eighth lesson. It is so audible to our ears, its voice is so distinct. Having ears to hear, why do we not hear? Its writing is so plain, so legible. Having eyes to see, why do we not see?

The coming of any patient a second time, the appearance of trouble the second time, shows that we have to put down our heads and let the Spirit speak over us.

"I have not been deceived into seeing evil in anyone or anything. I see good in all things and in all people, always, without delusions. I never accuse anyone or anything of seeming

imperfection in any way. I never accuse myself of seeming imperfection, or of hiding imperfections. All is the light of Truth in Jesus Christ."

This is standing aside in the mortal for Spirit to speak. You ought to wait a moment and see what treatment comes to you strongest. If you have devoted yourself to letting the Spirit speak of never accusing of deception, you will suddenly find a treatment spring into mind. You will feel very bold about giving it, for taking off the veil of hypocrisy is very emboldening.

Afternoon thoughts should be all about your environment. Morning thoughts should be about your own nature. "In the morning sow thy seed, and at even withhold not thy hand, for thou knowest not whether shall prosper either this or that, or whether they both shall be alike good," Ecclesiastes.

Now if you call to your mind the name of the friend you have treated, you may follow with me along the line of a second treatment. We will not stop to think whether we have treated him or her before or not. We know that one day is enough to give one treatment. We know that this is the scriptural second treatment which Scripture teaches, and we give it. Say to him or her exactly what I am saying to the one I have seemed to be deceived into believing to be a diseased person.

"I am not deceived into believing in you as diseased.

"You have not inherited the formulations of deception.

"You have inherited Truth only.

"You have not been deceived by a race mind forming deceptions around you.

"You have not been deceived by people around you formulating disease by the falsity of their beliefs.

"You have not formulated self-deceptions.

"You have not formulated deception between yourself and me.

"I do not believe in the formulations of deception, either by mesmerism, magnetism, psychology, auto-suggestion or hypocrisy.

"I believe only in the clean handwriting of God on every part of your mind, and standing forth from every part of your body.

"You are now showing forth perfection through every manifestation of your being.

"You have heard the Truth of God.

"You express the Truth of God.

"I see through you, and in you, and by you, perfect health throughout.

"You are every whit whole.

"You are therefore ready now to acknowledge that your health is perfect.

"You acknowledge it to all around you, to yourself and to me, now.

"In the name of Jesus Christ I pronounce you healed now and forever. Amen."

You may give this same treatment before sleeping tonight. Rewrite it from memory as well as you can remember it. Read it aloud. It is not what the flesh saith, but the everlasting voice of the Spirit.

These treatments react upon ourselves, and do us as much good as they do our patients.

Around us and before us, in the plain sight of our mind, our Spirit and our Soul, is our perfect power, ready to rise to accomplish the words of God.

Join with me now in saying:

"The words I speak unto you, it is not I that speak them but the Father that dwelleth in me, He doeth the works. God works through me to will and to do that which ought to be done by me. Amen."

Lesson Nine

Righteous Judgment

IT has always lain heavy on the mind of the race that holiness and health, sin and disease, bear a logical relation to each other. "I have been young and now I am old, yet have I never seen the righteous forsaken nor his seed begging bread," shows that not only health of body, but health of affairs have been laid back to the doorway of righteousness.

"Envy is rottenness of bones," says one. "My words are life to them that find them and health to all their flesh," says another one, when speaking for the words of the Spirit in man.

"The sins of the father shall be visited upon the children unto the third and fourth generation," said Moses. And Jesus said, "No man is your father upon the earth." Who then is visited by the sins of his parents? The Adam man. Who is it that shall have no consequence of sin visited upon him? The spiritual man. Did Jesus believe in sin? "Neither hath this man sinned nor his parents." Did he often address himself to the mortal man? Just enough to make it nothing. "Go and sin no more," he said to the man whose good sight sprang forth as a strong arm when the love of Jesus warmed it forth.

He put away the fleshly appetite, he left the Spirit free. He put denials and affirmations together for a right and left wing of the law of demonstrations.

It is often supposed that innocent young children are under the curse of their father's and mother's evil thoughts and character, and they may have lain down under the burden of scrofula and consumption because they thought it too heavy to carry, if their parents had lain down under it. Many have lain down under bad dispositions and kleptomania and intemperance because they believed their parents had left these things to them as their inheritance.

What kind of a God would visit his own people with such a law as that? Where have the followers of Jesus been tarrying that they have not risen out of thinking such things inevitable, with his commands ringing down through the written gospels, "Call no man your father." "The flesh profiteth nothing." "Follow me." "Keep my sayings." What a strange imagination against the Lord of hosts to think He sent our evil tendencies in the first place, and the consequences of them in the second place.

Where have we been lagging in the lesson of Mind, that we have overlooked Jeremiah's information that a man's word is his only burden? And the proclamation of Jesus that by our words we are justified and condemned? Could God, the principle of thought and speech, invest His people with a richer heritage than the power of the word? Is there anything more majestic than this great principle of every word being full of divine potency when true, and gifted with only seeming greatness when false?

Can a law be more stupendous than that a lie must seem to be reasonable in order to seem anything at all? If there is no law of flesh, because there is no flesh, must not all we say of flesh seem to be true, or not give us any claim on itself? Does it make any difference to you if a crazy man tells you that your mother stole his watch, when you know he never had one, and your mother is good and upright? But if a noble looking gentleman tells you that a shabby woman carried off his purse you believe him at once, whether he is lying or not, because his story seems plausible.

So when great and learned preachers stand in high pulpits and talk about a great being called God, who made a terrible satan to tempt good little children to steal and lie and die, we have felt that it seemed plausible. They were very wise indeed to describe the other side of such a God by saying that He sent His only son into a swarm of wicked men, who were none of His kind, though He had created them, to be badly used by the only wicked creations of His own hands. But the whole thing from beginning to end is false.

God is the principle of holiness, Goodness and Truth. Truth about God is expressing Principle. Lies about God express the opposite of principle, thus the opposite of holiness and Goodness.

The experience of the mind of the race concerning holiness and sin has been that they have been indeed the creators of their own destiny by their imagination. Some of the very great lovers of God have been mighty living demonstrations of words. One woman whose mind had become very quick in demonstrating words through constant praise of God, like the mind of Kurosumi, the Japanese, went through a hospital of plague-infested patients, and said: "In the name of Jesus Christ be ye healed," and many of them arose at once. Then she would say that if God pleased to afflict her with smallpox and otherwise torment her as he did his dear son, Jesus Christ, she was at that moment ready to receive the calamities. She put up such an expectant mind that she drew those very things to herself. Her words were quick and powerful.

"By thy words thou art justified and by thy words thou art condemned." For what the heart feels and believes, the words are sure to speak forth. Words are mighty signals of the heart's beliefs. Even if you say the man is healed, while your heart aches because he does not show forth health, you know you say he is healed because you believe he is if the Science is true. So, even in this case your belief is in your words, and if you say he is not healed, you speak from what you feel most strongly at that moment. So words are flags.

Jesus did not believe in having even our most vigorous belief in evil come forth expressed before the world. He said what to us means: Suppose you have said some violent words, expressions of your strong emotion, like "what a fool

I am," or, "I am terribly abused and an unfortunate person," and it actually appears today as if you had made some bitter mistakes, or were going to ruin, I say unto you, you may blast such words and never see any fruit of mistakes that bring hurts or misfortunes as I now blast that vigorous fig tree.

Right here let me tell you that if you are going to remember in your mind how sick your patient looks, you must turn that memory right out of doors. Look at a picture of some beautiful character, or speak some lofty principles over and over, for the memory of how your patient seems while sick will bring out that sickness plainly expressed.

If you are given to imagining how something would seem if it came to hurt you, you get right away from the imagination at once, for an imagination is determined to come out some way. If you have taken some good premise in mind "late in life," as we hear it expressed, you have struck the fears and imaginations you formerly held a hard blow. Possibly they may come out in your dreams. Be thankful they get no farther than your sleeping time in their exposure, for they were making ready to come out before all mankind in your affairs.

All evil is blamed to sin, but sin is only a mistaken idea of life, a mistaken idea of who you are, and what world you live in. This is all the sin you or anybody ever committed. You made your mistake in mind, and have lived out that mistake. This Truth erases that mistake. Then your life is free from the cause of its suffering and trouble.

You may often wonder why the Truth student, who claims to believe the doctrine of no sin, no sickness, no death, does not immediately show peaceful, satisfied conditions. Suppose the rain and dust have beaten against the plate glass windows until they are very dirty; do you think the mere cessation of the rain and dust will make the window panes clean? So it is with the mind that is covered with years of habitual imaginations. It ceases from imaginations, but practical daily washings of the dust of years must be made. This does not make the sin of imagination, the mistakes about life, a reality, but explains how real it seems to us.

The ninth stone is the Topaz, which stands for harmony between thoughts and externals. The world in which we live is the exact record of our thoughts. If we do not like the world we live in, then we do not like our thoughts. This is discord. There are thoughts which we can love greatly while we think them. They make conditions which we love. This is harmony. He who loves his thoughts greatly and loves his words greatly is sure to be a musician of some kind. There is much joy in his life. Let no one be surprised at his not being perfect in his science of music while he does not love his thoughts and enjoy the environments they have made.

Within each of you is the song of the Spirit. By thinking out that song within your mind, it will break forth over your affairs. Some Truth students sing their treatments, they sing their ideas. You can sing mentally until a joy of heart takes possession of you. This joy will come to pass in happy surroundings sooner or later.

Some of us fret because it takes so long to bring thoughts of good into our environments. This is discord. If we are given to discords, let us often say:

"I give thanks and glad praise that God hath given to the Holy Spirit all the joy and song of the universe, and she does not have to pray for it, beg for it, work for it, nor struggle for it; she is joyous and sings because she is joy, and sings as I am glad that the Holy Spirit is joy and harmony." You will uncover your spring of joy that lies within you, and soon you will sing and be joyous without trying to do so.

It is noticeable in almost all religious people that their first idea of goodness is to make life in some way harder for themselves and each other. They drive themselves to get up at five o'clock in the morning, with their families, and to go without sleep until one or two o'clock each morning, saying that as Spirit needs no rest and is strong enough to do all things, they are as able as Spirit to do that which is most harrowing to the whole family without murmuring. This may be what you will be tempted to agree to on one subject or another. It is forgetfulness of the way of Jesus, who slept and ate, drank and clothed himself exactly like other people, and only did differently when it pleased himself to do so, never even asking his disciples to share any of his self-elected hardships.

The yoke of Jesus upon us is easy. God is rest. The violets do not strain and struggle to be in harmony with their life. The mountains do not groan and labor to be great. The hurricane and the simoon of the desert do their mighty tasks easily. It is not being in adjustment with the Divine Mind to be thinking hard lines to travel on. Because we are Spirit, we do that which our own judgment prompts us to do, and lay no burdens on each other because of our ideas.

If it is hard for you to cure your case, you have made the mistake somewhere of believing in hardships for somebody or for yourself. A mistaken idea about God and your own life will break out somewhere.

Jesus Christ would not cast himself off a pinnacle to show how mentally powerful he was. He would not even heal a case to show how mentally powerful he was. He moved at the dictation of Spirit along lines not laid down by men or historic precedents. If you watch very carefully you will see that there is not an item of your life in which you are not guided by the Spirit into ways of pleasantness and peace. Any other way is one you have chosen independent of Jesus Christ principles, and is the sin of your life, that is, the mistake upon which you move about.

The ninth stone is the Topaz — harmony in peace, and delight with the pathway we are walking. There is one treatment which results in efficiency to manage environment easily. It is this:

"I do not accuse the world or myself of sin; all is well."

You have no idea how much of the inefficiency of mankind comes from thinking about the wrongdoings of others, and of ourselves. There is nothing more miserable than to feel that by some mistake in life you have not amounted to what you might have, and your misfortunes all hinge on that mistake. Now while a mistake seems to be so much, its right name is nothingness. God never made any mistakes in Spirit Your family never made any mistakes in Spirit. None of you can possibly make any mistake in Spirit. As Spirit is all that is real of you, the facing of the worst trouble of your life with the words that the mistakes that brought them being nothing, the troubles are nothing, will have a marvelous effect in putting them in a new relation with you. I do not mean that you will be hardened to bear them, I mean that they will be gone.

The day of the Lord cometh as a thief in the night, silently. God, the Truth, taketh away the grief and sickness as a mother comforteth. God is merciful. Be merciful with your people. The God acts only through mercy. Efficiency comes with letting the Goodness of the merciful and tender Spirit speak, instead of your condemning tendencies, wherever evil seems so plain. It is a sign of being farther on in Truth when you can make sin as unreal in your mind as matter. If Spirit is the only substance, matter is not substance. If holiness is the only presence, sin is not present.

You will be sure to be faced up with your case uncured the third time if between seeing them the second and third times you have harbored feelings of how wrongly people have acted, or how wrongly you have acted. There are a few claims of wrongdoing, or sins, which always bring a case in the third time. There is selfishness. We see that plainly in certain people, we say. By what right do we see selfishness? By right of the Spirit or of the carnal? We speak of enviousness. Who has envy? The Spirit? If the Spirit has not envy, of whom are we talking when we speak of enviousness in others or ourselves? Of nobody, most certainly, for Spirit is all. Then there is no jealousy. Have we accused ourselves of jealousy? We are the Holy Spirit. Do you wonder that accusation brings great infirmity to represent it? If we call anybody malicious, revengeful or cruel, we have spoken of Life, Mind, Spirit. That fairly ties our own thoughts in chains so that they do not heal well, manage environments well, nor do anything in the way of praise or skillfulness on instruments we so much wish they would.

If sin seems so real to you take every Wednesday afternoon and deny the reality of every sin you have ever heard of. Thus will your Spirit stand out in its uncondemned holiness, and, unchained, will do great works for you.

Plato taught that the whole world is a colossal system of shadows. The deepest shade is the belief in wrong doing. Its shadows throw long stretches of desert and forest over your pathway, which in Truth is all light with the glory of Goodness. It is said of elephants that they sometimes, in eastern countries, fight shadows on the rocks and beat themselves to pieces. Thus our missionaries and philanthropists, fighting the huge shadow of unbelief of somebody doing great wrongs in the universe, lie down with the feeling of how gigantic the monsters are who have the poor world in their jaws.

Learn that there is a divine harmony between the Mind from whence the true world is springing, and your mind; such a harmony that you yourself are that mighty and good Mind. "And the lion and the lamb shall lie down together; the child shall play with the serpent, and the sting of all that seems to be hurtful shall be removed."

"Behold the Lamb of God who taketh away the sins of the world." The Lamb is meekness, and the Lamb is not suspicious. The Lamb trusts to your goodness. The Lamb of God is Jesus Christ who condemned none, forgave all, suspected none, believed in no evil, feared nothing, loved everything. Therefore he healed instantaneously. Therefore he said, "All power is given unto me in heaven and in earth."

If you feel all the time as though you ought to be protecting yourself from mankind, either financially, or as to reputation, stop and think over these Wednesday afternoon words. You must not put up umbrellas against things which do not exist. Umbrellas are a burden in pleasant weather. By this I mean, if God is your Mind, if God is your world, what have you to fear? So your fears are a burden. Belief that I have made a mistake terrifies me. Belief that you have made a mistake terrifies you. And so with all the world.

If now we are told so strongly that it takes effect in our blood and our bones, and if we are convinced that it is true that we never could make any mistake, then our fear is gone.

"Thou wilt keep him in perfect peace whose mind is staid on Thee." "I will fear no evil for Thy rod and Thy staff they comfort me." Rod means activity, and staff means rest of mind. We act wisely and rest comfortably, therefore we are comforted. Deny the inheritance of sin." The son shall not bear the iniquity of the father any more in the land," saith the Lord. Deny the race iniquities. "For am I not God? Do I not fill heaven and earth?" Deny contagion of sin. Fear nothing from suggestion of evil. "There shall no evil touch thee, thou shalt be hid from the scourge of the tongue." Deny the personal sin. "Neither hath this man sinned, nor his parents." Deny that you ever wronged anyone, for in you is God only.

Socrates, being asked, "What is the most troublesome to good men?" answered, "The prosperity of the wicked." People who have made certain mistakes do not touch their finances or environments with those mistakes. They touch only their bodies. Some people's mistakes touch their environment entirely while their bodies are very well indeed. There has been no statement of cause and effect yet given forth which has been entirely accurate in describing how a selfish disposition or an envious one should affect the business of a man or the health of a man. Injustice in money matters does not always bring financial disaster to the actor. It may break out in his children instead of himself.

Each one of us has all he can do to look to the ways of his own heart, and make his harmony between his own heart thoughts and his world, by thinking as his heart is really thinking at its spiritual center, instead of from the mistakes of his thoughts about life and God, which are not his heart but his imagination. Let us imagine nothing, let us speak Truth. Sometimes people feel that all the talk about even the presence and character of God as Good, as Life, Truth, Love, Omnipresence, Omnipotence, Omniscience, is pure imagination, because nobody has seen or heard or felt such a being or such a principle. They resolve everything into imagination. Well, if imagination can take its choice between imagining life, holy and omnipresent, or death, evil and pain, and can bring out according to its ideas so imagined, we will see that it is a higher and nobler imagination to conceive of Omnipotent Good, than to conceive of evil.

Man naturally thinks there is a God. You think so. If every book that you picked up said there is no God, you would dispute it. It is not in anyone to dispute, however, if we point out the truth that there is no such God as some have imagined one sending afflictions and pain upon the good and innocent of the world. We are ready to give up such an imagination at once when the reasonable idea is presented, that Almighty Goodness did not create a satan, nor create passions and appetites and deceptions. He made only the Good and the Holy. The bad and the wicked are not made—they only seem to be made. They are the shadows of the sub- stance of the Good.

A good trait in you, like generosity, is seen to throw down a dark opposite to itself. You show jealousy. There was hardly ever a generous person without the opposite trait called jealousy showing its dark streak. Jealousy is the long headlight of generosity. The jealousy is nothing, it is not there. The generosity is something. It is God's presence. So, of all that is not desirable, the pure goodness being called substance, and the bad called shadow, the goodness comes into plainer sight, and the badness disappears altogether.

In spite of their high reasoning, often you will find some Truth students falling into begging a great being on a throne in the air to help them, even after they know that there is no such God, but that instead there is the Almighty Principle of Truth and Goodness. Paul's young friend, Timothy, was inclined to think sometimes in the old ways. It is a weak way to think. Take some wine of doctrine, stronger and warmer ideas of life.

Moses in this ninth lesson says, "Let the waters bring forth abundantly living creatures." Waters mean thoughts. The "living creatures" of the thoughts are the environments alive — the people, the friendships, the society, the children. Let your flowing thoughts, warmed at the fountain of pure reason, be rich in affection, love, life, joy, harmony. Swedenborg said that Moses meant affection by "living creatures."

The eighth lesson was about having light. Light is warmth. The brighter the sun the hotter it shines. The hotter the sun the surer the rivers are to bring forth living creatures in abundance. So, the hotter your religion, the warmer your love for the world, for God, for Truth. The warmer your love, the more friends and pleasures and conditions of joy surround you. This is confidence in your doctrine. It might be called self-confidence.

People who lack self-confidence are those who have not warmed into confidence in their doctrine. They are given to accusation of sin, but they as often accuse themselves of sin as their neighbors. Nothing alive and solid with success ever stays in the hands of people who are given to accusing others or themselves of sin. By this I mean, prosperity will always seem just ahead of you if you think of people or yourself as selfish, envious, jealous, revengeful or cruel. Your health will always seem just out of your reach. Your healing power will always be slipping through your fingers.

Just as you think your case is cured it is not cured. Every time it can be traced to your accusing of sin. Stop that, and your waters of mind will gather prosperity so tangibly that you cannot mistake it. Your waters of mind will breed new healing power, new judgments, new affairs, new schemes in some line which will please and satisfy you.

If anyone tells you of there being a principle of evil, deny it. If anybody tells you of there being a satan, deny it. If anybody tells you of there being a fall of man from his God estate, deny it. If you read of sin, deny it. You must not have a poor opinion of yourself. Your substance, your intelligence, your nature is God. If the Spirit of you arises in its strength, you will have great confidence in your own mission, your own work, your own powers.

Taylor, the General, called a council of Mexicans. They told him that in numbers and artillery his enemies were so far ahead that he stood no chance of victory. "We will dismiss this council until after the battle," he said. His confidence in his principle of action was so roused that he brought forth substantial victory.

Your principle of life is worth believing in with all your soul, or it is not worth believing in at all. Come, make up your minds decidedly. Do you believe there is any sin in the world, or the whole universe? If you do, but wish you did not, then you have light on your waters, but not heat enough to create good, tangible success.

People who ignore the sins of their neighbors the most are most beloved, and they love most. They are our best healers. People who believe in their own doctrine with all their might and main succeed every time. Make up your mind about this sin question, and you will settle the ninth point in Truth. You will polish the Topaz stone of harmony with your life. Discords and strife will cease. New creations will spring forth as the result of your new thoughts.

Klopstock, the German, who wrote the poem, "Creation," was waited upon in Hamburg by some students who walked all the way from Göttingen to ask him what he meant by a certain passage in his composition. "I do not just now recall what I meant, gentlemen," he said, "but it would pay you to spend your lifetime trying to find out what I meant." He had such implicit confidence in the accuracy of the genius that inspired him, that he saw it must have burned with a glory out of the reach of his own ordinary mind to have spoken beyond what, in calm moments, he could comprehend. Rogers, the poet, always read his own compositions. He believed in his own genius. He was greatly honored. Wordsworth always wanted to have his own writings read to him for he trusted and loved his own genius. He was greatly honored. Michelangelo, Dickens, Pericles — all believed in their own inspiration. "If I said it, it is so, and if it is so, I said it," said one who never opened his lips carelessly, never exaggerated, never misrepresented, wrote what he meant about God, human reason and satan, so that even his contemporaries listened to him. Hannibal swore eternal hate to Rome, and he believed so implicitly in the genius of his oath that when the Romans wanted to scare their children, they cried, "Hannibal is at the gate."

On every plan of your campaign believe in your principles, whatever they are. Hannibal's principle was destruction of the Romans. Poetry records of him that "The pages of his history with tears of blood are wet." It shows what confidence in the principle with which you work in your life will work out. Moses calls works of religious confidence living creatures of good things that make glad. No crying, no killing, no sickness, or death in them. Religious teachings at their best have no pain in them. They have living Good. So when you once wake up to conscious confidence in your religion, you bring forth works, great cures, great prosperity for yourself and for everyone.

Jesus Christ taught the making of gold by this law — stopping the conscious waters of mind with hot words full of substance. He taught the making of bread by the conscious confidence of mind in the Spirit that flows through it. You must believe that God works through you to will and to do some peculiar mission. Have confidence that if one man does to you what seems to be a wrong, that your genius, your Spirit, your God, is that moment working good for you. The man is the instrument. This is your religion taken exactly word for word from Jesus Christ: "For if you love them that love you, what reward have you? Love them that hate you, and do good to them that despitefully use you." God is then working the reward in the new delight right at hand.

Despise not the creatures of the sea. The rivers of Mind, flowing with true rewards, are legal creations. You have a right to rewards, said Jesus. They are the product of confidence in your religion, says Truth. Certain ideas produce certain conditions. If your confidence is put into a principle which you do not call good, that is, if you believe that something evil is going to happen to you, because you committed an injustice against somebody once in your life which you do not forgive yourself for, as you have not confidence in the Spirit of God as having made that wrong nothingness, and you keep believing evil will come to you, your confidence will bring forth, especially if you feel keenly about the matter. You won't like it, but you believe that way. Of course you know that fear of a thing is confidence enough in it to bring it to pass. Job said, "The thing that I feared hath come upon me."

It is a singular fact, but one that I will call your attention to, that people who lament much over anything always have liver complaint. Jeremiah wrote, "Mine eyes do fail with tears, my bowels are troubled, my liver is poured out upon the earth." You see he speaks of three maladies from lamentations, viz: poor eyesight, bowel trouble and liver complaint. This may often be a hint to you in denying the cause of these three sicknesses. But back of the lamenting there must have been something believed worth lamenting about, and that is always some wrong done by somebody. That wrong never took place in God's Kingdom, so there was nothing to lament about, and the Spirit never laments. Therefore, there is no disease. This reasoning put mentally to your patient is the flowing of a river of Truth through his dry lands. It will wash away the history of his disease. It will bring out living health in his organs.

The early practitioners of healing always got a history of the case of their patients, then they negatived it by saying: "You had no cause to mourn; having no cause to mourn, you never could mourn; therefore you have no failing eyesight, for there has nothing transpired to effect your eyes. You see with spiritual vision, which no mortal condition can interfere with." If, now, you remember somebody with failing eyesight, stop and repeat this treatment.

For these three maladies, so-called, we use a scientific argument for the whole race. Take yesterday's treatment, nullifying hypocrisy, deception, lies, psychological influences, and give it Tuesday afternoon to the whole world. And when your patient arrives for the second time you will not have to treat him against deception and its effects. Something will come very strongly to you, for your genius for healing is equal to the wonderful Gassnor of Germany, who cured thousands. And as you are bringing out your healing river by a scientific process, you can explain how others can heal as well as yourself. Tell that the whole world is absolutely well, "The inhabitants shall not say I am sick any more."

The reason so much is said about bodily cure and not about moral reformation and prosperity is because if the body is well the man can catch the tones of Truth on the larger and more intricate problems of life. Bodily healing often depends upon moral rectitude. It often depends upon prosperity. So you must focus your mind to the word "Health" for the world, expecting to touch each separate need of a man the moment you look at him.

It is a great principle to understand, that if we know the law of the Good, how it works when truth is told, that health and intelligence will spring forth from the face and through the bodily frame of whoever you speak to, whether mentally or audibly. The moment you see that the Good is really working through you, everything looks different to you from what it did before. The man's voice does not seem so rough as it did before. The child's cough seems free, it acts as if it were passing away, soon to be forgotten.

You have no idea how soon you forget evil when you have sight of the Good. The sight of Good surely acting with you makes you love it. Then you have confidence in it. Then you do good work. This is formulating Truth. When you see someone who seems to be selfish, what will you say? You will say, "Spirit never formulates in selfishness." Or you will say, "Truth never expresses in selfishness." And you will be sure to say, "I do not accuse myself or my world of selfishness."

Why do you say, "I do not accuse myself of selfishness?" Because every person you see is the expression of your own traits of character. When he is set right, you are set right. The business man you know best represents your business matters. Get him prosperous and satisfied, and you will be prosperous and satisfied. The musician you know best expresses one of your ideas on some subject. Get that idea right and he will be a fine musician. The singer whose voice you do not enjoy is one of your own thoughts out of chord with God. Tell her mentally that she is the voice of the Holy Spirit to you, and that you will not feel her imperfection. She will be gone from your ears, and her mission to you will be plain. You will feel a love, a warmth towards the Spirit that will soon bring the good news about something quite different from singing.

A woman was eating her dinner, and a telegram about the death of her son came to her. The telegram did not look like her digestive organs, did it? Yet the hardness with which she received the telegram hardened the food in her stomach, and for years afterward she had dyspepsia. A healer told her that Spirit never received bad news, never was shocked, was always free and strong. That mental message did not look like digestive organs or food, did it? Yet she was cured of indigestion that day. So this doctrine, always telling of God and life and health and prosperity, does not seem to be a tangible machine like a grist mill or factory, yet it grinds out the desires of the heart in happy conditions by its own mysterious lowliness.

We have new circumstances by its mystic fingers. It loves to feel you in harmony with it, for then it works freely through you to will and to do. All the time it is your own Mind speaking that which you call Spirit. Let this be clear to you: "There is a Spirit in man and the inspiration of the Almighty giveth him understanding." It is your own breath of Omnipotence when you think forth great thoughts of God. It is your own inbreathing of Omnipotence when you are pleased with something in your life. That pleasure came to pass because from the deeps of your Spirit along the way somewhere you spoke Truth or thought Truth.

People think more truly than you give them credit for. The grumbler has some great truth which he speaks or thinks often. It makes him successful, He has many happy moments. The rest is shadow, vanity, absence. The evil is nothingness. He would change his habits entirely if you would think the truth towards him, that he is searching so restlessly for the Good. The thief would drop everything and praise and bless Jesus Christ if you would breathe toward him the thoughts his mind is restlessly searching around for. The sick man would be well at once if you would breathe toward him the thoughts his heart has fainted for lack of.

You cannot cure sin by punishing it. "Who shall save us from our sin save he that seeth no sin in us?" If we punish sin by any other method than denying its reality, we make it more manifest than ever. So the Jesus Christ method of a blameless life, free from condemnation, peaceable, forgiving, mild, gentle, unpretentious, all the time shedding a fine radiance of inner light abroad, is the only way of setting free from sin. If you have a steady habit of thinking high thoughts, your presence will be helpful to people.

It was said of Socrates, you remember, that his presence, even without speaking, would regulate a man's judgment. If you have a strict moral rectitude, you can balance a man's health without treating him. You can clarify a man's ideas without speaking to him. Often you will have an entirely different effect upon people from what your treatments read. For instance, you might treat one for deafness and turn his habits into new channels, yet not touch his deafness. This shows that your mind works that way. You must be pleased with whatever way your mind works. Pleasure at even a remote good will bring other good into your manner of action.

I have been speaking to you about a supposed case of disease. You know very well that there never was any disease. Why, then, do I speak of one, and tell you to take a case of some kind to cure? Because we take all the appearances in one lot and tell the Truth. We look at the child's arithmetical problem and say "No" where it is not true. We say "Yes" to what is true. So we meet the children who are working out their life problems. We know wherein it is not the truth they speak by the sight they show. We know wherein we have not spoken the truth by the life we lead. If I am in bondage, I have had some extreme error about God and His relations to my life. The Truth tells me how to erase that error. Jesus Christ erased errors very rapidly. You and I will erase errors rapidly or slowly according to our nature. If we stumble at the calling of sin "nothingness," unreality, absence in this sea of omnipresence, we shall be slow in demonstration. We shall not be joyous. Our singing will be poor.

We cannot be like God until we speak and think of sin as God does. You do not believe that God looks at sin. You know that "His eyes are too pure to behold iniquity." You believe that God sees everything. Then he would see sin if there was any to see. What is this that looks like a man striking a child? There is no such action taking place. What was that when a man shot his little son? He never did. It is all the figment of the imagination. You have dreamed the stories. "Wake, thou that sleepest," shouted Paul. There is a Spirit in those you have spoken of that knows nothing of those actions which you name. Look toward the Spirit. Fix your eyes there. Hear now the direction of the Almighty as to what you are to do while you are looking toward that Spirit. "Their sin will I remember no more against them forever." *You need not harbor the memory of sin if God does not.*

A woman was greatly persecuted, as it seemed to her, by people who wished to get her position from her. Suddenly while she was riding in the street car amid the smoke and noise of the city where she lived, she said, "How would God regard persecutions? Would he cry and mourn about them, or ignore them? He certainly would not know anything about them. Neither will I." This treatment took away all her grief and fear.

Is it not to you a great rest that your true and real substance does not know anything about sin, sickness or death? When you are tempted to mix up with misery by feeling miserable, remember your noble Spirit, which knows no sorrows, no pains, no sickness, no unkindness, no burden. Is it not a joy to you that you have the power right within yourself to annul every evil thing? If there is no reality in sin, rise to agree with the Principle and love it. There have, as yet, been only a few to whom sin was as unreal as matter. They have had great power in healing where matter was the first unreality to them. Stopping at either of these milestones you do not harmonize with the world around you. Stepping past them, by the leading of the Spirit, you harmonize your life.

If you will notice the Topaz stone you will see it has a happy light. It is the peaceful light of satisfaction with your thoughts as they fold themselves around you in good friendships, good healing power and reformed conduct of men. I use the word *reformed* in the same sense I do *healing*. God needs no healing, therefore there is no healing to be done. God needs no reforming, therefore there is no reforming to be done. What then? We tell the truth, and as the whole and perfect man steps forth, he looks on the sense plane as if he were being healed. We tell the truth, and on the sense plane it looks as if the upright son of God were reforming his actions.

I know and you know that there is no work to be done. Does God work? Is not all finished in God? Yet this very saying that there is no work to be done, gives us the appearance of accomplishing miracles, because as the signs of the heavenly estates appear, they push the earthly estates aside The rolling of the earthly conditions away looks like activity. It is really the rest of God. Did you ever watch a star come into sight on a summer evening? It was there all the time, in solemn repose, but as the night deepens the star seems to be shot towards you. At first it is startling. Thus with the last day of earth. The heavenly land swiftly speeds into our sight, the earth rolls aside her curtains.

"Oh land beyond the sea!
Soon shall mine eyes see thee;
Soon shall my heart rest in thy shadow;
Thou art not for from me."

The Topaz light of your thoughts bringing out your word swiftly, is the leaping up of the heart into the mouth with joyous song. The joyous heart is a healing presence. Do you remember how Solomon said, "The merry heart doeth good like a medicine?" "Smile and sing ye the songs of Zion." Sing the thoughts of this Truth you bring out. Spirit can heal the whole world if it never yields to lamentations. Will you now take the case you spoke of yesterday, and call his or her name? Bow your head and let the Spirit say with you: *"I have never accused the world or myself of sin – all is Good."*

Now to the patient, your friend, speak as I am addressing my friend:

"*You are not covered with formulations of sin; therefore you are not diseased.*

You have not received an inheritance of sin in disease.

You came forth from God.

You are not surrounded by a race of sin; you are surrounded by God.

You do not hear sin, see sin, feel sin, fear sin, from anywhere; therefore you are free in purity.

There is no gathering of the consequences of sin around the Spirit; therefore you are free from the consequences of sin.

You have not gathered your own sins together in disease.

You are free from disease.

There is no cause for disease in Spirit.

I do not lay any burden of belief in my own sinfulness upon you.

The six sins of carnal mind I do not believe in.

I do not believe in selfishness. I do not believe in envy. I do not believe in jealousy. I do not believe in revenge. I do not believe in cruelty. I do not believe in the outshowing of these claims against mankind.

I believe mankind is God and God is mankind without sin, sickness, disease or death.

Therefore your life is Good, and cannot be threatened with death, nor yield to death, nor fear death in any part of your being.

Your health is Good, and it cannot be threatened with disease, nor fear disease, nor yield to disease in any part of you.

Your strength is Good; it cannot be threatened with weakness, nor fear weakness, nor yield to weakness in any part of you.

You are ready to acknowledge that you are healed.

You say this freely to all, to yourself, to me, now.

In the name of the Father and the Son and the Holy Ghost I pronounce you every whit whole."

Give this treatment three times before you sleep tonight. While you give it, write it out as nearly as you can.

Sing it to yourself. Have confidence in it. This is what Moses meant by, *"Let the waters bring forth living creatures."*

Lesson Ten

Fearlessness

ALL seeds have their seed within themselves, the scriptures tell us. Their seed is their ego, their vitality, their meaning. If you are treating a case you are apt to discover that you can see with another set of eyes than the ones you ordinarily use. You might be half awake and see something appear in your presence, yet not in your presence. Thus, while treating a man for lameness, you might see a star shining before you. Its meaning would be its seed. You are to take that meaning for your own use. It means that your word shines steadily like a star of hope to the man's helpless mind. He is feeling a little ray of hope. Its seed is the kindness of the law to you. It is your business to stop thinking about your treatment, about the man, and give thanks that your words have worked so well. If you are pledged to a principle it will work for you in loving kindness.

The tenth lesson of Science is the gift of skill in handling things with thoughts, so they record your thoughts perfectly. The instrument must record the singing and joy of the musician. The scroll must teach others what music can do. The machine must vibrate to the touch of the fingers. Your practice must tell the world what your genius can do. Everything you do must have its process of demonstration, which, by being recorded in plain sight, can show others how to do likewise.

While Paganini lived, he made the violin give forth tones, and semi-tones, of harmonies unheard of by ears of man, till, swinging his heaven-tipped bow in the fourth dimension of space, he thrilled multitudes to awed inspiration. But there is no record of these harmonies. They are not described on scrolls. No pupil received them. He had no skill in instructing in his science.

The tenth stone is the Chrysoprasus. (N. B. — A kind of quartz,, a variety of chalcedony, apple-green in color and sometimes used as a gem.) It is the color that stands for the true earth. It is the Heavenly City that descends. It is the bride, the Lamb's wife. The green fields and white gleaming mountains of Paradise are the new land into which we set our feet, if we have polished the ninth stone of our foundation.

If we have discovered how to be joyous and grateful, while yet on earth, which seems so dark and unreliable; if we have learned to smile and praise, while there was nothing, seemingly, to smile about or to be grateful for, there will come a moment when everything we can do we can teach others to do, and this is the stone of companionships — the Chrysoprasus — for dwelling among equals. The green stone polished and smiling with answering goodness.

Everything is as good to us as we have been to it. It records our skill. It tells our ability to discard symbol and realize reality, while we are giving forth thoughts, words, writings. Things and objects and people are the records now of ways we have thought in the past, also of ways we think now. We think new and joyous thoughts of people, of things, of life, and they presently begin to respond to our thoughts. The joyousness you persisted in has recorded itself, and answers back to you, as face answereth to face in the glass. This is the Chrysoprasus Stone.

When people and things respond because of your words, because of your thoughts, it is to your honor, your credit, your skill, they have come forth. It is quite different from having things seem to be mysteriously good, unexpectedly kind.

You must know that all the lessons in Science are lessons in consciousness, lessons in your pure intelligence. It is not the Chrysoprasus stone of your works when you heal blindness suddenly, as it were, accidentally. You must know how to heal when you heal; be able to teach others how to heal and understand keeping your cases well after they are healed. You must *know* to make a permanent work. You must play upon all the chords and anvils of appearances with the touch of one whose words will endure after him — endure forever.

Jesus taught his disciples how to keep alive, but Paul says they preferred death. In an old French book there is a record of a man who pledged himself to the Holy Spirit, and became so quick and efficient with his thoughts that there was nothing he could not ask for, as a child would ask for a cup of water, but what he got it as quickly as the child would get the water from its kind nurse. After a time he became tired of dwelling among symbols and asked that he might fold himself round with the mantle of death. He never seemed to have any idea of how to teach the process by which he entered into such union with the Spirit of God. He seemed never to have fixed his ideas into the surrounding conditions of his human lot, so that others were greatly benefitted because of his conscious intentions. He did not seem to be selfish, but only unconscious on this question.

The stones, spoken of in Revelation, all stand for living stones, as you know, by which is meant that your living Mind is your God. There are twelve evidences of entire consciousness. You must not be asleep on any point of doctrine. Every faculty must be awake and alive. Unlike the Frenchman, who helped himself by the consciousness of the presence of the Spirit, but who seemed to have been unconscious of the needs of others, not through selfishness but through not realizing, these lessons teach us to realize and to do, leaving nothing undone. This tenth lesson is on the subject of making your work tell. Making it stay by you, making it as definitely good, and as alive in its good, as your own Soul.

It has always been noted by metaphysicians that people who have diseases as the result of their sinfulness do not get well as quickly as those who simply catch maladies from surrounding mental belief in disease. The whole process is unreality, and the idea that people do not give up sin readily is only an imagination. When one imagines that there is a mixture of good and evil in the universe, he is sure to see a great deal of good and evil. If he lets his mind balance on the gloomy side, more than on the joyous side, he will see more evil conditions than good in his lot. He will not touch the tenth lesson. He will not see his world record joyousness, if he does not put joyousness forth from his mind as a steady stream into the world.

Moses said, "Let the earth bring forth cattle and creeping things." Earth means mind when it is formulated by persistent thought. The bringing forth of mind is cattle — which is a symbolic word for larger human relations, like governments, schools, homes, friends, family. "Creeping things" is a term signifying affairs like business, daily tasks, eating, drinking, sleeping. These things, says the text, come forth in a new beauty, by the persistent thinking of new truths. Cheerful breaths from the Spirit of the supreme cheer, being breathed again forth from mind, its destiny is assured.

All the world, and our close family relations, are Good beyond good. Let the mind see Good step by step. From mountain peak to mountain peak, let lofty ideas spring, never forgetting the splendor of one peak, but ever onward. Thus it is with the lessons of Science. One lesson seems to be all. The next takes us to another statement of Truth. The next still on, till the twelve gates of Truth are opened.

Our conscious, wide-awake thoughts, never off guard, must smile, and rejoice that our obedient world may be at last compelled to return our smile. Gentleness, love, cheerfulness, these may seem to be slow in conquering the world, but they have Deity, in all its enduring force, behind them. So Moses here would say, "Stand here and see your mighty principle carried out into government, churches, schools, homes, friends, family life, into daily tasks, eating, drinking, sleeping. Let everything that hath breath or moveth praise the Lord."

You know there is a natural strength within your mind to be your best, and do your most creditable thing. You choose to do and be successful. Some have chosen to be known as very rich. They would have that for their high ambition. Ward McAllister chose to lead society life in New York. Lady Vanderbilt wished to take Mrs. Astor's place as social leader. Mendelssohn chose to be known by his "Elijah" in music. Hayden will be forever honored for his "Creation." Raphael will be known as the Divine Raphael because of "The Transfiguration." So, at the height of your genius, there rests some masterpiece of splendor, laid out for you to do from the beginning, before ever the world was. It is the making your goodness or your Christ character, whose glory rests ever in the center of your own being, manifest in your own world.

Things are plastic substance your skillful fingers mold, as Michelangelo molded the marble. They are receptive to your finger touches as the canvas to Perugino, who taught Raphael to paint.

You must find out the secrets of every creature, and make them speak. Your mind is a greater work as the follower of Christ than Mendelssohn's, for there is music far beyond his masterpiece, but there is no music beyond that which you bring forth from the earth when you have proved that, to you, there is in Truth only God.

In setting forth to heal a man of his mental formulations, called disease, you disintegrate his accumulated ideas by true Principle. You reason his ideas right out of his mind. It is very much like ungluing them. His ideas fall all to pieces, and there is nothing left of them.

There is always a spot of time, a little moment when it almost seems as if a man would not let his old ideas go. If at that moment you are true to your Principle, stronger than ever, and ignore his conditions with more skill than ever, you will see him yield his false position without another struggle.

A very lame man was at a political meeting when slavery was called a "divine institution." This so stirred his mind that it held his body free from lameness and he jumped to his feet. The people laughed to see him forget his lameness, and when he saw them laughing he remembered it again, and sat down, as lame as ever. There was a time when this text would have been his entire healing, "Touch not the earth." His mind should have kept him from the earthly condition, and soared away on the ideas he knew were divine. So, when the woman who was being healed kept shouting how much worse she was, the healer took less notice of her than before, and praised God in her secret mind with harder praises than ever, till the patient ceased screaming, and after a few moments cried, "I am entirely healed."

If a patient comes before us the fourth time for healing, it shows there is a conflict going on within his mind and body. It shows that, before we saw him, we have been somewhat disturbed on the question of which is most powerful in the world, good or evil. Maybe we have been wondering if, after all, there is not a satan. Maybe we have thought it might be, in the long run, that good, and right, and justice, would prevail, but at present things were pretty dark. Things must have seemed very much mixed up to us. So on comes the patient for the fourth treatment, and up comes the undissolved business trouble again.

Well, the first thing to do is to bow the head, and let the Spirit speak of faith, confidence, steadfast-ness. We have come to the wall of partition. We are where we must let the Spirit say, "*I do not believe in mixtures. I do not believe in failure, I believe in success.*"

If you take Thursday afternoon and say all that the Spirit does not believe, and all that the Spirit does believe, you will not have a long treatment with a case when it appears the fourth time. You will see the good health stand out very plainly, right then and there. Or, if, when you begin to feel so mixed within your own mind on the question of evil and good, you have said strongly, "*I do not believe in evil, I believe in the Good. I do not believe it takes time for goodness to prove itself powerfully; I believe goodness demonstrates itself instantly. I do not believe in sickness, I believe in health. I do not believe in trouble, I believe in peace,*" you will bring the patient's good health out with great skill.

Let us stop the lesson right here, and rally our- selves and say, as strongly as the Spirit speaks it, "I do not believe in evil I believe in the Good. I do not believe it takes time for goodness to prove itself powerfully; I believe goodness demonstrates itself instantly. I do not believe in sickness, I believe in health. I do not believe in trouble, I believe in peace." If your business troubles face you, after you have treated faithfully three treatments, you certainly have been doubtful in your mind whether you could settle them by mental process or not. Doubt is sure to haul your lame business back into its lameness again. What you want to do is to refuse the lame side of the question. Don't touch it. "Touch not the earth," means keep your eye on the mark of the high calling.

God's prophet once told the Jews that it would not do for them to number the soldiers, or the people, because it was at a time when it would have discouraged them to know what a small army they had. So it is sometimes best not to think how your patient is at all, not to ask him a single question, not to talk to him at all, not even to answer his questions. Keep your mind only on one side of the argument. Keep it on the side of your faith. Ignore the rest. "I do not believe a word of it — not a word," you say while he mourns, or cries, or complains, or describes his ailments. So, too, you say to your affairs, when they keep facing you with what looks like disaster, "*I do not believe it, I do not believe that side of the question. I believe in success, victory, prosperity, for myself in the name of Jesus Christ.*" You say it to all that troubles you. You say it to everything and everybody that comes for a fourth time. You say it every Thursday afternoon. The old conditions must unglue, must go. God reigns. Believe it.

"God lives in me in his strength and glory,
He lives in me as my strength divine.
By the light of his love I read life's story,
And the key of the world is mine."

The Good Mind is your God. Let the Good Mind speak when you speak. Let the Good Mind speak its own glorious Truth through you. We all see things according to the mind we use. If we use the Good Mind in us, how can we help seeing how true the world looks? How can we help turning the key into every tree and rock and animal, by the light of the Topaz stone of cheerfulness, till its goodness stands out in eternal visibility? The ego of the stone is its God life. When it is plainly visible to you, by the use of your own consciousness, then it is visible forever. When you cure your case by your wisdom, you will cure him for all eternity. He cannot have the malady again. But you must remember that you are to make all mankind every whit whole. All creatures of the earth are to be obedient records of your conscious calling of their names.

The waters form the land. The waters of your mind must be left free to form your natural world. The land of your being is your present condition, it is your circumstances. The land, being once formed, it takes great and unusual force of the waters to change its shape and appearance. So the land might be called the doctrine of fate, as indeed your circumstances have been called your fate. Whatsoever you have thought consciously, your mechanical and obedient conditions of life must unresistingly record.

The land adhesion of your natural state of affairs is undermined, disintegrated, dissolved, by the true way of thinking. The true way of thinking, which we set to flowing through us, seems, sometimes, to be long in accomplishing its mission, but it comes to pass that our conscious thoughts get greater and greater impulse as we think on, till our whole earth falls to pieces. Friends change marvelously. Home reinstates itself. Maybe we seem to have no home. Business falters. Maybe we seem to fail. But this is the point where we are at the sepulcher in the beautiful garden of resurrection. We need not say, "They have taken away my Lord," simply because things look as if they were failing us. We must look up—up! Touch not the earth, touch God! We do not believe in material ways of thinking any more, and old conditions, manufactured by our material ways of thinking, must unglue for the conditions formulated by our true new ways of thinking to come forth.

"If the earthly house of this tabernacle be dissolved," no matter what part of our circumstances it represents, it has a spiritual house, eternal, not materially thought, not materially born, but spiritually thought out, and now showing its seed, its germ, its face, through the ungluing particles of the old, disturbed conditions.

Scientists, who have been very strong and steadfast, have seen everything change around them, because they have so entirely changed their thoughts. Holding steadfastly to some one principle, some one idea, they have gone through many, seeming trials with victory. Once a lady saw that her husband looked as if he were passing into another sphere. She said, "God is love." She did not treat her husband at all. Over and over she repeated the words, without being conscious that in Science we never treat anything violent directly, but turn our mind entirely to Spirit. She did this very way. Soon her husband rallied. One saw her family in great trouble and knew that she could not endure circumstances that were dissolving around her. She could think of no words to say except, "Jesus Christ," and they all came through safely.

Whenever any disturbed condition arises, do not believe in it enough to notice it. Behind you, over you, near you, there is a voice saying, "Touch not the earth, touch Me." So you look away from your environments, and with just the assertion, "I do not believe in evil, I believe in Good," you will put your mind entirely on the Spirit near you. All acute cases of sickness are signals for saying firmly what you do believe; and what you do not believe.

One woman had so much trouble that she felt that she was losing her mind. She said, "I do not believe it is thy will that I should be in trouble. Thou wilt keep him in perfect peace whose mind is stayed on Thee." Then she kept looking away from her troubles. She would not allow herself to think of them. Over and over she repeated Isaiah's promise, "Thou wilt keep him in perfect peace whose mind is stayed on Thee," till help came to her. She was saved, not only mentally, but conditions adjusted themselves. After you have determined to breathe toward you the Spirit of cheerfulness, the unbalanced and distracted state of your affairs will seem to make it impossible to hold your own in the midst of your changing and disordered-seeming world. "Be steadfast," said Paul, "immovable, always abounding in the work of the Lord."

He also noticed that it was just the same in a man's affairs as in his mind. If a man has determined to be scientific, he finds himself sometimes very ecstatic, very happy, then he gets despondent. He feels doubtful whether it is true, whether he can make his life a success on the spiritual plane. This is his mind in relation to doctrine. He must tell himself that he believes every word he has spoken, and believes it will all demonstrate exactly as he has spoken it. The same thing happens with your cases in healing. They delight you one day and discourage you the next, if you let them move your feelings by their ups and downs of conduct. This is where you must state that you believe your doctrine is working itself out in your own way, and there is nothing in the man working against your doctrine. Tell what you believe about your case, and what you do not believe. His actions are only the exposure of some doubts you yourself have been having, where you ought to have spoken: "I DO BELIEVE IN THE GOOD."

You cannot help noticing how chilling and depressing doubt is. It comes up and shakes you. Its name is fear. Many people call their doubt of the Good now working out with them in safety and power, fear. They speak of their fear, as they shake within themselves and hide it. Maybe some of you call it apprehension. Maybe you call it the blues. Its honest name is doubt. It is the dark shadow cast by the figure of faith, which stands so near you. You feel fear shake your hopes. Faith stands near. You know she can do anything. She can raise your hopes to highest heaven. She can fulfill your slightest wish. She is warming, strengthening, comforting. You can choose faith, or you can choose doubt. Both are near. One is the reality of life, the other is unreality. It is chosen by what you say most vehemently. I have heard of people passing through those seasons of unhappiness, caused by doubt of the Good if working with them, and almost without exception they have lain down and given up to dark and dismal feelings first, and then feebly struggled to lay hold of faith. The fact is you have to choose faith the first thing. Your first words determine your future.

But, you say, "I had my house burned down, my husband at the point of death. My two boys ran away. My money is all gone. My acquaintances deserted me. It is not possible to say that, I believe this all good. Here is where you are mistaken. This is where so many make their mistake. The Science does not say death is good. The Science says there is no death. The Science does not say the deserters are good. The Science says there is no such thing as desertion. The Science does not say poverty is good. The Science says there is no poverty. The Science does not say the changing ugly conditions are good. The Science says there is only Good. "Look not toward the earth, look unto Me."

It is a very important turn of the wheel of the law, this one of trying to make misery and death and poverty out to be good. They are not here. How can they be good? Their absence is good. That which is present is Good. If anybody abuses you (in the seeming) do not say it is your business to say abuse is good. Say rather, that it never transpired. Do not speak to any person mentally — speak to God. It is God who is Good. "There is only one Good and that is God," said Jesus Christ.

When you tell me your husband was so and so, your money was so and so, your children were so and so, and you could not say they were good conditions, you are at this important stone of your journey in Science. You must not think of a single one of these appearances. They are not there at all. God is there. Touch not the earth with thy mind. Touch Me. Not an evil is here. Not one. God is here. If you feel the shakiness of fear, you can say, *"There is nothing to fear. I am clinging to the loving God.* You can say, *"I will not doubt the Good. I believe in the loving God."* You can say, *"I do not believe in appearances, I believe in God here present in loving kindness."* In such seemingly hard set of circumstances as mentioned, you will find it the most comforting thing in the world to say, *"I do not believe in the power of a whole army of evil conditions. I believe God is bringing us all through safely."*

Why would you write a letter to your mother, or your uncle, or your brother, begging for help out of your misery, at a moment when the universe stands waiting for you to touch not the earth at an angle, but touch God? This is called "The valley of decision." The whole world finds it so much easier to talk and think and write on the dark side that Joel said, "Multitudes, multitudes in the valley of decision." The worse the condition, the less you are to turn your mind toward it. "Touch it not. Touch Me."

Goethe, the mighty thinker, writing of choosing between your pathways of feeling, said, "Here eyes do regard you in eternity's stillness, choose well, your choice is brief and yet endless." That which comes over us, about whether we believe in God in us now, comes over us when we put our cheerful doctrine upon the world. It seems as if our world all turns against us. But we have no right to agree with what comes. The Jesus Christ Spirit within us, and shedding its radiance around us, judges not after the sight of the eyes, nor after the hearing of the ears. There is no combination of circumstances so hard, so black, so complicated, but God can work a miracle in them.

Now, if we examine doubt a little more closely we shall see that it is not doubt of the Good at all. It is fear that the Good won't work NOW. We think the Good lets evil run on so long, and multitudes of good people pass away before their good deeds are respected, and ages go on before their character is believed in. You will see how we all have a sneaking feeling that we would like to know what good it will do us if our wrongs are not set right now. Come, face this adversary right up. Its name is belief in time, belief that it takes time for God to work. "No," you say, "I don't mean that I think God *needs* to take time, He does take it." This is the adversary then, belief that God always takes a long time to work out our cause for us.

Did you ever see anybody who, when they were in great trouble, never touched it with their thoughts, but touched only the God side? Did you ever see anybody who faced up that little sneaking fear that it would take a long time to set his affairs straight, and took the fear by the throat, saying, "I am not going to believe that the Almighty needs an instant of time, as I reckon time, to bring forth right conditions here and now." You must know by this time that it is the Jesus Christ doctrine that by a man's word he is justified and condemned. What can I expect but time, if I believe in time? What can I expect but fear, if I believe in fear? What can I expect but hatefulness, if I say hatefulness is good? All these things are my own imagination. Looking toward the

Heavenly City, I talk of the desert. Lo, looking toward the joyous peace of God's presence, I talk of trouble.

The Chrysoprasus is the stone which stands for your sight of the Good, where others see evil, your speech of God's blessed kindness, where you might feel deep bitterness.

It is singular how all the green tinted stones of John bear up on seeing the True Kingdom through the false appearance. In the midst of what seems to you to be your degradation, when you look old, feel sick, fear poverty, cry at failure, if you give way an instant, the green stone teaches you that the ego, the seed, the meaning of it all, is for you to know that you are a transcendent being, with transcendent powers. You were born of God. You go toward God. You know God. You have the power of God. It is the same with your patient. He is a transcendent being coming into your sight. It is the same with your affairs. They are Paradise coming into view.

When the storms come thickest (according to the seeming) the peace of your Soul is nearest. In the heart of the cyclone is the intensest peace. The ship only needs to make one turn to be in the heart of the cyclone. We have only to look away from turmoil, look unto Me, and the great storm will calm down, the sorrows will have nothing to exercise themselves upon. You have heard that the Brahmins once taught that the flower of the Soul springs soon after the storm, but the Soul's flower will not bloom if it chooses to be in the storm.

There is nothing can shake your patient's cure out of sight, except your own fears. You need not be afraid of his sickness. You need not fear you will fail. You have only to be afraid your family affairs will not come out right. This is quite enough to show a disturbance in his conditions. It is quite enough to bring him to you for the fourth time. All sudden attacks, and all our cases when they seem to be worse, need our fourth treatment for outside conditions. You need to be filled with the tenth lesson of Science. They all show we ought to be polishing the Chrysoprasus stone, which means taking our mind away from the earthly things entirely, fixing it upon heavenly themes, that our world, with which we in particular deal, may show here and now that our practice of joy is being responded to by our world.

All the lessons of Science turn to the side of joy and peace, strength, and happiness. There is not one that gives sanction for despondency on our part. Jesus was so cheerful and joyous that he was called a glutton and a wine bibber. He was so full of confidence in the Good of all people that he was accused of associating with people of bad reputation. He was so firm on the side of Good that he walked around among the most wicked circumstances. He went without food, without friends, without home, so much that they called him a poor man, and said he was a man of sorrow, and acquainted with grief.

All the time he was the owner of the universe. He was the Prince of Peace. He was the Central Fire of Holiness. He was the Joy Bringer. It is His doctrine that is coming out day by day. It is taking effect so rapidly now in the world that we have only to give it forth day by day, in order to see it demonstrate itself.

When evil conditions appear we do not have anything to do about them. We have only to see the presence of God in them. The child's diphtheria is not diphtheria at all. It is the signal that, by the right words now spoken, you can bring out a perfect character, a renewed intelligence, a beautiful health. You may say promptly, "I do not believe in diphtheria. I believe in the Holy Spirit. I believe in peaceful health, here and now."

If you have thought seriously of some great point in Science for a long time, you will be faced up with its mighty effects. All the opposition of your lot, your human nature, everything in your disposition, will meet your statement somewhere.

Take your premise, that the Holy Ghost will teach you all things. Treat your own self for freedom from stupidity and ignorance. Commence at the very day of your birth in the flesh. Deny that any cause, or result of any kind, leading to folly, or sickness, or trouble, has existed in your life. Pronounce yourself a spiritual being, with spiritual powers, untrammeled, unhindered, unrestrained, sealed from the beginning to preach the gospel, and demonstrate it through the universe; that the Spirit of Jesus Christ is salvation from evil for mankind.

There is no salvation for mankind except by the Spirit of Jesus Christ. In yourself is that Spirit. Let it always speak. Let it always think through you. By taking yourself in hand to be wise, you can quicken your understanding, exactly as you can cure yourself of bodily sickness. When you treat yourself, begin at the beginning, and come down to the present moment, always calling yourself spiritual and not material.

Jesus said that the Father would send the Holy Ghost, in his name, and that the Holy Ghost would teach us all things. How true it is that only the early disciples ever tried to prove this. Men have studied books and languages, machines and trees, but they have not practiced hearing the Holy Ghost through the name of Jesus Christ. So we have nobody on earth who can answer all the questions that are asked in science, art and literature, through the expression of pure spiritual wisdom, secured by speaking the name of Jesus Christ.

Whoever follows out this Science discovers that something about himself is soon healed. You will find that already you can point to different ways in which you are better for knowing this Science. If you have been healed of something, you can see that all things may be healed. One or two conditions may not go out except by persistence. You have to stick faithfully to something. There is a part of the doctrine that practically fits your poverty, for instance, but poverty does not go out with a little dose of that part of the

Science. You have to take a great quantity of it. They tell us that some people have to take a great deal of the water of Lourdes before they are healed, while others get well very soon after a little of it.

Jesus Christ told his disciples that they could not cure epilepsy except they prayed so earnestly that they forgot to eat. We often see Scientists leave their cases, and leave their important work, for the sake of their dinner, or their beds, when it is evident that, if they do so, their whole interest is not devoted to their doctrine. There is such a thing as forgetting all about everything, because you are so absorbed in your doctrine. You do not do this all of the time, but you surely do some of the time. Jesus said there were cases which would not yield till after we had been absorbed just so powerfully.

A German mother got down on her knees to pray for money to send her boy to school. She was so deeply absorbed in prayer that she did not eat or sleep for three days. Then, suddenly, she came forth, her face radiant. She had received a mental assurance of answer. That very day the money came. Go by yourself, alone with God, sometimes, and speak alone to Him. Reason with the Almighty as Job did.

A beautiful nature once wrote a little pamphlet about how he took every little item of his life to the Holy Spirit, and talked with God as a man would talk with his friend. The consequence was that he knew what he needed to know, and was helped all he needed help. His requests were very simple. He never asked for healing, and he never asked for the fullness of wisdom, which Jesus Christ commanded. I speak of him only to show you that if a little of the Christian doctrine, believed in, would do so much, if the short practice which people give to the Holy Presence will heal and help so much, what may you not expect from a life absolutely dedicated to the Spirit. If God will support a man who spends all his time in spiritual devotions, why not give all your time to the Spirit? If God will teach all wisdom to the man who converses with God continually, why not make God our Counselor, our Guide, our Friend?

When a physical or mental disturbance arises, as the effect of opposing Truth, it is called chemicalization. It is always met by keeping right on with the Truth. It is always the sign that Truth is working fast. It is something to tell what to say. It shows that we are to welcome the Spirit. We welcome the Spirit who has knocked if our friend seems to fall down in a faint. We speak rapidly: *"I do not believe in fainting and failure. I believe in life and activity."*

In a public dining room in a Western town, a man struck a waiter. The waiter struck him back. Instantly the guests rushed back and forth. There was great confusion. A Scientist, present, never looked up at all, but said within her own mind: *"It is nothing at all, peace is here. I do not believe in disturbance. I believe in harmony."* It was amazing how quickly people picked themselves up, and the man and the waiter settled the matter.

You can quell the very roughness of the ocean storm by sending your steady word of peace over the waters. They will respond. Response to constant treatment, on the part of the people and the affairs, is typified by the Chrysoprasus stone. The whole kingdom of God is here, ready to break into your sight. When one seeming thing comes forth, through seeming trials, as the result of our treatments, we have touched the tenth stone of our City.

The oftener you bring order out of chaos, the oftener you touch the tenth stone. The oftener you ignore mixed up and grievious states of affairs, the oftener you touch the tenth stone of your character To stand still and hold onto one statement, when another statement seems to have the whole battle, is to become a skillful workman, approved of heaven. While there is no great issue at stake we do not seem to have a great test of our skill. When the storm faces the ship, she is a good one, if she ignores the storm, and pulls all sound and clean into port.

The man who is on the point of bankruptcy and saves himself by his Science, touches the stone of his assurance. He hits upon his sure way of life. He knows how to work his Science. The man whose eyesight fails him, and his treatments only seem to put him into deeper darkness, knows, if he holds to one principle till it pulls him safely into light, just how to make everything yield to his treatment, Difficulties never daunt him.

The Chrysoprasus stone is the type of mind seeing land ahead—whether anybody else sees it or not. Columbus, driving on in spite of opposition, is the Scientist ignoring terrible appearances, and driving on with his doctrine. The Chrysoprasus stone stands for increase of seed, for enlargement of germs, for greater manifestations from lesser ones. One idea of Good, held in mind, is a deathless seed, for if it is in mind, it is there outside, in mind also. What you are thinking about is surely in your surroundings. They are obedient to your suspicions. Your doubts are on the shade side. They are obedient to your confidence, your faith, your steadfast ignoring of your own evil feelings. When a case comes the fourth time, tell it mentally what you do not believe, and what you do believe. When a disfigured state of affairs comes up, give this fourth treatment.

When you feel grieved or frightened at what is said or done in your world, give this fourth treatment. You may be interested to know that chemicalization means that things are coming out in a better state of affairs. It never means anything else. It is like alkali and acid in chemistry. When they mix they form a new base. So, when Truth goes singing over the thoughts of men, they have to begin to think in a new way. There is nothing to fear, there is no pain in chemicalization. There is no sorrow, if you do not believe in such things. You need not have a patient come to you the fourth time, but if he should come, you yourself are in chemicalization, and so is he. You have been mixed up and troubled about something which did not need to take an instant of your notice. Please, now, take your case you have been naming with me, bow your heads, and let the Spirit of Jesus Christ say:

"I have not believed in a mixture of good and evil. I do not believe in evil of any kind

I believe that all is Good.

There is no reality in trouble. All is peace.

There is no reality in sickness. All is perfect health.

I do not believe in anything wrong. I believe all is well."

Now, call the name of the patient and speak to him or her in this way, while I speak to the one who has been called diseased.

There is no mixture of good and evil in you.

All is Good.

I do not believe in an inheritance of any kind of sickness, disease or pain.

I believe in an inheritance of Good only.

I do not believe in a race of beings partly good and partly evil.

I believe in the universe of God.

I do not believe in contagion of evil through the mixed and confused thoughts of the people round about us.

I believe in their God Mind only.

I do not believe in your evil thoughts.

They affect you not at all.

If our mind is God.

I do not believe in my own errors.

They are not real.

They cannot affect you.

My mind is God.

I believe in God.

You are every whit whole.

Your life is God. It cannot be threatened with death, nor fear death, nor yield to death in any part of your being.

Your health is God. It cannot be threatened with disease, nor fear disease, nor yield to disease in any part of your being.

Your strength is God. It cannot be threatened with weakness, nor fear weakness, nor yield to weakness in any part of your being.

You are showing forth to the people around you that you are healed.

You acknowledge to yourself that you are healed.

You acknowledge to me that you are healed.

In the name of the Father, and the Son, and the Holy Ghost, I pronounce you healed now and forever."

I assure you that if you will focus all your mind to such a treatment as this, if you repeat it over and over, you will be so confident of the Good and the right coming forth victorious, that nothing can distract your attention at all. By such treatments as this you will see the whole world healed of grief, of sickness and pain, and of poverty and sin. It is, as you see, an orderly way of telling all the highest Truth you know. For my part, I feel it is a doctrine that needs only to be once heard, to take an everlasting hold on the heart.

I believe that it is so reasonable that when we even think it over all alone by ourselves, that, even then, the universal mind of man responds, and unconsciously they are all believing it. It is the perfect doctrine of prophecy. Let us once more bow our heads and proclaim to the universal mind:

"I do not believe in evil. I believe in Good.

I do not believe in poverty. I believe in the bounty of God.

I do not believe in sickness. I believe in health for all the world now. Amen."

Lesson Eleven

The Way of Wisdom

CONFUCIUS, the Chinese sage, who lived 550 B.C., said, "A man filled with Truth hath power over heaven and earth, gods and devils. Nothing in the universe can injure him. Water and fire cannot cause him to fear." Nothing can harm one who actually believes himself safe, though the one who tells him he is safe does not believe it. Then how much more will he be kept safe who, himself holding the Truth, believes what is true. This is what is meant; possessing life and thereby calling to one's self the life of heaven and earth.

The eleventh lesson has for its subject one of those experiences of mind where, having taken the basis, or premise, that a man is perfectly well because he is a spiritual being, not subject to material conditions, you come to an experience where it seems as if your premise, which has pleased you so much and had so much reasonableness in its appeal, is after all, much feebler than the premise, or mental position, of the man who claims to be sick.

You will notice that the last lesson showed the importance of holding your highest thoughts while the man's or woman's condition gives the appearance of holding onto evil. It is no kind of position to take, in mind, that sickness is more powerful than health. The strongest position you can take is on the side of the happy and peaceful state, as the real state. Even if a man tells you he is well when his liver is being destroyed (so his doctors say) and you cheerfully and innocently believe him, he will be recovered from his malady and his life prolonged (to use old terms) awhile, because of your simple faith.

In the Andover Review, for June 1889, you may read of an aged man, who went through the most extraordinary experiences, at the command of the people he thought were superior beings. His faith was so simple that it held his life unhurt, springing from pinnacles, or diving under seas.

Confidence, or faith, is a life principle. Always after taking a premise there becomes a time when it seems as if it would not work after all. Paul said: "Stand and having done all, stand." He also said that God is able to make a man stand firm to his highest premise, after he has once taken it.

You have not forgotten the fourth axiom, that mind will demonstrate as much Truth as it has courage to stand by its affirmations. The tenth lesson matches the fourth — only the tenth relates to the environments. Its axiom is also like the fourth, viz: The world will persist in exhibiting before you what you persist in affirming the world is. All dissolving, ungluing conditions, are your giving up your old affirmations.

If now you have become shaken up, and fall back to your old thoughts, that scientific statements sound better than they demonstrate, your new affirmations must come from your warm feelings, or the world will set itself to the old tune again. Paul said that God is able to make us stand. He means that those who have recognized that within themselves is God, must live the life which that knowledge kindles. We cannot possibly go back to affirmations of evil, when we know that by affirmations our premise of life is made just as we choose.

The Japanese have a teaching that the divinity within our own Soul may set aside the question of God, and, by faith in itself, work all the miracles ever thought of.

If you have heard this tenth lesson, of the law of the spirit of life in Christ Jesus that maketh free from the law of sin and death, you will certainly know what to think and to do in a time of special excitement, or in the time when you would persist in showing some ugly condition over and over. You persist as hard as it does, only you persist in ignoring it, and living on your side of the question. To you there is only one side of the question. Persistence is a wonderful manager. Daniel ignored Nebuchadnezzar's insanity three and one half years, before it fell into nothingness. Keely, the man who cures opium and liquor habits by his new liquid injections, ignored the idea of his brother physicians that it could not be cured, and held to his own premise that it could be cured, for fifteen or eighteen years, before their ideas fell down into nothingness, and his came out into visibility.

The call in Science is for you to take the position that your life, health, strength, support, defense, are from God. As God cannot fail, so these cannot fail. Cannot you persist in believing in your side of the question a few years? There is no need of its taking a few years to bring out your ideas, but if you have to stand by a premise, that Elisha and Daniel and Jesus and Kurozumi demonstrated, you can do it. Think that being true to your idea will be as wealth straight from the Spirit of God, so that you can feed all the seemingly poor people in the world; health straight from the Spirit of God, so that you can heal all the sickness in the world; wisdom straight from the Spirit of God, so that you can impart wisdom to all the seemingly dark minds in the world. You know by this time that this is only a mode of expressing that by your wisdom you see wisdom. By your health you see health. By your provisions you see bounty everywhere.

The eleventh lesson has for its axiom: *Judgment is as great and competent as will and meekness can agree.* This axiom, like every other one meets all occasions of life as well as some occasions of life. For instance you have a strong will. Naturally you feel like having everything go your own way. This is well, if you have meekness of character enough to yield your point instantly when you see you are wrong. Such a combination will make your judgment quick and accurate. In the first place your mind will unconsciously be trying all the time to protect your strong will, so that it won't have to be yielding to another man's quicker sight of the care than yours. Secondly, you will be consciously directing your will along the right so far as you can see it. We may always count upon it that we have exercised our will to carry out our notions, wrong or right, if we come to a particular point where we do not quickly know what to do. Or, we may have let ourselves yield to doing something we did not have a will to do, when our will was set right and the temptation was set wrong. We call this unbalanced condition of mind foolishness or ignorance, Nothing discourages a man like seeing what bad judgment he has used, and bad judgment always comes from turning to the way our best judgment disapproves, or, comes from carrying out our own will, regardless of everything, forgetting and ignoring judgment, or calling our vigorous will judgment.

Science teaches that you may take a base in your mind that you have consumption, and regardless of God's good presence of health, you may stick to it until consumption shows up, and ends in its own habitual way. Or, you may take a base that you are sound and well, and hold out on that line until your health is a miracle.

Some people can see this law better by calling it a premise that you already show signs of breaking down in your health. Every other thought that you have will bow down to this one. When you think you will work hard, your premise shouts out, "No, you must look out, you are breaking down." So, you knuckle under to a premise you yourself made up. What made you take that premise in the first place? "Oh," you answer, "because I felt my years." Who said you ought to feel your years? Mortal man or God man? How do you know but that these feelings you had were the quickening renewals of a spiritual influx of new strength? Was it necessary for you to take your premise with mortal man instead of God man? The siding with the low and dying side, instead of the high and living side, was not meekness, it was simply foolish yielding against your will, which blunts good judgment. I assure you, from the spiritual and omnipotent, you can make your judgment perfect by living up to the highest premise where your natural will leads you.

You can give birth to the divinest decision by compelling your meekness to unite with your will, as to your health, as to your strength, as to your prosperity.

Things look badly against your affairs—do they? Do you will it to be bad? No, a thousand times no. Your will is for good, but your poor will cannot carry the day alone. It has to be married to meekness. Meekness means yielding. This word "yielding" has gotten a good many Christians into misery. It has seemed to them to mean yielding to the evil and hard side of the appearance, when all the time it meant yielding to the spiritual doctrine, though appearances argue louder than spiritual realities.

A young man who had looked into the intentions of God with respect to man, found he had been thinking that he must yield to his poverty as sent of God. He saw his mistake. God does not send poverty. Whoever has said that the bountiful God is a giver of poverty has lied. He has been badly tempted, and has foolishly yielded to the temptation to judge against his will on the material side, as much as any person who ever dropped into lying or stealing.

All weakness of the body comes from yielding to appearances, when the man or woman ought to have yielded to spiritual doctrine. Therefore, when a man or woman asks you for help from weakness, you may know the mainspring to touch is foolishness and ignorance, which being unreality, nothingness, shadow, you can easily say, "Your will never fell through temptation." The doctrine of the fall of man came from believing in the reality of temptation, on the material side.

When the will is set to carry a point, whether the scriptural doctrine says one way or another, you will have more crosses than you can count, for it is materiality which you formulate yourself. You compelled what you knew to be nothing to seem real. This is foolishness. It is said to be harder to get rid of than ignorance. You can see this by the way an idiot and an ignorant child act. With the one you have pleasure in the speed with which he responds to your instructions, and with the other your heart fails, when you have labored as long for no response, apparently. Both of these children are the full bloom of the weed which you may call belief in foolishness and ignorance, or perverted will. It has both names in the Bible.

Solomon said: "The foolishness of man perverteth his way." Way is a word often used for will. When one does not respond to our treatments, he must be treated a fifth time. If he comes a fifth time, what makes him come, if that times does not find him joyously acknowledging his health? He comes because you have not touched his judgment. You have not struck the chord of his will. Why not? Because your own judgment has a veil before it. What veil is before your own judgment? I will tell you. It is your persistent habit of detecting ignorance and stupidity in people, and wailing about your own stupidity and ignorance. If you have seen that you did not know something, you have called yourself ignorant. If you have seen that somebody else did not know what you thought they ought to, or failed to be quick enough to please you, it was on your tongue, or in your mind, that they were either foolish or ignorant. It is the fall of man. It is all the fall there is. It is yielding to appearances. Spiritually, you have the power of discernment so strong that a child, man, or a woman can tell you anything you ask instantly. Judging that they cannot, and judging that you yourself cannot, keeps a veil before your mind. And you can tell when it is thickest, because your business comes up again and again, troubling you with not changing, and your patients come the fifth time, or they appear very weak and discouraged.

Many a practitioner has felt discouraged at once, when her patient has talked hard on the dark and feeble side. It was the final throw of the mind of old belief to hold its own.

It is the last grasp of the patient's belief in sickness, when he complains and whines in a discouraged manner, but it is the very best sign to you that his belief in evil is on its last legs.

How does your will want the case to talk? Of course you want him or her to talk buoyantly and audibly. Marry your will to the spiritual facts of the case. Rouse your judgment. This is the man of you. Notice the eleventh text. "Let us make man—and let him have dominion." Then put it with this one: "The father hath committed all judgment unto the son." The son is man, whom the Divine will and Divine meekness bring out as Jesus Christ. His will, he said, was omnipotent God. His meekness he said was God. There is the almighty judgment of Jesus Christ in you.

If, when your environments come the fifth time troubling you, you let the powerful judgment of Jesus Christ speak of the Spirit of the universe, you take down the evil that hides your prosperity. You can say *"I do not accuse the world or myself of foolishness or ignorance, therefore, I see clearly the prosperity of my new life now."* If your patient comes the fifth time, tell him the same principle. If a person seems very weak or feeble, say these words mentally, before you attempt to treat him.

I know that if you take every Friday afternoon to insist upon the Jesus Christ judgment within you, as knowing mankind as the expression of the wisdom of God, therefore, intelligent and wise at all times, if you positively take the premise that you do not accuse the world, or yourself, of foolishness or ignorance, nobody will ever come the fifth time uncured, and your affairs will never seem to wilt or hang heavy. Your own mind must be this man having dominion. Your own judgment must reign supreme. It must have no evil before it.

Do not let another man's discouragement pervert your judgment. Touch the chord of his will. Does he not will to be free, wise and strong. If you mentally unload him of all yielding to appearances he has ever done, he will spring up and respond to that touch of your judgment.

All discouragement, all feebleness, all fainting, halting, stopping, are signs to you to come forth with the fifth treatment. Come boldly forth. The powers of omnipotence are on your side.

John called the character which man exhibits after making the fifth treatment of his environment, the Jacinth stone of his character. Mind is composed of twelve powers. When mind exercises these twelve powers it has twelve characteristics, which shine like polished jewels. They make a perfect foundation for an absolute demonstration of Jesus Christ Spirit. The first time you go the rounds of these twelve powers, you may not show much difference in character. The second time, the third time, the millionth time around the statements, and how shining your life and mind become.

It is written that "Our daughters shall be like precious stones fitly polished." "Daughters" are meek statements of the spiritual side, when the material side tells a different story.

The first six statements are the beautiful powers of your mind as to your own looks, your own judgment. The last six relate to your surroundings. So when I say fifth treatment, I mean the eleventh lesson, or point of doctrine. Some call it the eleventh perfect premise.

The perfect Jacinth is the Ruby. The son of man is ruddy — is red with ruddy health, robust strength. His judgment is warming, kindling, reviving like the wine fires of the Ruby. When he speaks he helps you. The wine of prosperity is handed to you in the good news from your business. "Drink ye all of it," said Jesus, "It is my blood of the new testament." If you will bear in mind that the Spirit of Jesus Christ was health, life, prosperity, red with the reviving as the wines he gave at the wedding feast, you will understand the results of taking eleven right statements. You will have the judgment of the transcendent being that you are. You will be awakened. If I say to you that this is the only manner of thinking which has any practical effect in the life, on the triumphant and joyous side, you will have only the truth from me. It is in justice to this doctrine, that I acknowledge it is the only way you can think that will be every day safety for you.

There are twelve conditions of human life which may be met by twelve truths. These twelve conditions being met by Truth, you may be sure that your life will be free, glad and wonderful. The Brahmins had a teaching which read: "So dwell on the highest thoughts, this is the life of the awakened."

There is one thing which good judgment awakens, that has been brought out by some scripture writers, and that is beauty. The perfect in judgment are perfect in beauty. The beauty of Jesus Christ is because of his judgment. The Ruby is the beauty stone. The polish of meekness — that is the angel of beauty, who measures the City. She is bound to no traditions. What others believe she must be in order to be beautiful, she needs not. That which her own judgment decrees is her own charm.

So, no matter what others believe about the portent of your dream of the night, you must judge that it means something good for your surroundings —something others might call evil. Your judgment yielding to the good says some blessed good is coming to you. If you see symbols, speak of their good for your own surroundings. They all come for your benefit. They tell you that your environments are good. Then your ideas will be recognized as good by others sooner or later.

There is one universal mind which is the perfect Intelligence from whence all ages of men draw their stock of intelligence. Man may draw all this intelligence to his own use and not decrease it at all, as he might know all mathematics, and his neighbor might know all, and all the town might know all of mathematics, and not rob each other, nor exhaust mathematics. The more you speak according to this judgment, the more judgment your neighbor will have.

They may not see at first that you are wise with the Mind Divine, from which you are drinking each day, by taking these twelve lessons home to yourself, but after a time they will acknowledge the excellency of your judgment. Indeed you yourself may not always see why you say and do certain things, but afterwards you will see that it was your wisest course.

The refusal to call any man, woman or child ignorant or foolish, will uncover your dormant chord. You will leave the strings of your Soul exposed for the winds of God to blow over, and bring out the tones of music, the radiant beauty given unto your judgment from the foundations of the universe.

When you lay your judgment to the line, and your righteousness to the plummet of the highest truths you have heard, then, says the prophet, your old covenant with death will be disannulled, and your agreement with hell will not stand. You give up your old ideas in meekness, you talk aloud your new ideas, after you have thought them, and after you have written them. They are the outgrowth of solid soil.

Sometimes you will be astonished to hear people speaking rapidly and lightly of the lofty Truth that you could not speak until after you had been sown into your deep soil of profound meditation. Sometimes you yourself may speak this way. The fruitage of lightly handling these mighty principles is light. By the deep thought of the mind the word of the lips is solid judgment in ripe fruitage.

Isaiah told the City, which testifies of us, that when they had gotten themselves into captivity through careless speaking of their Science, they would be glad to have money to redeem themselves with. They should not be redeemed with money, they should be redeemed by their fidelity to their religion, entirely independent of money.

So, once in a while, you may find that nothing you do yourself causes your patient's cure. So far as you see, he gets his cure by reason of somebody else's treatments, after you have practiced with him. Or, you may find that money is not given to you to get out of debt with, yet somehow, by one deal or another, there are no debts there. There is really your will married to a kind of weak yielding to scientific statements. You did not make them your deep life, therefore solid assistance.

The whole of demonstration is the fruitage of your own judgment: "Ye have sold yourselves for a thing of naught, and ye shall be redeemed without money," is the voice to a half-hearted, insincere, timid, unprofound acceptance of Science. Even writing the Science glibly brings out the redemption, without substantial, solid aid coming. Even thinking the Science lightly does the same. Living it comes from thinking it deeply, writing honestly, speaking sacredly. When the outward life accords, then is judgment risen in her beauty. Then is healing instantaneous, Then, if you ask for help, it comes exactly as your perfect judgment would indicate. The point is to get your perfect judgment forward. It comes forward by handling this eleventh lesson.

It is signaled to be handled every time the fifth treatment is necessary. Judgment, when it is good, touches the loftiest ideas and plainest themes with equal respect. One often finds that his demonstration waits for him to give way his prejudices with respect to what is high or low. All must be alike to him, when they are names and descriptions of Spirit.

One lady, whose grief was because she was so ugly to look upon, and because she could not make herself highly thought of, insisted that her affirmation must be a high one. So she took "I am absolute Love." Another lady, to whom there was no high or low name of Deity as used by Jesus Christ, told her to use the interpretation of her own name for a constant affirmation. It was a meek one, "I am the King's daughter." It was the right one to soften and refine her face, and win her way for her. But it sounded so low down to her that she refused it. Yet it was the only treatment of meekness belonging to her, as the one of Jesus, "I am meek and lowly of heart," belonged to him.

Perfect judgment touches the life chords of each situation with the right word. Lofty ambitions are evidences of belief in high and low places. In reality there is neither high nor low in Christ Jesus. To the Spirit, all that is, is Good. That which is evil is not, never was, and never will be. So they who believe in high or low will have to take some statement which to them seems low, as that lady will have to speak her simple one in order to carry her point.

Scientific statements, held along in their order, will bring you to where you will see, no matter how unsuccessful you may appear, you are not unsuccessful, because Spirit is not unsuccessful. You have to fairly seem to be unsuccessful, practically, before you can see that success and non-success, all things, will work out to your pleasure, even in the old way of looking at them. The mind must agree with the Spirit; then is perfect judgment. This is man. Judgment hath dominion. The keys of heaven and earth are given unto perfect judgment.

The law and the Gospel must be one. In the gospel there is no material remedy for disease. In the law, Truth is the healer. In the gospel there is no disease, and not even Truth heals disease. In the law disease seems very real, and the law that Truth is its remedy seems so rigorous that it is accounted a terrible thing to take a pill for neuralgia. Whoever thinks anything is terrible must certainly believe in it greatly. It must have great power in his eyes. He may have to take a pill to see how unreal it is, how simple, how far from terrible. The law is against hating anything. Even stealing must not be hated. Why not? Because there is no stealing. We do not need to hate what does not exist. What is stealing? It is delusion of imagination. Is not God the only living being? Can God steal? This is a very awakening activity of mind. Thinking this way will bring forth wise judgment. Then this judgment will balance all things. Thieves, as they are called, will find there is a way of support they would like better than stealing.

When judgment is come forth, you will find you are not bound to methods of curing the sick, not bound to the modes of eating and drinking, sleeping and dressing. As judgment ripens with yielding the will to spiritual ideas, over and over, you will see great events and great circumstances yielding to very simple actions on your part. One man felt suddenly, after long practice of thinking spiritual ways, that he could as easily make gold as cure bones, but a voice seemed to say to him: "You would act foolishly with gold if you had it." He yielded the point at once. It looked meek and good on his part to yield to a warning voice, but no voice from the Spirit ever accuses a mind of foolishness or ignorance. Here is where he should have used the eleventh lesson, or the fifth treatment of environments. Here was one of his self-accusations formulated right close to him, and audible as a human voice. It had bloomed to be refused for the sake of the Spirit.

Judgment comes of compelling yourself to believe just as much as you hope for. If you hope to cure everybody that comes to you, you are able to believe all that you hope. If you only hope that you can cure them, you will be disappointed. Hope needs faith. If you cannot believe you can cure all, take a night or day for the statement of what you believe in Truth. Covenant with the Spirit to do all your cures for you. The government is on the shoulders of perfect judgment we are told. Therefore, let perfect judgment be born in you. The strong man says "I can!" The strong man says "I will!" The wise man says "I know!" The perfect man says, *"I know what to do, and I am able to do it, therefore I will do it."*

The state of mind that calls for you to state what you can and will do, is when you have steadily ignored the harsh and hard side of life, as it has been showing itself to you. When things looked dark and hard, you did not allow your mind to think about them at all. You thought only of God, the Spirit. You kept hold of the highest statement you had. You ignored the appearance. Then, after you had won the battle, or seemed plainly to have things coming out right, you had a feeling of blankness. You felt devoid of power, devoid of ideas. This is the blankness of a clear paper, upon which you may write what you like. Declare that, as the Mind of Jesus Christ, you do not believe in foolishness or ignorance. Declare that as the Mind of Jesus Christ your judgment is perfect judgment. Declare, *"I know all things, I can do all things."*

The blankness is like a smooth mass of protoplasm, out of which some idea will arise, which will govern all other ideas. Nothing can stand before that one idea which comes up when you feel blank, absent-minded, vague. If you can make it strongly enough felt that your main idea is on the side of Jesus Christ in you, then you will do the work of Jesus Christ in wisdom and strength.

There is no more potent opportunity for the use of judgment than this one. Have you not had something of this feeling lately? Let us take the fifth treatment together, to rouse your judgment away from the clutches of the old temptation to believe in foolishness and ignorance as belonging to us. Let us, as Mind, now state the eleventh premise:

"I never accuse the world, or myself, of foolishness or ignorance. I am the judgment of God. I know all things and do all things well."

This idea is a living amoeba, that arises from the protoplasm of mind, that lies still as the sea, waiting for the winds to blow over it, like the waters, which the angels troubled or stirred. So the mind is still, until the angel of Truth stirs it.

Right near at our hand is the Heavenly City. While we have called it distant, could we expect it to be near? Right here, visible to us, is the Heavenly Land. Could we expect it to show us its beauties if we talked of its being invisible? Right now you are wise and immortal, free, strong and at peace. Can you expect to feel your own true nature, and delight in your estate, if you keep talking and thinking of how little you know, how mortal your flesh and blood are, and how unhappy you are?

Buddha taught that Self is the Lord over self. If you and I do not speak from the spiritual Self of us, it will not act. We are the arbiters of our own destiny. The Spirit is truthful and takes us at our word. If we say, "I am foolish and ignorant," it lets us be what we say we are. Having endowed us with wisdom to know that we are the sons of God, with free will, does it suppose we could be telling we are something we do not want to be. The Spirit supposes nothing. It believes all things. Spirit brings its fountains of power to all words of *"I am,"* and *"I will."*

Buddha says, "A fool does not know when he commits evil deeds." Then there are no fools, for there is a Spirit in all men which pushes them away from all evil. The wise man breathes in his breaths as airs of omnipotence. He drinks his waters as cups of strength. He eats his food as the Spirit renewing itself. He knows all actions as spiritual, and so knows no decay, no failure, no death. The wise know no evil. They know there is none. They know no sickness. They know there is none. They set their faces like flint to know the ways of Good.

This is the true foolishness, viz., determination to know nothing among us save Jesus Christ. This is the true ignorance, viz., ignorance of evil, through knowing it is not reality.

The fourth strength of mind is the strength of inspiration. It enables one to see what ought to be done. It gives one wisdom to know it. There is the fire of wisdom and beauty in the sunshine of inspiration. John calls it the strength of the eagle, which is always a symbol of inspiration. We have no treatment which equals the denial of accusations of foolishness and ignorance, for causing the inspiration of wisdom. Buddha taught that all deeds wrought out by mind, and carried into the life as far as we can exercise our thoughts, bring happiness. "All forms are unreal." He said, "He who knows this becomes passive in pain; this is the way to purity." He advises the repetition of prayers. Repeat them often.

When you take your life in your hand, to speak of your own spiritual nature, as it was at the time of your supposed birth in the flesh, do not stop short of six days repetition of your treatments. Deny that there are any causes, or results of causes, in you or around you, that could lead to disease, poverty or failure. Take yourself for each year. If you set out upon the journey of treating a case, even if that one is cured of his malady the first day, do not let his high welfare escape your faithful mind for six days. This is a training process. Each day send your high blessing.

The ancient Bible taught that it is good to tame the mind, which is difficult to hold in, and very flighty, rushing whither it listeth, but once tamed, it will bring you great happiness.

One who had dropped all thoughts of evil from his mind, for a certain period of time, found out that if any evil of us is given to detracting from the merits of our companions, easily picking flaws in them, we get weaker and weaker, and cannot possibly destroy weakness in others. He found that there is no path to peace through outward acts. We must truly not see the faults of our neighbors as reality. We must not see ignorance or foolishness hiding the intelligence and freedom of our neighbors. This is called taming the mind.

We cannot crush out criticism. It will not be crushed. We can deny it, and this erases it from our mind. Being free from criticism, the mind runs only to repetition of Good. It is then perfectly tamed. The unity of mind is a great fact to recognize. There is but one Good Mind. All the good and the wise render this same verdict as to what is just and right, when their accusation is laid aside.

Accusations are prejudices against people, which keep the highly efficient judgment from speaking. They do not emanate from the One Mind. Prejudice against a religion will act against your business judgment, just as possibly as your health. Prejudices against people will very likely hit your business affairs. It does not always strike at your bodily health the first thing. The feeling we have against alcohol, tobacco, opium, is a prejudice against an imaginary substance. That prejudice held onto, is foolishness. That prejudice taken hold of, as a principle, because appearances teach us to fight the poor little ideas, is simply ignorance.

Therefore, we will take our cases and meekly say now:

"I have never, as the judgment of Jesus Christ, accused the world, or myself, of being foolish or ignorant."

Now we will speak to the case by name.

"You are not the result of inheriting foolishness and ignorance.

You inherit the wisdom of God, your Father.

You are not surrounded by a foolish and ignorant race.

You are surrounded by the wisdom of God.

Your daily associations do not burden and darken you by the weight of their foolishness, or the darkness of their ignorance.

All is wisdom, from which you draw wisdom every moment.

You do not weigh down your own mind with willfulness in thinking evil.

You know no weakness or failure of any part of your being.

You are the spiritual light that cannot fail.

I do not persist in thinking of you as faltering or feeble in any part of your being.

Your strength is Good, and cannot be threatened with weakness, nor yield to weakness, in any part of your being.

You are ready to acknowledge to all around you, to yourself and to me, that you are every whit whole.

In the name of the Father, and of the Son, and of the Holy Ghost, I pronounce you healed, now and forever, Amen.

Repeat this treatment before you sleep. If any other words come to you while you are treating the case, be sure to use them, for every new way of thinking that springs up out of the good soil of the old way, is the new plant which the heavenly Father hath watered. For this reason every teacher ought to be glad to hear of the success of his students— each in his own way, though all agreeing with the foundation Principle.

Lesson Twelve

The Crown of Glory

TO the Romans, Paul wrote the twelfth lesson of the Science of Christ: As Love worketh no ill to his neighbor, therefore, love is the fulfilling of the law.

Jesus Christ said, at the last lesson, "Henceforth I call you not servant but friend, for all that the Father hath told me I have told you." His life was His doctrine. Having so regarded it, He said, "Greater love hath no man than this, that a man lay down his life for his friend." Giving all His doctrine to His friends, He gave them His life. Seeing their heavy miseries, He descended into heavy miseries to show them how to ascend out of their miseries. A fireman goes into a burning building to bring out the people who are on fire, as a good physician goes into a plague hospital to cure the inmates.

Jesus was so full to overflowing with love that the plagues and dangers of this world did not terrify him in the least. He was not hurt by a single one of the miseries He threw himself into. Love is stronger than death. He that hath love hath freedom from every ill. He that hath abundance of love, wherewith God fills the whole universe, can save his friends from every ill. He is an atmosphere wherever he walks. Love diffuses itself with all its powers. Having love we have life, so we radiate life. Having love, we have strength, so we radiate strength. Pure love for a child will save the life of a child, so the life of all is saved if a man loves God, for God is all.

Jesus loved God. Thus he had all of life, all of love, all of truth, all of substance, all of intelligence, all of beauty, all of health, all of inspiration. He, therefore, saved the whole world. Even to look at Him would cure, even when He was manifest in the flesh. He never having gone away from our side, we can look upon Him now, and be cured of whatever ailment we cry about. Some people cry with lonesomeness. He will cure that entirely, if they look upon Him. Looking at Him mentally is the way we look now-a-days, though, it is certain that some people even in this century have seen Jesus the Healer, as present before them as He was before the two Mary's at His tomb.

Looking, mentally, upon Jesus Christ, as present, will cure poverty, it will cure blindness, it will cure deafness, it will cure palsy, it will cure rheumatism, it will cure insanity.

The Amethyst is the symbol of the miracle-working power of love. It is the love stone in the sense that the Chalcedony is the love stone, and in a still further sense than that stone. It is the stone of the resurrection, of ascension, of the New Kingdom, where love is filling man's mind, and overflows to the world, and awakens the same love to shine back. It is that love that is stronger than death, and when it enters into man's love, death is not possible. It is that love which, being entered into man's, is stronger than hate, stronger than poverty, stronger than swords, stronger than crucifixion and the tomb.

The Amethyst stone has the hues of all the stones. There is no stone, which, as you look into the heavenly face of the Amethyst, is not seen shining in beauty. Twelve works of God as Holy Spirit are all manifest in the Amethyst. John said the twelfth power of the gospel, showing forth in you, would be like the Amethyst stone.

Whoever gets into the state of overflowing, unquenchable love, is Jesus Christ manifest. He sees no evil in anybody or anything. He sees their Good only. He receives no injuries at anybody's hands. He rejoices at everything that occurs. Everything has a light and a life and a joy and a renewal of pleasure in it for him, which nothing that happens to him can kill.

If things grieve you, then you have not touched the twelfth sweetness of the Science. If things hurt you, then you are not in love with the Science. You are not alive with the ecstasy of the Science. If you are afraid of anything, you do not know the twelfth feeling of security. "Love casteth out fear." If you are poor, or in debt, or old, or discouraged, you have not touched the resurrection stone of love, that is stronger than death.

I told you that accusation would make somebody come to you looking sick and unhappy. Well, a joyous praise, felt in your heart, will bring somebody well and grateful to see you. If somebody comes the sixth time for help, you may be certain that you have been complaining and whining about something or somebody.

Complaining and whining are only exhibitions of great desert spots in your character. You must fill up deserts with rain and fertilizer. So you must fill up your moments of complaining with praise and descriptions of the Good in the universe. The desert has not had rain enough, so you have not charity and mercy enough, if you feel like complaining. If things in your past have made you feel sad and hard, you must say that the good they have done you makes you thankful. Give great thanks.

Nehemiah told the people not to grieve or mourn at all. They must eat the fat and drink the sweet of their lives, just as if it had come to them. Jesus Christ taught that we must look upon our life, just as it has come to us, and beautify and inspire it with the red wine of gladness. Nehemiah, 444 B. C., and Jesus Christ himself, knew that you and I need not mourn, if we do not choose to mourn. Jesus took the six stone water jugs and inspired the water to become wine. So you and I can take our conditions and inspire them with the twelfth lesson in Science.

At the sound of the twelfth lesson on the sands of the Sahara, roses and corn and grapes will spring up. At the sound of the twelfth lesson on the desolation of heart, happiness will spring up within you, and radiate around you. The twelfth stone is the Amethyst. Amethyst is the symbol of happiness. We may see the twelve lessons of Science are all intended to bring supreme happiness to the world.

Scientific Christian Mental Practice

Carlyle says there is a higher condition than happiness. He calls it blessedness. But blessedness and true happiness are identical terms. Nothing is left for us to wish for, when the twelve lessons of Science have poured out their twelve results upon our life.

It is a gratification to know that if an accusation will bring a sick person, a thankful and praiseful word, felt sincerely, will bring a happy and healed case to our sight. It is a good thing to know that there are thoughts we can think which will fill our mind when it gets to complaining and whining.

We need not deny, if we feel low spirited and dissatisfied. We need just describe the Good of our lot. We have lost sight of our Good for a moment. Describing our Good will bring it to our sight again. One thing remember: you will feel less spiritual inspiration when you are mourning, whining and complaining, but when you praise and describe the Good you will feel full of spiritual fervor.

If a case appears the sixth time you must praise him for every virtue, every power, every beauty you can think of. You need not deny his disease. You need not deny your complaining. You must just praise and describe the Good in him. The denials you have been giving have made some good chinks in his cottage, through which your sunlight can penetrate. Happiness will bubble over and glisten from you, through a mind that comes the sixth time for treatment.

A deaf and blind person stands for some willfulness of yours. You would not see a plain truth and you would not hear what somebody told you, once upon a time. You persisted in seeing things your own way. Then your daily denials of accusation will break down your stubbornness. You will listen meekly, gladly, willingly to every voice. You will be quick to detect the true and the false ring in what you hear. The false will not count with you — you will forget it.

Now, you know that accusation takes different forms of expression, or writings, on faces and in people. You remember that yesterday's lesson spoke of the Jacinth as standing for beauty and judgment. Good judgment marks the face with lines of beauty. Falling short of good judgment marks the face with weakness and homeliness. So, if you see a homely face, it is certain that you have been accusing people of being foolish and ignorant. If you, yourself, are homely, you have accused yourself of being foolish or ignorant. Homeliness and weakness come down to disease, they are so dependent upon accusations of foolishness and ignorance.

You see an immense herd of plain looking people in our cities. They do not look much diseased. This signifies that you have, all your lifetime, been accusing people and yourself, in a general way, not at all maliciously, but enough to show forth. You see many elderly and old people. They show your accusations against certain ones, that they know little, or nothing. Your own accusations against yourself will have the same effect as against others. The effect of praise of the spiritual intelligence is to bring beauty and good judgment to view everywhere.

We look at a strong man, and, if we remember how his strength looked to us, we catch his strength. There is a text which reads, "In thy light we shall see light." It can be carried out in the strength which people show. It can be the same with beauty, "In thy beauty we see beauty." Which means that as we recognize beauty, we soon show forth the same beauty.

There is a story of a child who kept a picture of a beautiful woman in her room and looked at it and talked to it so much that she became like the picture. A young woman found an ideal face of Jesus Christ, and carried it around with her. She looked at it and loved it so much that her face began to resemble the face of Jesus Christ remarkably – even to the fine shining light which always transfigures it when we think of it. Ingratitude is a painter of hard lines on the face. Soon all the curves and smiles will change. We must have a grateful feeling towards everybody, and everything.

In the story of The First Violin, by Jessie Fothergill, the hero, who was supernaturally handsome, is pictured as always grateful for everything that anybody did.

Cynicism is a spice of ingratitude that brings the most extraordinary people around us. Give thanks to the universe, to your ancestors, to your neighbors, to yourself, to animals, to everything that you have dealings with. Its spirit is your good, loving provider. Sometimes you must stop giving thanks to the supreme God, and name everything as giving you bounty, for God seems afar off sometimes, and not speaking and breathing through our world, and every object in it. By stretching the mind off to be grateful to our idea of God, we do well, but we do well to look at the God near at hand also.

The Divine Intelligence marks the orbit of the distant Canis Major and rounds the little moons of Mars with the same tender care. Divine beauty paints the North Star and the violet with impartial tenderness. So, you will be grateful to the man who steals your purse as to the father who provides for your youth. Why? Because God is the Life, the Spirit, the Intelligence of each alike, without difference of goodness from the hand of the Lord. If you have not seen this, it is true just the same.

Did you ever see a calm, benignant countenance? It shows how once you said calm, peaceful words, and thought that way, in harmony with your words. Look over your list of acquaintances, those you can call by name, and see what there is that is lovely in them. Then remember awhile how that loveliness looked. "Bring all the tithes into the storehouse," said the prophet of the Jews. If you gather all the beauty of one woman into your memory, all the smiles of a friend into your memory, you will have all the tithes in your storehouse.

The prophet said that whosoever should do this would spill over with blessings, for he would not have room enough to keep them to himself. This constitutes happiness. Happiness is the stone of freedom.

With the last polish of the lessons on your character, you see that there is nothing whatsoever to do. All was, and is, and ever will be, the finished work of the Divine Mind. "God saw everything He had made, and behold, it was very good." Divine Mind never sees any evil, and sees nothing to do. While we see evil, or see something to do, we must think according to denials and affirmations. When we love greatly, love supremely, we see nothing to do; and finished, beautiful life satisfies us, everywhere we walk. Like the clear innocent Amethyst, we let the happiness of the Divine Mind sift its innocent light through us.

As you look through the Amethyst you see all the colors of the rainbow. As you look through the Topaz everything looks laughing yellow—even the shadows look happy. As you look through the Amethyst the happiness of the Topaz is accompanied by the intelligence of the Sardius and the inspiration of the Ruby. The green of the green stones is to symbolize the completed work.

Now, do not lay too much stress upon stones, nor upon any other kind of symbol. Money is a symbol of the riches of God, the bounty of God. The Topaz tells you to laugh, because everything is supplied with its natural good. The Amethyst tells you everything is good and wise, and satisfied, as well as able to do all things. But none of these are the thing itself. Gold is the symbol of the bounty of Jehovah. When you look at gold, speak its meaning. That is its life and substance. If it does not increase for you, then you are ungrateful, cynical. Its nature is hidden from you as deeply as Lazarus was buried.

Do you remember how Jesus Christ gave thanks, when Lazarus was cold and still? Well, when your conditions are cold and unyielding, after you have been treating them faithfully, you must go into a room, by yourself, and give thanks to the Spirit that it always does everything good for you, that it supplies you, pays your debts, and in every way blesses you. Then speak to the gold, or your affairs, or to your sick neighbor, or to your family trouble, with a loud voice, praising its real meaning, and call it to come forth with new life, new kindness, new bounty and good conditions.

Read over the story of how Jesus raised Lazarus. It is in the eleventh chapter of John. It tells how Jesus tarried, when He knew that Lazarus was sick, in order to symbolize, or tell, how people sometimes neglect to give thanks and feel grateful so long that things get, seemingly, very bad for them. We have all the hardships because we have been neglectful of the praise and health vitalizing of right words. But, even here, said Jesus, there is a way to make things into new life.

"The last enemy to be overthrown is death." When you have learned the last lesson you will not only have power, but ALL power. You are not free from one accusation only, you are free from accusation utterly. You see the whole ground of the law beneath your feet, so, "Love is the fulfilling of the law."

George Herbert sang the twelfth light of Revelation:
"Oh, now I know how all thy lights combine
    And the configuration of their story;
Seeing not only how each world doth shine,
    But all the constellations in their glory."

You have run with the winged feet of mind from mountain top to mountain top of the shining lessons of Science without halting, but at the twelfth lesson you are like an eagle that folds its wings over the earth, so far beneath, and surveys the landscape in peaceful security. There is an absolute security, if you understand and feel the twelfth lesson of Science. The Amethyst stands for security. Only the heart that is above condemnation feels secure from condemnation.

The axiom of the twelfth lesson is: He that knows Me, transcends Me. It means that whoever truly knows Me is transcendently beyond the God he imagined Me to be. You know that even you feel that those who love you, find in you virtue beyond what you feel yourself to possess. The man who sees in his neighbor great virtues, has in himself those very virtues. It is himself he sees. He may not appreciate goodness and greatness as rich germs in his own nature, needing only to see goodness and greatness outside of himself to be fed with increasing food. Within yourself is the germ of beauty. If you see beauty outside of yourself, without carping at it, or complaining that you have it not, your germs are fed, and beauty begins to show in you. You have touched the twelfth lesson in Science.

This is the old art of animation of the particular from the universal, sought after by the ancients, but not found.

It is recognized good that makes us good enough to show goodness. The great wisdom-power within you is ready to spring up, fed with the increasing principle, when you see wisdom expressed in a book, or a man, or, even if you see for a second, the wisdom expressed by the flies and spiders in your house.

If you look straight into the face of the all pervading wisdom of the universe, you will feed your germs, which are like little mouths waiting for food, with their own kind of aliment, and your wisdom will increase rapidly. So with happiness. You look into the child's happiness, and do not lament because you are not happy, but just thank the happiness you see for showing itself to you, and your germ, or love of happiness, innate within you, will be fed.

If anybody speaks to you critically, listen carefully. There is a ring of Divine Intelligence at your door. You will get a piece of news about your faults, and you will take those faults and deny them. This may leave you a little melancholy. Now you want to thank God for speaking to you. Give thanks for His wisdom expressed to you. This causes your love of wisdom to feed in delight.

When you see adversity as the hand of God bestowing bounty, and give thanks to God, and call to the bounty of

God to come plainly to your sight, you have touched the lights of all twelve lessons at once. It is not that God chooses adversity to give you riches through. No, it is that, having neglected to give thanks and be grateful at the right time, you have covered your prosperity with a cold shell. But, there is no death of prosperity. It is alive in your adversity, and by your right dealings with this state of affairs, you can bring out your prosperity.

It lies within adversity to bring your bounty to feed your love of prosperity, innate within you, like a hungry germ. It lies within criticism to feed your love of wisdom, innate within you, like a hungry germ. The love of strength, the love of health, the love of security, the love of skill, the love of harmony, and all, abide within you. When you see health or strength or see prosperity, or see power of any kind, and do not whine or carp or complain that you do not have them, you are fed instantly, and soon will be all that you see. Also you will see more. It is the beauty of health that if you see it, it increases to your sight.

Have you never noticed that if you see a lame man on the street, you soon see half a dozen lame men? Things increase by seeing them. It never rains, when you let things come with ugly feelings, but it pours. When you see health, peace, prosperity, everywhere, you are in the absolute Mind of God. If you practice every Saturday afternoon, praising your world, telling you are satisfied with it, describing it as the perfect creation of Divine Mind, you will soon see more good than you have been accustomed to seeing.

So, I believe there is a "Don't" in the Science which has no denial with it, but only Science, and that is: "DON'T COMPLAIN."

It was a secret of Jesus that He never condemned anything in the world. He certainly had as much occasion to condemn the world as anybody.

Haggai, the Prophet, says that "The desire of the nations shall come and Glory shall fill the whole earth." You can see that, like the rest of the prophets, he saw that the time would come when the doctrine preached by Jesus would be understood. You can see that if the air, the skies, the trees, the men, the women, all are filled with the Spirit of Good, that we shall drink our love of God full to overflowing by seeing the Good. It is the opening of our eyes, ears, mouths, to be filled with satisfaction.

Sometimes it is wise to say that everything we see, hear, smell, taste, feel and think, delights us, we are satisfied utterly. This is breaking the barriers down. Our eyes have power to see much beyond what we use them for, and it is so with all our faculties.

Ibsen, the popular play writer has written a play called the "Master Builder," in which his motive is to prove that man is a limited being, and must not aspire to get beyond his limits. This is quite opposite to Jesus Christ's instructions. "Behold I set before you an open door which no man can shut, all power is given unto you." "I in you," "That where I am there ye may be also." The twelfth lesson sets aside the doctrine of limitations.

You can see for yourself that if a man sets his mind steadfastly to the premise that he is a limited being, that word "limit" will stop his career somewhere. You have seen great men rise to heights of knowledge, like Emerson and Ruskin, and then drop suddenly to nonentity. All the powers of intellect, which intellect is the simulation of spiritual Intelligence, fly to sustain any premise put by mind. So the world intellect has flown to support the ideas of limitation. But the spiritual nature of man has no doctrine of limitation. Take your choice which nature to take your premise from. By the spiritual law you have no bars put anywhere to your expansion. The love of harmony within you may be fed with harmony itself, till the great Masters are left far behind.

The wisdom within you is the love of wisdom. Feed it by sight of wisdom itself, and your wisdom will expand and multiply to the omniscience of God. If you are capable of eating some of God, are you not capable of eating all of God?

Jesus Christ said: "God is within you," and "I am within you." Then you are able to take in all of God. This is only one form of expression which gives a different turn of the mind. It is not that you eat God in a material sense, but Jesus Christ called it '"Bread" which he would have all the world eat of—speaking figuratively.

We have a marvelous birthright. We do not show our intelligence, our judgment, until we lay hold upon our birthright. We can hold this knowledge within our mind and then it will work through all the mind of the world. A false idea falls somewhere and fails. A true idea lives on and on forever. If we take the premise, within our mind, that there is no limit to our power, even though each day we see things seem to act against us, we nevertheless have the doctrine that will triumph.

A piece of ice may be found in the crucible of intensest heat. If the ice holds its own, and increases by constant renewal, the crucible heat must fail, leaving clear ice. So in the fires of the Martyrs, they kept cool and steadfast. Pain got no hold upon them. Even racks and the flames could not hurt them. In the center of the blazing, violent sun, there is a place that is beyond expression, absolute stillness. This stillness will conquer the violence of the sun eventually. So, the Spirit that is within you will conquer the miseries of the human lot. They shall be visibly nothing—just as they are truly nothing.

It is our business to translate the spiritual Truth within, into visible manifestation. We do this first by thinking the absolute Truth, then speaking it, then fixing it into everything around us. We must mix the idea we have in our mind with the right word that expresses that idea. For instance, if you mean that a man is well, but you say that he is sick, you carry, for the time being, the meaning of the word "sick," and your mental report of it does not work with the man to heal him as quickly as the words you speak work to keep him sick. We are told by Solomon that the thoughts work, but Jesus gives us to understand that not only do our thoughts work, but words, which have certain meanings, will convey those meanings sooner than thoughts which dispute them. We must mean exactly what we say. "By thy words thou art justified."

A man said this Science was true enough, but it would take a hundred years for it to work out with mankind. So, every attempt he made to do anything was slow. He mentally thought that Spirit could act instantly, of course, but his mental reservation counted for nothing for the time being. The heart must agree with the lips. Zoroaster said, "Taking the first step with good thought, the second step with good word, the third step with good deed, I enter Paradise." If the thought and the word agree, we cannot help good deeds. The lessons of Science lead you to absolute freedom from the results of the thoughts of the world, and from the material actions of the world.

Men may gather all the gold into a lump, and suppose you cannot have any, but by some way of the Spirit you will come out with more abundant riches than all the rest put together. They may hold arguments and try psychologic processes to chain your mind, or change it, but the Spirit will make a way with you to keep you free from all such attempts. You will elude every mental opposition as easily as you elude material things. Jesus came through their belief that he was dead.

Spirit does not need to go to school. It knows all things. If we speak and think from the Spirit, we are also wise without schools. The Spirit does not need commandments not to lie or steal. It is out of reach of commandments. The Spirit does not need to be told to be Good. It is above even goodness, The goodness that man deals with is badness under some circumstances. For instance, you can hate stealing so much that your goodness in not stealing is no virtue at all. It is a very subtle form of badness.

An old lady said she thought it very wrong to drink tea at church suppers. She did not drink tea, she hated it. Many people hate tobacco, until their hatred is far worse than chewing and smoking, for their own health, and the happiness of their families. Sometimes people hate the wrong-doing of others so that they can not possibly see their virtues. It makes an acid in the blood and eats up the strong gray particles of the brain. Hate is the premise we have to let fall entirely. Hate nothing. God sees everything good. What are we that other peoples' actions are so bad in our eyes? When we have a notion to which we would like to tie all the world, we are tied to that notion. It is as much bondage to be tied to an idea as to a stake. Martin Luther believed in freedom from other people's ideas, but he wanted to tie all the world to his ideas. In Science we do not get chained to a single statement. They are all good, but we do not drag ourselves around by any of them.

As you know, faith is good. Faith is the salvation of man. The idea that faith will save man is a good idea, but when Luther would not shake hands with Zwingle because he did not think faith would save a man, he needed an idea beyond the idea of faith. He needed love. He needed the idea of love as the greatest of all. He tied himself to the stake of an idea and would not go on to the mountain of love.

The twelve lessons of Science are all ideas. The ideas have living meanings. Luther's idea of faith had a living meaning, which he never got at all. The living meaning of salvation by faith is that faith in the Good enables us to see Good everywhere and in everything. Faith is God. God is Mind. Mind is Good and Mind sees Good. Mind knows God. The mind that has not the living essence of its ideas is as dry as sticks. Zwingle did not believe in the doctrine of faith, so Luther wanted to lift him out of salvation. So, our ideas of God have kept us chained. God is free. He is the skill of the healer. God is the Spirit that works out the health of the sick. God is the skill of all things. All action has a skill about its action, and that skill is the moving Holy Spirit. God does not see the outer actions. God sees only the heart.

The springs of life are fed by the meanings of words. Some people do not quite feel the meanings of the words they use, but the use of the words, by and by, breaks their meanings out over the mind. Precious ointment was shut in the alabaster boxes. Striking the boxes broke them, and the precious ointment fell out. So, striking the right words together breaks them open after awhile. It is the meanings of the words that go over the world like angels of mercy, changing all the thoughts of men. The higher the truths we tell, the finer and more precious their meaning. Breaking open the twelve lessons of Science, and receiving the ointment of the meanings, is getting at the actual teachings of Jesus Christ.

Looking at your state of mind, you will see how full you seem to be of heavy ideas. Your breath seems to have brought in anxieties. Now hardships meet you at every turn — you think.

The ancients advised people to breathe outward, to entirely empty their lungs of breath, and then draw in the breath with some affirmation of Good. Then, when they breathed outward again, they would only have a healing breath going through their bodies and affairs. The breath, they said, is vitally connected with our happiness.

You will sometimes find yourself praising and blessing your affairs for your prosperity, their life in God. You will find yourself consigning all your affairs into the hands of the Spirit. Whatsoever we do, we are not to lament, not to wail, not to mourn. There is nothing that will slice out of your feeling of power like grief. You cannot cry and heal at the same moment. Shakespeare said; "Grief, that's beauty's canker," and judgment is beauty. People make the worst mistakes of their lives when they are wailing. All the time the Spirit sits in calm security — in perfect happiness.

When we are happy, through some accomplishment directly from the hand of our doctrine, we have the Amethyst stone of character. We are in intelligence and peace. They together make happiness. All despondency, all melancholy, all depression of feeling, must be met by breathing in and out words of praise of the great realities of life. The spiritual nature of man is his reality. The reality is understanding. Understanding is formless, but it formulates. This is very metaphysical. Let me repeat it; "My understanding has no form, but it formulates me and my affairs. I have no affairs and no substance except what my understanding formulates."

Now, those affairs formulated by pure understanding are not visible to my fleshly eyes, which see things imperfectly, since they are limited. This sight in itself is a fine piercing ray from my understanding. Let me give the right word, and that sight will extend to touch perfect objects. So with hearing. It is no good to limit my hearing by not giving my understanding its absolute sway with me. Understanding can radiate through us till our faculties touch things in an entirely different way from what they do now.

The more freedom we give our understanding, the more delight we have in life. Our understanding being set free, feeds upon the great universal light. There is enough understanding in the universe for feeding our faculties forever. The step towards setting free our understanding of the world in which we live, and the understanding of ourselves at the same time, has been taken, when the eleventh lesson of Science has been practiced. It is being set free from accusations of foolishness and ignorance. There is no acid in the mind that has no condemnation, either of itself or anybody else. It is the acid of thinking evil that makes the blood corrode, and the bones and skin and sinews to fail. It is possible to nullify all our strong feelings by some exactly opposite idea. If you find yourself thinking that somebody is entirely wrong for using material remedies, when you know that the word of the Spirit is the only healer, let the idea fall out of your mind. It is the same with not using them. You will find you are free as God is free, if you depend upon nothing at all for your health. Your simple freedom is enough of a spread of the Truth.

Some find themselves having new diseases, new pains, new trouble every day. They can all be traced to the bondage of the mind, to some one idea or another. The Sunday affirmation of Science is good for such people. It is one you must also keep for Sunday. It is *"While knowing all things and doing all things, I am independent of all things. I am absolutely free."* This will take you out of the clutches of your old drugs. It will take you out of the clutches of your new idea that it is wicked to use drugs. You will be free from the need of remedies bodily, and free from any idea of remedies mentally.

The same with old age. The word of the Spirit is eternal life. There is no old age in Spirit. The knowledge of this will set you free from the clutches of old age physically, and from the clutches of old age mentally. The same is true of riches. Outwardly you will be well provided for, then you will feel free. Mentally you will never think of coming to want. You will never get to imagining what you would do if you should come to want. This is real freedom.

We must get free from our ideas. God is freedom from ideas. God is the free substance that penetrates and pervades all things. If you are afraid to do anything, because somebody might not like it, you are tied to their ideas. You must do as it is right to do because you are pleased with the right, or you have not learned the twelfth lesson of Science. You are not happy if you are not free.

You must begin the description of the perfection of the world in which you live. You are glad that the free Spirit is flowing through the airs. Tell it you are glad. You are glad there is a way to speak to the Spirit to bring it into your being. Tell it you are glad. You think your neighbor is a beautiful Soul. Tell her Soul, mentally, that you are glad it is so beautiful. The skies are lovely. Their loveliness is spiritual. Tell their loveliness how glad you are that it is visible to you. The stars resting on their black beds are wonderful. Their wonderfulness is spiritual. Tell it how glad you are that it is visible to you. The deep night, half towards morning, is stately peace.

Though you stand on bare sand, there is Mind whispering rich secrets. You do not need to be lonesome. Jesus Christ is whispering every instant some wonderful message into your ear. It would be a good plan for you to listen to the Voice of the Spirit. No matter if you are riding in the street cars you can be listening to what the free Spirit is speaking, as plainly to you through the earthquake as through the stillness. Only we do not think we can listen to a voice within a sound as well as to a voice within stillness.

There is a chance for the most unhappy person among you to breathe out your unhappiness and breathe in descriptions of the things you are glad about, till you hear the finer voice of nature, till you see the finer side of all things. You get above the ideas of your world. You are free from them. You get above even the idea of freedom. You see, the idea of freedom takes with it the idea of bondage of some kind. So you are neither free nor bound. You are not on that plane. You do not talk about riches, for that idea conveys the idea of poverty. You are neither rich nor poor. You do not live on that plane. You do not say you have dominion over all things, because the idea of dominion is the same as the idea somebody is inferior in some way. You are neither inferior nor superior. You do not live on that plane. The Spirit never gets caught on any of those hooks. It is not inferior to your understanding, nor superior to it. The Spirit is one with your understanding. So the Spirit has no dominion over you. It is one with you. You do not talk of destroying your temper. You have no temper to destroy. You do not talk of getting free from poverty. You have no poverty to get free from.

This is the effect of using the twelfth statement of Science. You sometimes hear Scientists make these statements and they sound dangerous. They only show that they are thinking just as the twelfth lesson led them. Every Saturday afternoon you ought to have a special proclamation. If you have a good realization of the meaning of what you say that afternoon, you will keep free from complaining about your disappointments or troubles, even within your own mind. Why should you tie your mind to a stake and swing back and forth like a rag in the wind? If you tie your mind to a single idea, you will miss the twelfth lesson. There have been many people who have missed the twelfth lesson, because they have stopped to whine and to wail. They tied themselves to an idea that they did not like one thing, and howled all night long over it. Of course, their case came for a sixth treatment and said he was not cured. Of course the same old affair faced them again for the sixth time.

You must not tie to an idea of anything being bad. If we speak of it, let us quickly give the twelfth lesson law to our mind. That is, we say nothing more about it. *We think nothing more about it.* We ignore it utterly and talk about something we like. We think about the true premise we have taken, whereby we propose to think that, if evil is not a reality, we do not mean to deal with it.

Now, whatever proposition you have made up your mind to, can you not stick to it? Of all things, if it is true that there is a substance of delight called Mind, within ourselves, and we can make whatever thought we please by thinking that way, we shall be very silly indeed if we do not choose a noble thought about ourselves, instead of an ignoble one. It is a noble thought to say:

"*I am satisfied with the world in which I walk. All things please me. Near me is the presence of Good and afar off is the Good. You are all creations of the living God, perfect, harmonious, satisfying.*"

You will find this a good idea with which to work out your happiness. Having your mind filled with this idea, you cannot have another idea in it. This idea results in happiness. It is the one to take when you feel like complaining. It is the one to take when you feel like comparing your lot in life with what you wanted it to be. It radiates your work with the green of the Amethyst stone. It will gladden your home with the yellow sunshine of the Topaz stone. It will make peace and harmony among your friends, like the Sapphire blue of heaven. It will redden your business with the wine of prosperity.

It is what nobody has demonstrated except Peter and John. They sang with great songs of joy, when they might have wailed because they were in prison. If you will notice people, you will see that they can hardly be made to laugh and sing, when they contrast their lot, as it seems, with what they wanted it to be. People say they would be satisfied if they had this, or that, or the other. No such thing! If they mourn now, they would find something to mourn about then. Happiness is something that must come from the mind within, being fed and renewed by the Truth of life. Nothing but Truth will satisfy the mind. Complaining kept the Israelites of old from large inheritance: "They provoked the Lord with their complainings."

The pleasant, happy mind is a health-giver, without trying to be. It knows its value in the world. It does not heal without knowing what it heals. Jesus perceived when he was healing people who were behind him. It is intelligence. Nobody is so wise as that man or woman who has refused the temptation to complain, and has, in his mind, spoken the twelfth lesson of Science. Melancholy, being met by this statement, is the best mixture for happiness that can be stirred up.

If your case comes the sixth time, tell him that you rejoice that he is giving the free Spirit unrestrained freedom through him. Knock at all twelve gates of his being through which he ought to be shouting healthy life. Say to the case that claims to be cured the same treatment as to the case that seems to hang on, because you have felt hurt, or grieved, or forgotten, or neglected to give the right thoughts that would have made you an intelligent healer. It should have the same treatment as the one that has been cured. It is the time for you to give thanks to God, and call out loudly to the true state of affairs to come into your sight. The cured case is easily told mentally that you rejoice in his health as God. The case that you are finding fault with keeps on the sick list, does not seem so easy, but if you have made it hard, you must soften it.

I might truthfully say that the case which comes the sixth time for cure, is the outshowing of your disposition. A good disposition through and through, is a happy disposition, and a happy disposition will cure anything. A happy disposition, mixed with scientific words, makes a quick understanding of how to speak mentally to a sick or unhappy being, and bring him instantly out into the right state. A good disposition, mixed with these lessons of Science will make a perfect memory. A good disposition mixed with thoughts of the truths of life, put forth while you are along each day, will make you very good and quick at speaking and writing the Science.

If your disposition is bad, or seems so to yourself or friends, the repetition of the twelfth premise in Science will make it good. Another thing, you will be able to quickly see if a man's disposition stands in the way of his health. A lady, who had trained her disposition to be smiling and cheerful, had been treating a patient, who believed in sore eyes, for a long time. One day, she spoke mentally, very impetuously; "You, as Spirit, have no bad temper." The next day the patient came, all cured.

That practitioner said she would sometimes be six weeks treating a case, and not stir it, then, she would suddenly say, mentally; "You never could, as a Spiritual being, feel dissatisfied with your son." Or, she would say, "You, as Spirit, can say that you, as Spirit, cannot be unjust with anybody." These sudden thoughts, she said, seemed to cut a tough thread that was holding the patient's mind from thinking of health. These little cuts at the strings that hold a case in pain or sickness, are what comes from your mind as naturally as seed comes up into corn and wheat. Nobody can tell what to say in particular to a case. They can only

Scientific Christian Mental Practice

give the general treatment. The general treatment leads up to the particular one. There is a verse that has helped a great many people into good courage. It is this:

"He who hath led me to this way,
 Still on the way will show.
He who hath taught me of this way,
 Still more will make me know."

It means that if God, in his infinite kindness and mercy, has put this Science before us, and led us into it, He will see that we go on to its end. It is as David was taken from the sheep-cote, from following after sheep, and put into the King's Palace. God elected him and fitted him for this place. So, if you have chosen to learn the Science, chosen to practice it, God, the Infinite Mind, will give you strength and fitness to fulfill each task set before you. Sometimes you will seem to be in great trouble, but you will never go under. Calamity will never overtake you. Probably the most prominent Scientists have had the very hardest troubles to encounter, but they never go under. They are always lifted safely over. A ship on the ocean dips low, and rides high. So you are built, if you have these lessons in your mind. They have gone out, like angels, to prepare your way for you. They have taken deep eternal hold on your mind and body. Jesus said; "Fear not little flock," and so I say to you, be faithful to the lessons. Be faithful to this last lesson, which goes down into your deep nature, and takes hold of your disposition and makes it divine.

If a case comes cured the sixth day, it is a -sure signal that you have gained a victory over your disposition. You have won the Amethyst stone. A very simple, trusting Scientist, who had entirely given her life to the spiritual doctrine, had an Amethyst given her. She took it as a signal that she had been victorious over her disposition. She thought, to herself, "It is a sign that, when I wanted to complain, I promptly spoke the last treatment of Science." She had a Topaz given to her. She took it as a sign that she had put cheerful, buoyant words out into her affairs, when they troubled her. "The outward conditions are so dependent on my thoughts," she said, "that I feel as if they were sermons in brooks and books in stones, telling me how I am getting on."

One Scientist used to begin to talk to herself as a newly born, perfect child of the Spirit. She would speak to herself, as she was when one year old, then two years old. She told the little thing what a miracle of God would be wrought for her some day. Then, when she came to the year of her age, according to the world's reckoning, she would pronounce the whole miracle already wrought. She felt that it was very important that she be every whit whole in her mind, if she was to teach Science.

No matter what that patient of yours would say to you personally, if you were to see him or her now, you may give him the sixth treatment, which is the last lesson of Science. You will be faithful in giving it to your world every Saturday afternoon, and you will treat every case, no matter how it seems, to this teaching, if it comes the sixth time. Follow me. I will speak to that one who used to believe in disease:

You are a perfect creation of the living God spiritual, harmonious, fearless, free.

You reflect all the universe of Good.

From every direction, everywhere, come words of Truth, making you know that you are free, wise and happy.

You are satisfied with the world in which you live.

You show forth to the world health, wisdom, peace.

You show to me perfect health in every part of your being.

You are fearless, free, strong, wise, and able to do everything that belongs to you to do each day.

God works through you to will and to do that which ought to be done by you.

You are a living demonstration of the power of Truth to set free into health and strength for living service to the world.

You acknowledge to the world that you are every whit whole.

You acknowledge to yourself and to me that you are well and strong and alive through and through.

God is your life, health, strength and support forever.

In the name of the Father, and of the Son, and of the Holy Ghost, I pronounce you well and strong.

As God saw the works of His hands Good, so I see you Good. All is Good. Amen.

High Mysticism

studies in the wisdom

of the sages of the ages

The original 12 volumes from her writings, published by the High Watch Fellowship

Contents

1ST STUDY: THE SILENT EDICT	249
2ND STUDY: REMISSION	271
3RD STUDY: FOR-GIVENESS	285
4TH STUDY: FAITH	305
5TH STUDY: THE WORD	329
6TH STUDY: UNDERSTANDING	357
7TH STUDY	389
8TH STUDY	421
9TH STUDY	448
10TH STUDY	473
11TH STUDY	496
12TH STUDY	521

1st Study: The Silent Edict

NOTE

Consider now with me in joyful amazement the unity of discovery throughout the centuries, which the illuminati have made, as to that practice of the presence of Deity most surely leading to divine imbuement.

E. C. H.

From the Divine Heights there has been vouchsafed to all ages One Heavenly-Edict. All the everlasting pages struck off by men under the white flames of inspiration, have been the results of knowing or unknowing obedience to the Soundless Mandate of the Lofty One inhabiting eternity: "Look unto Me, and be ye saved, all the ends of the earth."

A clearly unified instruction runs in almost verbatim language through all the sacred or charmed books of the world. It is the live wire insulated by absurd dogmas and ungodly imaginations. It is the footpath of the immortals. It is the mirific science. Whoever can read its supernal lines, undiverted by their company of errors, is in the way of salvation. It concerns that swift, subtle faculty pos-sessed by us all, whereby we look whithersoever we will; to the Deity ever beholding us, or to the dust beneath, without the aid of our physical eyes.

> "Thou canst not behold Me with thy two outer eyes, I have given thee an eye divine."—*Upanishads*.

This fleet, subtle sense is our incorporeal eye. It is the one faculty of our immortal soul which we continually make use of. It is the creature made subject to *maya*,[1] not willingly, but in the hope of redemption of the body, as Paul wrote to the Roman Christians.

The exaltation or lifting up of this sense toward that vast, vast Countenance ever shining toward us as the sun in his strength, is our way of return to the Source whence we sprang forth. It is the Path of Light. It is the Tao.

> "Make use of the light, returning again to its Source;
> Thy body shall be free from calamity's course,
> And thou shalt train with the Eternal at length." —*Tao-teh-King*.[2]

> "Man alone of all the animals goes in quest of his Origin, and perceiving that the highest good is to be sought by him in the highest place, looks to his Maker." —Lactantius.

This looking faculty antedates mind, and though offering itself to the service of mind, transcends it in achieving power. For it is primarily what we most see, and not what we most think, that constitutes our presence, power and history.

"It is not possible for anything to take place save in connection with an onlooker," reads an inspired line in the Vedic Hymn.[3]

If we exalt this swift sense, or look unto Him whose ever-repeated mandate is, "'Behold Me, behold Me,'" we receive back over the track of our vision tonic and viability to the mind, endurance and beauty to the body, joy and fearlessness to the emotions, integrity and intrepidity to the moral character.

---

[1] *Maya* is a Sanskrit word referring to the changeable, malleable nature of material stuff. It's usually translated as "illusion" but that should not be taken to mean that material experience has no validity or utility.

[2] Today, this is usually written *Tao te Ching*, and refers to the masterpiece ascribed to an ancient Taoist philosopher whose name we don't know but who is usually called *Lao tse*, which means "ancient master."

[3] This is remarkably like the idea in modern quantum physics that says that the stuff of the universe only becomes particles (matter) in the presence of an observer.

All that we think, is made up of the objectives, toward which we have directed this deathless, achieving visional power. All that this posit[4] we call body, exhibits, is the set of accretions that have come over the inner visional track.

"That thou seest, that thou beest." We collect sadness and depression from directing this mystic eye toward human faces. For this attent did Solomon weep so loudly his retainers trembled. Sanity and soundness are the characteristics of the mind of those who do not project their prehensile vision toward objects that gratify the five outer senses. They who see toward the heights are invulnerable to honor or contempt, praise or dispraise. Their probity, sincerity and courage lapse not.

> "For that thou seest, man,
>
> That too become thou must; God if thou seest God,
>
> Dust if thou seest dust."

With closed eyes, still let the gaze be heavenward; there on the fair unspeakable heights is the home whence we all came hitherward to view the ways of destruction:

"Thou turnest man to (see) destruction, but sayest,

'Return ye children of men.'"—Psalm of Moses.

To look upward with the mystic eye is to start on the saving Tao: "Look unto Me and be ye saved—I will turn away your captivity from before your eyes—when ye turn unto Me seeking My face," wrote the two great prophets, Isaiah and Jeremiah.

"With the flash of one hurried glance I attained to the vision of that which Is. And Thou didst not give me any peace till Thou was manifest to the eye of my soul," cried St. Augustine of Tagaste, in one of his illuminated moments.

The farther toward the celestial zenith we send the limitless eye, the deeper is our assurance of our own divine

---

[4] "this posit" means "this hypothesis" "this temporary position held for the sake of experiment or argument" "this assumption."

origin eye can find. Order and beauty hide their sublime mysteries till on the Tao's magic path the tireless vision speeds toward the Origin of beauty and order.

> "In heaven there is laid up a pattern which he who chooses may behold, and beholding, set his own house in order. The time has now arrived at which they must raise the eye of the soul to the Universal Light which lightens all things. With the eye ever directed toward things fixed and immutable which neither injure nor are injured,—these they cannot help imitating. But I quite admit the difficulty of believing that in every man there is an eye of the soul which by the right direction is reillumined, and is more precious by far than ten thousand bodily eyes."—Plato.

As down the sides of Hermon the unapproachable, trickle cooling dews to refresh the hot valleys, so falls a reviving miracle of newness upon the children of earth, when they penetrate beyond the stars to Him who proclaimeth forever, "Behold, I make all things new."

As balm from the trees of old Gilead in far past days soothed the hurts of the Jews, so the dayspring from on high doth visit them that sit in darkness and in the shadow of death, to guide their feet into the way of peace. Nothing we can do, or say, or think, can quench the down-falling reconciliation and empowerment, the preserving and healing, while to the high edict responsive, we lift up our eye to the hitherward smiling Countenance of the Lover ever with us, the Lord of Hosts His name.

He abiding as the Great Different gives peace which nothing can invade. His benedictions confer resistless might. Therefore, "Behold, as the eyes of servants look to the hands of their masters, so our eyes wait upon Thee."

This deathless visional faculty is our only achieving power. It is not dependent upon thoughts of mind or bodily actions, though to them it yields itself day by day in omnipotent servitude. Left to itself it flies away to the Elysian Fields, its rightful resting place.

So eagerly did the untaught seers of the past long to have this immortal faculty find its rightful direction, they willingly practiced mortifications of the body, denied self, affections as well as appetites, to give it freedom. But it asks no such sufferings on the part of the mind or body to give it power to tame and glorify them. It asks only their will that it go homeward.

It is the immaculate of us. Though age and decrepitude have cramped the flesh, senility has sapped the mind, and sickness has blinded the eyes and thickened the ears, yet the wrecked old man lifts up his sightless eyes and smiles. With the immortal and ever young mystical eye he beholds things celestial. And then he drops the robe of clay, hastening to be identified with his joy-giving vision. Had this eye been lifted to the mountains of help in earlier days, he would have trans-figured and renewed his flesh, instead of leaving it to the moth and the sod.

All the other faculties in daily use are maculate. The mind can become vitiated, the body can become diseased, but though this all-accomplishing sense can bring back on its beams the nature of that upon which it may be stayed, itself has received no tinge of similitude. The same out of itself, the same in itself — aseity.[5]

With it we are to repent — to return.

"And now commandeth He all men everywhere, to repent," declared Paul to the Athenians.

"Repent, and turn away your faces from all the abominations which your own powers have made," was Ezekiel's admonition.

"The eye of the soul, which is literally buried in an outlandish slough, is by the right science lifted upwards."—Plato.

And this is that return which hath divine reward: "Return unto Me, and I will return unto you," said the heavenly voice to Malachi.

---

[5] Aseity is from the Latin *ab se*, which means "of (or from) itself."

The mind cannot return, for as high as the heavens are above the earth, so are My thoughts above your thoughts. The footsteps of flesh cannot return, for as high as the heavens are above the earth, so are My ways above your ways.

> "For these are but the distance of the strengthless from the Stronger, the shortlived from the Eternal, and the fantasy from the Like-to-Itself-only." —Hermes Trismegistus.

But the heavenly vision rests her fleet splendor in the high Source from which the flawless and immortal soul sprang forth:

> "I have given thee an eye divine with which to behold My power."—*Upanishads*.

By turning the celestial faculty toward the heights we are taken above the thought circuit to the watch:

> "Watch ye therefore. What I say unto you I say unto all, watch."

> "Blessed are those servants whom the Lord when He cometh shall find watching."

All miracle workers have practiced the principle of watching. Moses, the genius for leadership, speaks unto the nation of slaves.

> "Stand ye still, and see the salvation which the Lord will work for you. For the Lord shall fight for you, and ye shall hold your peace."

And this is forever, inevitably, the prayer of the supernally inspired leader of men: "Look down from Thy holy habitation, from heaven Thy dwelling place, and bless this people." And they shall pass in safety through Red Seas of difficulty, though all the powers of mind and matter oppose them.

And this is forever the joyous chant of the liberated people: "He looked on our affliction, and our labor, and our oppression, and He brought us forth out of darkness, with a mighty hand and with an outstretched arm."

High Mysticism 255

Elisha the seer stood with gaze transfixed toward a seraphic host in the mountains round about Samaria. "They that be with us are more than they that be against us," he said to Gehazi, who watched with him. And though the king of Syria had sent soldiers to slay the lonely prophet, they were not able to hurt him, for mystic defense transcends the sharpest swords.

Is it not promised, "I will give power to My two watchers"—new powers, miraculous powers?

Saint Bernard, the abbot of Clairvaux, rose to almost supreme power in his church by persistently gazing toward the twelve stars in the diadem of Mary in Paradise. He urged others to do likewise:

> "If the winds of temptation blow fiercely upon you, look to these stars. If you find yourselves in a sea of trouble, look to these stars. If you are tossed on the waves of pride, ambition, or envy, look to these stars, and invoke the name of Mary."

Hosea, making note of such as St. Bernard, cried, "They return, but not to the Most High."

Savonarola pictured before his inner eye a monastery for a holy resting place from turmoil and strife. Its monks should all be men come not to be ministered unto, but to minister. And it is recorded that so influential did the outcome of his vision grow, that great citizens begged to join the Dominicans, and riotous processions, idle songs and fightings ceased on the streets of beautiful *Firenze* [Florence, Italy]. With his inner eye on the commanding form of a warming visitant from the shores of mystery, Savonarola drew order out of chaos, and established a new form of government in the city of the Medici. In a time of dearth and danger, loaded wheat ships arrived, and the enemy's troops were not able to reach the people under the protecting ministry of Savonarola the seer.

All the forces of the universe cooperate with vision toward beatific ideals. It is not till the eye descends to prowl among the viciousness and crimes of men that war and martyrdom succeed. So descending did Chrysostom, the golden mouthed, forget to show the glories of the heavenly land, and he perished in exile. Jeremiah lamented so profoundly over the mistakes of the Jews that he was martyred in Egypt.

But Elisha never lost his high watch, and even his bones were life giving. His whole pathway on earth was strewn with miracles. For no weapon formed against the comrade of angels can prosper—radiating forever what he assimilates. Hufeland secretly eyed the unspoilable region of spiritual health in his diseased patients, and they recovered. The hidden actual readjusted the molecules and atoms of the manifest, to harmonize with Hufeland's untaught visional practice. Gordon noted that those who reported to him their procedure while demonstrating miraculous cures, mentioned seeing with their inner eye some gesture or image symbolic of, or identical with, the healing about to show forth. Maxwell watched the fleet, ethereal light which he discovered filling all quarters of the universe, and he declared that by watchful use of it the ailing among mankind might all be made whole.

The difference between the great men whose names have attracted the attention of mankind, as to endurance in memory, and strength in perpetuating their doctrines, has depended upon the uplift they have given to the hidden eye whereby the mind receives elation or depression.

Socrates came not to teach any positive doctrine, but to convince man of the ignorance of his mind. His highest science got no higher than that men act wrongly because they form erroneous judgments. Upon being told that he was the wisest man, he said it probably was true, for he knew enough to know that he knew nothing, while no one else seemed to know that much. The ignorance of man's mind is a dark zone to fix the all-collecting eye upon. No joyous inspiration fulgurates from that Ethiopic field.

[Gautama] Buddha cried, "I will now seek out a noble law, unlike the worldly methods known to men. I will

High Mysticism

oppose the scourges of the world, old age and death, disease and poverty." And at last he proclaimed that in order to be blest, man must keep eight conditions, and the first is right view: "For it is not possible for anything to take place save in connection with an onlooker." Thirty thousand miracles of achievement followed in his wake, and one-third the human race hold him and his sayings in loyal reverence to this day.

The world-conquering Jesus crowned the doctrine of the exaltation of the supernal sense with immediate demonstrations: "Father, I will that they may behold my glory." And multitudes came unto Him, and He healed them every one. To the blind man with the clay upon his eyes, He said, "Look up." To all people in times of calamity, He said, "Look up, for your redemption moveth toward you."

This is the arcane way. It is high mysticism, whether knowingly practiced, as science, or unwittingly and spontaneously exercised, as inspiration. By science, which is the knowledge of invariable orderly processes, inspir-ation follows speedily. By inspiration, to which great works are easy and masterful deeds are simple, the science comes slowly following after.

The mystics of all ages have trusted to their inward eye. While turning it to behold their own personal emotions or affairs they have wrought out no beauty of action or quickening language. While directing it toward the Unnamable and Undescribable King of Kings, they have astonished their own age, and all ages, by their miraculous performances and noble aphorisms.

What made the shoes wax not old upon the feet of the Israelites forty years in the wilderness? Their gaze was ever toward the High Imperishable One, and even their garments partook of His unspoilable beauty. What saved Hezekiah from dying, when even the powerful Isaiah had declared, "Thou shalt die, and not live"? His outer eyes with their dimming sight were following the uplook of that sense which we are all in constant use of for life or for decay. So swiftly did the life river come rushing down that flume of immortality, that even the death-dealing Isaiah felt it, and turned to cry, "Thou shalt live!" He must now speak in tune with Hezekiah's resistless vision, for in the pathway thereof there is no death.

What turned Jacob from destruction, when reasonable terrors shook him all night long by the Jabbok Brook? "I have seen God face to face, and my life is preserved."

What lifted Job out of his boils, and set his feet in joyous security, at a time when the children of fools and base men held him in derision, and the days of affliction had taken hold upon him? "My witness is in heaven, and my record is on high." What saved Daniel from the jaws of famishing lions, giving him answer to the lamentable voice of the king, as from within a calm tabernacle? He had watched the untrammeled God and His fleet angels.

Turning his gaze from the faces of men to his own divine ego, Julius Caesar wrought over his fellow men like a god. "It doth amaze me," cried Cassius to Brutus, "that a man of such a feeble temper should so get the start of this majestic world!" Though Caesar's gaze be high, yet it is not to the Most High, the Hebrew Hosea would explain.

High Mysticism calls for highest uplook toward the glory of the Highest.

> "Thou canst upraise thyself by thyself, and rouse thyself by thyself; for self is the lord of self, self is the refuge of self."
> —*The Bhikshu.*

Cervantes beheld with persistent inner eye the image of his mad Don Quixote, and ended his life in a mad-house. Why not, if "that thou seest, man, that too become thou must?"

Elisha set his watchful eye toward the Cause of Elijah's greatness and not toward the prophet speeding starward in the fiery chariot. "Where is the God of Elijah?" he calls, and down over his fingers fall curative ethers that change poisoned pottage to nutritious food; into his breath runs quickening fire that the dead cannot resist; salt takes in a new savor, bread and corn forget their limitations, at the new tones of his voice.

> "He that looketh toward Me, though least among men, his words shall be regnant. ...And also Me whoso worships, he, completely transcending the qualities, is able to become the Supreme"— Krishna, in the *Bhagavad Gita*.

A meek man prayed, "Show me, then, O King of all those mystics of superhuman powers, Thy Exhaustless Self." And the meek man cried, "I behold Thee! Thou art greater than Brahma! Thou art of Infinite Valor and Immeasurable Power! Thou art the Primeval God! Thou art the Knower! There is none equal to Thee! O Thou with majesty unimaged! I behold Thee on all sides!"

By vision toward Transcendence the meek man became awake to Immanence. Omnipresence is but the garment of the Highest. None can find the Tao by way of discoursing of Omnipresence, Omnipotence, Omni-science. By the uplift of the inner eye toward the countenance of Him that weareth these garments, the two outer eyes are baptized with high altar fires to see the glowing land of splendor through which we ever walk, the finished work of One who saith, "Behold who hath created."

As the mystically opened eyes behold the everywhere-completed splendor, the shadows of disorder are not remembered. But this glowing land yields not its sights to him whose mystic eye has not brought back over the pathway of obedience to the heavenly Edict, the soft alkahests that dissolve the films of blindness.

Ideal philosophy strikes the lofty note of the Sacred Edict when it forgets to maunder and prowl among reasonings begotten of unlifted vision. Now and then its voice rises like the sound of an invisible choir on the airs of night: "Keep your eye on the Eternal and your intellect will grow."

"Honor and fortune exist for him who remembers that he is in the presence of the High Cause."

The Egyptian thrice-great priests of *Amen Ra* caught the soundless teachings of the heights:

> "He is by Himself, yet it is to Him that everything owes existence. Becoming eye-witnesses, behold Him, and in beholding be blest. He is not light, but the Cause that light is. He is not mind, but the Cause that mind is. Nor spirit, but the Cause that spirit is. Let us lay hold of the Beginning, and we shall make way with quickness through everything. For the spectacle hath something peculiar; those that shall attain to the contemplation, it detains and attracts as the magnet stone the iron. But now as yet we are not intent upon the vision. So many men are body devotees they can never behold the Vision of the Beautiful. Why, O men, have ye given yourselves over to death, having power to partake of immortality?"—Egyptian *Book of the Dead*

The Chinese of old had sages who spoke of returning to the High Deliverer:

> "Returning to the Root means rest. He who regulates his attitude by Him will become one with Him. He is the good man's treasure and the bad man's deliverer. If princes knew the Tao the ten thousand things would of themselves reform. They would be restrained by the simplicity of the Ineffable. Homeward is the Tao's course. Who knows the way that is not trodden, and the argument that needs no words?"

The Hindu watchers toward the fronting horizon sometimes lifted their forward-caught, *kundalini*[6]-bound sight, to

---

[6] *Kundalini* is the Sanskrit term for the life energy that moves up the spine through the nerve-centers that are called, in Sanskrit, *chakras*, and flows out along the nerve system through the body. "Awakening the *kundalini*" is a process by which the initiate, under careful guidance, learns to enhance the flow from the lower, body-oriented chakras to the higher, spirit-connected ones. There are many stories of people who've attempted to do so on their own experiencing great distress and discomfort.

High Mysticism

the topless heights, and hymned the rise of man from death and reincarnation:

> "Whoso worships Me, committing to Me all actions, regarding Me as the Supreme End, and to nothing else turning, for him I become without delay, the rescuer from the ocean of death-bearing, migratory existence. By reason of My being the Onlooker the universe revolves.
>
> Those devoted to the gods go to the gods; to the ancestors go those devoted to ancestors. Those go to the evil spirits who worship them, and My worshipper also comes to Me. I am beyond the destructible, and superior even to the indestructible; therefore in the Vedas am I called The Supreme. Whoso sees the Supreme, sees indeed."—Krishna, in the *Bhagavad Gita*

The ancient Hebrews filled their scrolls with prophecies of the day when all mankind should look to the far heights for the opening of their outer eyes to see the supernal lands through which, ever stumbling, they with downcast gazing do daily travel. And the pages of their sacred books blaze with inspired urgings to greet the onlooking Deity:

> "The eyes of man, as of all tribes of Israel, shall be toward the Lord. The Lord shall be seen over them, and the Lord of Hosts shall defend them. "Say unto the cities of Judah, Behold your God.—Seek ye Me, and ye shall live."

The Taoist declared that this is the rest for which the earth-wearied are panting. The prophet of Israel saw that the coming rest from competition and struggle would be irksome to the age of hurry:

> "The burden shall be rest, in the day when the eyes of man shall be turned toward the Lord."
>
> "This people refuseth the waters of *Shiloh* (rest) that go softly, and rejoice in *Rezin*" [warfare, strenuous exertion].

The saving effects of the exalted attention are oft-times proclaimed by the Jewish psalmists:

> "Because thou hast made the Most High thy habitation, there shall no evil befall thee, neither shall any plague come nigh thy dwelling."

> "Who is like unto Him who exalteth Himself to dwell on high? He raiseth the poor out of the dust that He may set him with princes."

History discloses that no word of self disparagement or thought of fear counts against the saving grace that hastens to defend, or against the tender mercy that upholds, when that deathless soul faculty, the inner eye, lifts toward the Absolute beyond the Light, where not Spirit, but the Cause that Spirit is, doth ever call, "Behold who hath created."

"We have no might against this great company that cometh against us neither know we what to do; but our eyes are upon Thee." And the Ammonites, Moabites, and Seirs, or the difficulties, inherited difficulties, and causes for discouragement, fled away from the besieged Jehosophat.

In simple meekness the king had stated his humiliating status, but he did the one thing he with all his army knew how to do — he looked, not with some mysterious sense we have to search for, we who are commanded to lift up our attention to the same all-accomplishing One, but with the everyday-used inner sense with which we can look back to our native city, or forward to the sunset.

This subtle faculty, swifter than the fleetest thought, being steadfastly rested upon any unknown point, can bring back to the waiting mind all the facts that pertain to the resting place. That we have let it fall most abidingly upon already transpired events, and drawn it away from the unexperienced, has been our own choice, indicating not at all the inadequacy of the able sense.

Columbus set his eye toward an unknown and unbelieved-in shore, and landed his ships upon it. Thus goes he toward the unknown I am, who sets his eye Himward.

> "Take sanctuary with Him alone, O Bharata's son, and thou shalt find the eternal abode." —Krishna, in the *Bhagavad*

Gita.

Speech follows the direction of the visional sense. A man's words therefore soon expose why he is unfortunate or triumphant, great or inconsequent.

> "Therefore will I direct my prayer unto Thee, whom my outer eyes behold not, and I will look up. Early in the morning will I lift up mine eyes unto Thee."—*Psalms.*

> "The ruffian looked at me, and wrought against me ... diseases. So mayest Thou heal me, Thou most glorious One."—*Zend Avesta.*

It is the lifting up of this sense out of the network of materiality, the wheel of incessant grind that takes man above his disasters and difficulties. "Mine eyes are ever toward Thee, for Thou shalt pluck my feet out of the net," cried David.

David's net was the wheel of events that harassed him, exactly as untoward events and disappointing circumstances worry the sons of men today. Down into these shadows streams a divine radiance, discovering to such as turn their gaze toward the Source of the Light Hypostatic, another outlook over affairs, more than compensating for the failures that menaced while the gaze was buried in misfortunes.

One above looketh toward man and his affairs. He is of purer eyes than to behold evil. Looking unto Him giveth some gleams of His view, for, "In Thy light I see light."

Nothing he could say disturbed these effulgent beams from doing according to their own upholding ordinance, when Ezra was fearing his downfall: "When I said, My foot slippeth, Thy mercy, O Lord, held me up," he gratefully acknowledged. Had he not practiced the precept of the sages of the ages, by which practice he must experience that they who look to the far heights never falter? Had he not looked to the Source of the mercy that saves?

Notice how the Greeks and Romans thanked the merciful beams from heavenly Mercury, touching them with magistral to poverty, and removing from their heads the guilt of their deceits.

Innocentius of Carthage, overcome with speechless emotions of fear and grief, looks to Him who alone can strengthen him for his crucial hour. Suddenly he finds that the surgical operation he has prayed for strength to survive, has been performed by invisible agency, and the saws and knives of material science are not necessary. For the angel of the Lord encampeth round about them that have the single eye that filleth the body with light, and delivereth them.

> "Thus shall all the bodily world become free from old age and death, from corruption and decay, forever and ever."—*Vendidad.*

Ignorance counts nothing against one whose attention is steadfastly set toward the Countenance that shineth as the sun in his strength. Each one of us is darkly untutored on some vital point. In the day of effulgence from above, the ignorant master and the ignorant scholar shall perish out of the earth. For they shall all be taught of the High Supreme, not wisdom, but the Cause that wisdom is:

> "Thus will I magnify Myself, and I will be known in the eyes of many nations."

> "And I will show thee great and mighty things, which thou knowest not."

Of new information has the Original of wisdom abundant store, to give in liberal measure when He is sought as the Author of intelligence. Therefore exalt Him and He shall shed new light upon thee, and upon all the inhabitants of earth. For by the obedience of one shall many shine forth.

Speak unto Him face to face, and no longer speak of Him. Speak unto Him over and over, as Asaph the seer. Three times in the midst of his song did he chant "Turn us again. Cause Thy face to shine, and we shall be saved." By repetition he welded the attention of his wandering-eyed, weak-minded people toward the saving and illuminating heights.

No sage of earth has ever declared himself any other than a seeker after the way of the Light that can raise the dead and heal the foolish; but Jesus of Nazareth said, "I am the way." Appollonius, who cured the diseased and called back the dying, traveled far to find if Indian or Egyptian priests could give him the law of life. But none could declare it, for all that they had spoken of the life-bringing Light had been spoken in moments transcending their natural reason. "I am the life," said Jesus of Nazareth.

Guatama, who wrought many miracles, proclaimed himself a seeker after truth. "I am the truth," said Jesus of Nazareth. "We look for one to overcome nature's dominion," said Plato. "I have overcome the world," said Jesus of Nazareth. "When Messias cometh, He shall teach us," said the woman at the well, echoing Plato's expectation. "I that speak unto thee am He," said Jesus of Nazareth. "I know that my brother shall rise again at the last day," said Martha. "I Am the resurrection," said Jesus of Nazareth.

This Man demonstrated His declarations by prompt proofs. He set the bands of death at naught, saying, "No man taketh My life from Me, I lay it down of Myself." He nullified the limitations of matter, as, looking up, He multiplied food, and walked upon the waters.

And whether this Man is speaking as an historic character, not yet having shown that in His own person He transcends death, or as a risen and triumphant glory, exhibiting to all beholders a body that cannot be absorbed into death, He is ever setting His seal upon the doctrine that had preceded Him, that all great transactions come into manifestation by reason of the right view of some steadfast seer.

"When disasters of nations come, and earthquakes, with seas and waves roaring, then look up."—*Luke* 21.

And He, looking up, spake with a loud voice, and the dead arose.

On the three circuits where He found mankind struggling, He met them with the reviving elixirs of the heavenly vision, and caused them to outdo themselves. He put into living text the lost old Persian declaration, that with right glance and right speech a man superintendeth the animate and inanimate.

On the first circuit, He stretches out His hand and touches wine, bread, and clay, and they obey His will to step out of their captivity to habit. The wines of the mystic islands rise through the Cana waters. Bread unfolds from the ether's mysterious opulence. Clay hides the sightless eyeballs till the eye divine sends healing light, and clay shows strange hidden fire as the child of Nain quickens to life.

On the second circuit, He sends forth His voice and there is overplus of increase for the needy, and His hearers learn the mystery of the Logos, alive in every spoken word baptized by beams from the life-giving God.

On the third circuit, He warms the fishermen with coals which no man's hands have kindled, and prepares them to live henceforth by the dispensation of daily miracles wrought from above, that they may be the joy and enlightenment of ages to come.

On the first circuit, He finds people appreciating the tangible and material things of life, and He blesses the material things with something from above, but He says, "Flesh profiteth nothing."

On the second circuit, He finds certain among His bearers advocating the power of thought, urging the dominion of mind, and He blesses the thoughts of mind with something from above, as He says, "I give you mouth and wisdom," but He adds, "In such an hour as ye think not," and, "Take no thought."

All the transforming power which He uses on matter and mind He draws from above, teaching plainly that matter and mind must forever keep within restricted bounds of

High Mysticism

performance, till all the world looks up and draws down authority to unseal their limitations. "Canst thou by taking thought (alone) make one hair white or black?" "Blessed are those servants whom the Lord when He cometh shall find watching."

Those who set their attention toward the Count-enance of the high and lofty One inhabiting eternity, are in the way of the ransomed from sin, disorder, and death. And the ransomed are offered two songs: "The Song of Moses, and the Song of the Lamb."

A song is a perpetually recurring note of speech or singing, concerning some one theme. "I am become their song," cried Job. The ransomed return with singing. They know the Name of the Highest which stands among men for The Absolute as Origin of Being, Might, Majesty. This Name was the song of Moses and of Zoroaster, those personifications of strength in leadership by the inspira-tion of Deity.

It is the Name taken up by all who lift the incorporeal eye toward the Author of Being, Might, Majesty. It was the Name the earliest known Egyptians had buried with them in their tombs, as full of the significance of immortality. It is as immaculate as the vision that is uplifted.

It is not the final name of the Cause of Being, Cause of Truth, Cause of Spirit, for proper name for the Father, the Unbegotten, there is as yet none known among men.

> "These terms, Father, God, Creator, Lord, are not names, but terms of address derived from His benefits and works."— Justin Martyr.

But the Name which is called the Song of Moses, is the highest name speakable by man at his present stage of expression. It has no reference to benefits or works. It stands by itself alone. It is applied to no other but One. It is, I Am that I Am. The term of address, or name God, stands for many objects of worship; the substantive Spirit, has many significations, it may mean one of twenty different descriptives; the name Lord, is employed in ten different ways, but the I Am that I Am is One. "When the children of Israel shall say: What is His name? What shall I answer. Say the I Am hath sent thee."

And He led them with His glorious arm, dividing the waters before them, to make for Himself an everlasting Name.

The Name I Am, addressed to the Highest, wakens the spirit of authority, majesty, undefeatable courage, in the breast of even the meekest and weakest of men. "I have wrought with you for My Name's sake," spake His voice to Ezekiel.

The Name I Am that I Am, brings up from the deep wells of hidden strength in all men, the sincerity, boldness and intelligence of leadership, and that originality of action and language which have characterized the heroes of the ages, whose names have lived so long in history that they have become myths.

It is recorded of one of these, that in deepest humility, asking of the Self-Existent face to face, His most order-bringing Name, he heard the words, *Ahmi Yot Ahmi* — I Am that I Am. And this man became ruler of a kingdom, and founder of the Wisdom of the Magi. He had touched the leading note of that Ineffable Name which is key to the mysteries of the universe.

This Name is the first utterance of those who set their attention toward the Heights, whence fall the kindling sparks that burn away the films hiding the finished splendor of the realm through which we walk.

And the Song of the Lamb is the second utterance of the upward-visioned among us. It is the name Jesus Christ "In My Name" said he that was slain. "In His Name," said his disciples. And it is declared that they never preached any doctrine except the power of His Name, This was their Song. It is a Name as immaculate as the Name I Am. It always means, God with us. It is the *Amita Buddha*, the *Ahura*

Mazda,[7] the *Emmanuel*. It is that Name of the Lofty and Everlasting I Am which represents his nearness and immanence. Name above principalities and powers, it is the Name of newness, of healing, and of comforting tenderness. It gives the baptism of the quickening Spirit. It is the greatest and quickest God-formulating Name.

It is the Name that restores the lost word, the now unspeakable Name of the Self Existent Deity. The Moravians hymn the power of this Name:

"Should I reach my dying hour,
Only let them speak that name;
By its all prevailing power,
Back my voice returns again."

And they tell of miracles of calling back from the dark defile of voiceless death to sunlit life, by the resurrecting energy of this Name.

The rulers of the Jews in Jerusalem, Annas the high priest, and Caiaphas, and John, and Alexander, and as many as were of the kindred of the high priest, A.D. 33, knew well the Magian power contained in certain names, and they asked, "By what name have you wrought this miracle?" "By the Name of Jesus Christ," answered the Christian Apostles.

The risen Christ, appearing suddenly, said, "Preach repentance, in My Name, beginning at Jerusalem." And Jerusalem means The Self.

Begin with yourself, to repent, to return. Lift up the willing inner sight toward the Supreme One, whose soundless edict through the ages is, "Look unto Me, and be ye saved." Taste the first manna which the upward watch sprinkles over the unfed brain and heart.

This is reasonable service. It is mirific obedience.

Facing toward the Heights, where the smile of the Comforting One begins its beaming Omnipresence, Omnipotence, Omniscience, speak from the heart the two greatest Names ever written or spoken on earth. They are the only

---

[7] *Ahura Mazda* is the Zoroastrian name of the divinity in personal form.

response the heart can make when the mystic eye is first uplifted. Without the uplift of the deathless sense the Names may be but heathen repetitions. For liberation is not achieved by the pronunciation of the Name, without direct perception. But consonant with the upward watch, these terms of address to Deity are the planting of the feet upon the rock of power and the transmeable hills of security.

> "He sent from above, He took me, He drew me out of many waters. Thou also hast lifted me up on high, above them that rose up against me."

Whatever comes upon you this day, or threatens to disturb or overthrow at any time, turn then away from it toward that High Deliverer looking hitherward, and within the silent heart sing the two Wonderful Songs of the Seers of the ages:

> O high and lofty One inhabiting Eternity! Clothing Thyself with Thine own Omnipresence, Omnipotence, Omniscience, as with a garment, hiding Thy goodness and majesty with names, and unspeakable names! I know Thou Art, and the Name of power and glory I must address to Thee is I Am.

> O Countenance beholding me! Looking toward me through the ages—Breath of the everlasting life in me, and manna to my fadeless substance—Thy Name that folds me round with tenderness, and lifts me high above the pitfalls of my human destiny, is Jesus Christ.

2nd Study: Remission

NOTE

The Practice of the Presence of Deity, through obeying His one great commandment, Look unto Me, removes the sense of limitation and danger. This second Chapter tells us to persist in obedience till we thoroughly experience the five liberations. E.C.H.

We are so constituted that when we are told that the divine edict is, Look unto Me, we lift our inner visional sense to look toward the High Cause. The Spanish mystics urged mankind to look a thousand times an hour toward the Vast, Vast Countenance that shineth as the sun in his strength.

The beams of that Countenance are hot with healing. Proculus the slave felt them melting both his sickness and his chains, and Severus the Roman Emperor chose Proculus to live in the palace with him, because an ever-falling grace from above undid the disorders of those who came near Proculus.

Something is ever gently wooing us. It is the sin-undoing Saving Grace. It rides swiftly to our freedom on the thrill of our recognition. It exposes the Elysium which the saints of old told of in song and sermon. Every beam of light and every waft of air from sighting toward the Unsullied Heights is the touch of the dissolving alkahest, the remitting mystery, the saving grace, removing some suffering, exposing some joy. Is it not written, "Look unto me, and be ye saved"?

One who had been utterly set free from the might of the flesh and its death, rose, an un-trammeled being, and said, "Preach Remission." Preach the removal—the putting away of the consequences of the downward vision, which appear as evil, matter, lack, pain, decay. Preach the freedom of those who notice that Deity onlooketh them.

A principle is a comprehensive law. As Jeremiah was brought to sickness and martyrdom by gazing much toward affliction, so they who look to the Unweighted First Cause are unweighted of sickness and the possibility of martyrdom. "Behold, I lay thy foundations with sapphires"—liberty. "They shall fight against thee, but they shall not prevail against thee."

The mind is not capable of bringing anything to pass except it be transfixed by inward visioning. Inner vision is the vital essential to the mind. When this faculty is exalted, the mind quickens with original ideas and has high instructions.

Hegel, turning his attention toward causes, got deeper than thinking, and wrote in his "Introduction to Logic" that we secretly perceive toward an object before thinking it, and it is only by having constant recourse by inward viewing that then the mind goes on to know and comprehend.

The High and Lofty One that inhabiteth Eternity offers to undo our weakness and our wretchedness, the laws of matter and the veneers of time, if we undiverted seek his face. He offers a new language, and the end of the world: "Look up, to the fields white for the harvest. The harvest is the end of the world." "They shall speak with new tongues."

As we are like those we face, dropping their unlikeness, it is not strange to find the mystics of all time joyously exclaiming that the Undifferentiated Self-Existent, the Abyssal Naught, has remitted for them the five dark unlikenesses to himself into which their aberrated watch had warped them. They have not been seeking liberation from bondage, they have only been seeking his face, according to the sacred edict, "Look unto Me," yet liberation has been as complete through the ecstatic moments of their contemplation as if they had entered Paradise. Read how the cosmic laws of matter and mind let go for Parmenides while seeking the High First Cause, "not life but the cause that life is."

The experiences of the mystic have been reported as the shouts of the free. Their shouts have been the creedal

High Mysticism 273

formulas of philosophical and religious organizations without number. The zealous lovers of the formulas have often forgotten that matter does not loose the grip of its law if the vision is not toward the heights; that evil lets go its claims only when the dayspring from on high drops its dewy sunshine into the heart; but all the same the world has loved to hear the lovers of the formulas sing the *non-est-ness* ['is-not-ness'] of evil, matter, pain, decay. The world has always sought its mystic nihilists when it has wanted its prison doors unlocked: "I will turn back your captivity from before your eyes, saith the Lord."

High mysticism is divine nihilism. Truly, there is no knowledge except what is taught straight from him who saith, "I will instruct thee, and teach thee." Truly, there is safety from drowning for any Peter who looks away from the stormy waters of human existence to Him who saith, "The flames shall not kindle, the waters shall not overflow, nothing shall by any means hurt you," sang the prophet Isaiah.

It is preaching remission when we tell the Unweighted Light face to face, that we know our surety of unburdened life under his healing smile. It is prayer; and prayer is ever a psalm of freedom: "Am I not an Apostle? Am I not free?"

If the vision be on high where the illimitable skies in untrammeled buoyancy shine chastely down, purity of moral tone and flawlessness of body are manifest. Vanity, dissembling, cowardice, are remitted, dissolved; sickness, weakness, disease, are removed. The original self, denuded of its crass teguments, forgets its history in matter. The former earth is forgotten. It does not come into mind any more.

He unto whose face we look hath vouchsafed to no man his name, and none as yet knoweth his nature. We know his promises, his gifts, his responses; but as our only carrying energy, the inward visional sense, has been engaged in fetching either gladness or sorrow from other objectives than his glory, we have nothing sublimer than Life, Love, and Spirit, of which He is the Giver, to describe. These being his gifts, and already among the tangible and practical experiences of man, it is not surprising that the subtler triumphs undergirding those who have sought the Giver and not the gifts have not been understood. For only the original of knowing can say, "I will show thee great and mighty things which thou knowest not."

Under the worship of *Amen*, the Unknown and Unknowable High Cause, Thebes, the Metropolis of Egypt was the seat of kings, and triumphed over all the world. Under the worship of *Aton* — Life, Truth, and Love, or Truth, Happiness, and Sunshine, Thebes flourished in splendor for a period, was rich, magnificent, and pompous, and then suddenly went out. Life and Love may not say, "Look unto me and be ye masters of life." They may not go higher than repletion with their like. Only their Author is their Master, and he only can confer mastership.

> "All the nations shall fear and tremble for all the goodness and for all the prosperity that I procure thee saith the Lord."

> "Thou canst not behold me with thy two outer eyes; I have given thee an eye divine."

"Concerning the Almighty we cannot find him out. With him is terrible majesty — Behold God is great and we know him not," chanted the awe-struck Elihu.

Paul, in his Mars Hill address, declared the Unknown God who giveth life and spirit. He could not describe his nature nor name his greater name than I Am that I Am. But it was immortalizing to Paul himself to call the gaze higher than life and spirit, to the *Ain Soph*[8] of the Kabbala, the "Great Countenance of the Absolute, above thinking and above being."

"My Father is greater than I," was the upward-calling statement of Jesus; and his eye being ever toward the Divine

---

[8] The *Ain Soph* means the "Source of Wisdom" or "Highest Knowing" and is the aim of those who study the Kabbala, the Jewish mystical tradition.

High Mysticism

Original, he was ever Master of life. "I can lay down my life, and I can take up my life," he said.

As there is rich newness over the Tao, or Highway, we need not fear to let go all that goes under its dissolving beams. Is it not written that no man can see that face and live according to his former estate? That his former estate shall shuffle off—be remitted?

Sell all, let all move aside—let go, and give to The Poor, The Unknowable Absolute, the Unhindered God, The Unweighted I Am, The Predicateless Being. This is the universal insistence of inspired mystics. We have only one thing to give, namely, our attention. There is one Poor, namely, The Unencumbered First Cause. "Who holdeth fast to The High First Cause, of him the world shall come in quest."

Preach the deliverance of the captive. Acknowledge high. Tell the One High Cause, that being Untrammeled Freedom in himself, all who look to him are untrammeled. Tell him that fear and doubt depart. Tell him that captivity itself is led captive, and only unvanquished Soul salutes Him.

The dissolving alkahest, the gentle grace that falls down over the track of the vision, has been praised by the sages of the ages, for there is surcease of world pain in its white softness: Behold the gentle neutral that taketh away the mistakes of the world.

Five grievous shades slip off the earth. They are the foolish virgins with no oil of healing and no oil of illuminating in their most eloquent declarations. No one describing them was ever to himself or to his neighbors, the oil of joy for mourning, nor ever the inspiration of wisdom while detailing their processes. It is the passing of these five shadows that has caused the five great shouts of liberty, the high sounding *Pehlevi*, the psalms of remission, the prayers of the released:

1 Steadfastly facing Thee, there is no evil on my pathway.
2 Steadfastly facing Thee, there is no matter with its laws.

3 Steadfastly facing Thee, there is no loss, no lack, no absence, no deprivation.

4 Steadfastly facing Thee, there is nothing to fear, for there shall be no power to hurt.

5 Steadfastly facing Thee, there is neither sin, nor sickness, nor death.

Preach remission, said the Risen Christ. Preach that the iron gates open of their own accord for upward gazing Peter.

Preach that the stone of interference looming on our life path is rolled away, as for the two Marys.

Preach that palsy falls off Aeneas, and death falls off Dorcas. Understand what the Vedas are hymning —

"O thou Unshaken One!

By thy favor my delusions are destroyed!"

Matter and its laws of mind are the fictitious generations of oft-time downward glancing with our efficient visional sense. When this sense is lifted up, what seemed external exists no more at all. The inner vision leads off the other senses and if it is exalted toward the Healing Onlooker all the senses aver health. "For I am the Lord that healeth thee." "The way of life is above to the wise, that he may depart from hell beneath." "Seek ye my face and live."

It is a very subtle doctrine, that man is like that to which his inner eye is oftenest directed.

It has been called the secret doctrine, because whoever discourses on the laws of mind, or describes the omni-presence of Life, Truth, Spirit, has not touched the secret of Deity's look toward him and his look toward Deity. In this sight, or science, is denuding, even of spirit. "Blessed are the poor in spirit." Something transcending Spirit smiles. Let the spirit blow where it listeth. "There is no man that hath power over the spirit," said Solomon, for Spirit is the servant of the High Deliverer — the I Am that I Am. "Behold, I will pour out my spirit upon you."

After years of austerity and singleness of eye, the Hindu mystic finds that the Deity who looketh toward us, saying,

High Mysticism

"Look unto me," is not Spirit, for Spirit arises in opposition to matter, and Deity is above distinction. He notes that he only who perceives the Lord as Difference-less, goes to the Supreme End.

"He is not Being," says Erigena, the Irish mystic,
"for here is an arising of contradistinction; he cannot be called goodness, for goodness is opposed to badness, and God is above this distinction."

Proculus, learned in the ritual of the World's invocations, concludes that Deity is best described by negations, since only his gifts are knowable. "He is not that" we may insist to all men's descriptions of Deity. Job finds his swollen flesh dissolving, when he sets his witness in the heavens. "Thou dissolvest my substance, he cries." Then the strong man of him springs up under the remitting but energizing light, and his last days are more triumphant than his youth and prime.

Specialists multiply that which they investigate. There shall never be an understanding of how fadeless health is roused, so long as the physical system, that faithful register of woe and vigor brought on the wings of secret viewing, is sought as the informer. Only by the study of the Uncontaminated One that inhabiteth Eternity shall unspoilable wholesomeness laugh in the substance of living creatures. Only his way upon the earth is the saving health of the nations.

The material body is a hard taskmaster. What it ought to be fed with and how it should be housed and trained — see how it worries us with never telling us. The sons of the Tao know that neither if they eat are they the better, nor if they eat not are they the worse. Every mouthful shines with new mystery, and buoys up the system as on wings of might; every abstinence leaves the veins free for the sunshine of the Beatific Uplands to flow in radiant strength along. Who can prove this till he has oft-time torn his gaze from the wheel of things to behold the Unencumbered Highest?

The mind is a wearisome objective. Its thoughts have laid claim to great powers of destruction and great powers of building.

With the brightness of the I Am beaming upon them, even their wrath is praise of the Unthinkable Absolute. Jesus can look around with anger, being grieved, and the withered arm stretches forth, restored whole as the other. Under the baptism of the Divine Smile, the wickedness of the wicked shall not destroy, and the righteousness of the righteous shall not save. The tender mercy, the day spring from on high, remits the thoughts of the mind. Man's inheritance of things that have not been conceived by mind comes into sight by looking to the Unknowable, who originates new knowing. "I will teach thee." "I will turn to the people a pure language."

He who watches for the erroneous thought that caused the malady of his neighbor shall find it alighting upon himself: "The watchers for iniquity shall be cut off; that make a man an offender for a word."

"We wrestle against the rulers of the darkness of this world," said Paul. He is speaking of the wrestle of the morning of health that dawns on the upward watch, with the midnight of disease that glooms with looking toward mind and body. All the ways of darkness are removed by the Light that falls with remitting grace upon him who notices that the Deity looketh upon him. "Look up to the fields white for the harvest." "The harvest is the end of the world." "Speak ye comfortably to Jerusalem. Tell her that her warfare is accomplished." There is one universal dissolvent. It is the falling alkahest, the whiteness that makes death let go, that looses the bands of palsy and of pain. There is no pain facing Thee.

Steadfastly looking for high news, Origen finds that "evil has no substance." Plotinus, on the same quest, becomes aware that "matter is nothing." Hezekiah, more awake than they, rises in free majesty, because, "The earth and all the inhabitants thereof are dissolved." Isaiah, greatest of the seers, finds that "All nations before him are as nothing, and they are counted unto him as less than nothing." Job, meekest of all under the ever-beholding Solvent, yields himself in joyous dissolution—"Thine eyes are upon me, and I am not."

The assurances of the stately scholars called mystics, have ever been, that all the hurting powers are nullified—remitted, for him who looks away to the Divine Original:

"No weapon formed against thee shall prosper."

"No bad fame can hurt thee."

"Thou shalt be far from oppression."

"Terror shall not come near thee."

Their accepted formula has not been that the world is divine, and all things are God, but the world is nothing—the Lofty One inhabiting Eternity is The Alone—The All.

Looking downward, we weep at loss and lack, while the offer has ever been that there shall be no lack for the beholders of the smile of the *Ain Soph*. Obeying the sacred edict, "Look unto me," woman's cry of no wine of life—the health, strength, praise, of which she never feels she has a plenitude—ceases. She hungers no more. She wants for no good thing. "Woman, what have I to do with thee?" says Jesus, when Mary declares, "They have no wine." Woman has ever been the propagator of lack. She is to be first to declare, "They shall want for no good thing facing Thee."

Man's strenuousness on every line desists; he labors not, he takes no thought. There is a way that looking toward labor and lack has hidden. Looking to the Heights, away from labor and lack, the way is visible.

"I will lead thee by a way that thou hast not known."

"The people shall not say, I am sick."

"They shall not see death."

"I am the Lord that healeth thee."

This truth of the nonhindrance of matter and mind, as the beams of the shining countenance penetrate to the hidden man of the heart, has the testimony of many sages of the ages. It is the Mystical Vision and Union which Dionysius discovered gave him "that most divine knowledge of Almighty God, which is known through not knowing."

It constitutes that union which Plotinus declared, "Enkindles our life flame, giving rest to the soul now fled up, away from evil, to the place free from evils." How worth while to view above time and sense, preaching the inevitable remission, taking the instructions of the sages of the ages who have experienced it!

Sometimes these great forerunners have called our mental, moral, and physical characteristics and comports, "our garments folded around in our descent to view the not-God." And they show how one by one these garments have fallen from them on their upward-fleeing vision. "Love of honor is the last garment to be stripped away, as we show ourselves more and more like the Divine," is the remission preached by Proculus.

According to all these illumined ones, it is the Omnipotence through all things that binds them all in such sympathy. The crawling worm is brother to the archangel, in the fact of his central spark being God. And wherever remission is experienced, there is the miracle of the creature divinely transcending environment. Preaching remission uncovers the divinity at the center, because it entices the eye heavenward, whence the uncovering day-springs hail.

The illuminati of the world, each manifesting according to his own recognition of the Supreme, have been at all times living proofs of the efficiency of setting the look toward the Self-Existent Heights. Unto some it is the manifest readjustment of environments. Unto others it is the forgetfulness of environments. Unto some it is joy in shining health of body. Unto others it is forgetfulness that the body exists.

Union with divine Freedom, the heavenly Poor, is fraught with resultants near and far. The world receives a treatment as the pioneer on high plains unifies with the free light. For the watcher shines forth as the sun with the healing glory of his Father above. Why may not the dead rouse past their cerements, if some pioneer abides undiverted in sight of that peace which Cosimo di Medici saw folding round Antonino, to such effect that it stopped earthquakes? The world awaits the great Peace Treat-ment.

Whether the Unweighted Heights are sought in coldly scientific mood, or in religious warmth, to inspire the particular from the Universal, that which would hedge the free self removes. "Watch the Way," said Nahum, "so fortifying thy powers mightily."

Ezra is scientific: "I will lift up mine eyes to the hills, from whence cometh my help;" but he makes haste to be religious: "I have gone astray like a lost sheep; seek thy servant, Lord. Great peace have they which love thy law, and nothing shall offend them."[9]

He who learns that gazing upward toward his Father's face is a liberating act, rouses with fresh hope. He senses that he is greater than what has heretofore happened to him. He forgets his calamities. He is on the pathway of salvation from the causes of calamity.

The free, wise, immortal center of man is the begotten of God. Only this uninjurable and shining principle is offspring of I Am that I Am. Not only the free and unspoilable soul, spirit, of Jesus, but the soul, the hidden spark, of Nero, is Son of the Highest; Jesus being unclothed of matter with its mind and temper; Nero, being heavily garmented therewith. The upward vision saves Nero or Jesus. There is no respect of persons on the high watch. "Mine eyes are ever toward the Lord; for he shall pluck my feet out of the net,"

---

[9] These lines are from the Psalms and are usually attributed to David, but Emma seems here to be attributing them to Ezra, the man who some believe integrated the various "books" and oral traditions into what we now call the Hebrew Bible or Old Testament.

may be proclaimed by bad and good alike. "God is the bad man's deliverer," gratefully sang the ancient Chinese sages.

The remission loved by Proculus was the disappearance of memory and idea while raising eyes to the Predicateless One. The remission loved by those who lift their eyes to the Predicateless One in this age, is the removal of the hurting powers of life and death, riches and poverty, sin and virtue. They look for the day of Wisdom to break, and the shadowy night of ignorance to flee away.

The ordinance of the Highest, "Look unto me," requires an individual practice. It compels a life of its own. It exposes the doctrine known to Jesus of Nazareth, who said, "If any man will do his will, he shall know of the doctrine." At the point of knowing right doctrine, an influence emanates which clarifies all atmospheres. The neighbors of the knower drop their errors of thought and conduct. They start to seek the highest good at the highest fountain.

This is that cognition which irradiates, till kings consider that which they have not been told, as Isaiah prophesied.

Gazing toward the One and Indivisible, Parmenides learned that the phenomenal world with its origination and decrease, multiplicity and diversity, is non-being, and illusion. This knowledge extended forth from him, rousing sublimity of character and conduct in his adherents. Leading a noble life was denominated the Parmenidian life among the Greeks for centuries, so influential had been the remission preached by Parmenides.

But if, indeed, there were no radiance from the watcher's clarified being, he would love and preach the High Eternal I Am, whose assurance is union by vision. The heart would praise and extol Him whose look toward man remits all unlike His own nature. To the real heart there is joy in the divine fact that there are treasures of knowledge laid up for him whose true foundation is freedom by the look of his God upon him, dissolving his mentals, and setting aside his bodily hindrances. To the heart there is gladness in knowing that remitted conditions leave exposed the secret original Self from which transcendent character springs forth, daily honoring the Father with the beauty of Soul Integrity.

The second angel sounds; man acknowledges the liberty that he senses by obeying the high mandate, and the mountain of all personal obligation rolls into the sea. The I Am that I Am, of Unspeakable Majesty, is seen to be the Only Responsible One. Like St. Augustine, in his hurried glance, man attains to the vision of that which is: trouble as a shadow has flown; he cannot find it. Only untrammeled God is Real. "Is there any beside Me?" Anxiety is no more. With Maimonides, Spinoza, and Gerson, in their diviner moments, proclaiming that evil has no existence forever, the obedient watcher heavenward walks the buoyant path of fearlessness. He bursts the bonds of desire and its attainment. He breathes above ambition. The wonderful God makes him a preacher of the heavenly remission. He tells of Him above Truth, whose works are truth; of Him who saves from old age and death, disease and poverty, ignorance and competition. He joins the singers of the God-born Vedic Hymn:

"Destroyed is the knot in the heart;
Removed are all doubts:
Extinct are all the hidden longings,
Upon beholding Thee." —*The Vedas*

Let us set aside a day to telling over to Him unto whose Divine Countenance we look, the wonderful remissions, the heavenly liberations promised to those who oft-time turn away from smothering environments, to face the Lover inhabiting Eternity—the Lord of Hosts is his name. Let us boldly acknowledge, as we lift up our eyes unto the Deliverer, the Limitless: "Because Thou art the Unconditioned and Absolute, I also am unconditioned and absolute. Because thou art The Free, I also am free. Because Thou art The Self-Existent, I also am self-existent."

3rd Study: For-Giveness

NOTE

This Third Study is prepared so that even those who have not heard its subject matter orally can understand that the High Vision which awakens high thinking and incites to noble living has been the Vital Theme of the preceding studies. Something always antedates thought. That something is Vision.

"Look unto Me" is the Sacred Edict.   E. C. H.

When Aristides, wise Archon of Athens, was so ill that his physicians left him, he saw as in a half dream the goddess Athena/Minerva with her shield. She was to him in his dream even more beautiful than her Athenian statue by Great Phideas. He called out to those about him to hear her words relating to honey from Mount Hymethus and the new diet he must observe. His family could not hear or see the goddess but they prepared the honey and arranged the diet exactly according to his report, and he soon recovered. Aristides declared that Aesculapius was with Minerva at the time, shedding healing breaths over all her balmy words.

From unprejudiced standpoint there does not seem to be any striking difference between the experience of the Archon of Athens attending to his two gods, and the Christians later on attending to their one God.

"When earthly helpers fail and comforts flee,
Help of the helpless, O remember me!"

Two gods with benignant smilings; one God with smiling benignance!

Throughout all time there has been tacit understanding that when half gods go the gods arrive. Some let go of their half gods with tears and lamentings, bemoaning the departure of all earthly helpers and hitherto comfortings; and some take hold of unseen help with groanings and grim determinations, whereby they terribly earn their blessings, heroically forgetting, "Cast all your care." "My yoke is easy and my burden light."

It was easy for Aristides, wise Archon of Athens, to let go his earthly helpers for they all forsook him and fled, and it was easy for him to receive healings from his gods for he was half asleep when they dropped their sweetly worded balsams on his head. It is the wisdom of Jesus that he enjoins being wide awake and easily letting go, and wide awake and easily catching on, to the sprinkling alkahests, all soundless nepenthe ever falling on all our heads: "Hurt not the oil of letting go; nor the wine of healing inspiration."

Repent for remission, receiving the Ghost that maketh whole.

John the Revelator is not choosing haphazard the chalcedony stone as the third lesson of divine law. The chalcedony signifies awakening strength: "Awake, awake, put on thy strength, O Zion!" Look up to fields white for harvest; so shall old conditions dissolve; so shall Holy Ghost arrive — white breath that maketh strengthening wholeness.

Mankind sticks to a triune of some kind. It is his mysterious instinct. Pythagoras called Three the number of Divine Law. The Jews have always regarded Three as a specially complete and mystic number, and we may note that this Lesson Three with its wide application, holds all the twelve lessons in its norm, or pattern, if we read its purport aright. It is but interpreting the story of three-faced Hecate to our own generation. Whatever way men regarded Hecate, that way or face would she show herself to them.

So also God the Father Almighty, miracle-working Jehovah-Triumphant to the great prophets: God the Son Almighty, miracle-working Jehovah-Triumphant to Apos-tolic Christians: God the Holy Ghost Almighty, miracle-working Jehovah-Triumphant to the Apostles of the Mystical Dispensation just winging its white influence across our awakening planet.

So far, this third dispensation of the Triune God in the Universe has not shown forth the mighty miracles of the first

High Mysticism

or prophetic dispensation: nor did the second, or Apostolic, dispensation show itself equal in grandeur of performance to the first: but the halt in splendor of achievement has had more universal promise in all that has been done, as if a whole globe were being bathed in softly stealing Brahmic Breath where astonishing whirlwinds had once glued the world's awe-struck attention.

When Moses, legislator of the Hebrew nation and founder of the Jewish religion, called to God the Father Almighty to divide the Red Sea before the two million Israelites fleeing from Egpytian bondage he heard his God saying, "Wherefore criest thou unto Me? Speak unto the children of Israel that they go forward, and lift thou up thy rod, and stretch out thine hand over the sea, and divide it: and the children of Israel shall go on dry (ground) through the midst of the sea."

When Joshua needed that the light of day should keep on while the Amorites were fighting his people, till his people should win in the battle being waged against them, "Then spake Joshua unto the Lord . . . Sun, stand thou still upon Gibeon" — and the sun stood still till the Israelites had shown supernal fighting genius to the five kings of the Amorites with their combined armies.

When Elisha chose to open the eyes of his servant Gehazi to see the Army of the Lord of Israel encamping in the mountain to defeat the army of the King of Syria, horses, chariots and soldiers a great host, then Gehazi saw the Army of the Lord with their chariots of fire filling the mountain of Dothan, movelessly and soundlessly fighting for Israel till the Syrian hosts had no more power to hurt the army of Israel.

When Ezekiel, worshipper of the Father Almighty raised the dead, he raised a whole valley full.

When the Apostles, worshippers of Sonship Almighty, preached the Risen Christ Jesus, they raised dead Eutychus and cured many taken with palsy and lameness.

When worshippers of the Holy Ghost, whom the Father Almighty hath sent because of the name of The Second Dispensation, or the Jesus Christ Dispensation, do works, they do them on a small scale, but being determinedly related to Universal Spirit, or Brahmic Breath, which is Holy Ghost Influence they sweep the globe with inspiration. For now is come that Great Spirit, the wind in the wings of the messengers of Jehovah-Triumphant; and everywhere the sound as of a mighty wind from heaven.

Has it not been declared that a Breath of Brahma wafts through our common atmospheres, breathable by all who choose to inhale it as strengthening spirit?

> O hither wafting breath of strength
> In Brahmic ether's keeping!
> Man may wax stronger day to day
> By the mystic way of reaping.

The Breath of Brahma was what Job was volitionally inhaling till it healed his mind of grieving and his bones of soreness.

Inspiration, or inbreathing of the air-encompassed Ghost, or heavenly Breath, is sure healing of the mind of man; sure transforming of his thinkings; sure healing of his body throughout all its flesh and bones; sure healing of his affairs also; but who is found indrawing winds his nostrils take no note of, gazing towards a hither wafting white breath his outer eyes see not? But truly, such only are those revivingly healthy among us who have learned that the healing breath never faileth, changeth never, abideth forever in miracle-working competences exactly as Job reported: "The breath of the Almighty giveth me life."

Why, O mankind, so decrepit, having power to partake of mystical renewal by quickening inspiration? "Ye shall receive power after that the Holy Ghost is come upon you" — quickening inspiration that waketh the hidden God-Seed; inspiration that cureth the mind of thinking; inspiration that draweth hitherward that Mind which no man as yet knoweth, the instantaneously working *Ain Soph* above thinking and above being; for-giving the mind of the world; hurrying along the promised speech that distills new health like morning dews.

With the sounding of the first angel, writes John the Revelator, there fall hail and fire, mingled with blood.

The first angel is the first call to Look Up.

Obeying the call, the resistless rule of the skies with soft alkahests dissolves opposition. The strenuousness of the laborer and the anarchist lets go. The strain of human existence is hailed upon with blessings from above. A new fervor glows in the speech. The heart of man fires up with knowledge of a right outshining the law of "Thou shalt not."

The sense of plentitude wakes the shout "All hail sweet riches!" for the groan "I want!" This is forgiveness. It is the beauty given for ashes that Isaiah saw across the ages.

In everything Hesekiah King of Judah, did, he was prospered, because his heart was in it. But though Amaziah did the thing that was right there was no enchantment in his deeds because his heart was not enlisted. The fire that John saw mingled with hail is the kindled heart.

And the blood that commingled was the new type of man that is even now already among us, healing and protecting when he appears, as the young man in the furnace protected the three friends of the compassionate king and presented them to him unharmed.

And one-third of the trees and all the green grass are burnt up by the fire of the new heart and speech, continues John. All the competitives that constitute the ginger and glow of human encounter, flourishing like trees for strength, give way to the miracle that sets each man into his right place. The hastening periods of childhood, youth, old age, forego. The man standing in the fiery furnace knows nothing of the seasons of life that are like the grass. Obedience to the mandate, "Look unto Me," introduces a new order. "I will give power to My two watchers" was the promise John heard from above, meant for any two of us who now begin the high watch that wooeth the God power.

"These are the two olive trees." These are those enriched and set in authority from above, not by effort, not by worthiness, but by resistless grace falling over their high watch, as Moses and Aaron of the upward-visioned Kohathites. "These are the two candlesticks," priests taught from above, speaking with new tongues, needing not that any man should teach them. These are the two olive branches, whose golden pipes send forth the golden oil of healing all unseen but resistless as the sky stones called healing hail; the golden oil of enwisdoming till kings know that they have never read, and understand that they have not been told; the golden oil of prospering till the poor lift up their heads with comfortings, wooed to comrade with those angels who minister cure to poverty. So shall the nations seek and find *Ain Soph*, the Great Countenance above thinking and above being.

With the sounding of the second angel, writes John the Revelator, the sense of personal responsibility, of heavy obligation, rolls softly away. Look up whence the high laws hail, unburdening the tongue of talk of hardship. If the tongue is yet speaking of hardship its owner has not sensed the second angel's message.

With the sounding of the Third Angel, said John the Revelator, the star called "Wormwood" — ware-mood, the mind preserving principle — wraps the conscious mind in sane security. The mind is forgiven its suggestibility to foolishness and ignorance. It is gathered to Unsuggestible Illumination, *Jehovah-tsid-kenu*.

Hitherto all healing has been directed for the body's benefit or for the lightening of hardship. Now it is that the mind no longer thinks, "I walk on the earth, or on the floor." The mind is cured of such thinking. It gives way to the sight of that foundation under our feet that is God Eternal. The mind is cured of thinking "I put my head on my pillow." It gives way to seeing underneath the God arms everlasting.

High Mysticism

The mind no longer thinks "I breathe common atmospheres." It gives way to glad discovery, "The Spirit of God is in my nostrils and the breath of the Almighty fashioneth me."

We always become like those with whom we associate. Did not the observing Herbert Spencer conclude that man is more like the company he keeps than that from which he is descended? The youth, Evison, who associated with sellers of salves and plasters, never grew any eyeballs in his empty eye-sockets till he began to attend faith-cure meetings, where his attention was steadily urged toward the curing sunshine of the Vast, Vast Countenance ever beaming toward him. Iamblichus noted that certain men had taken on majesty and superhuman accomplishing powers from constant association with the powerful gods.

Associate with the alkahest and its remitting abso-luteness is ours. Like Proculus at the king's court we bring dissolvings to pain. We associate by converse. "He that communicateth with me strengtheneth," saith the Lord of Strength. "He that speaketh unto me wakeneth. He that toucheth me is cured. To him that holdeth his convers-ation aright will I show salvation."

The third star was Wormwood, or the tonic of divine contagion. "Repent, for the remission, and ye shall feel the contagion," said Peter to the brethren. Repenting himself, he caught the curing contagions. "Now let signs and wonders be wrought!" he shouted. "The stretching forth of Thine hand, O God!" he said, as the curing flakes fell even upon his shadow.

"Hurt not the oil and the wine," cried the angel of the third seal. Hurt not the doctrine of denial, the cathartic oil of unburdening recognition and its speech, as, "Facing Thee, there is neither sickness nor death on my pathway." Hurt not the strengthening wine of affirmation, as, "there is none beside Thee. Thou Hast forgiven my mind."

"My bark is wafted from the strand

By breath divine.
And on the helm there rests a hand
Other than mine."

"The third, the face of a lion," writes the entranced Ezekiel. The lion is emblem of strength, sovereignty, and princely achievement. We are as strong as sovereign, as able, as our backing, our consort, our aid-de-camp. "I can kill a thousand snakes! I can build a house!" shouts the tiny child clinging to his father's hand. He feels the strength of his father. "By Thee have I broken through a troop! And by my God have I leaped over a wall!" proclaims David, clinging to his Father's hand. He feels the strength of his Father God. We all know how it has been prophesied that by associating with angels, man shall know new music, new architecture, new laws of life.

And the third stone in the foundation of character is the chalcedony, further describes John the Revelator. The chalcedony is copper-emerald, strength by associating with Strength: and sky-tinted opal, emblem of circumambient, quenchless life. Now have I bitten off a leaf from the tree of Immortality. Now have I partaken of Eternity's reviving breath. Now am I wise with high inspiration.

Fortify thy power by the contagion of Power, preached Nahum. He was proclaiming contagion, or forgiveness, beginning at the self, or Jerusalem, seven hundred years before the undestroyable Christ gave orders to declare strength for weakness and life for death, beginning each man with himself.

"Therefore I will look unto the Lord. Rejoice not against me O mine enemy! When I fall I shall arise again!" This is Micah, stronger than himself by reason of association with Sovereignty.

As the needle is nerved with magnetic power by communing with the magnet, so are we nerved with God-power by converse with the I Am that I Am, Author of Omnipotence:

"Thy influential vigor doth reinspire this waiting frame.

Thy lamp of hastening Omniscience shines newly on my liberated brain."

The Hindus drink always the cathartic oil of rejection. The Hebrews quaff deeply of the wines of acceptance. "Deity is best prescribed by negations. Life itself is to be denied till we are independent of life. Substance is to be rejected, till we, like Nanak the guru, are all invisible; sensations are to be disregarded till we can eat live coals, or lie buried in the ground unheeding that we breathe not." This is the religious exhibit of the Hindu.

"Preach the gospel, heal the sick, cast out demoniac dispositions, raise the dead." Welcome the contagion of All-Efficiency. Behold, God exalteth by his power; who teacheth like Him? This is the religious exhibit of the Hebrew.

"Making the great surrender, Spirit Almighty acts in our behalf," was the Christian discovery of the Spanish mystic Alvarez de Paz.

We can imbue with peace by recognizing the ever presence of everlasting Peace. We can separate our self unto any one force, or energy, or attribute, and by per-severing attention to it can become the embodiment of it. Did not Taglioni become the embodiment of rhythmic motion by practicing it? Did not Margaret of Paris become the embodiment of suffering by separating herself unto suffering? Did not Simon Magus imbue himself with the levitating principle emanating from the earth, by focusing all his attention to it till he was levitated thirty feet in the air?

Now is the time for us to choose the power, or force, or energy, we would embody in ourselves, and make essay at it till all its characteristics are ours and the efficiency that lies in it is our efficiency. Is it not written that "the works I do, ye shall do."

"Sing and rejoice, O daughter of Zion! For lo, I come, and will dwell in the midst of thee saith the Lord." Let us choose to be identified with the Lord strong and mighty, with Him able to keep us from falling, whose is the kingdom, the power, and the glory. For our contagion we will separate unto "the great, the mighty God, great in counsel and mighty to work."

The Lord Unknowable, All-Knowing, originates all knowing. The Intense, Inane All-Power, is the Author of all activity. The Mystical Stillness wakes tongues. Is it not written, "I will give mouth and wisdom which no man can gainsay"? Was not Stephen charged with Spirit so that he wrought spiritual miracles? Did not Peter speak with resistless eloquence to the converting of three thousand people in one day? Thus have the Real mystics of all time been tongues of fire, uncontrovertible logicians, magazines of scholarship, and the most virile and masculine energies of the age they have invigorated.

Every objective to which we give our attention has its storage of possibilities ready to spring forth and proceed *in extenso* [radiating outward, extending] through its devotee. Tennyson chose himself as the objective to his inner eye and made permutations and combinations of the stored vocabulary of "I Alfred Tennyson," till he was prince of song, so strong in his tones that all the world's harsh criticisms could not drown his supremacy.

Mind follows the visional sense. Hannah's grieved mind was suddenly transformed to joyous proclamations of the glory of living, and to praise of the prayer-answering God. But it had taken years of her obedience to the mandate of the forgiving Presence to have this sudden trans-substantiation by contagion of Divinity; not by contagion of the levitating principle emanating from the earth, nor by contagion of the "I Hannah, elder wife of Elkanah the Levite."

Jahaziel had elected to identify with Miracle-Working Spirit, and at the battle with the Ammonites he proclaimed that the Jews need not try to defend themselves for his Lord would fight for them. Like Hannah, he had come to the day of Fulfillment. Schopenhauer chose ascetic morality as the redeemer of the world. By this choice he finally struck the hard note by which his name is known: "God is the gigantic evil." The poet-scholar Leopardi taught mankind that a pitiless nature has man at its mercy. By this election his life, mind, and affairs were chased by poverty, despair and illness. These are all demonstrations on the blackboard of existence. They prove the transmuting energy resident in all objectives. They prove that what we now experience we need experience no longer. Our weakness waits transmuting for-give-ness. Our ignorance stays with us till our vision toward the Author of Omniscience comes to us with our own right knowledge. Come, gather to Him ever near, who for-giveth us altogether, so that we find ourselves holding our conversation aright: "O Thou Hast for-given myself with Thyself!"

There are unspoken wisdoms awaiting our separation unto the Giver of Wisdom. There is imperturbable health awaiting our separation unto the Imperturbable Author of Health. There is authority over the transactions of daily encounter by separation unto the Unconditioned and Absolute. "No oppressor shall pass through them any more, for now have I seen with mine eyes," declared Zechariah whose eyesight had been baptized from above. "With right glance and with right speech man superintendeth the animate and inanimate." Here we have Hebrew Prophet and Parsee[10] Sun-worshipper heading up with dominance by contagion with the Absolute. Is a man poor, he shall be poor no longer if he but separate himself unto the Owner, Chief Presence in the Universe. Is he witless, let him lift his vision, and like Elihu the Buzite, he shall fetch great knowledge from afar. He shall breathe that

"Breath of heaven all truth-revealing,

Kindling in him life divine."

---

[10] Parsee is the term used to describe the Zoroastrians from Persia who migrated to India. They aren't technically sun-worshippers, but the sun, and all flame, is the closest approximation to the divine nature and so is honored and often the center of rituals.

We always become negative, soft, plastic, to that objective unto which we oftenest give our inner eye. "God maketh my heart soft," said the devotee to God, Job the patriarch of Uz. The most powerful of the Babylonian kings, living at the time when metaphysics was the chief study among philosophers, softened his brain by the practice of reasonings such as Parmenides was giving in the science of *Ent.* and *NonEnt* [being and non-being]. "But at the end of the days I lifted up mine eyes unto heaven," he said;

> "and mine understanding returned unto me; and at the same time my reason returned unto me; and for the glory of my kingdom mine honor and brightness returned unto me, and my counselors and my lords sought unto me, and I was established in my kingdom."

He does not state how long a time he had spent lifting up his eyes to the King of Kings, the Author of Right Judgment, before he was true exponent of High Watch to the counselors and lords of his realm. But he knew that Daniel had been for three and a half years establishing the Healing Name in Babylon for his sake, and that by finally becoming amenable to its baptism he had identified with Daniel's King. "Now do I extol and honor the King of heaven, all whose ways are judgment; and those that walk in pride He is able to abase." Thus was his proud mind for-given. And thus "Proclaiming Him King, we are happy in His kingdom," promised the Sibyl Cumasan.

A photographic sensitive film steadily exposed to the night skies takes imprint of stars which the telescope cannot discover. So he who becomes sensitive through steadfast attention to the Wisdom-Countenance ever shining upon him knows laws which the books have not recorded. He shows forth activities of unhistoried aspect. "My servant shall deal prudently, he shall be exalted and extolled, and be very high." This is the result of attention to the High and Lofty One inhabiting Eternity, as revealed to the sensitive Isaiah.

To become sufficiently sensitive, negative, tender to an objective, is to be its servant, doing its will. "I came down from heaven not to do mine own will, but the will of Him that sent me." This was the secret of the heroism of the Redeemer. "Ye cannot be negative to two opposites at the same time," was his science.

The triumphing I Am is not vitally promulgated by man, because man has been negative, sensitive, tender to the untriumphing opposite to the I Am "I said, Behold Me, behold Me, ...all the day long ...to a rebellious people ...that turned on Me their backs and not their faces." These are the explanations of Paul, Isaiah, and Jeremiah, concerning all who are attentive toward the destructible unlikeness to that One ever offering joy for mourning and victory for defeat.

"Only Thou mayest heal me, Thou most Glorious *Manthra Spenta*" [the Zoroastrian name for the High Good].

In the days when the proud opposites to the Great Fact have rule, shall the King of Kings be chosen — was Isaiah's view of this moment. When "*Labor omnia vincit*" ['work conquers all"] is the motto of men, "Labor not" shall be the risen watchword, "Take no thought" shall be the law. In the days when hospitals are most beloved by reason of their agreement with the destructible opposite, the inhabitants shall stop saying, "I am sick," and the angels shall save all feet from stumbling.

In the days when nations are leaning upon their armies, "Put up thy sword" shall be obeyed. While prisons are yawning for criminals, "Neither hath this man sinned nor his parents" shall everywhere be declared true of all men, every eye on the uninjurable Soul Self fathered by Jehovah The Glorious.

While money is the substance most desired, for which kings and scholars are bartering their titles, the sensitive to divine Substance shall "cast their silver in the streets, and their gold shall be removed." While scholarship is at its highest pitch of repute, men shall rise taught of God the things that the schools discuss not. "The master and the scholar shall perish." "*In vocavi, et venit in me spiritus sapientia*" ["I call within and the wise spirit (or spiritual wisdom) comes to me"] shall be each man's scholarship.

Neither shall the powers and capacities of mind be science. "The righteousness of the righteous shall not save him, nor the wickedness of the wicked destroy him," touches a tonic chord of the miracle above thinking and its resultant conduct. God enthroned above the pairs of opposites is the bad man's deliverer and the good man's glorious liberty.

"Thou shalt be hid from the scourge of the (silent and audible) tongue," strikes beyond the range of human effort. "The watchers for iniquity shall be cut off, that make a man an offender for a word," shows a rule of relationship transcending criticism. "Take no thought." "Lift up your eyes," is Christian mysticism. "What I say unto you I say unto all, Watch," is Jesus Christ magism.

"I have a way that no fowl knoweth and which the vulture's eye hath not seen," saith the Rewarder of the diligently watchful. The "fowl" is the looker for right words and their outcomes. The "vulture" is the searcher for sin and its consequences. This was the patience and the faith of the saints of old, the observers of badness and goodness, the strong believers in rewards and punishments, the unknowing of the law that "that thou seest, man, that too become thou must."

Until the High Redeemer inhabiting Eternity is made the objective of the all-achieving visional sense, he that taketh the sword must perish by the sword, he that leadeth into captivity must be led captive, and no power can ward off the victim's exactness of duplication, for all the time the mystic law is printing on life and mind and body the inner eye's telltale *intaglios* [signs, clues].

The One served by inward beholding gives for our former nature Its own nature. Milton wrote that converse with angelic spirits etherealizes the body and turns it by degrees into Soul's divine essence. Xavier of Navarre, the celebrated

High Mysticism 299

missionary, often seemed to be on fire during his prayers to the Supernal Presence. Today there are those who by contemplating the Healing God rather than their own pains, have had given for their diseased bodies vigorously healthy ones; for their depressed minds buoyancy of heart, thus bodily preaching forgiveness.

The thing we fear is the objective our inward beholding touches with contagion. The lightning, the draught, the miasma; loss, deprivation, sickness — they soon find lodgment, embodiment and expression. "Oh! Why will ye die?" cried the Hebrew prophets. Can ye not read the divine decree, "Look unto Me and be ye saved"?

There is a ground of ready affiliation in our constitution in which the germs of contagion find strong root — God if we contagion God, misery if we contagion misery. Jesus of Nazareth had no consenting ground of affiliation with Satanic cowardice, feebleness, inefficiency. "Evil findeth nothing to tie to in me," he said. His ground he had kept sensitive to the Ruler in the heavens and the earth, so that he could speak forth experiential evidence: "All power is given unto me in heaven and in earth." "Where I am, O all mankind, there ye may be also."

"Preach forgiveness," he urged. We now know that "We cannot help preaching forgiveness," was the secret salient of the urge. Preach to men to stand and feed in the strength of the Almighty. Preach to them to breathe in the Almighty; to wake the God-seed by vision, by breath; for the inspiration of the Almighty waketh the waiting under-standing, stirreth the God. Agree with One who is Adversary to pain, misfortune, defeat. Agree with this Adversary quickly — now!

"Behold, I am against thee," saith the Highest Lord . . . "I am against your feasts .... even your solemn meetings." This is Isaiah feeling horror as of a man dreaming, seeing as in a trance the false fodder of low viewing with which his beloved companions are feeding to their destruction. He senses the now well-known law that we feed on what we inwardly behold. He sees the saving Substance that his neighbors might feast upon by lifting up their eyes to the fields white for the harvest, but he cannot make them look and taste; like as in a Sibylline dream, he speaks for the waiting Substance. His neighbors know his vision is Truth, but they obey not. They were uninformed that long before Isaiah's time, the Parsees had proclaimed that nine-hundred ninety-nine thousand, nine-hundred ninety-nine diseases spring from low visioning, but that the most Glorious Highest being sought, the diseases should all fall away.

"The ransomed return with singing," in their joy affiliating with the Author of joy. The taste of joy gives sense of success with a new leverage. The deaf man who spoke with passionate earnestness to the Presence of God in the Universe, felt a great cleavage in his head, and blood flowed forth from his ears. The gates of his imprisoned hearing being opened, he shouted for joy. The kingdom of heaven cometh and findeth something to tie to in him who touches the God-estimates. *Scire* meets *scire* — knowing meets knowing.

Honor and fortune and knowledge are forgiveness by recognition of the Glorious Presence of Victorious Divinity. Health and strength and joy and peace co-operate as God with man, by upward visioning.

Did not Dionysius the friend of Paul find new knowing by upward viewing toward the Author of knowing? New knowing starts with mystically sighting toward the Original Knower by whom our knowing roots are quick-ened. Let us know from our own base, and poverty and foolishness and evil have nothing to tie to. Thus do we find our original goods. So are we for-given. For, "Behold, God exalteth by his power; who teacheth like Him?"

Paul called the day of joy the Day of Atonement. "We joy in God through Jesus Christ by whom (accepting our sonship as he declared) we have now received the atonement." Jesus called it the day of for-giveness. To the man let down through the roof, all calloused with misery, he said,

High Mysticism 301

"For-given." To the woman bruised of heart, he said, "For-given." And thus were these both brought to conviction; not of sin, but of Sonship.

Agreement is harmony; harmony with the Adversary to pain, ignorance, disorder, means success like the Adversary.

> "I will contend with them that contend with thee. He that striketh at thee striketh at me. Thou art my servant, fear thou not. They that war against thee shall be as naught."

"O I Thou and Thou I!"

High success denotes entire harmony, entire for-giveness. He that is entirely for-given speaks with resistless inspiration. He has the *hestia vestia*, the heavenly hearthfire. He is a world kindler. No opposition daunts him. Like the deformed French child who knew that the doctors in the hospital would cure her, in spite of their "knowing they could not," till the unbelieving doctors did indeed cure her, so we, for-given, know that life, health and joy are eternally native to us all, and our positive fervors warm past all doubts. The Third Angel's burning Lamp is the speech of the Imperturbable Knower. It is mind tonic, wormwood to the vitals, ware-mood, mind-preserving acquaintance with the Presence of the Healing Christ.

"He that humbleth himself shall be exalted." He that letteth himself go to the Finished Fact, as the inconsequent needle yields to the magnet's empowering, is a new character on the earth. By his utter meekness he is liberated from himself, and works the works of the Worker unto whom he has yielded himself.

The Sacred books, uttering the inspirations of the God-taught, the Theophoroi, lay great stress on voluntary surrender to the Divine Trend. "Put on humbleness... meekness." "Because thine heart was tender, and thou didst humble thyself before God ... behold, I will gather thee." "If my people shall humble themselves ... I will for-give ... and heal all their land." "Thou shalt walk prosperously because of meekness."

It was while Daniel was voluntarily casting himself down, to be taken possession of by the Saving Sovereignty in the Universe, that the angel being caused to fly, touched him with heavenly inspiration, and said, "Ho, Daniel! I am come to give thee skill and understanding. Stand thou upright on thy feet."

We gladly offer the sum total of our unlikeness to the Almighty Giver. We gladly offer the initiation fee of our contrary tempers at the courts of the Healing God.

The Third Angel's voice wakes the will to let go the last vestige of opposition to the Mighty Trend. What matter how unlike to our way is The Way our life seems to be moving? We take with us words and return, looking steadfastly unto The Great Mover. Is it not assured that when the Lord returns our returning our mouth is filled with laughter, and our tongue with singing? How else save by being free inspiration can we warm the world into health? How else than by being God-glowing can we go into all the world preaching the gospel and raising the dead? How else than by High Association can we contagion free inspiration, the Holy Ghost influence that sweeps down all aftermaths of low visioning?

The Hindu sometimes touches the law hymned by the Third Angel:

> "Bow down to Me, and thou shalt come even to Me ... Take sanctuary with Me alone ... I shall liberate thee from all sins by the resplendent Lamp of Wisdom."

Milton immortalized his acquaintance with the Third Star's supernal import:

> "What is dark in me Illumine.
> What is low raise and support,
> That to the height of the great argument
> I may assert Eternal providence,
> And justify the ways of God to man."

The all conquering Jesus passed through the gates of voluntary lowliness, and taught us all that identifying worship when it touches the conquering truth has come up out of the baptismal font of humility. "They that worship the Father must worship him in spirit, (of humility) and (the bold words of) truth."

Now are we ready to cast our self and all our wills and demandings in lowly yielding up to Unseen High Sovereignty and His own Providence. Who is not glad to surrender his proud mind's muddy *wadis* [swampy areas, watering holes] of foolishness, its dark pools of ignorance?

> Here is my mind, I spread it out before Thee. For-give Thou its foolishness and ignorance with Thy bright wis-dom.
>
> Here is my life impulsion, I offer it to Thee. For-give Thou all its contrariness to Thee.
>
> Here is my heart; it is Thine only. Forgive Thou its dissatisfactions; for-give its restlessness. For-give its dis-couragements; for-give its elations. For-give its hopes and its fears; its loves and its hates.
>
> Here is my body, I cast it down before Thee. For-give Thou its imperfections with Thy perfection.
>
> For-give me altogether with Thyself, so only can I be the life and inspiration of the five bold words of Truth, Hymns to the Eternal—glowing Virgins with oil of healing and oil of illuminating in their everlasting lamps—Thou art and there is none beside Thee, in Thine own Omnipresence, Omnipotence, Omniscience.
>
> I am Thine only and in Thee I live, move, and have being.
>
> I am Thine own Substance, Power and Light, and I shed abroad wisdom, strength, holiness from Thee.
>
> Thou art now working through me to will and to do that which ought to be done by me.
>
> I am for-given and governed by Thee alone, and I cannot sin, I cannot suffer for sin, nor fear sin, sickness or death.
>
> My soul doing obeisance unto the Wonder of Thee wakes again these hymns of the Morning Stars in praise of Thee.

High praise of Him all For-giveness draws hither-ward the promised New Language, and brings into view "The New Race to be sent down from heaven" for-seen by enrapt Sibyls, keepers of the five hymns that should some time "sing-in" The Golden Age.

4th Study: Faith

NOTE

This Fourth Study has treatment quality for all who read it, even though they may not have heard its subject matter discussed orally. Practicing its lordly formulas wakes victorious energies.

E. C. H.

Every number held profound significance to the ancients. Number Four held the fire of convincing energy. It was the Uriel angel of divine telepathy. Beresford, the English writer, declared that he caught belief in survival after death from the mass faith at a meeting of Spiritualists. He did not report that the sparkling up of the faith center in man is the waking of his hidden miracle working genius; the great outfiguring of number Four to Pythagoras, sign of the fertile square according to the Cabala, the touch of fourth-dimensional strength, the change from Moses meek to Osarsiph bold according to Egyptian Hermetics.

The fourth stone symbolic of character according to St. John of the Revelation is emerald. It was once called the *smaragd* and held radiations for sharpening the memory, even to the recalling of our heavenly beginnings, making us mindful of "that country whence we came out," as Paul wrote to the Hebrews, assuring them of it as a country to which we all may return.

> "Not in entire forgetfulness,
> But trailing clouds of glory do we come
> From God who is our Home."

Everything about Four was fourth dimensional to the wise men of old. Notice them telling how man is comraded by angels from the city of God when he finds himself touching the fourth side of the city that lieth four square. Things have never satisfied his seat of sacred starvation; nor yet noble thoughts, high statements, even the highest; nor practice of ectoplasm and its astral shadows of departed friends. Only by laying hold of The High Adequate has man laid hold of that which satisfies his heart's desire. Notice the wise men telling of Jacob by the Jabbok brook sensing the angel of God who called himself God, changing him from Jacob the frightened to Israel the fearless, and causing him to found a dynasty of kings ending in earth's final King — The Nazarene Jesus!

The phoenix bird which fell into helpless ashes and rose into winged majesty was once the symbol of man's helplessness in the face of death, rising into daring renewal above death by the sacred touch of heaven's Uriel fire on his yearning heart's despair. Not only did the phoenix signify survival after death but revival out of death, even as the King of Judah rose while yet Isaiah the mighty was laying the ban of death upon him.

As the mariner on the sea steers his ship's course by a needle which points to a magnetic north, not to the north of polar bears and icebergs, so man is truly steering his hopes by an inner needle pointing to a country unseen from whence in time of danger or despair miraculous succor may swing toward him.

Something within us innately hopes great things from the self-existent kingdom to which king David turned crying, "Mine eyes are ever toward the Lord, he shall pluck my feet out of the net;" to which the sage of India gazes and is touched with long life because the kingdom is ageless.

David was rewarded for his bold insistence, his persistent high watch — "I went through fire and water," he cried, "but thou broughtest me out into a wealthy place."

It was the business of the Levitical singers in David's time and in Solomon's time to sing the ways of the kingdom unseen in its miraculous workings with this visible world and its people. "Thou shalt ride prosperously because of meekness," they chanted to the high-pitched, rich-toned sackbut of many strings.

High Mysticism

David had been meek even to sorrowing daily in his heart before the Lord of his hope who seemed sometimes to hide His face from him. Therefore was the promise fulfilled upon him. "Thou shalt ride prosperously because of meekness." "I will sing unto the Lord because he hath dealt bountifully with me," he triumphantly proclaimed.

There is a mystery about meekness, gentle receptivity, which even the merchants of Rome and Athens knew, as centuries before the Christian era they bowed their heads before unseen Mercury the god of magistral to poverty. And as Hesiod the Greek taught, bowing his head to angels that they might sprinkle him with wisdom-glory or with gold, not according to his human will but according to their own heavenly decrees.

Sometimes we read that those astral pictures which Homer called shades may meekly be yielded unto, but truly if there is presence of King of Kings and Lord of Lords with givings and workings supernal ready to let fall upon our human lot, why choose shades of the dead? "Hast thou faith, have it to thyself before God" had better be our starry choice on this our plain of Esdraelon. So shall He give his angels mysterious ministerings in our behalf!

The Levitical singers of David's time and of Solomon's time sang that the daughter of Zion should be Uriel-fired with Kingship. "Daughter" was the Levitical singers' figurative word for the Most Meek among the people. Was not the daughter of the old Hebrew house the most meek member of the family? Was she not handed over to her husband as docile and adoring, as seeing in him her "lord, her governor, her friend"? Was it not recorded that her confidence in his greatness caused him to be known in the gates, when he did sit among the elders of the land? As lighted candle lights candle so conviction fires conviction. Elisha was lowly in his conviction of Elijah's Godlike greatness as head of the schools of the prophets of Jehovah in Gilgal and Jericho. So Elijah, showing forth that Godly majesty, touched Elisha's meekly receptive being with conviction of competence, and he rose up head of the schools of the prophets of Jehovah in Gilgal and Jericho.

Long before the time of Elijah and Elisha it had been taught in mystic language that we rise up with that authority before which we have been meek. Was not Isaiah meek before the Lord of Hosts till the Lord of Hosts told him to command the Lord of Hosts as an Obedient Servitor? Was not Jeremiah meek before the Ruler in the heavens and the earth till the Ruler in the heavens and the earth told him to show himself ruler over the nations and over the kingdoms?

Did not Jesus say, "Have the Rulership of God himself," when he told his disciples to have the faith of God? For is not faith rulership? Is not faith kingship, or confidence to command? Is not kingship always associated with confidence to command?

> "If ye have faith as a grain of mustard seed ye shall say unto this mountain, Remove hence to yonder place; and it shall remove; and nothing shall be impossible to you."

Peter found by his own obedience to the bright angel who smote him on the side, saying, "Rise up quickly, Peter, gird thyself, bind on thy sandals, cast thy garment about thee and follow me," that the bright angel was obedient to him, opening the barred gates and loosing the chains of the four quaternions of soldiers to whom he was bound. It is no wonder that Peter wrote it down for an eternal verity that angels, authorities and powers are subject to the hidden man of the heart; the waiting authority principle lingering in the being of every man, woman, child, on earth.

The mystery of obedience to authority as surely rising as authority is every instant manifest. Do we not have to obey the authority of the door knob before it works for us? Or have to obey the rigid law of our feet before they do what we wish of them? So the Mighty King we call God gives orders to which we must yield obedience before His sublime service in our behalf is sublimely manifest: "The Lord lifteth up the meek"—the gently receptive to burning God

High Mysticism

conviction, which is confidence to command, which is kingship ever waiting to find its meek sparkling tinder within us.

Was it not wonderful of the gentle Japanese to discover that if one had faith, which is confidence to command, no larger than the point of a needle, he could say to a dead sardine's head, "Walk me over the water," and it would obey? Was it not astonishing that Count Puysegur of Buzancy could rouse up confidence to command a strong tree to heal all who touched it, and it meekly did his bidding? Was it not mystic inspiration in Maxwell the Scotch metaphysician to find that he could rouse confidence to compel the secret Spirit of the universe to do blessed healing ministries for him?

Maxwell did not know that he was practicing inborn, native kingship by such bold commandings; neither did the Japanese, nor yet the hundreds of daring new missioners, who go about the world saying to the lame "Walk!" and they walk. Or saying to the deaf, "Hear!" and they hear. But none of them can tell us like the Hebrew prophets and the masterful Nazarene the practice that rouses the living dominance called by Peter the hidden man of the heart, our secret Jehovah Nissi (Jehovah my banner).

The prophets and Jesus teach us that being insistent and firm with The Waiting Adequate we shall find The Waiting Adequate most willing and competent. "Is anything too hard for Me?" He saith. "Hast thou faith, have it to thyself before God." "Lo, I am with you always." "Let the Lord be thy confidence: he will never suffer thy feet to be taken." "Concerning the work of my hands, command ye Me."

Note how universal God majesty awaits the rise of man majesty universal!

Joseph in the prison house of Pharaoh of Egypt was meek to the fulfillment of the prophecy that he should save the Jews from starvation. He stopped his own thinking for the Unseen Knower to strike the hour for divine wisdom to touch his brain with words not known on all the earth. So great Pharaoh set him over all the provinces of the realm and gave him the handling of all the gold and silver of the realm, and today every Jew on earth owes his life to meek Joseph rising to kingly authority by reason of being touched with sprinklings of gray matter from above till his speech did distill as the dew.

Napoleon was also an example of letting his own thoughts stop for the thoughts of those higher in authority to sift on his brain. Catching their dominance he proudly said, "The only difference between me and other men is that I have confidence to command." It was not 'til he began to study the science of battles that he lost victorious confidence caught from Victorious Confidence. We find on looking over the people on this earth who have been baptized with originality that they have let the world's thinkings alone, and even for no telling how long have stopped, perhaps unwittingly, their own thinking also, and so creative new knowledges have been free to touch them. Here we come upon the magic wisdom of Jesus of Nazareth: "Take no thought" — "In such an hour as ye think not."

Even in print we read how some clergymen admit catching their thoughts from the thoughts of their congregations. So they are not original in their instructions. The world now needs fresh news from Universal Wisdom. Who can stop studying Latin enclitics and ages-old vivisections long enough to bare his meekness to new distillations from Divine Beneficence, sparkling gray matter-drops charged with healings from on high? Has any heavenly distilling reached mankind from the Sultan Amurath's striking off one hundred Persian heads that his physician Vesalius might watch the spasms in the muscles of the human neck? But note what the voice of inspiration declares to Amurath and Vesalius: He that taketh the sword must perish by the sword. He that leadeth into captivity must be led captive.

High faith is confidence to command the Working Executive standing up in the universe to the point of hearing

High Mysticism

as good response as Jacob, forebear of royal Jesus, heard: "As a prince thou hast power with God, and hast prevailed."

Or, as John of the Christian Apocalypse heard, "In Christ Jesus there is no more curse" — no Karma, [the consequence of past actions or thoughts].

Jesus discussed the mystery of forgiveness. He proved the mystery of bold use of the Working Executive facing us through all things, ever saying, as Iamblichus discovered "Boldly tell me what to do, and when to act."

When shall the fig tree, symbol of all flourishings, fruit for the one who discovers his own bold authority? Never! When shall the fever desist for such an one? Now!

To what was Joshua speaking when he stopped the sun and the moon in the midst of the heavens? To the Lord facing him, as we read in the book of Joshua, tenth chapter. To what are the little children of India speaking when the sticks and the stones with which they are playing do actually move here and there at their orders? To the same Lord facing them that faced Joshua the daring "I am captain!"

Why did not Bjerregaard go on with his discovery that "the earth is creating and destroying because it knows no better," and boldly tell it better, as the Jewish Bible with its vigorous miracles offered him precedents?

"Prosper Thou me!" commanded King David.

"Prosperity is of Thee." "The silver and the gold are Thine." "Riches and honor come of Thee."

Such truthful recognitions caused plenteousness of gold and silver to come to him exactly as such truthful recognitions would now cause plenteousness to come to any one of earth's multitudinous sons of the Highest. By this fourth lesson with its grand offerings, we see that Deity is no disciplinarian giving us hardships and refinements of deprivings, but a Beneficent Presence awaiting our use of everywhere-facing-Beneficence by bold insistences, like the "Glorify Thou me" of Jesus; the "Prosper Thou me" of David; the "Answer Thou me" of Job; the Stand Thou still" of Joshua.

"Come boldly up," said Paul. Why not come boldly up if "boldness hath genius, power, and magic in it"?

This One everywhere and through everything facing us is no hound of heaven hounding us to starvation, cold and death. Neither are we His hound dogs beaten into submission to His ceaseless disciplines. Let us take right view of Him: "Ask what ye will," He saith. "What wilt thou?" He asketh. "Concerning the work of My hands, command ye Me" He urges. "Is anything too hard for Me?" "I will work, and none shall hinder."

When the Belgian writer tells us to be frank with the God Presence and tell Him we are dissatisfied with our lot, the Belgian writer does not seem to know that such assurances multiply our dissatisfactions because they pick up the formulating substance charging the ethers and embody according to their recognitions. Tell him to speak boldly, looking into the face of the answering Substance,

"Deliver Thou me from evil!" "Give me this day my super-substantial bread!" "Give me courage, confidence to insist! Bless me with life, wisdom, divine efficiency!"

Tell him this recognition picks up the formulating substance and translates it into the mystic's fulfilled assurance, "So shall thy life renew; so shall inspiration teach thee; so shall thy affairs go newly right with thee." We light our inner vision by exalting it. Lightened vision wakes all our faculties to sense the Supernal Good-Willing surrounding us, forever wooing our positive, "Give me for my weakness, strength to command Thee!"

Some things will never square right with man till he takes Deity at His word, "Command ye Me."

Stop talking *about* God and His Idea Man, and speak unto majestic Deity face to face! So shall majestic man arise, victoriously daring!

As Adam and Eve were not only individuals but perceptions, so are the Angels of the Apocalypse not only winged messengers but high perceptions and their activities.

The Egyptian Magi changed the name of the neophyte at the fourth perception, because at this his nature changed. From being a meek listener he became a bold speaker; from being a timid follower he became a daring leader.

The fourth angel smites one side of the sun and on that side it is dark. So did the same angel smite Jacob and one side of him was withered, not for use but for super-use. So did this mighty angel smite Peter in the prison, and the smitten side of him being now supernal perception and not common intelligence, even as Angels of the Free Adequate, opened the bolted prison doors and undid the chains and manacles that human animosity had welded. The Roman soldiers guarding him four quarternions strong were smitten, and the miracle proceeded onward uninterrupted.

The fourth perception, setting aside the common law, exposes the unmanageable fourth dimension in space, which makes locks and bars and lions' teeth and adverse criticisms of no account.

Job the stricken was searching for help with his watch toward heaven, when suddenly he sensed the fourth dimension, and life for him became a track of victorious light to lighten all generations after him.

Jacob sensed the presence of the angel of the miracle, the angel of the helping, and wrestled with the angel, enduring as seeing the invisible, and his name was changed to Israel. He was no longer Jacob the cringeling, but Israel the Prince whom God Himself served. To any daring wrestler with the ever present angel of the miracle any man may hear that Angel Servant responding, "Concerning the work of My hands, command ye Me." "As a prince thou hast power with God."

At the fourth perception David found the same servant: "Bow down, Thine ear to me; deliver me speedily," he cried. "Thy gentleness hath made me great," was his astonished acknowledgement.

At his fourth perception Isaiah implores all mankind to practice the formula of the fourth dimension, whether they themselves have been entranced by the fourth angel's smiting or not. "Thus saith the Lord, Ask Me of things to come, and concerning the work of My hands, command ye Me."

Jesus the Redeemer gave the formula of the fourth verbatim. It is the speech of the fundamental knower risen up out of the waters of humility. It is the speech of the hidden man of the heart, without age and of no nationality. It is the genius of Massini at seventy, singing Gounod's "Sanctus" to an enthralled congregation. It is the genius of Elman at seventeen drawing a magic bow across a magic instrument to enraptured throngs. How thirstily the people put their lips to the troughs where living waters flow! What hearts of love they lean close to fires celestial!

All the world travails for the fourth angel's birthmark — the parting of its common mind for its uncircumscribed genius to act. "Who is this that cometh from Edom with dyed garments from Bozrah? I that speak in brightness, mighty to save." I that have dyed my language in the word of The High Supernal. I that have dipped my will in the Heavenly Trend. I smitten by the angel of the miracle and his delivering might. "Arise up, quickly!" the angel says. Now am I as Jacob, not for visible but for mystical usefulness. Now am I as Peter, free Spirit.

A principle is a comprehensive law or doctrine from which others are derived.

That is, obedience is vested in the Supreme I Am or there could be no obedience in the dog or horse. Authority is resident in the King of Kings or the General-in-Chief of an army could not command with success.

When Iamblichus of Chalcis found that the weather obeyed him and eagles flew hither and yon at his insistence, he supposed there must be an order of obedient invisible powers in the universe, altogether at the bidding of man.

High Mysticism

By reason of triumphs which certain men of old achieved after speaking with commanding determination to their invisible gods, they sang.

"Cease your fretful prayers,
Your whinings, and your tame petitions;
The gods love courage armed with confidence,
And prayers fit to pull them down.
Weak tears They sit and smile at."

Something concerning the mystery of man's inborn authority has ever been the fourth theme of such as have consciously or unwittingly obeyed the Supreme edict, "Look unto Me." By snatches of what Luke the Apostle called sunrisings from on high, the illuminati of the ages have known that the will to command the Obedient Supreme Presence rises up after obedience to the will of the Supreme Presence.

"If man avoids regarding himself as king of the universe it is because he lacks courage to recover his titles thereto," wrote one of the illuminati after having been by meekness dissolved into recognition of the Majesty of the Commanding Supreme, and felt its quickening stir as likeness triumphant in his own breast.

The law is plain enough. If that nature before which we have been negative, soft, meek, plastic, draws forth and stirs alive in us its own kind, it is not surprising that the meekest and lowliest of all men rose up with the bold proclamation: "All power is given unto me" — "I have overcome the world." It is not surprising that his disciples, catching his assurance, found that satanic tempers fled at the sound of their bold commands, and the willing angel of the miracle stood by them to save them from prisons and swords.

"Tell ye the daughter of Zion, Behold, kingship cometh in meekness." This is Zechariah agreeing with Jesus across the gulf of centuries. The mystic law is one and its way is one as mathematics is one. Does the relation of the hypotenuse to its base and perpendicular ever alter? Pythagoras sacrificed an hundred oxen of rejoicing when he discovered that eternal relationship of the hypotenuse. Jesus gladly sacrificed himself to call the attention of mankind to the root of Divinity, the spark of identical substance with the Unconditioned Absolute inherent in them each and all.

Job's saying that the root of the matter was in him had not sufficed to call the attention of men to their own Absoluteness. The prophet's assurance that "He hath made of one blood (or root and stalk) all the nations," had not given the serf and bond woman inkling enough of their own right to dominion over that mysterious Servanthood standing up in the universe.

As in mathematics the time came in with Pythagoras for knowing that the root of the sum of the squares of base and perpendicular was forever the diagonal, so in with Jesus came the time for showing the root of divine authority bone of bone in men forever, in their relation to the Supreme Good Will occupying Omnipresence: "Thus saith the Holy One of Israel, and his Maker, Concerning the work of My hands, command ye Me" (Isaiah 45). Therefore, after this manner pray ye:

> Give me this day my super-substantial bread—bread for my eternally innate authority with the God that standeth in the congregation of the universe!

When Saint-Martin told us that it is lack of courage that keeps us from acting with kingship, he did not tell us how to rouse that courage. When Jeremiah was shown that it was a sign of arrested development to tarry as a cringeling in the face of the waiting Good Will, he did not understand that he was to instruct all the Jews in rousing their courage to speak as lords of the Obedient God. He heard it as for himself only, "Say not, I am a child—See, I have set thee over the nations and over the kingdoms—to throw down, to build, and to plant."

But Jesus, the Bloom in the Garden of Man, rising up out of authority-breeding lowliness, said, Speak like Masters to the responsive stately God of Lazarus; to the stately responsive God of the man with the impotent arm; to the stately God of the mountain; to the obedient responsive of

High Mysticism

the sycamore tree. After this manner speak ye: "Thy kingdom come! Thine is the Kingdom forever. Stretch forth thine hand! Make straight the path!" His God did not overdiscipline man. His God awaited man's bold insistence, "Make straight my path!"

This is the rise of the Hidden Man of Job, of Joshua, of Jacob—the great triumvirate of J's on the commanding heights of courage to command the willing Omnipotence ever whispering to all mankind, "Concerning the work of My hand, command ye Me!"

Did not Job hear the Supreme Authority in heaven and earth speaking with sternness, "I will demand of thee and answer thou Me"—over and Over, till the intone of it smote his root of divinity, and he turned with the same address, "I will demand of Thee, and answer Thou me!" And is it not recorded that the Lord was pleased with Job?

Was it not to the Lord fronting him through the sun and moon that Joshua spake with bold commanding, "Sun, stand thou still on Gibeon, and thou moon in the valley of Ajalon! And the sun stood still in the midst of the heavens, and hasted not to go down about a whole day. And there was no day like that, when Joshua spake unto the Lord." With the rise of his inborn Root of authority spake he to the Willing Obedience facing him as the Omnipotent One!

And did not Jacob wrestle to give his hidden boldness dominion? "I will not let Thee go except Thou bless me I" And the yielding Angel of Victory did vouchsafe the blessing. "I have seen God face to face," said the trans-muted Jacob. I was afraid, but fear had no annulling strength against my vision of God.

Napoleon Bonaparte was docile and promptly obedient to his superior officers; watchful of their genius at commanding, till his latent generalship stirred and he turned on them all, Head of the Army of France.

Hannibal was from infancy meek and plastic before Hamilcar, General-in-Chief of the Carthagenian army. Every hate and every love of Hamilcar stood forth in Hannibal at its proper moment. Is it surprising that at twenty-eight he is head of the Carthagenian army like his father?

How docile was Joan of Arc to the wills of the angels with whom she had converse all her life, dauntlessly repeating their directions to the awe-struck generals, soldiers and statesmen of France, till she at the age of sixteen was *tete d'armee* [head of the army].

We must choose well the objective before which our inner eye oftenest pauses, for if the objective has not commanding boldness, resistless authority as its savor, when the moment of identification transpires neither will there then be any commanding boldness, resistless authority rising up out of its sleeping place in us.

Gather a hint from the slow rising Moses, docile, teachable, tractable, before the tutors of princes in Heliopolis at a time when the tutors and priests of Heliopolis were famed for their learning and manners. Is it not written in secular history that Moses also was famed for his learning and manners? But at forty years of age he fled like a cringing Jacob at the threats of two Israelites. No confidence to command and be obeyed had leaped like a fountain of fire from its slumbering pit in him. How could it, if the tutors to whom he had been religiously attentive had never waked their own fearless dominion? Can a stream rise higher than its source?

Now, as an exile among the mountains of Midian, he has spent forty years humbling himself before the High Deliverer, the Noble Counselor, the Almighty Champion, and though he is eighty years of age two million Israelites obey his lightest word of command. Notice the mathematical increase, afraid of two, dominant over two million! The Lord of Lords and Ruler in the Heavens and the earth sends him forth Law giver, Governor, Mighty Champion, High Deliverer like Himself. He sends him forth with youth in his genius, the stamp of Fadelessness on his body.

"Here eyes do regard you

In Eternity's stillness:
Choose well, your choice is
Brief and yet endless."—Goethe

"Let the Lord be thy confidence,
He will not suffer thy feet to be taken."

This is the principle of attention to the Highest Lord to the point of rising above prisons and lions' jaws. This is the principle of making them of none effect. The lordship that causes the iron gates to open of their own accord, that rolls away the stones from the pathway, must hail from above the three dimensions.

Joan of Arc was left to be burnt at the stake at twenty years of age, because her vision had not sought higher than the faces of the flying messengers. Napoleon is in common exile at forty-seven, because he has never sent his vision higher than Emperors' faces and heads of armies for its snatches of quickening dominion. Hannibal is in durance at sixty for the same reason. But Jacob and Elisha and Paul finish their course with the words of the light still on their lips, and the crown of the conqueror still shining on their heads.

And the kings that shall arise after them shall be lords even over the Sabbath, or the stopping place of death. "There is no Sabbath keeping in the temple," whispered the rabbis. The Lord of the temple is Lord. He says to the obedient Executive standing still and tall in the flourishing fig tree of fever or dying, "It is finished!" and nothing can resist the Lord's command to the eternally present Obedient God.

The rise of boldness, authority, is the rise of inborn superiority to surrounding conditions. It is wresting the tongue from outward descriptions to conform to heavenly fact. Authoritative speech brushes aside the cobwebs of outward appearance. It is backed by the mystery of the conquering kingdom of The Inmost Actual.

When Solomon said, "The opening of my lips shall be right things," he meant that he would speak forth from the hidden man, as free Spirit that knows nothing of defeat or poverty or sickness. By this speech he would lift his head above conditions. At a certain moment the hidden man of the heart, gifted with dominion, leaps like the lightning to expose its magical independence of the length, breadth, and thickness of matter, mind, sensations and their world maneuvers.

Does Habakkuk say that he yields to grief when the fig trees blossom no longer in Judah? "Although the fig trees shall not give blossom — the labor of the olive shall fail — yet will I speak rejoicings — my feet shall walk on high places — let the chief singers chant with me!"

It is the failure to stand by the things of Almighty Spirit to the leap of authority that accounts for the seemingly unmanageable misfortunes of aspiring men in all ages. They have supposed, in unguarded moments, that the yielding they must make was to the overbearing three dimensionals of misfortune, old age, and dying.

Let us heed the voice of inspiration. That yielding which the sons of earth are dimly tending to make, is not to the three dimensions but to the God law that works above them. Although now, apparently, by my past downward viewing I have walled myself into feebleness, sickness, defeat, yet, speaking boldly from my bright secret self, I am Strength itself — I am flawless confidence, I am Master of the Willing Good of my universe. This is the opening of the lips with right things, and all the divine forces stand ready to minister to my leaping Word.

As the young eagle presses his leathery joints against the cracking shell, all nature waiting in mute sympathy, expecting to be governed by his new born demands, so the Still God of the universe waits to move through all visible and invisible items to minister in willing docility to my undiverted high confidence.

"Although the flocks shall be cut off from the fold, and there shall be no herd in the stalls, yet will I joy in the God of my salvation" — still forever we hear the voice of the poverty-surrounded Habakkuk singing through the night watches our steadfast example through the ages.

The meekness of the mind, the will, the heart, opening to The Healing Good, is their moving aside for a lordship not of the flesh to act. Watch ye therefore, for ye know not what hour your lordship rises.

> As when by drastic lift
> Of pent volcanic fires,
> The dripping form of a new Island
> Springs to meet the airs,
> So from our deeps we rise.

"Now will I rise, saith the Lord, now will I lift up myself" — and "at the lifting up of myself the nations are scattered."

It is the rise of the divine will to see, when the blind beggar throws aside his ragged garments and runs to the waiting Jesus. It is the rise of its pent up fragrance when the tightly closed petals of the rose fall back and the hidden splendors of color and perfume face the sun, uncramped forever.

"Dost thou ask what Christianity is?" says the Mohammedan Sufi, forgetful of creed and country: "I shall tell it thee: It digs up thine own ego, and carries it up to God."

It is the rise of the divine ego that makes a man victoriously bold. "Come boldly unto the throne," said Paul. [Goethe, the German transcendentalist, tells us,] "Boldness hath genius, power, and magic in it; what you can do or dream you can, begin it. Therefore be bold!" Persist like Jacob.

Though my low views have sent me loss of friends, pain, humiliation, yet truly am I strong son of God, with dominion in all my vital sap. I am at my roots greater than my environments and the shadows of hardship with which by turning from the Highest I have darkened my path! And Omnipotence stands before me and behind me, at my right hand and at my left, above me and below me, to serve my rising commandings, as He Himself hath voiced by priests and prophets, and the young eagle's springing.

So we are to look upon the man who threw aside the wrappings of the grave, the stone-sealed tomb and the soldiers' swords, bursting their three dimensional bind-ings with risen divinity, as law for the whole of us, world without end.

After this commanding manner speak ye:
Let me not turn aside from facing Thee!
Deliver Thou me from evil.
Thou art empowering Obedience.
I owe Thee bold command,
O Thou Owner of all the kingdoms!

There is a noble triumvirate of D's on the self-authorizing rock of conquering confidence: David, Daniel, Darius:

"Show me a token for good, that they which hate me may see it"

"Let my Lord now speak to me"

"Thy God whom thou servest, He will deliver thee."

They show how at the first upspringing of this confidence, this bold certainty, the God in the universe serves promptly. The symbol of this upspring is the emerald stone; stone significant of walking free from common law, unified with the miraculous, where he that would hinder thee cannot discover thee.

This is the science of high visioning — of looking unto the Vast Vast Countenance with healing of our tardy recognition of our own inborn kingship as its fourth gift.

Is not faith the gift of God, according to Scriptural instruction? Is not faith the confidence of things chosen according to the same high information? And does not masterfulness rise with confidence? And are we not told to have the faith, which is the masterfulness, of God himself? "Have the faith of God,' Jesus.

"'Thou hast a strength of empire fixed." The exaltation of lifting up of the vision is "Fear of the Lord." "Pass the time of your sojourning here in fear," preached Peter. It is written that the fear of the Lord is the instruction in Wisdom. It is written that it is the beginning of wisdom, or light. If thine eye seek The Lord only, thy whole body shall be full of wisdom. If thine eye seek The Lord only, He will fulfill thy desire. If thine eye seek The Lord only, He will be thy strong confidence. If thine eye choose the High Deliverer, thy dominion shall rise up.

Thus have the inspired among men written in their own risen moments, always showing by their instructions that heir risen kingship stirred forth from the bed of lowly-heartedness. And always lowly-heartedness before Supreme Majesty else how should genuine kingship rise with its scepter? "To this man will I look, even to him that trembleth at my word," saith the Supreme Lord.

Jeremiah trembled at sight of the danger streak in the Jews' sum total of character. The wicked and foolish trait deplored by all the Jewish wise men had glued Jeremiah's unmitigated attention. Out of the molten depths of his anguish he forged the prophecy of doom in which that trait would lawfully ultimate. It has taken centuries on centuries for the Jews to labor out from under the black bar of Jeremiah's decree:

> "Your inheritance shall be turned to strangers.
>
> God is wroth against you, O people of Zion!"

Jeremiah sometimes forgot the sin streak of the Jews, and looking above them saw them above themselves, for seconds of time, as the High God saw them:

> "In a day shall Judah be saved. Thus saith the Lord. And David shall never want a man to sit upon the throne."

Note that Jeremiah prophesied coming greatness and glory while his vision was toward the High and Lofty One that inhabiteth Eternity, who cannot Himself look upon evil.

Seeing sometimes as God sees he sensed the liberation of the Jews from the stream of their forefathers' sins, but never long enough to sense their right to their present Victorious Sonship to their Heavenly Father.

Jesus the star out of Jacob, bright with the morning of the liberation, told them that no man upon the earth was their father; one Only was forever the Father of all, even God. He dipped his speech in the truth of high birth and victorious life.

> "Neither hath this man sinned nor his parents"

> "The flesh profiteth nothing"

> "And they shall see His face—And there shall be no night"

> "Go ye, and make disciples of all nations."

He taught that he that is steadfast unto the day of believing, commanding confidence, faith, shall be saved from the law of cause and effect, the *karma* of past vision and thought. For though foxes have holes of resting, and birds of the air have places for their pause, the risen soul belongeth not to their order. There is no set outcome to the vision toward the Infinite. Though "envy is rottenness of the bones," the loss of envy has no stopping place of freedom. Before the Son of Buoyancy the doors are all open. Though "the hypocrite's hope shall perish," forever, in some particular disappointment, the loss of hypocrisy has no limit to its good and perfect gifts from above.

The great aphorisms of men wrought out from looking away from the Highest, cease from being true, but the high truths that belong to the vision above the aphorisms of downward visioning cannot cease. All the aphorisms of men are like unto "no royal road to learning," but according to the lore and law of divine mysticism, the road to the learning that falls on the face of the upward watcher is royal. The upward watcher knows things which before he knew not, and which neither teachers nor books have mentioned.

High Mysticism

The downward watcher wades through seas of trouble and is chided for not having faith. How can he have faith, the substance of things hoped for, when it is the fourth smite from above, reaching down over his own isolated vision to the roots of his own being, and rousing his own untaught spark of authority over an undescribable Almighty Executive?

When the spark of faith like a lightning for splendor spoke from the masterful lips of the Unkillable Redeemer, the quickening Mystery back of the tomb and the soldiers' swords flung them all aside for his free feet to go into Galilee, where the eyes of five hundred might see him alive and not dead.

Let us write it with a pen of light dipped in the fountain of everlasting truth, that we have found a new Servant — the Able-to-do all things. "Is there anything too hard for me?" he saith. "Before the day was I am He, and there none that can deliver out of my hand." "Concerning the work of My hands, command ye Me." "Kings exercise lordship," said Jesus. How shall one be king except his kingship be roused? And true kingship, one ray of which is as strong as the decree of Darius concerning the lions, comes from above: "By Me kings reign," saith the Great Voice that John turned to see. If lions do not stand back, and warrings do not cease, and diseases do not retire, the true kingship is not among us. Only its crude symbol, working through the heavy machinery of army and navy, and jailor and hospital faces us.

Then the disciples asked him to increase their faith. But he answered them nothing. For faith, which is kingship exercising to call the God of Lazarus to come forth, and the God of the withered arm to appear, is the deepest secret of all the deep secrets of the *Magia Jesu Christi*. Seeing then that after speaking with commanding earnestness to Unseeable Majesty he made insanity and poverty drop their grip, they said "Lord, teach us also to pray." So he taught them to speak firmly and sternly to the Great Servant.

He that is greatest among you, let Him be your servant. He that is greatest among us through all eternity is the Lord, Strong and Mighty. None other is greatest. Your brains do not make your inborn Self greater than the Self of your serf; your money cannot make you greater than the pauper; for God is no respecter of persons, and He surely hath made of the blood all the nations. Only One among us is greatest. Our Father is He—with name unspeakable on the lips of the downward watcher. His is the kingdom ready to show its finished presence. His is the will to command and the will to obey, identical with the inborn root of obedience and authority inherent in man, the highest God and inmost God being one God.

He feeds with super-substantial bread all who rise up like Marcella to demand it. He rouses the payment of the debt of confidence to command owing unto Him since ever the world caught us in its wheel. He delivers us at our bold command. He prevents our speech when it chooses the path of disease in description of evil. And this is His way and His glory though you believe it not and take not hold of this key to His kingdom. "He shall feed thee on the Heights of Confidence" prophesied the exiled Ezekiel, writing by the banks of the Chebar.

The speech of the Lord's Formula being understood as the word of command, acts like nutriment to the hidden Jehovah nature. It is that feeding on strength which Micah was exalted to foreknow: "Man shall feed in the strength of the Lord." It is the end of that feeding on descriptions of goodness and badness, poverty and riches, the pairs of opposites, which Solomon noted as the foolishness that only fools feed upon.

As the savage can be taught mathematics and become proficient therein, centuries before he could evolve mathematics by himself, so are we taught the obedience of the Good Will fronting us by the gold formula of the Prayer of our Lordship long before we would have formulated it. "I know that His commandment (or the commandment of

Him), is life everlasting" said the Messiah. "Thou through the commandments hast made me wiser than mine enemies," cried the glad psalmist. For when I demanded that Thou bow down Thine ear to me, to deliver me speedily, and be my strong rock, then Thy gentleness made me great.

"This is the whole duty of man," said Solomon in one of his moments of speaking above his mind, "Fear God, and keep His commandments."

"God manifests His word according to the commandment of God," wrote John the lover. "The commandment of the Lord is pure, enlightening the eyes," wrote one who had touched kingship by watching toward the high I Am who makes kings.

At the Waters of Lourdes, some patients are taught to repeat the great formula of the hidden Lord in man, called the Lord's Prayer, fifteen times while the curing waters are being tasted. Has anybody explained to them that the waters of tribulation begin to subside for him who touches the fifteenth cubit above them? Has anybody explained that Paracelsus the miraculous healer of Zurich, caught all his flashes of genius from much repetition of the seven stately commands of Matthew's Lord's Prayer, or prayer of our own lordship?

1. "Hallowed be thy name.
2. Thy kingdom come
3. Thy will be done.
4. Give me this day my super-substantial bread.
5. Forgive my debt of confidence to command Thee.
6. Let me not into temptation.
7. Deliver me from evil."

Who is not glad to utter these words of insistence the number thereof, that he also may be healed of his cringing to old age and death, disease, and poverty?

The fourth Angel, being caused to fly swiftly, smiteth all of them of the mystic formula. They are they that keep the commandments of God and the faith of Jesus, as John on Patmos foresaw. The fourth Angel is the bright angel smiting Jacob, smiting Peter, smiting Job "on the left hand where He doth work."

Look unto Him of power to establish according to the mystery which was kept secret since the world began, but now is made manifest according to the commandment of the everlasting God, for the obedience unto faith, as did Paul, writing to the Romans with the pen of that same Victorious Confidence, even to the quickening of dead Eutychus.

Faith is man's *El Shaddai*, his risen recognition of himself as Jehovah Soul, seeing the mystery of Divine Obedience everywhere awaiting the kingly rise of his heaven planted boldness to command, "I will not let thee go except thou bless me!" "Thine is the kingdom, and the power, and the glory, forever and ever."

> A Shape looked up from eating herb and grain.
> It chanced to see the stars, and with that look
> Came Wonderment, and Longing in its train.
> The food untasted lay. A beating pain
> Smote at its forehead, but it looked again.
> And yet again.
> And then it thought. Lo!
> Man stood upright as the stars did wane!

5ᵗʰ Study: The Word

NOTE

This Lesson is self-active in its treatment power. Do not try to delve into it; make the acknowledgments and let it have its Apostolic way with you.

E. C. H.

PROLOGUE

When the Greek and Roman peasantry cried aloud to invisible Mercury, "Grant us magistral to poverty!" they received magistral to poverty. Their confidence was effectual. Confidence, or faith in anything, makes it work according to the "Faith in a dead sardine's heads healing power would make it heal," declared the ancient Japanese.

Higher up in the scale of authorities there was Carlyle insisting that "conviction is not properly speaking conviction till it develops into action." Then there was Paul the Christian convert finding that "faith without works is dead," by which he meant that unless some kind of work takes place we haven't believed anything.

Our globe has been called Number Five, the planet of works, since everybody and everything must accomplish something or be nobody and nothing: Sun, Vulcan, Mercury, Venus, Earth. Each to his feat, or opus, till some crowning bloom in earth's garden of man cries, "It is finished!"

Earth, as Number Five, must perform The Great Achievement. The most wonderful achievements of mankind have been brought to pass by confidence in some wonder working Unseen Power. Moses and Aaron had a five-pointed star at the end of their mystic wand which they swung high into some unseen perfect land. And when the workings of that land touched this earth they were called miracles:

> "And Moses stretched forth his rod toward heaven ... and fire ran along upon the ground ... and hail smote every herb of the field ... only in the land of Goshen where the Children of Israel were, was there no hail ... and Moses spread abroad his hands unto the Lord and the thunders and hail ceased"

even over all great Pharaoh's land.

All work is redemption. It redeems a place or a people or a situation from one status into another status. And redemption is historically associated with Number Five: With five loaves did Jesus redeem five thousand people from hunger. With five measures of parched corn was Nabal redeemed from death. With five measures of parched corn was Abigail redeemed from common-placeness to queenship. With five encounters with the terrible Archelaus did Heracles redeem the whole land from misery. With five sling stones did David redeem all Israel from Goliath the terrible. With five men did Joshua give his people rest from their enemies on the side of Jordan toward the sunrise. With five wounds did Jesus redeem common mankind from ignorance of His Sonship to Royalty Triumphant.

> "If a man steal one ox, let him give five oxen for the one ox and he shall be redeemed from the stigma of thief. He shall be restored to his former estate. He shall be reinstated. It shall be as if he had never stolen."

The sardonyx stone, which was the fifth stone of character building according to John the Revelator, was worn by the ambassador of the King. To him was given power to redeem such as were appointed to destruction. We read that Joseph wore the sardonyx stone as Vice-regent for Pharaoh king of Egypt; that Haman wore the sardonyx stone as representative plenipotentiary for Ahasuerus, king of Persia; that Philip wore the sardonyx stone as ambassador for

Antiochus king of Syria, and that each of these had power to redeem such as were appointed to destruction.

It has even been traditioned that Jesus wore the sardonyx stone as ambassador plenipotentiary for the King of Kings and Lord of Lords, but there is no written history for this tradition as there is history for the lesser vicegerents of lesser kingdoms than the whole earth.

"Five truth mumblings are self-active." Five eternal words were traditioned as written on the shining garment of Jesus the Glorified.

If we please to look up all that has been written about the mystery of Five we shall see how worthy is Number Five to be called The Works Lesson. It answers the Hindu discovery that the best doctrine is that which removes pleasure and grief from the mind; showing that doctrine is self-active. So the Fifth, Works, must be a working doctrine, acting on the mind, which affects the body; which body is the working field of mind. Vision affects the mind. Mind is the working field of the vision, as body is the working field of mind.

Notice Hegel finding that "we always look toward an object before thinking it." Mind glorifies or cramps the body according as the visional sense runs high or low.

Nine hundred ninety-nine thousand nine hundred ninety-nine diseases and pains were declared by the Parsees as having been formulated by low visioning acting on mind to afflict its body.

The best ambassador for any king would be he who should best understand his king's mind and best carry out his king's hidden wishes. There is One King of Kings and Lord of Lords, whose whole purpose toward His kingdom has ever been peace, health, wisdom, majesty even to the greatness and wisdom of His Own Self: "Look unto Me." "I extend peace like a river." "I am the Lord that healeth thee." "I will instruct thee and teach thee." These are the words of the High Redeemer inhabiting eternity, whose way upon the earth is the saving health of the nations. The Ambassador

Plenipotentiary for this High Redeemer said that the same fountain sendeth not forth both bitter and sweet. So when we have pain or poverty or sickness or misfortune of any kind we must have been looking away from The High Redeemer, who hath counseled, "Seek ye My face and live."

Let us not be deceived by the poetic eloquence of any great poet or theologian who tells us that The King of Kings suffers or is grieved. For if He suffers or is grieved He must shed suffering and grief around Him, even as we when suffering and grieved shed suffering and grief in all directions. Those who speak of The King of Kings are not ambassadors understanding The Great King's mind when they report that He is angry with the wicked every day, or that anything grieves or dismays Him. They are ambassadors for their own kind of king, and their own kind of king works his own way with them.

Notice that high potentate who spoke of Jesus Christ as a fable. Bespeaking no balm of Gilead in this "Fable," the potentate was afflicted with an incurable malady; his fortune melted; friends failed him; his great ambitions faded on all sides. For there are some wounds on life's pathway that only the Real Christ Jesus can heal.

Hear the Erythrean Sibyl prophesying of the Real Jesus Christ seven hundred years before He appeared: "All who style Him King shall be happy in His Kingdom." Read the words of Zoroaster of Persia eighteen hundred years before the coming of the Anointed of The Heavenly King:

> "A virgin shall conceive and bear a son, and a star shall appear at midday to signalize the occurrence. When you behold the star, follow it whithersoever it leads you. Adore the mysterious child, offering Him gifts with profound humility. He is indeed the Almighty Word. He is indeed your Lord and everlasting King."

There is a science that runs like a river of light above all the sciences. It never changes its assurances. It tells of the Working Efficiency of One Lord Supreme and of how the language runs that describes the Working efficiency.

High Mysticism

It is the Mystical Science. According to its practice we never say we fight for The Lord Supreme, but "The Lord shall fight for us and we shall hold our peace." We never say we trust a friend, but "All my trust on Thee is stayed."

For, "Put not your trust in princes," is the language of the Lord Supreme;

> "I will contend with him that contendeth with thee"
>
> "No man shall set on thee to hurt thee."
>
> "Fear not, I will help thee."
>
> "Look unto Me."

Mystical Science starts the New Language promised sometime to break forth from the lips of mankind:

> "I will turn to the people a pure language."
>
> "They shall speak with new tongues."

Whatever language mankind starts up with it shows that his visional sense has preceded his speech. He can throw a vision out toward assassination like Carnot of France and glue it with acknowledgment like Carnot. For "I have made thee like unto Him, even God who calleth those things which be not as though they were."

He can throw his vision out toward damage for some neighbor and silently mentioning the damage in definite terms he will find it formulated in the experience of that neighbor. But "Add to your strength, knowledge," said Peter. Is it not written that the man who imagined the damage of his neighbor, fell and injured the very limb he had imagined himself using with neighbor-damaging violence? David found out this law: "How long will ye imagine mischief against a man? Ye shall be slain all of you; as a bowing wall shall ye be, and as a tottering fence."

See how we need high watch with its high language!

People must learn the law of lifting up the face to The Lord Supreme who worketh noble conditions of life into view.

Who shall tell that potentate who set forth to paralyze the world that his own bodily paralysis is reaction? How shall we get it to the potentate who is doomed by wasting disease that his wasting is reaction from wasting a nation by viewing it as easily suborned?

How shall we make it plain that power and vigor and plenty hail from above, with no need to maltreat or suborn our neighbor?

Things and people are often troublesome. Mystical Science teaches us to let them alone as if they did not exist, and look up to "The Vast Vast Countenance" for one second of time; may be two seconds; to have nothing to do with them; to cut the threads of attention toward them. The Vast Vast Countenance saith, "I will set them in order before thine eyes," "I restore to you the years that the locust hath eaten." Have not locusts always been symbolic of domestic tormentings? Restorations hail from above. Expect greatly from above, and greatly shall restorations multiply. "Prove Me now herewith, saith the Lord of Hosts, if I will not pour you out a blessing that there shall not be room enough to receive it."

So is Self-recognition awakened. So is new mind built. So is hidden ability set astir. So ariseth the new race of which Jesus was the forerunner.

No man has ever stood so boldly forth for the Redemption of the God Self of man from the clutches of the mortality self as that young man of despised old Nazareth nineteen hundred years ago! No lover of his brother man so willing to die that he might show man his own God transcendence has ever appeared on this earth! He knew the ancient doctrine preached in many ways that man was the offspring of Satan with only one God glow in his being, and that the angels dwelling in glorious Paradise had asked each other who was willing to leave his heavenly home to Redeem the God

High Mysticism

of man from the Satan of man and daringly declare to man, "For this cause came I forth." Why should not now the angels,

> On heights of untold glory
> Sing oftentime the story
> Of the greatest one among them,
> Christ Jesus and His love.

It was practicing inborn authority over the Universal Servitor, when the wonderful Jesus cried, "Glorify Thou Me!" And when on the cross He acknowledged, "How Thou hast glorified Me,"[11] He was seeing the obedience of the obedient God to His orders. His eye overlooked future ages, when He should stand to mankind as the embodiment of divine insistence — His Name above principalities and powers, and above every name that could be named.

Abraham was practicing inborn authority over the Invisible Servitor, when he said. 'I lift up mine hand unto the Lord, the most high God, the possessor of heaven and earth. — Whereby shall I know that I inherit the land? Show me a sign." And he was experiencing the obedience of God when a deep sleep fell upon him, and he saw himself famed for spiritual and material riches throughout all succeeding generations.

David was practicing innate authority over the Universal Obedience, when he said, "Be Thou my strong rock! Deliver me speedily!" And when David's little band of warriors had swelled into "a great host, like the host of God," and he

---

[11] This phrase is usually translated: "why hast thou forsaken me?" as if Jesus, on the cross, were quoting a Hebrew scripture from the book of Daniel when he said in Aramaic *"Eli, Eli, yani sabachthani!"* Aramaic is a language with many possible meanings, and it's unlikely that the Master would say something in Aramaic that he had always read in Hebrew, so a number of scholars today agree that he was probably intending something other than the traditional translation. It could also have meant "for this was I born (separated from you)! Or "by this am I fulfilled!" Emma's is as valid as any other and fits both her thesis and the Gnostic interpretation.

had been three times crowned king, he was in the thick of God's obedience.

Gideon was practicing the same inborn authority, when he spoke to the Universal Servitor, "Show me a sign that Thou talkest with me." And when fires rose up out of a rock, and the Midianites and Amalekites and all the children of the East fell down at the sight of Gideon, then the Great Servant was obeying Gideon's bold prayer of lordship.

Authority with the Universal Servant is roused in us, as in Gideon, to accomplishing vigor, by repeating the prayer of our inborn lordship, with firmness and sternness. (See the Fourth Study.)

Authority with the universally present Divine Servant discloses authority with the particularly present divine Self, or Spirit of God vivifying each frame. "He that ruleth his own spirit is better than he that taketh a city," wrote Solomon the discoverer of spiritual activities. This individually present Godship is that self which obeyed Kossuth, when he addressed his own body, seeing it as charged with an intelligent entity, saying to it whenever it fell into weakness, "Rise up strong and active; be competent to do all my work this day; throw aside pain!" It was the God charging every molecule and atom of him with competent obedience that slowly stirred from its quiescence into energetic activity, intelligently obeying his orders, making him strong and healthy for the day.

"The self of the man who is self-subdued is as the Supreme Self, or God," wrote the Theophoroi of old. The Eternal Immanence is in the present tense exactly as in the past, and the still intelligence that waits at every infinitesimal pore of our human frame, today, as yesterday, leaps into action if we command with firmness and sweet sternness. So now let us according to orders, "Upraise the self by the Self; for Self is the friend of self."

Every night of the life, before the eyes close in slumber, the immanent Godship, swelling the self with possibilities, should be commanded what work we choose our self to accomplish, and what type of character we choose to exhibit.

"Awake up, my glory!" commanded David, and his glory awoke. "Shake thyself from the dust; arise, and sit down, O Jerusalem; loose thyself from the bands of thy neck, O captive daughter of Zion!" shouted Isaiah to himself. And Isaiah transcended all the prophets that have ever lived on the earth; he was loosed from all dependence on the instructions of mankind.

The Self of our self has a voice. Its answer is, "I can all that and more," to every command we give it. Why should we fall asleep regretting the day or dreading the morrow, when we have an eternally abiding Self, quiescent, still, instinct with executiveness, waiting our firm insistence on Its action in our behalf?

Apollonius realized that he must be up and about the business of managing his own Godness, and he commanded the vitality of his own mind to remember all things, and the vigor of his own heart to beat with steady hardihood. And his mind did remember all things, even its relation to Universal Spirit that raises the dead; and his heart beat so in rhythm with the universal possibilities of himself that he was able to be in two places at once, whenever it was necessary.

"The upright man shall have dominion." chanted the Hebrew choirs under the leadership of David.

"Praise is comely for the upright man," sang the same Hebrew choirs; for the "I," the Soul-Self, the God-Self is one with praise as with command, ready to demonstrate all excellence for which It is praised, as all accomplishings to which It is commanded. The voice of inspiration teaches us to praise Soul, the upright Self charging ourself like a

Shekinah[12] pillar of fire by night, and a straight cloud of glory by day.

Let us not speak dispraisefully of our I, our secret free Spirit, saying, "I am sick," or, "I am discouraged," or "I am inconsequent" — for this is speaking out of key with high truth. "I was free born," said Paul, speaking in key with truth. So were we all free born, upheld by Free Spirit forever. By recognizing this we bring It to the front.

Lysias said, "With a great sum purchased I this freedom." He had had to struggle to appreciate his free born "I." Paul saw that no strenuousness is called for; that truth is mighty in itself, and whoever fights for high truth has forgotten its almightiness. Lysias represents those of us struggling to sense our freedom. Paul represents those of us sensing our free estate by simple recognition of our free Divinity.

"Lo, my sheaf stood upright," praised Joseph, visioning ahead when the Jews of all ages should owe their daily bread to his fidelity to praise of his own Self, maintaining his own vision of himself, even while in prison, as one instinct with majesty and virile with omnipotence. He had once had his ordinary senses entranced as in a dream, while his sense of Godness rose like an incense, and, remembering this, he told his fellow prisoners the import of their dreams, while yet his own dream was unfulfilled. He knew that truth is truth whether we are as yet embodiments of it or not.

Poets by setting their words and thoughts into tune with the soundless whispers of their own laws of Soul life, have often struck the chords of Self-praise like wonderful antiphons:

> "Thou shalt flourish in immortal youth,
>
> Unhurt amid the war of elements,

---

[12] *Shekinah* is the name of the divine Presence in the Jewish mystical tradition, the Kabbala. It is the feminine aspect of the Creator, whose presence is hinted at in Genesis.

The wreck of matter and the crush of worlds."

"Wingless upon your pinions forth I fly,

My words begin to breathe upon your breath:

Shorten half way my road to heaven from earth."

"It were a vain endeavor, though I should gaze forever

At that green light that lingers in the west;

I may not hope from outward forms to win

The passion and the life whose fountains are within."

The muscles of the body can be trained to be so strong that they can beat down giants in gymnasiums and pugilistic encounters. Thoughts of the mind can be trained to be so strong they can strike down opposing ideas on invisible mind fields, and paralyze the judgments of the brain so that judges and juries speak nothing, or, speaking, speak only nonsense. Muscles highly trained have won out against natural muscles, and thoughts highly practiced have wrought mental havoc.

What shall we, who wish to be free and not to engage in warfare, do, when our peace and safety are menaced by foes of such giant physical and mental stature? We will seek unto God, the high presence in the universe not affected by thoughts: we will seek unto Him present at our own headquarters, Whose years alter not, Who saith,

"These all shall perish but I, Soul, Self, shall endure."

"Seek ye Me, and ye shall live."

"No weapon formed against thee shall prosper."

"It shall not profit a man to gain the whole world by the prowess of his arm or the might of his thought. It shall only profit him to know his own Soul, uncontaminated offspring of Eternal Majesty, whose triumphs are already complete, ready to manifest."

"Highest God and inmost God is One God."

Let mind no longer claim creative powers or accomplishing energies. The true work is already complete in Spirit—the Self that we praise. "I am all that and more," answers Soul, our own I, to our highest descriptions. "I can all that and more," It answers to our highest mandates.

Soul hath a strength of empire and an influential glory which it hath not entered into the heart of man to conceive:

"Thou hast a strength of empire fix't,
Coterminate with God."

Our own Soul, our own free Spirit forever says, in bold faith, "I am Truth, I am God—Omnipresence, Omni-potence, Omniscience." The outer appearance, the cocoon, the hard chrysalis, vibrates when the words of Immortal Soul are spoken silently or audibly, as the chandelier hums when its key note is struck, or as the brim of a bell resounds when its hidden tongue hits it.

Paganini said he could shake any building by maintaining the note that caused it to vibrate. By speaking the truth of and to our own Soul, or Self, we strike the true key tone to the body of flesh and its mind and emotions. We can speak in silent language or audible words the truths of the transcendental Self that cause health, happiness, and helpfulness to radiate; and this speech wakes the Soul type of man to walk on earth.

A great modern philosopher says, "The Spirit is ever rising up in wrath against the forces that would brutalize it; the Soul is ever striving for independence of matter." But the truth of Soul is, that It ever dwells in calm majesty, striving against nothing. The heathen philosopher spoke more wisely: "Nothing can injure the immortal principle of the soul."

"Truly my soul waiteth upon God," sang David to a noble tune on a stringed instrument—"Truly my soul waiteth on God." And the angry javelin of the angry Saul could not reach him, for he had keyed himself to Uninjurable Immortal Soul, by voicing Its invigorating truth.

High Mysticism

It is not what happens to us that makes us healthy, happy, radiantly helpful; it is what we harmonize with, and we harmonize with what we describe. The winds of misfortune and pain hit every one sooner or later; but they do not touch our Self. "Truly my soul waiteth upon God," we sing. "My soul doth magnify the Lord," we chant. We set ourself to the heavenly Soul key by praising our innate Lordship, our eternal identification with Divinity:

"'Tis the set of the soul
That decides the goal,
And not the storms of life."

The Hopi Indian praises the great power that shines behind the sun. The Parsee praises the great power whose shining creates the sun. We praise the great free Spirit that stands back of our mind, which mind was once to us the sun of our life. We praise the free Spirit that knows beyond the mind which is saying ever, "I am God — I am Truth — I am Light" — and so we touch the law of the "five." For when the fifth angel sounds, the sun and air are darkened to the vision of John the Revelator. He means that by recognizing our divine "I", our mind ceases to be our supreme guide, and the sensations are forgotten.

There is a consciousness of cold, there is a consciousness of heat, there is a consciousness of stinging, and of falling or rising; so there is a consciousness of God. It is consciousness as in a trance; and John calls this the darkening of the sun and the air; for John is always speaking in figures.

He who has the consciousness of God knows beyond his mind, and wakes a new kind of body, in tune with the Infinite Immortal, the Lord Supreme. Nicholas of Basle once had this consciousness transcending his mind suddenly spring forth through all his being, and he found himself for a moment one with the Origin of knowing; and he said strange things beyond his previous concepts.

Praise and command of the divine Self of our self always wakes the consciousness of our own superiority to environing disadvantages and ignorances. "Know Thyself" was written over the Delphic Temple. It is only the divine Self, Soul, free Spirit that is worth knowing, worth praising, worth commanding. Fight as though thou wert the fighter, but know that it is the free Spirit of thee that moves on the opposing phalanxes that try to make life difficult — and the free Spirit masters them though the mind and the flesh quake. Jacob trembled all night by the Jabbok brook, and his mind was afraid, but the Angel of God's presence, with whom he had identified himself, fought his battle for him. "I have seen God face to face," he said, "and my life is preserved." "The Angel that redeemed me, blesseth the lads."

In the Fourth Study we are taught to practice the prayer of our lordship. John the Revelator calls this the smoke of the incense arising from the pit of our own infinite possibilities, for the highest and the inmost are one in infinitude. "And the smoke of the incense, which came with the prayers of the saints, ascended up before God out of the angel's hand." And one came like a star from the skies, showing to all mankind their own infinite possibilities, through recognizing the identity of the Soul of each man with the majesty of Almighty God. The infinite possibilities of Soul, our God Self, are spoken of in the Apocalypse as "the bottomless pit."

When Naomi was recognized by Ruth as her leader and guide and the light of her life, she was recognizing Spirit and forgetting her unhappy mind and emotions. "Entreat me not to leave thee," said Ruth "nor from following after thee, for where thou goest I will go." And Naomi, by her acceptance of Ruth became forebear of Christ the Savior. So our Soul, our Ruth, is ever saying to us, "Where thou goest, I will go," through the ages — always waiting in quiescence, in shining *esse* ["to be" or "beingness"] for acknowledgment by praise and command.

"You cannot praise Me so highly that I am not more than you praise, you cannot command Me so greatly that I cannot work by you still more greatly," ever whispers our secret Self.

The young Jesus stood up in old Nazareth and spoke of the everlasting Son of God, the Immortal Youth, the Unconquerable Divinity of man, and the Nazarenes tried to throw Him off a precipice, to destroy Him and His words. They refused to recognize their own divinity, their self renewing fountain of immortality. So old Naomi, accepting what Nazareth rejected, was prophecy that the seed of the woman should bruise the serpent's head — or, that the vision of woman toward the ever fresh fountain of divinity should save the world from the hard rulership of mind and matter.

"When the mind no longer conceives itself to be the knower, recognizing that Free Spirit is the knower and the doer, then is man's liberation from the laws of mind and matter," intoned an illuminated Hindu sage.

It was by the recognition of His own Infinite Divinity, His own Godness, that Jesus of Nazareth discovered His ability to perform the greatest work ever accomplished upon this earth, and made Himself the Bloom in the Garden of Man of all efforts to accomplish great helpfulness by divine at-one-ment. He saw Himself as the fulfillment of the prophecies of the ages, that one should come who should be greater than death and pain and grief and all the hatred of all the human race. He saw Himself so identified in the flesh with flawless, unhurtable Substance, that He could take to Himself all the pains and discords of the human race, and yet be not slain, and yet be nothing less than Divinity. He saw that whoever should in future ages acknowledge His accomplishment, should be set free from his own pains and discords, and should sense that Jesus of Nazareth, charged with His own divinity, was the Savior of the world from disease and death, misfortune and decay, even here and now upon this earth, in the sight of all mankind. "Who gave Himself for us," said Paul, "that He might deliver us from this present evil world."

"Who hath believed our report, and to whom is the arm of the Lord revealed?" wrote Isaiah, visioning ahead when the Savior of the world, as the arm of the Lord revealed, should not be acknowledged as having destroyed death by taking into His own body the sum total of death, and not acknowledged as having destroyed disease and pain by having taken into His Divinity-charged body the sum total of disease and pain, that all mankind might go free by the acknowledgment. Yet,

> "Surely He hath borne our griefs and carried our sorrows—'that we might go free from grief and sorrow.'"
>
> "Surely He was wounded for our transgressions, He was bruised for our iniquities; the chastisement of our peace was upon Him; and with His strips we are healed."

When Jesus came, the Bloom in the Garden of Man, of all the divine doctrines of earth, and charged Himself to the complete with the Divine Presence in the universe, He fulfilled the prophecy of the Jews that one should come who should be so at one with Absolute God that He could be slain and yet not dead, and diseased and yet immaculate, who should chemicalize[13] out of existence, and thus make nothing, all the maladies of earth. The condition of other men being consciously and visibly saved by this exercise of His divinity should forever be, the acknowledgment of this accomplishment.

> "He that acknowledged the Son hath the Father."
>
> "When thou shalt make His soul the offering for sin... the pleasure of the Lord shall prosper in His hand."

What is the pleasure of the Lord? "It is your Father's good pleasure to give you the kingdom."

As we each of us have a work which is supremely ours and no other can accomplish this opus, or God-ordained work, save our own self, so Jesus of Nazareth had His work, and His work was the redemption of mankind from sin,

---

[13] To "chemicalize" was to experience an idea or belief in the body taking on physical form—usually as symptoms, but sometimes as excretions—as the person released it.

High Mysticism

sickness and death, by the withdrawal into Himself, by virtue of His supernal Godness, all the sin, sickness and death of the universe, leaving the universe entirely without sin, sickness and death, thus making us to walk through a redeemed world.

This was His chosen work; and as it would be only fair for mankind to acknowledge the fact, if we had composed the greatest piece of music, or had built the most splendid temple, or discovered a wonderful law of mathematics, so it is only fair to Him, Jesus of Nazareth, charged to the supreme with Christ power, to acknowledge the completeness and splendor of His finished chosen work.

The inspired Scriptures are explicit on the subject of His successfully accomplishing in the large, what Elisha and Elijah accomplished in the small, in the way of taking death into Himself, that He might deliver them who through the expectation of death were all their lifetime subject to its bondage, destroying him that hath the power of death, that is, the devil, the lie from the beginning, abolishing death once for all. "Who hath saved us, and called us with an holy calling, not according to our works—who hath abolished death."

Gautama Buddha offered to bear the sins and the consequences thereof, which the Kali Yuga, or age of spiritual blindness was bearing, but he could not accomplish it, because he had not sufficiently identified himself with Divinity Supreme.

Elisha took the death of the Shunamite child into himself, and because he was so strong and alive with the Spirit of God, he chemicalized the death of the child into non-existence.

Elijah took the death of the Zarephath woman's child into himself, and because he was so alive, so virile with spiritual fire, he chemicalized death into non-existence for the child.

It is a well-known law in some countries that certain people by putting themselves into certain attitudes of mind and sensation, which we would call the consciousness of God, can withdraw sickness and pain and disease and deformity and death into themselves, leaving the sufferer free from his sufferings. Manes, of the Manichean sect of Christians thus took the sufferings of a great many people into himself, leaving them free from suffering.

Catherine of Siena withdrew many diseases and other forms of affliction from unhappy victims, into her own self, and by virtue of her spirituality made them nothing for them, and for herself also.

John Joseph of *Cocenza*, a small city southeast of Naples [in Italy], received into his own body the two terrible ulcers with which the Archbishop Michael was afflicted, and made them nothing by the chemical action of his awakened spiritual Substance.

This vicarious suffering is often taken in our own day, by sensitive and spiritually illuminated men and women, who are not awake enough to chemicalize the condition into nothingness, and so every neighbor wonders why spirtually sensitive and divinely illuminated people are so often afflicted in mysterious ways.

It is only Jesus of Nazareth in the history of man, who has understood how to consciously withdraw the wretchedness of the people into Himself, and make wretchedness nothing both for them and for Himself. He did it by the consciousness of His own God Substance, His own majestic, untarnishable Soul. And Isaiah the prophet, gave the assurance that all should go free from their own sorrows and sicknesses, who should acknowledge that Jesus of Nazareth, by the Soul, or the Christ splendor shining through Him, had borne their griefs and carried their sorrows, taken their infirmities and borne their sicknesses.

Mistakes of mind and action may be conscious or unconscious on the part of mankind. When mistakes are unconscious people may never trace the mechanical

High Mysticism

consequences of their mistakes in the misfortunes of daily life. The mother compels the child to study his lessons, not knowing that his eyes or brain may be weak, and in after years, when he is insane or blind, she is totally unconscious that she had once pressed his brain or eyes beyond their bearing point. The father compels his child to eat food repugnant to it, not sensing that his offspring naturally divines its proper pabulum, and when later the child has scrofula or consumption, the father feels that it is a great affliction, but surmises not at all his own guiltiness.

"Art thou come hither to destroy my son, and call my sin to remembrance?" asked the weeping Zarephath woman, for she belonged to a people and an age of the world which knew that it is some one's mistake of mind or action, exhibited in result, when sickness or death or deformity or misfortune attack anybody at all.

Keshub Chunder Sen of the Brahma Samaj of India, told in England, that the mothers of India try to direct the sicknesses of their children into their own bodies, by gashing themselves and striking themselves, feeling that they are strong enough to bear the consequences of their own mistakes, which the Hebrews would call sins, quite certain that by this vicarious suffering the children are set free from pains and sickness.

It is a law which has slipped the attention of the scientific men of our age, with the exception, perhaps, of a very few. Charcot of Paris discovered in the hospitals, while practicing healing by suggestion, that the malady of one person set free by his hypnotic will was found lodged in the next ward in some other patient, or even in the body of some person mentioned by his liberated patient.

Sometimes mental practitioners of today wake up in the morning with the pain of the person they have so faithfully treated, silently, with the noble affirmation, "You are Free Spirit, uncontaminated by disease or sickness." If they are spiritually strong and healthy they throw off this vicarious bearing, but if they are not, they may keep this condition for some unpleasant length of time.

A certain New England healer of this sensitive type did not like to shake hands with sick people, because she caught their diseases, though they went free, and she was not aware of being spiritually strong enough to dispose of the condition she was thus vicariously bearing, and not acquainted enough with the offer of the Great Vicarious to acknowledge, "Himself took our infirmities and bare our sicknesses," and so pass it along to its annulment.

This is where the offer of Jesus the Christ — the vicarious bearer of all the sufferings and all the unwitting causes of sufferings, for all the world — the destroyer of karmic death and disease, should be acknowledged, which acknowledgement is the same as passing on all distress to the Healing Fountains: "Himself took our infirmities and bare our sicknesses" — "and redeemed us from the curse of the law."

There is no describing what world wide liberation from suffering might be manifested, by making His "Soul the offering for sin" and its consequences, since the sacred promise remains on eternal pages, that "God the Father giveth us the spirit of wisdom and revelation, for the acknowledgment of Him," which acknowledgment the world has not yet made.

Peter and Paul among the early Apostles of the Christian doctrine were the most definite and distinct in proclamations concerning the mysterious mission of the Lord Jesus of Nazareth.

To the Galatians Paul wrote,

> "God sent forth His Son, made of a woman, made under the law, to redeem them that were under the law."

> "Christ hath redeemed us from the curse of the law, being made a curse for us."

And to the Corinthians he wrote, "God was in Christ, reconciling the world unto Himself, not imputing their trespasses unto them."

And to Titus he wrote, "Who gave Himself for us, that He might redeem us from all iniquity." In calling the attention of the Hebrew Christians to the majesty of the fulfillment of the law in the history of the Redeemer, he said, "We are sanctified through the offering of the body of Jesus Christ once for all." "How shall we escape if we neglect so great salvation?"

He further explained to the courageous Christian preacher to the Cretans—who were the famous liars of Homer's time and of Paul's time—that Jesus had given Himself for us all that He might redeem us from all iniquity.

It was reiterating the insistence of Jesus Himself that the "Son of Man came to give His life a ransom for many," when Paul wrote so boldly of Him "who gave Himself for our sins, that He might deliver us from this present evil world," "Who though He was rich, yet for our sakes He became poor, that we through His poverty might be rich."

Paul does not try to argue us into the acceptance of the principles of vicarious suffering, and the liberation from suffering, accomplished by acknowledging who hath suffered vicariously, for Paul was a Jew of the strictest sect of the Pharisees, and it was to him the natural religion that one should be made sufferer for the transgressions of many.

David had slain the seven sons of Saul to stop the three years of famine in all Palestine, and no Jew of Paul's time doubted that the cessation of the famine in Palestine in David's time was accomplished by the vicarious suffering of the seven sons of Saul; and Paul had been brought up on the belief that the transgressions of many might, even as a religious sacrament, be solemnly passed on to some innocent animal in the wilderness.

He understood Jeremiah's lamentation that great and small in his time were dying in the land, because of the sins of their parents, their prophets and their priests; and Paul understood also the unbelief of the scientific Greeks, and the hesitation of the Jews in accepting the vicarious accomplishment of The Universal Redeemer, because he knew, that although it is a strict law of possibility, it is a subtle proceeding, and only the mystically visioned can truly see it in the worldwide as the old Jews had seen it in the national.

"For the preaching of the cross is to them that perish, foolishness," he wrote to the hard headed, heavily diseased Corinthians, "but unto us which are saved it is the power of God."

When we are told, every one of us, to make acknowledgment of our works before the Heavenly Father, it is a severe test of our knowledge of Scriptural information, for there we are told that no man has ever accomplished any work purely by the recognition of his own divinity, except Jesus of Nazareth,

> "who hath put all things under Him" ... "to redeem us from the curse of the law."... "being the first fruits of them that slept," ... "abolishing death."

Peter's words are vivid and emphatic like Paul's: "Who His own Self bare our sins, in His own body on the tree, that we, being dead to sin, should live unto righteousness, by Whose stripes we are healed," for "Christ hath suffered for us in the flesh," and "once suffered for sins, that He might bring us to God."

We are all posited on this planet for the one purpose of accomplishing some great opus, or work of a unique and immutable sort, by the recognition of our own divinity, our own free bold spirit, offspring of Almighty Jehovah, and we have the example among the multitudinous sons of men, of One who was the first fruits of them that slept in non-recognition of their own divine equipment.

> "For now is Christ risen from the dead, that both He that sanctifieth and he that is sanctified might be one."

There is no respect of persons with God, and though Jesus of Nazareth was indeed the first to accomplish the superhuman, by the recognition of His own superhuman

High Mysticism

equipment, there is no reason why each one of us should not rise up and accomplish the super mission which we came here to accomplish for the glory of our Father Eternal.

This is the great planet of achievement. Every individual upon it naturally seeks to accomplish some beautiful and praiseworthy deed. If we name the sun as the first globe of our constellation, we are the fifth of the round balls of our enfolding skies, and may easily be called the planet of works, achievements, accomplishings, labors: Sun, Vulcan, Mercury, Venus, Earth.

But although we are the planet of be-stirrings, we must remember and acknowledge that only One of us has really accomplished His native deed of unspeakable splendor by full recognition of His own unspeakable, splendid Divinity. Tauler the mystic was persecuted by the Beghards and Beguines, and grand convent ladies, for telling them that the only work they could acceptably present before the Majesty on high was the Finished Work of the Lord Jesus.

The early Christians associated Number Five with the vicarious sufferings and death of the first human being among us to recognize Himself as God:

"Come tell me truly, to what truth
Should number five be guide?
The wounds of Christ in hands and feet,
And in His bleeding side."

When David, who had read in Leviticus 20 that five should chase an hundred, would slay Goliath, he chose him five small stones, for he was about to accomplish the liberation of his people, a tremendous deed, by the recognition that his divine Self was coining up against an hundredfold powerful foe: "Thou comest unto me with a sword, and with a spear, and with a shield, but I come unto thee in the name of the Lord of Hosts."

Only David's secret Self, or heavenly intelligence, knew the name of the Lord of Hosts, but by recognizing that somewhat about himself was Sonship to Jehovah, he took his symbolic five stones of victorious accomplishment, and undid the heavy burdens, and let the oppressed go free. Had David not acknowledged the victory already inherent in the unspoken Name of the Lord of Hosts, Goliath, the embodiment of bondage would not have been abolished.

There is a divine executiveness accompanying all high acknowledgments, as Paul also understood, when writing to the magic loving Ephesians: "God the Father giveth unto you the spirit of wisdom and revelation, for the acknowledgment of Him."

As it has taken the light of some splendid stars thousands of years to reach our earth, so it has taken the best part of two thousand years for mankind to recognize the far reaching glory of the undertaking of the Divinity-charged Jesus of Nazareth. It takes the upward fling of all man's cognizance of the law of vicarious suffering, to make him at this late day give honor to whom honor is due, and proclaim to the High and Lofty One inhabiting eternity:

> Christ Jesus as Emmanuel, or God with us, has borne my mistaken actions and their consequences once, for me, that I might be unloaded of my life blunders and be free to accomplish my own great task.
>
> Christ Jesus as Emmanuel, or God with us, has once taken to Himself the mistaken thoughts of my mind and their consequences that I might be unveiled of my mind, and free with my bold Soul, my uncovered free Spirit, to speak new words of victorious truth.
>
> Christ Jesus as Emmanuel, or God with us, has once borne for me the burdens of my human lot, that I might be unburdened free Spirit forever."
>
> He is the propitiation for my sins, and not for mine only, but for the sins of the whole world."
>
> That it might be fulfilled which was spoken of by Esaias the prophet— saying, "Himself took our infirmities and bare our sicknesses. ... Bore our griefs and carried our sorrows" that we might not bear them.

All the learnedness of the world can not compass the wonder of the mind of Christ, who knew all things and needed not that any man should teach Him. And the acme of His wisdom was His understanding of how to be God, glowing and transfiguring through the flesh, even to the annulment of all its mortal liability; and how to transfigure the mind with new light, so that no more errors could darken it; and how to be so mighty with Omnipotence that all who should recognize Him should share His mightiness. Whoever confesseth that Christ hath thus actually once come through the flesh, partakes of the coming, and is himself sent as a worker of new work, and a speaker of new words.

Who is ready, by acknowledgment, to wash sometimes in this pool of Siloam, or complete negation of himself, in heavenly abandon to the great Scripturally proclaimed Neutral to the sin of the world, living, like Paul, only as "Christ that liveth in me?"

This is becoming dead with Christ that we may live with Him. "For if we be dead with Christ, we shall also live with Him." Jesus was truly unified with highest God only, as positive magnet is unified with negative magnet only, so only the God of man could gather to Him to abide, and only the Christ can gather to all who let themselves go with Him in full acknowledgment of His having put all things under His feet, tasting death once for every man, suffering, the just for the unjust, as Master of all things.

> "Turn ye even to Me with (this) fasting, and behold, I will send you corn and wine and oil. Fear not, O land, for I will do great things."

It makes a great difference to us what doctrine we mine out of the Scriptures, and the Apostolic Christians surely mined there from, the doctrine that Jesus blotted out the handwriting of ordinances against us, taking it out of the way, nailing it to His cross.

Abraham was the pivotal man of sustained faith in individual good due from the Universal Absolute. Antisthenes was the pivotal man of cynicism, the doctrine of the absolute responsibility of the individual as a moral unit. Zeno was the pivotal man of stoicism, the practice of stern personal virtue as followed by Aurelius and Epictetus. Jesus was the pivotal man of achievement of the humanly impossible by the identification of Himself with the divinely possible.

The Chaldeans had prophesied of Him as the Lofty One to arrive among men.

The Egyptians had foreseen Him as the Lord of the whole world to come among us. The Chinese had waited for Him as the Saving One to be born and die for the race.

The Hebrews had expected Him as darkness expects light.

The Sibyls had foretold that as a Savior of man from his ungodliness should a free denizen of heaven come to earth to teach mankind of their own God Nature, and so redeem it from its hiding place in earthliness. "But," wrote the Erythrean Sibyl seven hundred and fifty years B.C.:

> "hostile man shall spit upon Him; on His sacred back they shall strike; gall and vinegar shall they give Him to drink; on a tree they shall hang Him; a darkness of three hours from midday shall cover the earth. But on the third day He shall rise in joyful light, and all who acknowledge Him king shall be happy in His kingdom."

It is ours to let ourselves go bathe in the Siloam waters of yielding, under Scriptural orders, as meekly as the blind man bathed in Siloam of old, declaring the Scripture doctrine of Christ Jesus as the first Divinity-awakened laborer in the vineyard, redeeming the world from sin, sickness, and death, that we might perceive with open eyes that we are walking through a finished kingdom, the arm of the Lord revealed.

This is fasting from our sense of obligation to heal the sick, cast out demonic tempers, and raise the dead, since in

Christ Jesus these works are finished, awaiting only acknowledgment to be plainly visible. "Is not this the fast that I have chosen," saith the Lord, "to loose the bands of wickedness, to undo the heavy burdens, to let the oppressed go free, and take off every yoke?"

Let us go daringly free into Scriptural declarations, as this is pure Scriptural doctrine of vicarious bearing, mentioned distinctly to an age lost to all belief in the truth of the cross, though "all the light of sacred story gathers round its head sublime."

Great signs shall follow them that believe in the Redemptive labor of the Divinity-awakened Lord of Galilee. They shall disclose the heavenly health of the redeemed world their opened eyes descry — the world free from sin, sickness, death, misfortune, mourning. "For there is a kingdom on this earth, though not of it," said Balthazar, "that is a fact, as our hearts are facts, and we journey through this kingdom from birth to death without seeing it; nor shall any man see it till he first knoweth his own Soul."

"Speaketh Isaiah of his own Divinity-charged soul, or of some other man's?" asked the eunuch of Philip. Then preached Philip unto him, Jesus of Nazareth, the Deific Man of the first undoing of the shadowy mechanicals of human association, leading on the generations into new *gerenda*, new works, to shine forth with, through sighting with mystically opened eyes the Kingdom of Love and Life immortal and uncontaminate that lies all about us.

"When thou shalt make His Soul the offering...the pleasure of the Lord shall prosper." "...Your Father's good pleasure to give you the kingdom."

6th Study: Understanding

NOTE

This Sixth Lesson is a lesson in invocation. It is well to know what we are invoking. Whatsoever we desire we are invoking it, and sooner or later it arrives upon us. Let a man draw himself to himself, and leaving all else choose what he will, and so it shall be unto him.

E. C. H.

As a bar of iron gains magnetic virtue by being placed for a time in a special position, so, it has been opined, particles of matter arranged and long continued in a certain posture may eventually get surcharged with life.

As natural phenomena are mysteriously symbolic of mystical realities we can understand by the bar of iron and the particles of matter how it came to pass that the inspirationally taught Theophoroi of old discovered that the inner vision of man oft-time giving attention to "*Ain Soph*, the Great Countenance of the Absolute" would charge man with transfiguring newness of Divine Life in plain manifestation.

Great promises have been caught by awakening watchers toward the Vast Vast Countenance of "Him who exalteth by his power, none teaching like Him"

"Look unto me and live."

"Seek ye my face and live."

"I give life to the faint."

"And I will reveal unto thee the abundance of peace and truth."

Take a wide-wide view of The Vast-Vast. "He giveth to all men liberally and upbraideth not." Upbraiding and stinting hail not from him, "not life but the Cause that life is — not spirit but the Cause that spirit is."

The oldest science in the world is The Mystical Science. It came to primordial man from the Tao over the Tao, while wistfully uplooking toward the wooing heights for some direction on his seemingly inscrutable life path.

Whatever came to primordial man concerning his relationship to the High Eternal First Cause he called inspiration, as it seemed to come along with his inward breathing. "The inspiration of the Almighty waketh understanding,* he said.

Hesiod, poor, despised, lonely, felt the wooing of some higher influence and called it Spirit, or Breath of Heaven, and he founded a new school of poetry with some thing like the power of "thrice ten thousand spirits round our pathway gliding, rewarding some with glory, some with gold," as the key teaching of his successful school. Joshua set up twelve stones in the midst of the Jordan River to commemorate the dividing of the waters by heavenly influence where the feet of the priests bearing the ark of the covenant of the Lord of all the earth stood firm, rewarding the Hebrews with what Hesiod's poetry would call glory.

The miracle-working Unseen had been the glad theme of inspired men before Joshua and Hesiod. They all taught that a great unseen world swings close to this world, an imperishable world, whose substance is Zeus, or Brahma, or Ra, or God, or Gaea who sprang from Chaos, or Cimah the queen of heaven to whom the Hebrew women offered cakes and worshipping incense in the streets of Jerusalem. Jeremiah was angry with the women for not calling the ruling other world that swings so close to this world, Jehovah; but the women said that they had had plenty of victuals, and had been well, and had seen no evil while worshipping the queen of heaven, the nourishing Cimah, and they would not call the miracle-working Highest One Jehovah.

The breath of the unseen world was in the refreshing winds that hailed from above to primordial men as they bared their heads and purposely inbreathed the ether winds

High Mysticism

subtler than earth's common atmospheres which to this day wait actionless for man's inbreathing action:

> "Breathe toward me heavenly breath, till all this breathing form of me quickens with breath divine."

Father John of Russia felt the stirring of a breath full of curative elixirs quickening the bread and wine of the Eucharist. He cited cases of bodily healing while partaking of these ether-charged elements. Certain names of old were reputed to liberate the healing elixirs biding forever within the airs we daily breathe never noting their mystic offers:

> "Why, O man will ye die, having power to partake of the breath of immortality?"

Even watchers toward the winds that make forecasts for coastwise shippings and aerial flyings declare that there is one wind that comes from above which always fetches reviving. It is the northwest wind. But to them that seek all their good from above every wind contains over breaths of willing revivings or buoyant ethers of renewal. Ezekiel called for all the four winds to breathe forth their secret vitalizings that the multitude of dead in the Seir Valley might quicken through all their earthbound forms.

The cradle doctrine of the New Age, is "Thou God seest me—For I also have looked after Him that seeth me," as it was the cradle doctrine of earliest Hebrew prophetics, announcing the coming together of aristocracy and serfdom in The Christ above the pairs of opposites rich and poor, bond and free. Every man's hand has been against Ishmael the bond child, and Ishmael's hand has been against every man, yet Ishmael's cradle instruction was "Thou God seest me," and the Ishmael type did found a great nation and place twelve princes in the earth whose determinations are with us to this day.

And Isaac, the aristocracy of the world, with the same father Abraham that the bond child owned, though he has held the world in fee, must with the serf begin again, "Thou

God seest me, For I also have looked after Him that seeth me," that the time of their warfare may be shortened according to Christian decree.

Abraham their father looked for a city which hath foundations, and sought the wooing Unseen by looking up and hearing the voice of the Light of the city saying, "The land thou seest, to thee will I give it."

Why should serfdom and aristocracy fight for land, or houses, or precedence, when all that belongs to either of them they may inherit by lifting up their eyes to the world that swings close whose miracle-working winds may any time waft in miraculous new prosperings?

"The spider layeth hold with her hands, and is in kings' houses," says Solomon, speaking for those who seek their highest Best by highest Watch:

"By so many roots as the marsh grass sends in the sod,
I will heartily lay me ahold on the greatness of God"
The Miracle-working God.

Mystical Science brings the close swinging miracle-working uplands to our attention with perpetual urgings. To bad and good among us it declares the same: "Lift up your eyes to the fields white for the harvest." If we keep off the world's righting ground of good and evil in thought and conduct, the clinches of its estimates of what is good have no yea in us, and its estimates of what is evil find in us no agreement. Visioning toward the same country Abraham was seeking we swing in with The Miracle-Working Heights. "The land thou seest, to thee will I give it," whispers its unceasing voice. "Honor and fortune exist for him who remembers that he is in the neighborhood of The Great," wrote the truth-announcing Emerson, keeping step in a mystical moment with Moses the God-taught law giver, and Ezra the inspired reformer.

Seven million men and thousands of tiny children perished [in the Crusades] marching toward the Holy Sepulcher to take possession of it. Where was their inward watch? Remember [Hegel tells us] that "We always look toward an

High Mysticism

object before thinking it, and it is by having oft recourse by inward viewing that then the mind goes on to know and comprehend" — and the body, obedient follower, to show the concrete thereof. Who on earth was there to teach the pilgrims and crusaders sepulcher-ward inward viewing, that there was another country smiling over their heads, whose giving was prospering, unsepulcherd, joyous life?

He of highest vision rises highest even among the sons of earth. Samuel said, "I am the seer," and he went forth to choose a king for Judah and Israel. Jesse of Bethlehem-Judah was the greatest man among the Hebrews, and his sons the finest specimens of Judean manhood. Abinadab, Eliab, and Shammah were marched before the seer. One had a genius for war, one a genius for statecraft, one for language. What a wonderful gift is language! If your language were right you would be the desideratum of kings' courts. You would stop the warfare between Isaac and Ishmael, capital and labor, rich and poor! Samuel Johnson, uncouth, untidy, ragged, held the young peers of Oxford spellbound with his speech, and the masters gave him larger freedom of action than his confreres, because his words cut swaths like polished scythes. Djemal Pasha ruled the Turkish empire with his speech. The world awaits its master of brotherhood-cohering words. "A right word; how good it is, who can measure the force of a right word?"

But Samuel said. No, not one of these for king of Judah and Israel. For the one with genius for war has his inner vision toward men to marshal them for martial triumphs; the one with genius for statecraft has his inner viewing set toward men to place them as heads of tribes and territories, and the one with genius for compelling speech is observant of men's swaying emotions under his spellbinding oratory.

Now their youngest brother David took not much note of men. "Mine eyes are ever toward the Lord," he said, "for he shall pluck my feet out of the net." Not what he himself did, but what the Lord on high was doing, was David's aspiration. And the seer anointed David with kingship; and he was the greatest warrior on earth, the greatest statesman, the most victory-awakening speaker: "The Lord hear thee in the day of trouble — The name of the God of Jacob defend thee — send thee help from the Sanctuary — Strengthen thee out of Zion," was his national rallying cry.

In the time of the World War one nation shouted, "We are ready to sacrifice seventy-five thousand men any day." And it was soon recorded that that nation had sacrificed more men in proportion to those sent forth to battle front than any other nation engaged in the great conflict.

What should that nation have shouted? "We are ready any day to forward an army to the triumph of our righteous cause!" Why should they have called the attention of our globe to sacrifice? Are we not soon showing forth that to which our inner gaze is directed? Sepulcher 1000 A.D. or Sacrifice 1917 A.D.? Who shall rouse the world to choose the sepulcher-and-sacrifice-undoing High Watch?

Nothing shall by any means defeat us lifting up our eyes oft-time to Thee!

Elisha was enraged at Joash king of Israel, for not smiting the earth with his arrow five or six times, instead of only three times, when Joash was told by Elisha to smite the earth with his arrow. For five stands for successful labor, and six stands for laborless success, or the miracle of The Highest ever moving hitherward.

The hyacinth bulb planted top side down labors desperately to bloom Chinaward, and succeeds in making an anemic blossom, pale and small, but plain imitation of itself as it would be facing the sunshine and ambrosial morning airs. What does the downward looking hyacinth know of its own sun-facing, un-anemic wide-spreading beauty? So we have never seen a man of the Laborless Supernal order, facing the "Sun of Righteousness with healing in his wings," till the New Dispensation gave us its good news when he came toward us!

An inspired full victory, or the laborless miracle, was Elisha's hope for Joash. But Joash had only three small victories over Ben-Hadad king of Syria, enemy of Jehovah, as his three arrow-smitings prefigured — wide indeed of the mark of the high success his royal right might claim. "I fetch my knowledge from far," said Elihu, youngest of Job's advisers.

> "Behold, God exalteth by his power; who teacheth like Him?... He sealeth instruction while man slumbereth on his bed... He openeth the ears in the night time... Remember to magnify His work, that men may behold it afar off."

The more we look to *Ain Soph*, the Great Countenance of the Absolute, the Origin of knowing, the more we know of the influence of the close-swinging miracle-working world in its finished beneficence:

> "Listen, O isles, unto me, and hearken ye people from far"
>
> "I will show thee great and mighty things which thou knowest not!"

Solomon got him to the myrrh mountains of wisdom for the mystical daybreak, and to the hills of frankincense for the streams of healing hailing from above the sunrise. Beyond the margins of the mind supernal Wisdom waits. Over the dayspring of a glory from above the heavens' mysterious healings are distilling for those who obey the mandate — "Lift up your eyes — Look unto me — I am the Lord that healeth."

The greatest doctrine announced by the voice of inspiration, is that A Mighty One onlooketh us, wooing ever as, "What wilt thou?" — "Ask what ye will" — "Is any-thing too hard for me?" Who of us, uplooking, answers face to face as a man talketh with his brother? Who of us holds high converse with the Ruler in the heavens, who saith, "To him that order-eth his conversation aright will I show salvation?"

In ancient mythology the sixth god was Cronus, god of the harvest,, with two faces, one glowing white and one glooming dark, according as he set himself to harvest from the heights above or from the depths below. When the giants got six-toed from earth bound attentions they were destroyed. When the man of Galilee touched the six-stepped throne place by daily converse with what David called The glory above the heavens, such magian effulgence gleamed forth from him that multitudes coming unto him, he healed them every one.

We are all harvesting according to our inward viewings. "Why are ye troubled?" asked Jesus, and "Why do thoughts arise in your hearts?" We had to wait for the birth of Hegel, 1770 A.D., before we got the scientific answer to that question: "We always look toward an object before thinking it," wrote Hegel, "and it is by having oft recourse by inward viewing that then the mind goes on to know and comprehend."

High Mysticism is not a science of right thinking, or right conduct; these are strenuous labors. High Mysticism is the call to look up to what the Kabala of Jewry named *Ain Soph*, The Great Countenance of the Absolute, who ordereth thoughts and speech and conduct anew. "Behold, I make all things new," he saith. "I will return unto that people a new language." "They shall speak with new tongues."

The speech of man always declares where his inward viewing, laden with harvestings for life conditions, oftenest alights. The good woman mentions the shiftlessness, the sorrows, the sufferings of her neighbors, and she has some unpleasantness of body and of affairs formulated by the inward gazing her verbal descriptions betray. Is it not written that the wages of sin (or aberrated vision) is death? Mysticism is not a science of goodness and badness of conduct. It is the science of that which harvests as good or bad conduct. It is the science of the genesis of conduct and the genesis of thoughts. Secret viewings compose their own speech, rouse their own emotions and formulate their own actions.

Our initial and compelling faculty is our inner vision. Vision often Godward and live anew. So shall the body be

High Mysticism

like "a tree planted by rivers of water, whose leaf fadeth not." Vision often Godward so that affairs also may go well. Gaze often toward Our Father, and all thoughts shall be like morning music. Lift up an inward looking now and then to a country whose ether winds ever raying forth their healing aura, are fleet remedials for all the world's unhappiness.

Does not Dr. Jowett record that Bishop Westcott of Durham was a man of royal strength from gazing toward the glory of the Highest? How did he know there was a Highest to gaze toward? How did he know there was any glory to harvest from as royal strength of mind and body? What was he gazing with?

The kings of Tyre wore the sardius stone, sixth stone of Revelation, to signify that they had caught a threefold luster by invocation. The sixth stone of Revelation is the luster sardius, symbol of invocation.

By physical invocation the body may renew with the subtle elixirs that wait to mill within it to strengthen and uplift. The hills open in the daytime and at night pinch into themselves the circumambient vitalizings with which the daytime airs are charged. Then they bring forth grass and herbs and grains and cattle. The brain of man can open and close into itself the wisdom elixirs that hug it down like Sibyls' hoods. "Lift up your heads, ye gates (ye sutured brain), the King of glory waits to enter in. Who is the King of glory? The Lord strong and mighty, the Lord of Hosts, he is the King of glory." There is no part of the body that may not open and indraw the subtler-than-air stimulants that would soon burst forth as strength. This is physical invocation.

The mind is surrounded by distant knowledges that it may indraw by asking of awaiting knowings, and burst forth with answers as from unseen teachers. This is mental invocation. The sardius stone stands for mental invocation.

The luster sardius stands for mystical invocation — the way to know new things from the heights above the margins of the mind, where things hitherto untaught lie waiting our mystical invocation. Pythagoras said that there are magic mighty syllables making up an Ineffable Name, Key to the mysteries of the universe. Speak them as into upper ethers where the hitherto unknowns abide; and they will mill hitherward with new knowledges. "The Ineffable Name to key to the mysteries of the universe."

The Parsees called the magic syllables so equipped with drawing power, the *Ardai Viraf* Name, full of Revealings. "And the throne had six steps: and I saw in the right hand of him that sat on the throne, a book."

Every man's name is the book of his equipment, and the use he has made of his name constitutes the influence of his name, or its spirit, or its ghost. Would we not expect that he whose vision had lifted highest, and whose invocations had brought him to highest harvestings would shed the strongest and best influence, or spirit, or ghost, by the calling of his name? He who sat upon the throne, with the book in his right hand, announced to all the world, "The holy ghost, whom the Father will send in my name, shall teach you all things."

Surely the magic name for which Pythagoras was seeking to reveal to him the secrets of the universe must be concealed in the name promised to reveal all things by invocation! From its breathing forth power the Parsees might have caught the wisdom-wafts their longing aspirations forecast.

I wept much, said John the Revelator, because the world went on so long without noticing that some names are like alabaster boxes of empowering ointment. Break them open by invoking them, and mysterious new influences awake through body and mind and environments. Paul wrote to the Ephesians that revelations would be vouchsafed by the acknowledgment of Jesus Christ, and the eyes of man's understanding should open to know the hope they may entertain from the calling of him that hath put all things under his feet, with name above every name that is named, not only in this world, but also in that which is to come.

The one insistence of the Jesus who was Christ with the fullness of the Godhead bodily, was that his name sheds forth fresh life:

"My words (my syllables) are life."

"I came that ye might have life."

"I am the bread of life."

"He that eateth me shall live by me."

Tennyson wrote that "'Tis life, more life for which we pant," but he did not tell us how to get more life. Only the Christ Jesus man ever told mankind how to quicken anew with the "life of which our nerves are scant," and he declared that his name would stir the ether-breaths of the unseen eternal world to inbreathe with our inbreathing, as the ancients called the names of mighty warriors and wise saints and drew toward themselves their influential vigors.

There is no science of wealth or health so great as the science of inbreath, was the conclusion of the ancients. "Like to a sky cow for rich givings, is invocation," they averred.

"An hundred forty and four thousand had His Father's name in their foreheads," said John, which means that the right number to stir the world shall have cognizance of awakening Spirit, or Holy Ghost, or healing winds, or God breath from heaven that the name of the Lord of Life conveys.

O Hither wafting breath of strength, There's a heaven-taught way of reaping!

Shall we know less about invocation than the Greeks and Romans of old, calling, "O Mercury, grant me magistral to poverty—O Morpheus, come with celestial soporifics!"

Invocation is the greatest efficiency of prayer. Did not the voice of far past inspiration declare that the name of Deity transcends prayer? Jesus, of Nazareth called the Overlooking Deity Father! At the crucifixion he cried, "Father, forgive them!"

Why does the world persist in telling itself that the cry of the Jews invoking the blood of the cross to take vengeance on themselves and their children has been the only prayer answered through all these centuries? Why have we not been taught to lift up our eyes to the prayer-answering, forgiving Father, and partake of the now hitherward streaming Beneficence into which the glorified Jesus was then gazing? Should the offspring of the mistaken Crusaders be harassed world without end? Should our children's children be taunted on and on because of our today's foolhardiness? Though your errors were as scarlet, the for-giving answers to the Jesus Christ prayer on Calvary passing them along to the sin-undoing High Redeemer, they shall be as if they had never been.

"I will set no wicked thing before mine eyes; it shall not cleave to me," was David's song for our instruction.

In the science of numbers, Six is significant of complete manifestation, all the faculties raised to their highest exercise. And Sin is errant vision unified with errant words and acts. Errant vision, or sin, carries the banner of triumphant arrival at complete manifestation.

To the mystically wise the badge of triumphant arrival at the worst that downward vision can accomplish, is tantamount to telling plainly the possibilities of upward visioning.

To the mystic the victorious arrival of a bodily swelling, the result of somebody's downward viewing, at the strength of its ultimatum bursting and blasting with death, shows how sight upward toward the Author of strength would make manifest Undefeatable Omni-potence. "For the way of life," wrote Solomon, "is above to the wise, that he may depart from hell beneath."

> "And number Six, what mystic truth
> Do wise men find therein?
> As Six, Six, Six is Satan's mark,
> Six is the badge of Sin."

High Mysticism

The secret that sin tells to the wise, is that by vision toward matter and mind and their laws of pleasure and pain we get caught in the wheel of destruction, but by vision toward the Highest One above the pairs of opposites, we get charged with independence of matter and mind. It is ours to choose whether we will be blooms in the Garden of Immortality here and now, or blooms in the garden of apoplexy and failure.

To the mystic, the sensualist with his blazing sores of malefic contagion, is sign royal of the possibility of one charging himself to fadeless bloom with heavenly inspiration, till men round the globe to touch the hem of his garment of healing; till "the gentiles come to his light, and kings to the brightness of his rising."

To the mystic, the idiot, the heaviness of his neighborhood, breathing the common airs and dying like the rhinoceros, is sign royal of one charged with wisdom from Highest Jehovah, inbreathing immortalizing elixirs, till people brave oceans and deserts to enter his buoyant presence, to be lightened of their burdens of ignorance and catch the breath of his victorious life.

There is but one commandment issuing I from the Giver of Almighty Health, and that one commandment, is "Look unto me, and be ye saved, all the ends of the earth." — "Beside me there is no Savior."

Where did Elijah get strength to run barefooted all the twelve miles from Mount Carmel to Jezreel, ahead of King Ahab's swift horses, leading them by bridle and tiring not? From inbreathing winds of unceasing strength from above, where his inner eye was seeking the Author of strength, who giveth to all men liberally, even to unbreakable Omnipotence. "As the Lord God of Israel liveth, before whom I stand," he said.

Elijah did not touch the six mark of arrival at the best that the high watch could do for him, for he did his inbreathing of victorious energy intermittently, and unwittingly, and his upward watching halfway, unknowing of the secret of up-looking power. Like most human beings of this very day he spent more time viewing his troubles and describing them, than glorying in the immune splendor of the wisdom-imparting Jehovah.

To the true mystic the upward looking and the inbreath of heavenly atmospheres are volitional and scientific. He knows whence the energizing breaths come wafting their newness, and the healing elixirs come streaming with enlivening vigors, and he knows that if he is not rounded up with unkillable Omnipotence it is because he has neglected his science.

The world waits the six mark of unceasing acceptance of the divine Highest only; it waits the visible bloom of immortality in the Garden of Man — the Jesus point of plain demonstration that "No man taketh my life from me."

In the Apocrypha, we read that in the sixth place the Lord imparteth understanding. Understanding imparted from the Lord is the desideratum of man, for having touched this magian flame his life is kindled to glow forever. For "understanding is a wellspring of life." Mystic understanding is strength, identical with divine strength. "I am understanding," saith the Lord, "I have strength," and it is written that He giveth this strength to his people.

Habakkuk, reputed to be the Shunamite child raised from the dead by Elisha, could not help reasoning, in his first chapter of prophecy, that because the Lord his God was from everlasting, he need not die, though the Chaldeans, supping up their leopard-like strength from the east wind, scoffing at kings, and deriding every stronghold, should become dust heaps like as their swift horses.

In self-forgetting moments Habakkuk breathed from beyond the margins of the Chaldeans' powerful east winds. He breathed the ethers that lave the throne steps of divine arrival. He made it education to know sin's glorious secrets as his three mystic chapters reveal them, telling of the high watch and the low watch, and of saving and gathering and honoring as the time of unspoilable wholeness ripens, disclosing the bloom of arrival at the glory of the Lord's still, secret inbreaths, mighty to save.

Habakkuk's three chapters lay stress on the end of captivity, everywhere visible to the eyes of all watchers toward Him that saith, "Look unto me." They tell the story of the Holy First, who came from Paran, the hidden heights, whom the Gadarenes of earth implored to depart again into hiding. They tell how, when sin's vast secrets uncover, mankind shall choose to breathe from above, till they all bloom as unspoilable health made visible, in comradeship with the Lord of fulfillment, and the brightness of his completeness shall not be lost to their view.

These three chapters of Habakkuk tell of the presence of the Lord of demonstration now among us, back of the coasts of Gadara, or our unopened faculties, ready now to quicken to life in every part all who believe on his leadership and his nearness, and call upon his revealing name. "Who hath believed our report?" (see 5th Study) "That believing, ye might have life through his name." "Call unto me," he saith, "and I will answer thee, and show thee great and mighty things which thou knowest not—and all the nations shall fear and tremble for all the goodness and for all the prosperity that I procure."

Paul was told to rise up quickly, calling upon this name, and he knew Its ripening value, as the Gnostics of his time knew the gift-giving name *Abraxas*. "I press toward the mark, for the prize of the high calling of God in Christ Jesus," he said, "but if in anything ye be otherwise minded, God shall reveal even this unto you."

Many Christians have been "otherwise minded," in their calling, and have had what they called for revealed in full measure. [The British Bishop Thomas] Carlyle called, "O Fortune! Thou that givest to each his portion on this dirty planet! Grant me literary distinction!" And he declared that ever since he had been able to frame a wish, the wish of being famous had been foremost.

Eliphaz the Temanite enjoined upon all mankind the practice of the calling principle: "Thou shalt lift up thy face to God," he said, "Thou shalt decree a thing, and it shall be established unto thee." Every choice is a call, direct or implied^ Carlyle's call was so direct that literary fame was promptly "established unto him." William the Conqueror's call was not direct like Carlyle's, but so strongly implied that he laid hold of England with uncanny power, defeating the brave Saxons with astonishing ease. He had for years been claiming the crown of England as the bequest of Edward the Confessor to his father. Landing at Pevensey of Hastings with 60,000 warriors to take possession of his vision's crown, he fell forward upon his face into the sand. Then all his 60,000 attendants blanched in their faces, for to be apparently *hors de combat,* biting the dust on a strange coast, was evil omen. But William's vision was too strongly set toward England as his own possession to regard omens. Clutching the sand in his fingers, he used the words that tallied with his steadfast view: "By the splendor of God, I hold the soil of England in my hands!" he shouted. The historic demonstrations of important men give definite cue and clue to each individual's demonstration, on small or large scale, according as his choice has been powerful or puny, and his objective glorious or commonplace.

Paul and the Christians he gathered round him lifted up their faces to the Almighty, as Eliphaz had enjoined, and called to the Victorious One, till they were great conquerors together. "I am more than conqueror," Paul declared of himself. And he insisted that the victorious Christ Jesus he had so persistently invoked, charged him so near to the brim with Christ executiveness, that he could work miracles. "I can do all things through Christ which strengthened me," he said.

Paul did not round up to the six mark of unkillable Life and unbreakable Omnipotence, because of getting entangled in a downward watch toward sex differentiations, and foods suitable and unsuitable. He split on the rocks of sex and food. Though on his spiritual nights he proclaimed ' 'neither male nor female in Christ Jesus," yet he "suffered not a woman to speak in the Christian Church."

Though on his vision's scientific formulas he read plainly that, "Neither if we eat are we the better, nor if we eat not are the worse," yet he became explicit in explaining what might and what might not be eaten, and forbade any man who was not a strenuous worker to eat anything at all; as though eating were very important.

The glory of sin is its consistency — it keeps at its own stride toward full arrival and nothing diverts it from its six mark's grand completeness. Does any upward watcher catch heavenly health by his persistence heavenward, till his health breaks forth like the morning, and every sick person catches health from him, as surely as the downward watcher identifying with small pox, gives his neighbors the same by the hundreds, if they come into contact with him? It is only the Jesus among us of whom is it yet written:

> "Multitudes came unto him, and he healed them every one."
>
> "And as many as received him, to them gave he power to (visibly) become the Sons of God."

In mysticism we learn the law of our subtle visional sense. We find that we use our inner vision constantly, and we find that our thoughts follow its wake, and that physical conditions follow the thoughts. By knowing the law of the inward vision we follow intelligently Job's lamentation that his thoughts were only unmanageable shadows, till his witness was in heaven, and his record plain on high. We know how the seers read right descriptions of all that is transpiring far or near: "It was the labor of mine eyes," wrote Asaph the seer, after studying into the secret workings of his successful seer-ship.

For whatever is looked toward as an objective to the inner eye reveals its secrets, whether the lofty One inhabiting eternity, or the pyramids of Egypt, or the motives of our neighbors. There is but one law running along to the flowering of all steadfast visioning.

"The secret of the Lord is with them that fear him." "Fear" is singleness of eye.

"In the fear of the Lord is instruction in wisdom."

"The fear of the Lord is a fountain of life."

"And there is no want to them that fear him."

Fear, or singleness of eye toward any objective, is disclosure of its secrets, and experience of its working power.

"Pass the time of your sojourning here in fear," wrote Peter, after having wrought great miracles by obedience to the Mosaic law of fearing the glorious name of the Lord. Peter discovered with the prophet Micah, that there is great effect from singleness of eye toward names, as toward other objectives, and he chose the name of the Savior of men to stand by. Micah got it as an unfailing law, that, "My name shall (cause to) see that which is." And Peter proved it by walking with the angels, and doing their works, after fearing the "only name given under heaven, whereby men must be saved." For as the angels do wondrously, so also did Peter wondrously always by the power of the name he inbreathed.

The purpose of religion has always been to teach men to make the most of themselves. And at its acme of instruction it has taught that right thought and right conduct follow right view. To look steadfastly toward the Helper, and Healer, and Savior abiding unseen but always within calling distance, has ever been its injunction: "Endure as seeing Him who is invisible."

The Gnostics of old endured seeing and calling toward *Abraxas*, unseen Giver of tangible blessings.

High Mysticism

The name of one who has accomplished great works vibrates with his genius. Aristides, the wise archon of Athens, knowing this, set his eye toward Aesculapius, whose skill in curing diseases and restoring the dead to life, was traditioned to have made Zeus angry, lest he rendered men immortal; and Aristides called faithfully upon Aesculapius, till he came swiftly through the formless spaces, and stood in his presence, audibly counseling Aristides for the successful cure of his bodily disease.

"There is one operative virtue running through all things," was a discovery of Cornelius Agrippa of Cologne. "All things super-celestial may be drawn into the celestial, and all things supernatural may be drawn into the natural," was also his discovery, though the practice of drawing down the virtues ascribed to the different angels, into statues, and periapts and wafers, long antedated Agrippa's explanation of the magical drafts men may make on the good offices of nature and of God.

By much attention to material things, men make such drafts on matter that its mysterious operations seize upon them in more than conceivable manifoldness. They suck in the ways of matter, by indirect calling, as they look to it for their welfare and their knowledge. This is the way of which Solomon wrote, "that seem-eth right unto a man, but the end thereof are ways of death."

Let men but volitionally lift up their eyes to the Sender of the mystic cure currents ever hailing hither-ward, and make all their drafts on these immortal streams, and the mysteries of health, and prosperity, and incessant renewal shall be revealed and experienced. Jesus having demonstrated this, his name as the vanquisher of death, and the abode of all gifts of God, made him able to declare, "Whatsoever ye shall ask in my name that will I do." "Ask what ye will, and it shall be done unto you." For "all things are delivered unto me of my Father."

"This is the path which the lions' whelps (or the obedient followers of the masters of material science) have not trodden, nor the fierce lions (the masterful kings, and generals, and presidents among us) have not passed by." It is that lost old superstition, in which the world was nearer essential truth than ever in its so-called scholarly acquirements.

The Science of God reveals all science. The true name of God reveals the Science of God, and reveals all names, from the names of the stars to the names of the insects, from the names of the fearless arch-angels to the right names for the victorious earth walk of our children.

The name of one who knows the Great Revealing Name, reveals his knowledge. "The Holy Ghost, whom the Father will send in my name, shall teach you all things." "Thou holdest fast my name — I will give a new name which no man knoweth save he that receiveth it."

All that we as yet know of the Maker of the universe is the practice of His Presence. Of His actual substance and purposes we know nothing. "Touching the Almighty we cannot find Him out — with Him is terrible majesty," reported Elihu, who yet found the Almighty teaching and exalting him, and giving him songs in the night, as the result of his upward watch and the inbreath of the Almighty that waked the God seed of understanding within him.

Elihu seemed to know no other name of the Highest but "God." But he spoke of a messenger, an interpreter, a ransom, an atonement, one who could enlighten with living light. He could not speak the name, but fetched, he said, the knowledge from far, that by the recognition of the atonement, man should begin to breathe in lakes of joy and wisdom from the Giver of wisdom, thereby comrading on terms of equal arrival with the man whom the race of men had accepted as the flower of divine arrival on this globe. The recognition of the man of atonement, makes draft on the Holy Spirit, "The Holy Spirit whom the Father will send in my name." It makes draft on life: "I will put my spirit into

High Mysticism

you and ye shall live." Wherefore turn yourselves, and live ye."

The Holy Spirit is the ghost or spirit of wholeness; or breath of wholeness. Job speaks of the spirit of God being in his nostrils; and Job's whole life was changed by refusing to speak against the transformation which the inbreath of the healing ghost was making in him. Job was faithful to the high vision and the atonement, though he knew not the name of the daysman who should make the atonement. Evidently Job knew that to regard the breath he breathed as the healing spirit, instead of common atmospheric air, and never to speak of the outcome as anything but trans-forming, would fetch him out on to some upland that men who breathed just air, and called it air, would never reach. And he was right. His witness in the heavens and his breath always known by him while inbreathing it as the God breath, brought him to where he was blessed beyond his calculations, and with mysterious wisdom he knew himself well pleasing to the High Eternal.

The Apostles of the Regeneration knew the name of the daysman, and they knew their breath as charged with the ether wafts of healing, and they knew the law of the vision, and the reborn status that was to be the outcome. This was their Christianity. In the name of the Great Achiever they drew their breath as the Holy Spirit, which is the spirit of wholeness, and they were transformed characters. They walked in the fourth dimension in space, and no prison walls could hold them, and no lions' jaws could destroy them; and no former ignorance or common birth among the people who breathed common air, and sought their life from material productions could count against their being the wisest men on earth. They took up a life near us and yet above us, a life with the power of manifestation here and there, and now and then, through-out the generations, not unmet even in this twentieth century.

But their mode of arrival at the state of just men made perfect, on the unseen plane, is not the final arrival that mystical interpretation foretells.

To be charged to overflow with irresistible miracle-working while yet manifest in the flesh, to be the radiance of buoyant joy while yet walking among the sons of men, to shed the perfume of healing and strengthening and illuminating while yet speaking with us and smiling upon us — this is the final Christian ministry; this is the bloom of full obedience to the Sacred Edict, "Look unto me."

There is no warfare where the vision of God is. There is no disease where the healing name is called. There is no inadequacy or failure while the spirit of God is in the nostrils, inbreathed as the only breath. This is living truth.

If Pope Sixtus, as a ragged lad under the trees, could lift up his face toward the papal throne, and decree to be pope of Rome, and draw himself by his decree to the papal seat, equipped to perform all its high offices with intelligent determination and successful energy, so some lover of mankind can lift up his face to the Almighty, as Eliphaz counseled, and decree to be the healing and strengthening and illuminating of all the people whom he may look upon, or who look upon him.

If we would transcend our limitations, we must look above our limitations. And we always believe in what we look toward; and we draw what we believe in. Deep believers in punishment are unconsciously drawing it. All the prophets drew punishments..

Great believers in miracles draw them, s George Fox, Evangelist Finney, and Dwight L. Moody, drew pentecostal tongues, and spoke languages they had never studied. Irenaeus bishop of Lyons wrote that in his time there were "many brethren speaking all kinds of languages by the Holy Spirit." And St. Sauveur of Horta cured six thousand persons during the feast of the Annunciation, through his devotion to the healing grace his inner eye beheld and his mind so ardently decreed.

High Mysticism

The watch of the first Christian Apostles was toward the Lamb that in the midst of the throne is man's unfailing Provider; and they wanted for nothing, and all those who gathered to them were abundantly supplied. Their vision was toward the Highest, and no man could set upon them to hurt them, with power to defeat them, nor hurt the thousands obeying their injunction to continue in prayer and watch in the same. Their faces were set toward the Author of peace, and they allowed no man to be a slayer of himself or his fellow men. Their look was toward Christ the Triumphant, and no man could grovel in their presence, no man could lack joy, no man was foolish. They were the spiritual magistral, or sovereign remedy, answering the prayers of the ancients for a way of universal cure, opiate divine to the sorrows of the world. The high and lofty One inhabiting Eternity is above the pairs of opposites, good and evil, life and death, spirit and matter, therefore his ways that inspire us as we look toward Him are not our accustomed ways. We let Spirit go on its free way, to leave us poor in spirit; we are independent of Good; we do not hug tightly to Life, as though it were precious. For Spirit, Good, and Life, are gifts of the Highest.

Shall we be in love with gifts, like Nebuchadnezzar at the gate of the fiery furnace, calling for Hananiah, Mischael, and Azariah, whose names stand for the gifts of the Highest, instead of the Highest? It is not the gifts of the Highest that say, "Look unto me and be ye saved," though all the gifts of the Highest do come if we set our inner eye toward them and call their names, drafting on their waiting offers. Can we not call sleep, and inbreathe sleep, that subtle thing that Ezra said the beloved of God receive, till insomnia flees our being, and the poppy breath of heavenly forgetful-ness wafts us into Elysian fields? But sleep is not God. Sleep is a gift of God. To joy in sleep is to be like Isaiah's people joying in a harvest of grass and apples. The bloom of sleep is not the perfume of unspoilable health shedding itself abroad from the sleeper. We can call strength, inbreathing its offered vigors, looking toward its omnipresent smile, till strength nerves us to masterful handling of lions and elephants. But strength by itself is not God. Strength is a gift of God. No beams of the Almighty radiate unceasing renewal to the fainting from the heaviest weights among the powerful pugilists. To joy in strength is to joy as in a harvest of apples that lose their flavor, or corn that moulds. For all the gifts, sought with eagerness for their own sake, have their round of existence and disappearance, and those who receive them partake of the same. But thou O Highest Original! art forever, and the manna Thou givest for the calling of Thy name, is radiant beneficence scattering and yet increasing, till the world is alive forever-more!

The choice of the High Original alone instructs the mind, renews the body, engirds the affairs. "Call unto me, and I will answer thee." "Revive my Spirit in thee, and...nothing shall prevail against thee." Nothing prevailed against Jesus. "I can both lay down my life and take it up," he said. And he knew all things, and needed not that any man should teach him. His face was always heavenward, comrading always with the King of Kings and Lord of Lords.

Thus invoking the name of him calls toward us his masterfulness of life and death, knowledge and ignorance, health and sickness, majesty and insignificance. Has it not always been believed that invoking the name of a man of masterfulness and courage inbreathes master-fulness and courage?

"Go, my dread lord, to your great grandsire's tomb,
Invoke his warlike spirit."
"Let the king hear us when we call."
And that calling sleep brings it?
"Draw near and touch me,
Leaning out of space,
O happy sleep!
Enfold me in thy mystical embrace,
Thou sovereign gift of God, most sweet, most blest,

O happy sleep!"
And that calling the invisible goods with which the spaces are charged fetches them.

> "I will call for the corn and increase it."

> "I have made thee like unto him even God, who calleth those things which be not as though they were."

Call to the trees that lean and whisper against the far horizons, and they shall tell thee all their secrets, from the cedars of Lebanon to the hyssop that springeth on the wall. Call to the stars that lie on their black beds through the long north nights, and they shall tell thee what the schools have not discovered.

Call to the Lord of Life and Glory beyond the bars of human sense, and all the living fountains lying deep in thee shall quicken into stirring streams, and all the pent-up wisdoms that inhabit thee shall leap to meet the Universal Wisdom, shining forth as the sun with the glory of their Father.

"There is none like unto thee, O Lord! Thou art great, and thy name is great in might!"

When the disciples had associated with the Risen Christ till they knew that he had borne the griefs and carried the sorrows of all the human race, and by reason of his God Substance it had been as nothing to him, then "opened he their understanding, that they might understand the Scriptures." He dissolved the bars of human ignorance that hid their Lord-implanted inward wisdom. He dissolved cold foolishness and dark ignorance by the hot beams of his bright Righteousness, or shining Understanding.

Did not Aristides say that when he associated with Socrates he felt himself flashing with wisdom? Did not the Chaldeans say that when Daniel came near them, their doubts were dissolved? Does not the fearlessness of a bold and successful leader communicate itself to his associates? Do not the nightingale's pure tones kill the birds of mongrel notes?

The Risen Christ was weightless of body and thinkless of mind. He was Pure Understanding, hot with universal dissolvent to human heaviness, dewy with working mystery. Then was fulfilled in his disciples the inspired promise that they of understanding should do exploits. Then was fulfilled in them the promise that whosoever should draw out his soul to the hungry, and satisfy the afflicted, should have his light shine forth in obscurity, and the Lord should guide him continually. "To satisfy the afflicted" is to acknowledge the Lord of affliction. The Lord of affliction was Jesus the Judean, wounded for the transgressions of the world, bruised for its iniquities, bearing the chastisement of the peace of all mankind, that by his stripes they might be healed.

To draw out the soul, and to acknowledge, are noted as identical activities in the Scriptures, being followed by the same results—the breaking forth of the light, and the consciousness of daily guidance by the Lord of victorious living. "Acknowledge me in all thy ways and I will direct thy paths." "Draw out thy soul to the hungry, and satisfy the afflicted... then the Lord shall guide thee."

To acknowledge the Great Hungry is a mystical expression, meaning to acknowledge Him that swalloweth up death, and hell, and the Egyptians, and the ways of the paths downward. This is to acknowledge Jesus the Savior from death, and Hades, and darkness, and the paths downward.

And the only Scripture the Risen One gave the disciples, after their acknowledgment of his vicarious achievement, was his own name. "The Holy Spirit whom the Father will send in my name shall teach you all things." And to the world at large he prophesied: "Ye shall not see me henceforth, till ye shall say, Blessed is he that cometh in the name of the Lord."

No library on earth holds a book guaranteeing to teach all things. But the ancient wise men declared that there is an Ineffable Name that teaches the mysteries of the universe. The Rabbis said that Jesus of Nazareth did not know the Ineffable Name, therefore his miracles were wrought by sorcery learned in Egypt, "not by the power of the Great Name." Matathia, in the Nizzachon says this, writing for the Rabbis. But Jesus himself testified for all time,

> "The Holy Spirit whom the Father will send in my name shall teach you all things."

> "In my name preach the gospel, heal the sick, cast out devils, raise the dead."

He knew the Ineffable Name that is key to the mysteries of the universe. And he knew that whoever should keep his name as Jesus Christ should come into the Ineffable Name.

"Thou holdest fast my name — I will give a new name." This new name cannot be spoken without instantly accomplishing the raising of the dead or the healing of the sick, or the illuminating of the life. It can never be spoken in vain. "Thou shalt not take the name of the Lord thy God in vain," is a prophecy, like "They shall not hurt or kill in all my holy mountain."

To the Initiated, all the so-called commandments are prophetic utterances. They all mean that when the Ineffable Name of the Lord is known, we are at home in the perfect land, where the former things come not into mind any more.

The Valentinians by a cabalistic system called *notarikon*, made the name Jesus the equivalent of *Jehovah Shammain*, or the saving Word; and Osiander the Lutheran studied the two syllables as in themselves the Ineffable Name.

That the name Jesus Christ is even at this day, and in this age of regarding the historic sufferer rather than the victorious Peace-Presence, a mysterious power, many can testify. Notice the testimony of the Algiers woman converted from Mohammedanism to Christianity: She had been poisoned by her angry relatives to put her out of their way as being their religious disgrace. Having read that in his name the dead should rise, and if a Christian should drink any deadly thing it should not hurt him, she began to call the name. She persistently invoked it though the well-known symptoms of mortal hurt were increasing. Suddenly she felt as if a stream of pure water were flowing through her body. It kept on with mysterious swiftness, till every vestige of the poison was eliminated, and new life began pulsing through her being.

Who now is ignoring every disastrous state of affairs, and separating himself to the one name by which the first Apostles wrought their miracles?

> "And the throne had six steps. ... And I saw in the right hand of him that sat upon the throne, a book. ... I wept much," wrote John the Apocalyptic seer, "because no man was found worthy to open and to read the book."

It is the book effecting by the mysterious writing on its covering the unlocking ' of the doors of limitation, and the uniting of whoever reads the outer writing to unstinted blessings.

> "Seek ye out of the book of the Lord and read, no one of these shall fail."

> "For the deaf shall hear the words of the book, and the eyes of the blind shall see out of obscurity, and out of darkness."

Surely, the book in the right hand of the Lamb slain for the transgressions of the race, gives for its outer reading the name or revealing so vitally insisted upon by the first Christian Apostles, and so ignored as to its mystical potency by the Christians of today. And the opening of its inner writing waits upon the faithful reading of its outer form.

> "Blessed is he that readeth"

> "I will give him to eat of the hidden manna."

Faithful reading is always associated with understanding:

> "The mystery whereby when ye read, ye may understand."

> "Whoso readeth, let him understand."

And understanding is mystical light. It is the light pent up and hidden in all men as in the first disciples of Jesus, and it is the glorious light of the Lord of the wide universe.

"Then shall thy light break forth as the morning"

"And the Lord shall be unto thee an everlasting light."

The same law of light reigns for the unseen shining as for the manifest. Do not the men of science insist that the same light that illuminates the noon-day sky is present in the darkened chamber? And that the bars of hiding being removed, the light within springs to meet the light without!

Held our eyes no sunny sheen,
How could sunshine e'er be seen?
Dwelt there no divineness in us,
How could God's divineness win us?

The breaking forth of the pent-up light, which is our hidden understanding, is associated with the bursting forth of our pent-up health: "Then shall thy light break forth as the morning, and thine health shall spring forth speedily."

It is associated with rising: "Unto you that fear my name, shall the sun of righteousness arise, with healing in his beams,"

"And the gentiles shall come to thy light, and kings to the brightness of thy rising."

"Tarry ye in the city of Jerusalem," said the Risen Lord, "till ye be endued with power from on high"

"Ye shall receive power after that the Holy Ghost is come upon you"

"... the Holy Ghost whom the Father will send in my name."

Then the obedient disciples tarried in Jerusalem. They tarried during the forty days of the Lord's ten appearances, plus the days to the fully come Pentecost, the Sixth day of Sivan, the feat of the harvest; coming together often, with one accord, to call upon the Spirit-imbuing name. On the sixth day of Sivan, the house where they were gathered trembled in the rushing spirit they had invoked by their persistent calling. Tongues of mystic fire whispered to them the powerful mysteries. They were ready to greet the outside world with a new ministry.

Six is the number consecrated to final equipment for heavenly offices. No equipment transcends the effulgence that wakes in us the healing word, the tongue for speech with angels. Even the shadow of Peter, most name-distraught, caused joyous forgetfulness of pain.

Jerusalem is symbol of the Self. To tarry at the self, invoking the name that wakes magian majesty, inbreath immortalizing, medicine of God, is labor worthy the sons of men.

Judas of Judea set his eye toward secret cheatings, and inbreathed them with the Palestinian winds. He shut the gates between himself and the offered higher laws of success. Jesus of the same Judea set his vision toward the Author of success, and inbreathed the airs of Paradise. He opened the gates between himself and unstinted transcendence. Judas hanged himself, and his name is full of suicide. Jesus rose to immortality, and his name is full of life-giving, miracle-working energy; it opens the gates between man and his native kingship.

Choose this day the objective for your vision's oft-time gaze, and your calling's precious good. Be as hotly intent as Carlyle toward literary distinction, as Judas toward the bag of silver, his own bold business, as Jesus toward God. Whatever we look toward, we come into identification with.

> He that seeks Me identifies with Me.
>
> He reigns with Me.
>
> He lives as my life, he strengthens as my strength, he understands as my understanding. What I Am He is.
>
> He calls upon my victorious Name, and whatsoever he does prospers, reminding mankind of my ever present, ever friendly, ever available Supremacy.

For I send the Healing Ghost, the Enwisdoming Breath, to him that calls my Miracle-Working Name Christ Jesus, bursting through which is the other name, only known to them that invoke His Anointing Name.

7th Study

NOTE

Let us recognize the Jesus Christ Self of this planet as The Victorious One ever present.

Let us be insistent about it. Even distant nations must measure up to life-giving peace by our persistent attention toward the Radiant Solitary whom God hath set in their midst.

E. C. H.

The angel of his presence accompanies every man. It is his kingly self. Two are ever in the field, one shall be taken the other left.

"I will send an angel before thee," said the voice of God to Moses. Because Moses knew this he daringly followed his leader. Once the angel led Moses into Marah where waters were bitter and the people complained that Moses was a deceiver. But the angel pushed him to a tree to cast into the waters and its absorbent qualities picked up the bitter globules leaving the waters limpid-sweet. Then the angel led him on to Elim where there were twelve wells of water and three score and ten palm trees.

This high leadership is every man's heritage. He need not fear dangerous days or vicious circumstances while he is aware that his angel goes before him, pleads his cause and defends him. High vision causes sense of nearness of The Highest. It is the closeness of the *Ain Soph*, the Great Countenance of the Absolute, above thinking and above being, which the Hebrews called Angel of God, the Brahmins called Divine Self, or Stately Soul, the mythologists called Aesculapius, or Apollo, the Christians called Jesus Christ.

Some reality, or closeness of the Universal, has always been the human insistence of mankind. To the earliest man The Angel of God was the happiest name for the closely near, ever ready helper whom man might throw his arms around and unto whom he might cry, "I will not let thee go except thou bless me." Jacob got what he cried for; Moses got what he cried for; Samuel got what he cried for; Abraham Lincoln got what he cried for; many today are getting what they cry for putting their heads against the close presence of the All-Competent One who hath surely said, "He shall cry unto me and I will make him higher than the kings of the earth."

"Who hath God so nigh unto them in all things that we call upon him for?" asked Moses, who taught High Attention and the close Angel of the presence to the Israelites, thousands of years ago.

Always the angel does wondrously, flies swiftly, mighty in strength, ministering life to the faint, help to the defeated, comfort to the despairing.

But we must notice the angel. Attention is the secret of the success of the combination. We combine with what we notice. We produce something worth while by combining with the Angel of God's presence.

There are some unitings or combinings even among mankind that produce success, victory, splendid achievements. The unassuming Cadijah made the greatness of Mahomet to out-shine himself. The unassuming Stier made the genius of Pavlova to transcend herself. The unassuming John made the speech of Peter to stir living sparkles through dead nerves. Many a great man owes even his ability to make money to the unpretentious mother or wife or child who lives in his house.

There are occult combinations that win outward honors. The science of the future will unveil the combinations. The Hebrews knew that Raphael was the angel of healing; Gabriel was the angel of comforting; Michael was the angel of good overpowering evil; Uriel was the angel of convincing doctrine.

That is, they named the miracles by their angelic names, as the Greeks named the healing that worked in their bodies

High Mysticism

Aesculapius, the strength that roused up in their nerves Hercules, the sleep that rested their bodily frames Morpheus.

Sleep was to the Greeks an entity. So also was health. Strength was a god by itself. All these were callable, that is, they could come by being called. The Christians united all the gods into one God, all the angelic ministries into one ministry, viz., the Sonship presence of the Universal Redeemer whose close visibility staid longer than any god of Greece or Rome was ever reported to have remained visible.

The Christian dispensation gathered the multitude of gods into one Lordship, Savior visible for three years, then Savior invisible but blessedly near for the rest of time. "Lo I am with you always," he said, which promise not one of the gods of mythology ever made, though forever and ever strength as a distant entity might be called near to stir the sinews, and health as a distant entity might be called near to charge the bodies of human beings.

These white gods had each his own ministry, but Christ Jesus had the combined ministry of all the gods. "All power is given unto me," he said, "Whatsoever ye shall ask in my name, I will do it."

All the gods with their several ministries were known to be representatives of some Universal Vast Vast. It was chrysolite stone of character to know how to be charged with the invigoration of some supernal deity and then, further, to cause the same invigoration to wake in one's neighbor. It was the ministering power of only a mysterious few who were called priests of Zeus, or priests of Aesculapius, or priests of Apollo, according to what god quality they could best awaken. We read of a priest of the Egyptian goddess Neith whose beautiful daughter was married to Joseph the Hebrew. Also in The Acts of the Apostles we read of a priest of Jupiter in Lystra who brought garlands to honor Paul and Barnabas for having healed the feet of a lame man crippled from birth, whom he as priest of Jupiter had not helped.

Those who had been sprinkled by Chronos the god of time did great things even in their old age. Evidently they would have said that Titian had unwittingly been sprinkled by Chronos for he painted The Battle of Lepanto at ninety-eight years of age; also that Michelangelo must have been sprinkled by Chronos for he was still painting great canvasses at eighty-nine. Whatever characteristic one could inhale from the ethers, or be sprinkled with from the gods consciously or unconsciously he was privileged to cause to rise up to some extent in his neighbors. He could pass it on as the contagion of his aura, or atmosphere, consciously or unconsciously, as was reported the cure of a love for intoxicating drinks passed on to an inebriate while he sat near a lover of The Free God in a public meeting.

Give attention to The Effulgent One like Parmenides and radiate effulgence. Gaze toward the glory of The Highest and ray forth some new aspiration. Seek him that turneth the shadow of death into morning and ray forth reviving ethers that "spiritualize even injured backbones. Be strong in the Lord and in the power of his might and ray forth peace and confidence in the midst of life's hardships. Be in love with some Truth of The Self Existent till the scent of its Rose Garden reaching thee thy garments carry Balm of Gilead for pain. Is it not written, "I clothe my priests with salvation?" There is healing victory for every one in love with The Uplifting, Awakening Highest. His influence is irresistible.

> "Listen, O isles, unto me, and hearken ye people from far
> —I will give thee for a light to the Gentiles, that thou mayest be my salvation unto the ends of the earth."

Beresford writes that some people's secret emanations or influences are very strong, so strong that they can be photographed. Let us note that only those who have been in love

High Mysticism

with Divine Rulership ray along divine influence, doing angelic ministries mighty in strength, flying, swiftly.

Calling unto the Name that smites the ethers into new activities creates new conditions.

> "Ye shall know that I am the Lord when I have wrought with you for my name's sake."
>
> "Therefore, turn yourselves and live ye—Turn others and live ye," calling upon my Name.

There is a miracle working Presence. It is man's privilege and obligation to make identification with The Miracle-Working Presence, till he himself is a miracle-working presence, spilling over with new radiations as the opened flower spills over with new perfumes. All miracle workings are angelic ministerings.

It is well to notice what we are oftenest visioning toward, as it accounts for our personal conditions and our atmospheric influences. Tell the vivisectionist that his own bodily anguish hurries toward him, and that his subtle personal influence is pain breeding. Tell the worshipper of The High Redeemer that the liberty of the Sons of God hurries toward him undoing all sly contagions, and that his subtle atmosphere is pain-undoing.

Give the whole world the message, how that on his golden bed Solomon with eyes tightly closed gazing out over his unhappy subjects became so unhappy his groanings could be heard afar off; and how the greatest surgeon of Italy on his last bed of torture, with the instructions of another world touching his mind, declared that he must expect that to happen to himself which he had caused to happen to others.

The vision of man is persistent. It records. And it must formulate somewhere *nolens volens* [nothing willing, without our willing it]. "Look unto me and be ye saved." "Thine eyes shall see the King in his beauty—and the inhabitants shall not say, I am sick, any more."

Isaiah writes of priests and prophets who by erring in vision stumble in judgment. He deplores their covenanting with their own unprospering imaginations. He insists that in this way they cause their people to dwell in the paths of destruction.

But the golden thread of a healing doctrine runs all the way through his denunciatory messages. He is teaching the Hebrew prophets the curative ministry of the High Watch: "Behold, your God, he will come and save you."

Notice how all inspired writers put the vision before the judgment; and the outward conditions of the people's experiencing as results following judgment: "Where there is no (saving) vision the people perish."

Man's inward visional direction creates his judgments, or mentals; mentals then translate into manifest affairs and manifest bodies. Mentals unvitalized by high vision are but compoundings with phenomena that never get anywhere. "Canst thou by (such) thinking make one hair white or black?"

It is the glory of Mystical Science that its fundamental and first instruction enjoins the exaltation of the inward visional sense, in order that exalted thoughts may formulate and immortal bodies and joyous affairs be made manifest.

David was teaching according to mystical law when, looking up, he talked to the Author of the Wooing Edict, "Look unto me:"

> "Thine, O Lord, is the greatness, and the power, and the glory and the victory, and the majesty. Thou art exalted as head above all. Riches and honor come of thee. Keep this forever in the imagination of the thoughts of the heart of thy people."

The Greeks were clutching at higher things than their minds when they glanced up to Aesculapius the white god above them, who caught and held them tightly and performed even surgical operations as god of healing ever ready world without end, the sweet gods' envoy.

The new education that is coming slowly to the front, tells by one or another mode of impartment, that whatever is oftenest viewed with the inner eye reveals its secrets and hands out its gifts. On this principle a certain choir master taught his boys to remember how the notes looked on the staff, and it was remarkable with what accuracy the boys sang the notes when after some days they came to voice practice. The notes had handed out their best to their attentive onlookers. Mozart lifted his inward gaze again and again to the sky's angelic choirs, and heavenly strains gave him mental musical ecstasy.

The Parsees taught that every man has a rich boon destined for him, but that hardly ever any man receives his boon; he repels it, instead. Ostensibly the Parsee gives no hint of how a man may draw the boon destined for him; but going deeper into the secret doctrine threading its way through the Parsee, as through Hebrew writings, we find the sweet urging and the plain direction to set our vision high toward Him that turneth the shadow of death into morning: "Every good and perfect boon cometh from above."

Some people by untaught fixedness of inward attention have occult vitality in visioning. They hasten their objective points to be plainly extant in the world of nature at large and in the world of their own human experience. W. T. Stead described the shipwreck of a White Star liner on an iceberg at sea several years before he experienced it. This was not a very prompt arrival, but J. A. Bartlett's vision of the Omnipresence of One Flawless Spirit caused a lame man sitting nearby to suddenly throw down his crutches and walk with flawless freedom.

"I have said, Behold me, behold me, I have spread out my hands all the day long unto a rebellious people," saith the Lord by Isaiah. "To a people that turned on me their backs and not their faces," saith the Lord by Jeremiah.

Occult vitality, or swift formulating vigor is cultivated by steadfastness of attention to the High Helper, the Supernal Giver, who evermore is saying,

"Look unto me"

"I restore"

"I help"

"I instruct"

"Is there anything to hard for me?"

There are objective points to focus the attention toward that Isaiah calls covenanting with death. Peter the hermit set his inner eye toward the Holy Sepulcher in Jerusalem and with impassioned descriptions drew the steadfast attention of millions of men, women and children toward it as their rightful possession. They endured as seeing an invisible sepulcher and nearly all fell into sepulchers of their own while journeying toward the eloquently described far distant Sepulcher of Jerusalem. How wonderful would have been the hermit's record had he used his hot eloquence to invite his people's attention to the Lover above ever calling to them,

"Seek ye me, and ye shall live."

"Look unto me and live."

"The way of life is above to the wise."

Why has no eloquence described the countenance of the over-looking Father in whose light we may breathe the light that infuses with the untellable life of the splendid Eternal?

The mother says, "You will catch cold." She does not say, "You will catch health." As the child has native identifying speed he soon exhibits the objective of his mother's errant vision with the threatening name cold. If the little Ludovico could tell what page in a book his mother was looking at, even when he was not near her, why could not a child catch his mother's fears or her foolishness, why even could he not catch her fearlessness or her wisdom?

High Mysticism

It was from persistent attention toward the All-Wise and Ever-Living Jesus Christ that Tertullian became the creator of Christian Latin literature, and was given to know the ministering assurance that "We shall all go on forever being the same persons we now are, and shall so continue forever clothed upon with the peculiar substance of immortality."

It was by observing the disasters in the earth that the unministering Epicureans contended that "God is inert, and a nonentity in human affairs."

> Christianity came after Epicureanism, teaching that the kingdom of God cometh not by observation of earth's disasters; that we must
>
> "Look up to the fields white for the harvest"
>
> "To the God who giveth to all men liberally"
>
> "And He shall wipe away all tears."

True mysticism in every age and every land calls the spreading appearances of earth mirage and delusion. What inspirations, what instructions, can possibly arrive as the results of much study of mirage and delusion? What noble cures, what divine immuneness from necessity for cure have arrived, or ever will arrive from the observations of men in the torture chambers of vivisection? On the contrary, is it not written that "He that killeth with the sword must be killed with the sword?"

True mysticism teaches a practice that results in cure for all its devotees, and exposes to them the immune offspring of Jehovah-All-Peace on every side. He that looketh toward me doth everywhere behold me. "I the Lord will hasten it."

In the eighteenth psalm David proclaims that he called upon the Lord, and was delivered from his enemies and his wisdom candle was lighted. Solomon his son explains for us that David's candle was the Spirit of the Lord shining upon him: "The spirit of a man is the candle of the Lord."

Job in his identification with affliction lamented the lost days when he had seen the candle of the Lord shining on his head, which candle he himself had hidden by much gazing toward suffering.

The secret of a man is his candle of lordship, his spirit of wisdom. Dr. Arnold of Rugby studied every class lesson faithfully in order that he might bring out the responsive intelligence — the candle of lordship common to the class — the Solitary that God had set in that little family. To his lasting honor, by addressing Responsive Intelligence he brought forth leaders of men, statesmen, presidents.

An instructor must bring forth lordship of some sort or he has not accomplished anything. "He has gained nothing who has not gained the Soul," proclaims the *Vendidad*, mystically teaching men how to rise free from the clutches of defeat as stalwart lords over evil by oft-time lifting up attention toward The High Redeemer, whose way upon the earth is the saving health of the nations.

Soul, Spirit, Light, Wisdom, are all names of the Responsive Intelligence filling the universe, ready to break forth everywhere by recognition. "With right glance and right speech man may superintend the universe, animate and inanimate."

"In the seventh day the Lord called to Moses." He responded plainly to the speeches of praise Moses had made unto him. And he taught Moses how to build an ark-symbol, which should to the Hebrews be sacrosanct testimony forever that the Lord Jehovah does dwell among men, their Leader, Defender, Provider, Inspirer.

Praise of the ever over-looking, ever fronting Provider, Defender, always meets with response. Was it not promised of old that the scepter should never depart from Judah? Judah means praise. Praise of earth's bountiful productiveness has caused the earth to teem with plenty. Praise of gold has hurried gold in rich masses to show itself to praiseful gold seekers. Praise of labor has overrun the globe with laborers planning world conquest.

Recognition is a form of praise. Description is a form of praise. Even to describe what we do not like magnifies its importance and spreads forth its capabilities. "Mine eyes are ever toward the Lord," said David, and "my mouth shall not transgress."

Did not Fechner discover that Responsive Intelligence looked upward toward him through the earth, as he called it "Angel Mother"? Did not Simon Magus experience earth's levitating strength, when, by praising Responsive Intelligence as upward bearing strength he buoyantly rose high into the air? Did not Iamblichus draw the distant eagles from their crags to come near to him, by speaking firmly and confidently to the Responsive Intelligence shining through the eagles? Does not Bjerregaard declare that the whole earth is awaiting orders to change its perpetual destructiveness?

"Let your speech be seasoned with salt," said Paul, by which he meant stern confidence. We learn stern confidence by facing the Author of stern confidence, speaking praisefully to the High Original, whose word changes not, whose finished works, instinct with agreement that firm praise shall surely make manifest, endure forever and alter not. Concerning the work of my hands offer praise and thanksgiving. The scepter shall never depart from praise.

"I send to you Epaphroditus," writes Paul; "He was sick unto death; receive him therefore in the Lord, and hold such in reputation" (or, "honor such").

Paul may not have known how near he was bordering to Hinduism while saying they must receive such as Epaphroditus in the Lord and give them good descriptions; but the word of the mystic Hindu had for centuries before Paul's time been, that, "He that beholdeth all creatures seated in me, shall behold me on all sides."

"Behold me, Behold me," this is the never-ceasing heavenly edict. "Whoso offereth praise glorifieth me;" this is the law of magnifying by description.

"Let none of you imagine evil," said Zechariah the prophet who had understanding in the seeing of God. Zechariah might have detailed the sickening imaginings of the mother, the death-dealing imaginings of Peter the hermit, the defeat-bringing imaginings of people like Cleopatra at Actium who, when in the midst of victory suddenly lowered her gaze and brought defeat. But Zechariah specified nothing in particular. He gathered all false imaginings against ourselves and our fellowmen under one head, and warned mankind forever to speak only truth to his neighbor: "Let every man speak truth to his neighbor, let none of you imagine evil in his heart against his neighbor."

What is truth? High praise of the lordship, the shining wisdom, the divine wholeness of every man, woman, child, animal, tree, plant, stone, star, throughout all the near and far stretching expanses, visible and invisible — this is truth. For back of each visible is divine reality. In the Hindu *Lanka Vetara* we read, "What seems external exists not at all."

What made the Christian Apostles so mighty in works? Their secret visional direction, forming right judgments quickly, making sudden outward demonstrations, being certain of a countenance shining as the sun, raiment white as the light as the only ever facing reality.

"I am determined not to know anything among you save Jesus Christ," said Paul to the Corinthians. The Corinthians were famous for their strange diseases, but so long as the Lord Jesus Christ was standing up in the midst of them why should Paul set his eyes on strange diseases?

> "After six days Jesus was transfigured before them, and his face did shine as the sun, and his raiment was white as the light—And lifting up their eyes they saw no man save Jesus only."

The time always was and is now that the divine Self, the shining Spirit, the Jesus Christ Lordship stands ever before us, but only by having had our eyes lighted by lifting them to the *Ain Soph* the Great Countenance of the Absolute, can

High Mysticism

we see face to face who our neighbor is in the sight of the over-seeing Father, and give our neighbor the honor due him as shining Spirit, flawless Lordship.

This was the secret of the wonder working early Christians. He who had said, "He that hath seen me hath seen the Father," was the perpetual objective to their inner eye. He was to them the Angel of God's Presence, identical in office and authority with The Father. His promise to be with all men to the end of the dispensation of lower imaginations was a reality to them, as it is now to all who believe his words, "Lo, I am with you alway."

There always comes before us the Angel of God's Presence whenever any man, woman or child appears. "I am the truth," he is saying—"Judge not according to appearance." It requires that strength of character called the seventh stone to answer, "I will not judge according to appearance. Noticing only the Angel of the Presence I can firmly declare, I know you as free, wise, immortal Christ Jesus here present; neither sin, sickness, nor death, can touch you."

Once having started on this truth, the glory of truth so quickens our hearts that to us as to the upward visioned Apostles, there is no man save Jesus only, with face shining as the sun, and raiment white as the light. Nobody, even a Corinthian-plastered enemy, can resist the praise of his victorious free Spirit, his candle of Lordship, his angel of God's presence, his own real Self. He has to drop all his delusions, his diseases, his griefs, his misfortunes, even his death. Two are ever in the field. Choose ye.

"Go, I pray thee Joseph," said Jacob, "and see the peace of thy brethren." And Joseph went out into the world seeing only peace, the Jehovah Shalom ever present, the Lord of peace, and speaking only peace to his eleven brethren. From the standpoint of the unenlightened eye the eleven brethren were liars, thieves, murderers, disease threatened hypocrites. But Joseph on about his father's business, saw peace, spoke peace, went forward toward the light of peace, till the eleven fell down before him transformed into lovers, friends, light bearers to the world.

The bringing forth of the Jesus Christ type, spiritually bold and executive, is the fruition toward which all religions and philosophies are bent.

The recognition, the acknowledgment of a Christ Jesus in the universe, focuses the inward attention to the greatest character-formulating objective the universe holds. It acts like heat on invisible ink. Mary had been with the inner eye looking steadfastly to her Lord as above in heaven, till he stood beside her, even while she with outward eyes beheld him as the gardener. He called to her as he had called to Moses. Then with opened eyes she saw Him, and not the gardener. "The secret of the Lord is with them that fear Him; and His covenant to make them know it."

Some later day philosophers tell of "The Soul, the Spirit, rising up in wrath against the natural order that denies its autonomy;" and of its "defying the principalities and powers that would brutalize it." But the Hebrew sacred teachings declare that Soul, in calm majesty, defying nothing, doth truly wait on God. "Nothing can injure the immortal principle of the Soul," wrote the watchful illuminati among the far past Theophoroi.

He who is the Strong Son of God, standing ever in our neighbor's stead, manifests as health and strength in mankind, when glorious truth is spoken to him as The Wonderful facing us everywhere. Nothing that we praise the Omnipotent Christ as being shall fail to manifest somewhere, somehow, among the sons of men. Why should we speak to him, free Soul, free Spirit that he is, as rising up in wrath, or fighting with defiant zeal to hold his own among us?

Sometimes we read in writings of greatly influential men, that God suffers at sight of our wickedness, and is distressed at our ignorance and stubbornness. For the moment the writers seem to be forgetting that "God is of purer eyes than to behold iniquity." By such teachings concerning

High Mysticism

suffering and distress on high, they turn the eyes of their docile people to an inadequate and despairing Deity who needs help and encouragement from us. They must study again the written inspirations of men in their diviner visions, when, as the Greek high watcher averred, they are "above their proper wits," unhypnotized by outward observations. There they will read of the High and Lofty One inhabiting Eternity, who healeth the broken in heart, who bindeth up their wounds, who teacheth men what before they knew not, who exalteth by his power, great in counsel and mighty to work, who cannot look on evil.

"The Lord will raise up a prophet from the midst of thee, of thy brethren; unto him shall ye hearken," was the Mosaic prophecy. "And Philip findeth Nathaniel, and saith unto him, 'We have found him, of whom Moses in the law and the prophets did write.'"

"And in his name shall the Gentiles trust."

"And he shall show judgment to the Gentiles."

"Watch ye therefore—to stand before the Son of Man."

It is necessary to right accomplishment that we have a definite goal to reach, a character standard to emulate. Failing a unital standard of finished high achievement, whole colleges of men have gone on year after year without graduating a single man of high achievement.

It is not from gaze toward the inchoate mass of men as brotherhood, or the mass of women as sisterhood, or the mass of labor as leaderhood, that we catch the sound of a distinct moral tone or discover a pivotal health centre shedding forth resistless health. It is from gaze toward one victorious, indestructible Minister of the Almighty Original ever standing in our midst, saying, "Lo, I am with you alway," that we catch the key note to victorious ministry.

He has gained nothing who has not gained sight of the ministering Solitary whom God hath set in the family of earth.

Joshua saw the Lord Jehovah standing up in Jericho; and moon-worshipping Jericho became a school of the prophets of Jehovah. "As the Lord God of Israel liveth before whom I stand," said Elijah, not noticing Ahab and Jezebel and their warrior-strengthened animosity; and Elijah was independent of the angry king and his army of haters.

"In a very little while Lebanon shall be a fruitful field," wrote Isaiah with figurative profundity. Lebanon stands for the Soul type, the Jesus Christ standard, Strong Son of God, Everlasting Friend, always with us, asking only recognition by praiseful description to be promptly fruitful after his own pattern, till earth's cities and plains are filled with men fulfilling untellable triumphs by new laws discoverable only through association with an altogether triumphant Prototype.

"I turned to see the voice: and being turned," reports John the Revelator, "I saw seven golden candlesticks. And in the midst of the seven candlesticks One like unto the Son of Man."

Candlesticks are definite divine messages. To know the seven definite messages of Pure Mysticism in their straight line of revealment, as decipherable through the many insulating or mistaken injunctions of the Sacred Books of all time, is to come like John, face to face subjectively with One All-God, whose objective reality makes haste as the fulfillment of inward certainty. For, except what we recognize subjectively, has its counterpart outwardly, we have not consummated our convictions. Inward conviction is not alive till it demonstrates on the human and manifest blackboard of daily experience.

Make a note of John's final hardy exhibitions of what he saw on the Isle of Patmos, with inner vision unrelated to the harsh passing Patmos days: Men denied the truth on which his faith rested, and with railing and malignant temper disputed his authority; but Polycarp, Ignatius and Papias rose up ready for martyrdom for the truth of his preaching. Boiling oil had not power to hurt his Christ-imbued body; even

High Mysticism

robbers turned glad Christian healers at the sound of his confident word, "Thy Soul prospereth." At Ephesus, where he had been maligned and denied, he was carried into the Christian assemblies bearing on his brow a plate of gold with the sacred Name engraved on it; and he was named "Apostle of Love," not as a character feminine, yielding, softly benevolent, but as one who recognized the Lord Christ ever present as the only reality of every man everywhere.

Jacob saw the same Son of Man, and called him "Angel," and "God," and keeping his vision steadfastly set toward the Angel, he blessed with effectual blessing all his children and grandchildren to the present generation, and to all the mysterious generations hastening along. "The Angel of his presence saved them — in his love he redeemed them."

And the seventh foundation stone of character (the heavenly Jerusalem) is chrysolite. This was one of the symbolic visions of John toward the Son of man merging into manifestation. The chrysolite is the golden stone symbolic of right communication — the tongue of the wise that is health. Does not Solomon say that he that speaketh truth showeth forth righteousness, and that the lips of truth shall be established forever, and that the words of the pure are pleasant words, winning the Soul — the divine Selfhood, to show forth?

The divine Selfhood always accompanies every man. It stands with him, back of him, or near him, instead of him, un-contaminated by his human mistakes; indestructible though he himself appears to be broken; omnipotent though outwardly he appears weak; poised, wise, joyous, though uncertainty, stupidity and grief are now his manifestations. Who is there determined not to judge according to appearance, but to judge according to the Selfhood of every child of earth, praising the ever-present upright man whose right is dominion?

Those willing like Paul at Corinth to know no man save the Jesus Christ Self only, touch the seventh stone — the golden speech of right association. "Two shall be in the field," said Jesus, "one shall be taken, the other left."

"Choose ye this day whom ye will serve" by description. For all description, silent or audible, brings to outward exhibition; speedily, if the inward conviction is alive, slowly, if the inward conviction is not yet vivified by persistent attention. The downward watch calls for descriptions of death and defeat, disease and dementia, the shadow system, insubstantial, untrue, ever waiting the message of its own undoing.

True descriptions are the New Gospel. Praise the true Self, is the Right Message. Do not wail that little false notions, little errors are always creeping into your mind, though truly you want only God. Do not complain that your body is not sound, though you really love the Highest. Can you not see that your vision is on the terrifying errors creeping in, and on the body's non-refreshment, rather than on the "bad man's Deliverer," "the Lord that healeth?" The sacred edict calls for looking away from error and from human brokenness.

What shining conversationalists and clever describers of human conditions are among us! What gospels of healing they might be turning their splendidly equipped tongues into, by praising the free, wise, immortal Son of God standing up Solitary and Glorious in the family of earth! Every listener would be enchanted with his own divinity and forget forever his low estate of ignorance and pain. But even if the learned and eloquent of today refuse their privilege of chrysolite speech, the "Desire of all Nations" shall surely come, as response to some voice of praise of Reality, as the prophet Haggai foresaw.

Though the people were tired of Aristides for talking so much about Aesculapius and Minerva, his undaunted speech brought Aesculapius and Minerva into his own plain sight, with their ministry in his behalf, one to teach him

High Mysticism 407

statescraft for the people's benefit, the other to bring him health to continue helping the people.

Though they were tired of Paul for teaching Christ Jesus, yet by persistent praise of the "Desire of all Nations" Paul raised their dead for them, saved their proud officials from drowning, and cured their people of life-long maladies.

> "Thou didst keep my word and didst not deny my name— and I will make (men) to know I have loved thee."

> "But in the days of the voice of the Seventh Angel, when he shall begin to sound, the mystery of God should be finished. And the Angel said unto me, Thou must prophesy again, before many people and nations and tongues and kings."

In his tenth chapter John tells the whole story of the Universal Christ ever present for manifestation. To prophesy is to proclaim truth, the same today as yesterday, and the same tomorrow as today. The eternal verities have no tense.

The first six angels, or announcements, insist on our looking above to the High and Lofty One inhabiting eternity, King of Kings and Lord of Lords. The Seventh Angel declares that with the inbreath of the Victorious Name, the speaking tongue and the thinking speech are newly alive.

The Victorious Name awakes vital breath and vital prophesies.

The old injunction of the magi to animate each particular life from the Universal Life is native activity to one who has caught the messages of John's mystically heard six angels. The Seventh Angel's voice telling us to preach the truth of the ever-present Son of God coming before us whenever our neighbor faces us, is the call to us to speak to free Life till free Life shines forth.

Philip of Macedon kept a servitor near him whose business it was to be often saying in his ear, "Philip, remember thou art but mortal!" This worked so on the secret springs of

Philip's outward activities that he rushed downward into assassination at forty-six years of age. Israel of old kept Ezekiel often reiterating what Israel should experience in the distant future. Ezekiel told Israel over and over that seeming national death should finally eventuate in upbuilding and regeneration.

A captive himself on the banks of the Chebar, he proclaimed a far-off future liberty for Israel by a new Law, or Torah. Futurity worked so on the secret springs of the Israelites that they are still waiting regeneration by a new Torah.

So under the Jewish mesmeric descriptions of futurity were the early Christians that Paul said they would not accept deliverance from martyrdom, hoping for a better resurrection later on. And Paul, under futurity's spell, said that God himself foresaw that the martyrs would not have been made perfect by suffering if they had not received the promises of futurity. Paul often forgot that "today is the day of salvation."

He who has awakened his speech by the Holy Ghost that comes by the Mystic Name, talks only to the awakened. He sees the Master Spirit wherever he looks, and he describes Victorious Spirit with the bold tongue of unhushable conviction. He looks to the Christ Jesus Spirit of the man who hates, and comrades with the Lover only; then nobody can find that man of hate. He talks to the Christ Jesus Spirit of the man who offers to "die for the Right," and he converses only with the Indestructible Master for the Right; then nobody forevermore can think of "dying for the Right." It is unthinkable. He thinks only that Right is Its own Life victoriously unkillable.

Right vision so regenerates judgment that the tongue and bodily activities regenerate in all directions. This is not more than Joseph did with seeing Peace, nor more than John did with seeing the Angel of the Presence, who told him not to do obeisance, but to know him as Mighty Brother, Master for Right, without hurting or being hurt.

As far as John went in his convictions born of his vision he demonstrated among men. As much as he visioned distinctly he proved. To him the Seventh Angel was the proclamation of the complete — the finished: "And the Seventh Angel poured out his vial into the air. And there came a great voice out of heaven, saying, It is done."

"And the servants informed the nobleman, 'Yesterday at the seventh hour the fever left him.' So then the father knew that it was the same hour in the which Jesus had said unto him, Go thy way, thy son liveth." The words of Jesus had been spoken to unfevered free Spirit, and outward conditions had tallied with unfevered free Spirit.

John prayed that his neighbors might prosper and be in health as he saw their soul prospering, and he declared that the greatest joy he had was hearing that his converts walked in truth, doing faithfully to their brethren and to strangers.

"In the seventh place the Lord imparted them speech, an interpreter of the cognitions," writes the Son of Sirach, in Ecclesiastes 17:5. Seven is thus implied when we read that the "Lord hath brought forth our righteousness, and we must declare in Zion the work of the Lord." "And the Lord shall bless thee out of Zion, and thou shalt see the good of Jerusalem all the days of thy life." "Zion" is man's divinity-Self, the upright that hath dominion. And the greatest blessing we can bespeak Jerusalem (our neighbor) is his divine freedom, as all sacred lore and law insist:

> "In that day shall thy mouth be opened to the free."
>
> "In the seventh year let him go out free."
>
> "Ye have done right in proclaiming liberty every man to his neighbor."
>
> "That thou mayest say to the prisoners, Go forth, and to them that are in darkness, Show yourselves."

Always high vision stirs right speech silent or audible; and right speech silent or audible stirs right convictions, and the accomplishment of the seemingly impossible is the outcome.

The upward watch of Benezet the shepherd of Savoy stirred in him such vital conviction of the presence of a living Christ that the Christ spoke plainly to him, giving him orders to build a bridge across the river Rhone. The public monuments of Avignon attest that Benezet did build the bridge which even Charlemagne would not undertake.

The upward watch of Dorothy of Brixton stirred in her such vital conviction that the same Lord Christ spoke plainly to her, telling her to rise off the bed of death and show herself strong, sound and sane. And she rose up strong, sound and sane. These both heard the same Responsive Power speaking to them that Moses heard "in the seventh day," as we read in Exodus 24:16.

Everywhere majestic divinity faces us. Speaking to majestic divinity stirs celestial instinction. Celestial instinction is that secret spring to right conditions which all the world is seeking. Instinction, vital conviction, is some-times called the will. Has it not been declared that nothing ever really wins the will from its native bent? But High Watch wins the will to work the kingly ministry of the flawless Deliverer standing up in the earth. "Did not we cast three men bound into the midst of the fire? Lo, I see four men, and the form of the fourth is like to the Son of God." And seeing thus the Saving Other, the king found no hurt in the three men of the fiery furnace in the plain of Dura. Was not that an exhibition of the worthwhileness of sighting the Son of God, the Radiant One ever present?

"And Enoch the seventh from Adam prophesied, saying, Behold, the Lord cometh." Enoch was mentioned of old as a type of perfected humanity. He was described as one living a prophetic life and having constant con-verse with the unseen world. He taught our true human existence in glory, and the resurrection of our body in beauty. The voice of early ecclesiastical tradition regarded Enoch as one of the two witnesses John mentions in Revelations, eleventh

High Mysticism

chapter, to whom should be given power to prophesy twelve hundred and sixty days in the midst of world-wide unbelief. Enoch was the Scriptural forerunner of all who look out over the earth toward the Angel of God's presence, the Christ Jesus of Mankind, harmonious, wise, immortal, and keep on describing the Saving One though war, ignorance and destruction throw their shadows across the shining majesty.

Out of John's vision we gather the straight instruction that the word concerning the Lord's presence among us shall prove itself to be the most mighty word, for he shall surely be seen taking to himself his great power and reigning visibly among all the kingdoms of the world. Why not, since what we persist in praising must surely stand forth?

Ezekiel once had this mystic vision of the Son of Man, the Lord-Self among the seeming dry bones in the valley, as he prophesied divided Judah and Joseph as soon to be one great kingdom alive with the word. His speech to the dry bones has the vitality of some unseen ocean's morning winds. He is a phonograph of the Voice of the Master Builder:

> "O ye dry bones, hear the word of the Lord. Thus saith the Lord God unto these bones, Behold, I will cause breath to enter into you, and ye shall live. And I will lay sinews upon you, and will bring up flesh upon you and cover you with skin; and put my spirit in you, and ye shall know that I the Lord have spoken and performed."

Benvenuto Cellini sent his inner eye out lowering down into distant space and caught the form of Charon. He painted the form and features of Charon on plaques and vases and shields, till he feared Charon as a dangerous entity. Martin Luther sent his lowering inner gaze into dread space and described Satan, till Satan became real to him — so real that at this very day an ink stain on a castle wall shows where Luther hurled an inkwell at the prince of darkness his mother had so often described.

And to this day other human beings are still setting their eyes toward menacings that do not menace, when, like Enoch and Ezekiel in their great moments, they might be viewing the ever present king in his beauty, to the transformation of human existence into glory, and the revival of the human form into beauty and vigor. For at the sounding of the Seventh Angel's message, great voices shout that "The kingdoms of this world are become the kingdoms of our Lord and his Christ, and he shall reign forever," transforming war into loving kindness, and anger into chants of praises of ransomed man.

To gloom or glory is the tending of the inner eye. And all human beings and all events of human existence are gloomed or glorified to us by the direction of our inner eye. Luther at one period saw Satan overshadowing everywhere. Every direction then became so gloomed to Luther that Catherine asked him if he thought God might be dead.

Choose not to set the inner eye toward menace. Choose to set it toward the prize of the Lord Christ's healing face ever looking toward us—Strength of the nations, joy of the world.

> "Here eyes do regard you in eternity's stillness;
> Choose well, your choice is brief and yet endless."
> "Let a man contend to the uttermost
> For his life's set prize, let be what it will."

In one of Isaiah's dreams his tongue was touched with prophetic fire from off the altar, because his eyes had seen the king in his beauty. And all sorrow fled from before Isaiah's face, and sighings he could not hear, for the songs of the unshadowed were in his ears, and the sight of the lame man leaping, and the weak hands strengthening, filled him altogether with joy.

If Isaiah with his will to concentrate all the energies of his being to the salvation of mankind from war and pain, had had the science of making visions immediately tangible, instead of always throwing them into futurity, Israel and Judah would have made manifest the sons of peace and

High Mysticism 413

healing in all directions, as Isaiah's delectable demonstrations of the *radio in extenso* [extended arm, or radiating outward, extension] of a finished vision firmly and sternly declared. "Believe in the Lord's prophets so shall you prosper," counseled Ezra the reformer; and the Hebrews believed in the prophets of futurity and prospered. Let now the world believe in the prophets of what already is, in the already presence of One who redeemeth all life from threatenings for the seer's sake, that mankind may visibly prosper every-where, and be in health, as Soul, the Only Reality of man, his Sonship to the Highest, already prospers.

"By the bright Soul's law learn to live;
And if men thwart thee take no heed;
And if men slight thee have no care.
Sing thou thy song and do thy deed,
Hope thou thy hope and pray thy prayer,
And claim no crown this does not give."

Every spiritual law calls for steadfastness. There is but one edict but we must steadfastly maintain obedience thereunto. Thus only are the practices signified by the voices of the angels our own spontaneous practices. But having scientifically learned the voices of the angels, it is scientific for us to maintain them day by day under all the circumstances of daily living whether or no they have as yet proved themselves. Strike the iron till it is hot. Is it not reasonable to speak often praisefully and with firmness to the upright, ever present Lord of Cure, if by so doing the radiance of the sun of righteousness with healing in his wings shines forth, affecting all in our vicinity, as the wonderful Fourth affected Azariah, Mishael and Hananiah for the king of Babylon's sake?

"Man has the enunciative reason; if he makes use of this for what he ought, he will be guided into the choir of The God" prophesied thrice-wise Hermes. "Do thou thy work betimes, and He shall reward thee in his time."

"My praise shall be of thee in the great congregation," said David; "That thy way may be known upon earth, thy saving health among the nations." Could any enunciation be more calculated than positive praise of the Lord ever facing us, to guide us into the choir of The God? Why should we not joyfully practice the Seventh Angel's orders, "Prophesy again, before many people and nations, and tongues and kings." For "He healeth the broken in heart, he bindeth up their wounds. His understanding is infinite."

> "I will praise thee among much people."
>
> "On the harp will I praise thee."
>
> "Forasmuch as there is none like unto thee, thou art great, and thy name is great in might."

Let us take our eye off cheapness and incompetence, the wounded in life's battles, and the defeats of strife, and look often to the Saving Other awaiting our praises.

"He shall deliver the island of the innocent. It shall be delivered by the pureness of thine hands." Hands are powers. No powers so pure as unqualified praise. But, notice, He shall deliver the island of the innocent. Some law as mysterious as that by which the trees leave forth, makes the unseen divinity of man, his island of innocence, kindle forth as health and newness of life, when the divinity is called Jesus Christ, the everlasting, ever present, omnipotent Self, the Christ in you the hope of glory.

Note that David praises him on the harp for the might of his name. We may never speak the name Jesus Christ. We may always speak the name Spirit, or God or Love, and describe Spirit, God, as Omnipresence, Omnipotence, Omniscience, and do quite great things by such praise, but there will be some nameless flavor lacking in the health and strength that come forth thereby. As the actinic ray in the sun is the secret of the sweetness of the grape, so Jesus Christ who stands up in the universe as the one man having demonstrated the fullness of the Godhead bodily, is the human touch to the divinity of man. And being recognized as the health of man, there is a vital kindling forth as health

High Mysticism

and happy vigor, fearless of death and misfortune, not translation but transfiguration for humanity.

"God hath given him a name which is above every name." The preaching of the mysterious might of the name and the healing presence of the Jesus Christ is the risen doctrine. It is not the province of the risen doctrine to insist on a verbatim formula of praise of the far radiating presence. The recognition, the acknowledgment of a pivotal character transcending all limitations, irresistibly acting as invigorating energy, causes right words silent or audible to formulate, sweeping their original meanings into the affairs of the world.

"Now therefore go," said the voice of the Lord to Moses, "and I will be with thy mouth to teach thee what thou shalt say." Moses was slow of speech, but he spoke and thought and wrote words that have caught the ears and hearts and actions of millions of strong men throughout many centuries. "The Spirit of the Lord spake by me," said David, "and his word was in my tongue." And David's words have been radiant with beauty and vitality since ever he thought and wrote them forth, kindled by the Spirit of God. "For I put my Spirit in you, and ye shall know."

"I will give you a mouth and wisdom which all your adversaries shall not be able to gainsay or resist," said the prophetic Christ to his first disciples. "And they were not able to resist the wisdom and the spirit by which Stephen the miracle worker spake."

The ever present Jesus Christ is a resistless healing and strengthening centre.

How can we help speaking the name and describing him as the burden bearer of the world—the one Almighty Substance upbearing our sick neighbor and his sickness — upbearing our unfortunate neighbor and his misfortune— upbearing our insane neighbor and his insanities—upbearing our wicked neighbor and his wickedness—upbearing our palsied neighbor and his palsy—upbearing our burdened neighbor and his burdens — upbearing us and our obligation to help our neighbor, till all the nations fear and tremble for all the goodness and for all the prosperity the acknowledged Son of Light procures them, as Jeremiah foretold in his chapter 33.

No address to our neighbor's mental constitution (conscious or unconscious, so called) by the brave, bold insistences of mental suggestions of freedom, peace, strength, can equal the curative activity of the Son of God acknowledged as up-bearer, order-bringer and healing peace.

> "It is He that giveth salvation to kings."

> "He maketh doctrine to shine as the morning, and sendeth forth her light afar off—and leaveth it to all ages forevermore."

It is the nature of the rose to shed forth perfume. It has faced the sunshine that causes heavenly breaths to smile forth from unscented leaf capsules:
"How sweet the breath beneath the hills Of Sharon's dewy rose."

It is the nature of wine to refresh and revive. The grape has faced the sunshine that wakes reviving wines. It is the nature of man who faces the Countenance that shineth as the sun in his strength to shed forth beautiful descriptions that fit only the ever-present Sun of righteousness with healing in his beams. And he who is full to the brim of his being with silent descriptions of the Lord of Glory now looking toward us sheds healing perfume, curative breaths, reviving elixirs through even his garments. Did not Paul's aprons and handkerchiefs cure the sick? Did not Peter's shadow revive the faint? The Lord of life and health was their comrade. They kept high company. Not a new set of men and women came to them to show forth their unseen comradeship, but the same men and women came before them, clothed and in their right minds.

> "For thus saith the Lord, I will extend peace like a river, and glory like a flowing stream."

High Mysticism

"And ye shall know that I am the Lord when I have wrought with you for my name's sake."

"And when he had opened the seventh seal, there was silence. ...And I saw the seven angels which stood before God, and to them were given seven trumpets."

The seal of man's being first stirs to opening when he silently addresses the God that standeth in the congregation of the mighty, the shining One ever in our midst; and the seven trumpets are his when he boldly speaks aloud that the Jesus Christ of man is the only reality of man. The trumpets of God are the tongues of his prophets speaking in heaven-taught moments, when no com-plainings or denouncements caught from sights of evil spoil the music of their tones.

In the days of the voice of the Seventh Angel John was told that the book he must eat, which was the name that should teach him all things, would be sweet in his mouth but bitter in the vital centers of his being. If John had not known by the third angel's speaking, that the wormwood of mind cure was the blessed bitterness of the book, and that the seventh angel's voice was only emphasizing the former prophecy, that his influence should be as a river of mind cure if he assimilated the Mystic Name, he could not have understood the glorious gospel reiterated by the Seventh Angel's instructions.

But John understood that he was being told anew that his inward speech should relate him to the great Jesus whose fame went throughout all Syria as healing the people, and throughout all Judea where the multitudes had only to touch the hem of his garment to stir with newness of life. John felt himself blessing countless generations by reason of comrading with the great central figure of cure and blessing. He felt the river of mind cure flowing forth from his own inward speech.

And the Son of Sirach prophesied, "Whoso feareth the Lord it shall go well with him."

To fear is to keep the eye single: "If thine eye be single thy whole body shall be full of Light" (wisdom). "The fear of the Lord is the instruction of wisdom."

The Lord is the resistless Law of the High Deliverer making manifest among mankind as the result of upward watch. Looking to the High and Lofty One inhabiting eternity we bring to pass a new order of outward appearance to represent our high vision. It is always a masterful appearance. Nothing can hold opposition to it. If by our steadfast watch in obedience to the high mandate we suddenly see peace before our inward gaze, that peace will prove its lordship by quelling pain and discord. This is the Lordship of Peace. Jesus Christ ever standing before us is forever the prince of peace. His name is the mystic name of the resistless lordship of peace. The Lord maketh it go well on all sides for them that recognize Jehovah Shalom.

"Who by this vision splendid
Is on his way attended,
Great peace shall mark his way."

And the Son of Sirach further said that his right tongue, his new tongue, was his reward for praising the Lord, the Savior with the Great Name. And this reward he called the time of the Seventh.

"And the Lord turned the captivity of Job when he prayed for his friends." And his friends were praying for him. Throughout all the mystic teachings of the divine law of cure, there is mention of prayer and praise in behalf of the brethren of the faith. Notice John's instruction, "Do faithfully whatsoever thou doest to the brethren, and to strangers."

Jesus began by sending his disciples out among strangers by two and two. "Two did build the house of Israel." "Two did put ten thousand to flight." "How should two put ten thousand to flight except the Lord had shut them up?" asks Moses, calling his people's attention to the miracle working Lord. "If two of you shall agree on earth as touching anything that they shall ask, it shall be done for

High Mysticism

them," said Jesus; and, "It is also written in your law that the testimony of two witnesses is true."

Happy in our own day is everyone who has a comrade to go forth with him, keeping the high watch and praising the divine Self facing them, the Angel of God, the unweighted flawless Reality of every neighbor every-where without respect of persons. They are surely like Peter and John at the Temple gate, speaking to the Jesus Christ Self of the impotent everywhere, to walk and praise their Lord.

Zechariah, the seer of God, prophetically beheld two women with wings, bearing an *ephah* [shield with a pattern on it] between them. And the wind of Divine Spirit was in their wings, and they bore the *ephah* to build for it an house in the land of Shinar (hostility). Somewhere among the books earlier than Zechariah's time, it reads that two women together bearing the same message or *ephah*, could bring all the world to their doctrine. But surely the doctrine must be divine truth to be strong to hold out in the land of hostility (Shinar) to the day of the world's acceptance. Only divine truth can survive the Shinar hostility of downward-visioned mankind. Two bearing the heavenly *ephah* of high vision and the praise that make up its ministry shall have speech with Responsive Intelligence, the Jesus Christ Self, standing free, wise, immortal, before them always. "Behold, he goeth before you," said the angel to the two Marys.

Job was one, and his friends together made another. Peter in the prison praying for his friends made one; his friends in an upper chamber praying for him made another. The great quarternity of sorrows, the dark D's of the downward looking of man's inward eye, disease, death, demonism, darkness, like a four-thicknessed veil, dissolved always before the heaven-sent two, the two standing before the Lord of the whole earth. "Even the devils are subject to us," reported astonished Peter.

The law of the way of the mighty miracle has never been abrogated. To all who read the words of the Seventh Angel, or the Seventh Chapter of the divine law of cure, all the miracles are free grace to the praiseful. Each reader makes the first of the two bearing right praises, the new *Ephah*, the rest of those who love and agree with high praise of the Lord in the midst of us mighty to save make the other of the two bearing the *Ephah* or the praise message.

It wakens a new and more spontaneous dealing with the flawless divinity of the distressed and ill, if we first look, to the Divine One standing Solitary and Glorious in the midst of the people of the New Age, saying boldly to that Shining Presence:

> I see you transcending all human conditions, unweighted by matter, unshadowed by fear; free flawless, triumphant. I look now to the Son of God, the Angel of God's Presence, the cure and peace and strength of all mankind. I look to Everlasting Life, shedding forth the radiance of the Everlasting Kingdom. All are gathered into life ever renewing, into health ever restoring, into wisdom ever brightening and rejoicing—gathered and upborne in beauty and love and might by thee, O Free Spirit, victorious Christ Jesus facing me, with face shining as the Sun and raiment white as the light, transfiguring the whole earth with living triumph!

To address Responsive Reality in this way is to come into ready praise of the victorious divinity, the Angel of his presence of each claimant for our help. Praise of the ever-present Son of God distills as wine for the faint in the wilderness, sweet friendships to the lonely, blessed restorations to hearts sick of earthly hardships, for there is ever a baptism from high praise. It falls like gentle healing rains on human beings. It unites them to that which causes them to transcend themselves. Enduring as seeing the Invisible Solitary is greeting That which sees us, and the outcome is Health that rays forth Health.

> "The healing of thy seamless dress
> Moves past the ways of men,
> They feel thee in life's throng and press
> And they are whole again."

8th Study

NOTE

By practicing the high directions of this Eighth Chapter as concerning everybody everywhere, and concerning every thought and every thing, we bless them all by undeceiving them all.

E. C. H.

The point of each chapter or lesson in Mystical Science is its practice point. The practice point of the fifth lesson for instance is not the acknowledgment of the Vicarious Jesus, but the Self recognition that He practiced and urged all mankind to practice, that each one might do something great in his own line as He Jesus of Nazareth had done in His line. His leadership in Self recognition was His credential to special acknowledgment and special praise on the part of all mankind. Self recognition follows recognition of the Angel of The Presence as Miracle Working Nearness. "I will not let thee go except thou bless me" should be the Jacob cry of all the world, face to face as all the world is with its Jacob Deliverer.

The practice point of the Sixth lesson is our own inspiration or inbreath of the Breath of Brahma.

> "I put my breath in you and ye shall live. I put my spirit in you and ye shall know."
>
> "Why O man will ye die, having power to partake of the breath of immortality?"

The practice point of the Seventh lesson is recognition of the Angel of God's presence as the original Self of every man, woman, child. Two are ever in the field; one should be taken the other left, as Jesus himself discovered.

To notice the unweighted, flawless, everlasting Self, or Angel of man is to notice the Christ Self, strong son of God, lover divine. It produces a change in the bodily and mental presence of anybody to notice his unweighted, everlasting divinity with praiseful acknowledgments silently spoken or audibly declared.

> "A right word, how good it is, who can measure the force of a right word."
>
> "With right glance and with right speech man may superintend the universe, animate and inanimate."
>
> Notice always how potent is a glance:
>
> "Glance up often, so shall thy life renew."
>
> "Look unto me and live."

An eminent bacteriologist found that the indicator in a delicate instrument moved back and forth with the direction of the eye looking at it through a sighting slit. The mystery of vision will some day be declared by science in such a way that mankind will know that to set the eye toward the divinity Self of the neighbor is to find its tangible beauty coming forth; and to sight toward Deity is to experience the workings of Deity. "Seek ye the Lord and his strength, Seek his face evermore," will not be a beautiful sentence on a page, but a living fact according to high science. "Deity onlooketh thee. Onlook thou Deity. This to thy salvation." Or, "Look unto me and be ye saved, all the ends of the earth."

To endure as seeing the invisible is to fetch it into visibility. That means that we see toward what we cannot see till it arrives into our living experience.

A certain set of people choosing to see toward health, wholeness, unspoiledness, declare that sick people are made whole by their practice. Another set of people are seeing toward riches, and riches come into their living experience. "Seek ye first the kingdom of God, and all these things shall be added unto you," said Jesus. The whole and beautiful kingdom of which he was speaking was noticed by Brahmins: "Above this visible nature there exists another, unseen and eternal, which, when all things created perish, does not perish," they said. It was "The Perfect Land" looked toward

High Mysticism 423

by Egyptian seers of most ancient times. "The Archetypal world, the *Yesod*, the nourishment of all the worlds," wrote the seer of the Kabbalah.

"The mother of Moses saw that he was a goodly child," reported Ezra, the illumined priest of Babylon. And forth came the all-competent Moses, learned in all the wisdom of the Egyptians, a matchless warrior, a godlike law giver, a miracle worker unsurpassed. That mother must have had inner vision toward the flawless, victorious Angel of the presence to have brought forth such a victorious man. It is written of him that he was a finished mathematician, the inventor of boats and engines, instruments of war and hydraulics; also the author of the accepted Egyptian hieroglyphics, ever leading by his lonely self the ascetic life that he might pursue high philosophical speculations and prophetic insights. Secular history presents him a noble example of the effect of noble vision — so noble that critical intellectuals have not been able to believe that such a character ever really lived on this earth.

Whoever glances upward toward the countenance that shines on his face begins to be lifted upward. Why should he not be lifted upward out of ignorance and feebleness altogether by oft-time returning the ever Seeing toward him of The Perfect Deity? Does not the hidden oak tree of the rotting pulp inside the splitting shell come up into another country and another breathing space by oft-time glancing upward toward a sun it sees not and untold homecoming for which its heart is ever dumbly yearning?

Mankind yearns for a country and a comradeship he cannot find except by enduring as seeing toward that city which hath no need of the sun or the moon to lighten it, for his own Beloved is the light thereof.

St. John of the Cross looked up toward a finished kingdom, and the furrows in the Monastery field were found to be miraculously plowed.

Even the most intellectual critics of mystical claims acknowledge that "the concepts of future creation are present in their completeness in the eternal Now before being brought to birth in the material sphere." But they neglect to mention in such splendid assertions how to fetch to birth in the material or tangibly visible sphere the heavenly eternals already finished. For this we must look to Mystical Science. "And he brought him (Abram) forth abroad and said, Look now toward heaven, and I will give thee a son of her (Sarai) and she shall be a mother of nations; kings of people shall be of her."

The finished kingdom, the "Archetypal World" is forever wooing the sons of men to look toward it that they may find themselves and their environments blessed with supernal newness.

The stone was rolled away for the two Marys because their inner gaze was wooed heavenward. Lavater's gaze was upward toward The All-Knower, and his mathematical problems became easy. Martha's gaze was toward pans and brooms and bread for supper, but Mary's gaze was toward The Perfect Country, and Jesus said she had chosen the better part, or the visional direction that brought better results.

The Wooing Countenance shining into our faces from above was called *Agni* by the Parsees of old. They declared that man must have been formed out of the eye of *Agni*, because his initial and compelling faculty was his eye faculty. Wherever his vision was directed, there his other faculties caught their sensations.

This explains why the great Catholic Saints caught such tangible experiences. Lukardis of Oberweimer secretly gazing toward "some delicate invisible refection which the Convent could not afford, there came to her one day the most loving Infant bearing in his hand food, and begging her to eat it for his sake. She did so and was wonderfully strengthened." So writes Baron von Hugel, among other mentions of visible things appearing from invisibles with tangible outcomes, because of sighting toward.

Francis d'Assisi saw the invisible five wounds of an invisible Jesus on an invisible cross so perseveringly that he the visible Francis had the five wounds visibly present in his own visible hands, feet, and sides.

The point of the Eighth lesson or chapter is the executiveness of persistence, perseverance. Seek ye my face ofttime evermore.

"Persistence of vision" is a scientific term. It was called one-pointedness by the Brahmins. Man may behold the face of The Father in the Eight, wrote a lover of numbers, meaning that persistence in oft-time glancing lightly and quickly toward the Onlooking Deity, the God Countenance beneficently looking forever upon us, gives us the sense of friendship divine, effecting our awakening into our own flowering greatness. By persistent attention toward the Divinity Self, the Ageless Son of God, Plato found that "nothing can injure the immortal principle of the Soul."

By watching toward Apollo, the invisible god of good gifts, for nineteen years, the Greeks and Romans saw him visibly present and heard him promising happy harvests and safe child-births. By much asking outward toward some invisible informant a great chemist saw as in a trance the form of a stranger who answered his question. By oft-time setting his inner eye toward the One Invisible One filling the Universe, Parmenides saw himself as unified with that One so that the forces of nature desisted from their wonted operations for his sake.

> "After eight days the disciples were within; then came Jesus, the doors being shut, and stood in their midst, saying. 'Peace be unto you.'"

Everything that has to do with the visible ministry of the invisible Jesus blazing forever with The Christ Substance acts quickly, for that Reality is already complete. The Suffering Jesus is an imagination of the heart and takes more time to tangiblize, as witness all the bearers of the stigmata, so long in manifesting the five wounds. It is high time for us to take our inner gaze off the suffering Jesus and set it toward the Risen Victorious, Christ-empowered Jesus. "I if I be lifted up," he said. It is time the world took its inner eye away from an angry God and set it toward "Him who healeth all our diseases, who redeemeth the life from destruction, who crowneth with loving kindness and tender mercy."

It is time we took our eye off the grave and set it toward Him who promiseth forever, "I will ransom them from the power of the grave," "Seek ye my face and live." Let us remember that the grave cannot demonstrate our acquaintance with God; only "the living, the living shall praise Thee."

Even the ancients of Parsee India discovered that watching things that spoil and die affected them with spoilings, but oft-time upward glancing blotted out and washed away the spoilings. "Lift up thine eyes." "I even I am he that blotteth out thy transgressions for mine own sake."

The point of the ministry of the eighth lesson is, "He sent me to preach deliverance to the captives." All the world is groaning for its rightful deliverance. Some are groaning in the bondage of bodily pain. Some are groaning in the bondage of financial limitation. Some are groaning in the bondage of mental inadequacy. Some are groaning in the bondage of bodily inadequacy. It is no use trying to get free by any other attempting than upward face to face with Self-Existent, Untrammeled "*Ain Soph*, Great Countenance of the Absolute, above thinking and above being." "Thou hast redeemed us out of every kindred, and tongue, and people, and nation," acknowledged the high visioning John.

In the *Dharmapada* we are told that wisdom cometh from above and the wise man casts off all shackles; that right religion leads to escape from pain, and deliverance from destruction. Also that the best doctrine is that which removes pleasure and grief from the mind. As mind is mirror of the vision it stands to old-fashioned reasoning that Visioning toward Free, Unattached, Unhindered God the mind must be free. And as body follows mind's agreements body must be free also.

"Lift up your eyes on high and behold who hath created," said the heavenly voice to Isaiah. "Behold the Lord God will come with strong hand, and his arm shall rule for him." The coming of the "Lord" is near, our own near angel of deliverance. Something mighty to save is near at hand to do the saving. "The angel of his presence redeemed them." Always the Universal Absolute seems near as a strength beyond strength doing for us. Who notices the touch of The Almighty to save? "The hand of God hath touched me," said Job.

The Brahmins called the Wonderful-Competent our Real Self of our self. The Hebrews called it the Angel of God's presence. The Chaldeans called it The Stately Soul. The Christians called it the Christ Jesus ever present.

Some people are trying to show that Jesus of Nazareth did not claim to be The Promised Messiah, The Christ, The Savior. But he did. Notice him saying,

> "The Son of man came that he might give his life a ransom"
>
> "I come not to judge, but to save the world."
>
> "The woman saith unto him, 'When Messiah cometh, which is called Christ;' Jesus saith unto her, I that speak unto thee am he."

They also declare that he did not teach The Trinity. But he did. Notice him saying. "I and the Father are One." "The Holy Ghost whom the Father will send in my name, shall teach you all things." "Go ye, therefore, and make Christians of all nations, baptizing them in the Name of the Father, and of the Son, and of the Holy Ghost."

They also proclaim that he did not urge any sacrifices or sacraments. But he did. Notice how he said, "If any man will come after me let him deny himself, and take his cross" (the practice of denial of all that is not Free God). The ordinance of the Lord's supper was his sacramental ordinance to all time. "This do in remembrance of me," he said.

Keep the eye single to One Free Self-Existent God and you cannot help believing in Free Grace. You cannot help having a mind devoid of the pleasure and grief which worried the Brahmins and Buddhists. A new joy such as New Visioning gives causes the queer saying, "I believe hardships fall away of their own weight," in place of, "I am in bondage to hardships. I cannot cure myself."

Nobody is asked to cure himself of his particular bondage. He is asked to look up to him who redeemeth the life from destruction, taking off every yoke. To him whose only order has been,

> "Look unto me, and be ye saved, all the ends of the earth."
>
> "The windows from on high are open, the earth is clean dissolved."

To regard the Countenance that shineth into our faces from on high is to be aware of the Countenance as shining from all sides into our faces, and from below as the foundation under our feet.

All is promised to follow the high watch even to a new heaven and a new earth.

Therefore, leaving all the shows of human misery ofttime and oft-time rejecting them, seek ye the Lord and his strength, seek His Face evermore.

"The Eighth was Simeon the hearkener." It is certain that the inner ear back of our outer ear does hear statements from every direction where the inner eye directs itself. The Siena Saint heard a voice from out the silence saying, "My daughter, think of Me, and I will think of thee." She knew it was Jesus the martyr, for the voice further informed her that he left her sometimes in order that she might feel herself deprived of consolation, and afflicted by pain.

How far this is removed from the voice of the High Deliverer speaking to Jeremiah, "They shall fight against thee but they shall not prevail against thee, for I am with thee to deliver thee"; or from the heavenly voice speaking through

High Mysticism

the transfiguring Christ Jesus, "Nothing shall by any means hurt you" — "I am with you alway."

It is sign of ongoing in relation to that hidden objective toward which our inner all compelling vision is oftenest set when we have inner auditions. And inner auditions from that direction we most certainly shall have. If a voice sounds on our inner ear that a boat is to be shipwrecked and we must not set sail upon it, we may surely infer that our inner vision has been oft-time turned toward danger of some kind, or menacings of catastrophe. If we hear a voice on the inner ear saying, "Fear not, I am God thy Savior and I am thy people's Savior"; we may know that our vision has been toward the High Deliverer, the Miracle working almighty to save.

The Eighth lesson declares that oft-time glancing upward toward the Saving One we are saved, and as Paul was told, all they that sail with us shall be saved. Nothing shall have power to hurt them.

Is it any wonder that the wisely inspired of time have found themselves saying, "It is not so," when tales of danger and descriptions of calamity have been declared in their presence? "Nay, Nay," said the Brahmin high watcher.

"I sign it all away by the mystic activity of the cross I carry on my shoulder, symbol forever of blotting out, erasing, undoing the heavy burdens, taking off the heavy yokes," whispers the four-thousand-yearo-ld voice of the miracle-working high watcher of forgotten old Egypt. The cross was once the symbol of such strong agreement with joyous Reality that all differentiations from joyous Reality were denied, rejected, blotted out.

Suffering, disappointment, poverty, degradation, death, those hieroglyphics against The Beautiful God, The Prince of Peace, The Miracle-Working Angel, are all erasable by denial, rejection, when they confront us as evidence of our past downward visionings. "If thou wouldest accurately put away all contentious words, O Child, thou shouldst find that truly the Soul dominates" — The Free Unspoilable Self makes manifest.

"Salute no man by the way." Salute no mighty claim except to wash it off the *Ain Soph,* Great Countenance of The Absolute, above thinking and above being.

All recognitions react. Notice the mysterious reactions that come from gazings toward a tormenting god: "A great desolation, the Lord increasing grief, pain that grows to such a degree of intensity that in spite of oneself one cries aloud," wrote the Carmelite Teresa, steady-watcher toward a terrible presence.

High Science recognizes only the God who extendeth peace like a river, who, like as a mother comforteth so comforteth He, saying, "I am the Lord that healeth thee," "I give life to the faint, and to such as have no might I increase their strength."

It makes a mighty difference to mankind what description of God he looks toward. The tormenting, angry, partiality-showing God of old Sainthood made them most miserable in mind, body and affairs. Their consciousness of their own wickedness was terrible. "Wheresoever thou findest self drop that self" wrote one of them. But he did not say, drop that imaginary God whose impress on thee makes thee dissatisfied with thyself.

"All the gods of the nations are idols. Sing unto the Lord a new song. Declare his glory among the heathen," shouted Ezra the learned descendant of Hilkiah the priest.

To endure as seeing Invisible Divinity is to extend all the faculties and sense the identity of all like with the Unlimited Supernal, the Free Self-Existent. To endure as seeing Invisible Divinity is to become one pointed. "Only the one pointed succeed," said the old Buddhist priests. When Sir Isaac Newton tried to explain the reason for his own great success he used words which meant that he had been one pointed.

The seventh law of mysticism broaches the original heirship of all the sons of earth to One Divine All-glorious

High Mysticism

Father. In the seventh we are told to keep our eye on the Lord Jehovah standing stately and majestic on the earth as the Self of our neighbor ever facing us, as Joshua saw the Lord Jehovah standing in the midst of moon-worshipping Jericho, and as king David foresaw the Lord always before his Isaiah speaks of the great rebound of such faithful ministry: "He that stoppeth his ears and shutteth his eyes from seeing evil, shall dwell on high."

As evil is a weight, how can we help rising to happy heights as we reject evil? "No!" says the Sage of India. This is his way of putting away contentious words spoken against his neighbor's original Self. "I make the sign of the cross as if erasing marks on a tablet," signals the priest of Isis. And the gods of ancient Egypt were sculptured bearing crosses to signify that they stood for accurately putting away contentious descriptions of the glorious Invisible ever facing mankind.

"Be not deceived," said Jesus. This intimates that Jesus was brushing aside contentious descriptions and being one pointed to the unspoilable Invisible. "Judge not according to the appearance," he said. This shows how persistent he was toward the Invisible as a waiting splendor.

Attention is the secret of success. Would Peace have folded all *Firenze* in its victorious arms, if Cosimo de Medici had not noticed it with his inward viewing, as a moveless Irresistible radiating forth from the non-resisting Antonino?

Would the hidden Lazarus have burst the bars of death if Jesus had not looked toward the One Life Undefeatable? Was not Cosimo ignoring the cries of hunger and fear in all his city, while the vision of Peace was holding him spellbound? Was not Jesus ignoring death while the vision of Triumphant Life held his gaze?

"Every tongue that shall arise against thee in judgment, thou shalt condemn," said the prophet Isaiah. To condemn is to declare useless. Is not a bridge declared useless when the authorities have condemned it?

When the attention is wholly engrossed with peace, or life, or strength, there is a tacit rejection of turmoil, death, weakness. When the attention is strongly distracted toward the cocoons woven by the dusky "I am's" of the downward watch toward death, disease, discord, we are told that we must use positive words of rejection to truly accompany our watch toward the Invisible.

"If any man will come after me (the Inviolate Unseen), let him deny himself," said the great Seer. Let him refuse the evidence of his outward senses, and "Watch, what I say unto you I say unto, all, Watch."

Their watch toward glory despite outward horrors has made the mystics of all time the most powerful engines for miraculous good that the world has held. They have all been miracle workers. They have not forgotten that outward and objective signs always manifest when true inward viewing is married to true positive speech. "Tabitha, arise!" said Peter, addressing Unkillable Vitality, paying no attention to visible death. "Your son lives!" shouted St. Anthony of Padua, disregarding the messenger's death report.

"Thou, Lord, holdest my precious gem! It cannot be lost!" said one facing the Owner of the spheres, and ignoring loss. "Thou art the Savior of this woman from her own speech," said another stopping both ears from the hearing of evil. All these endured as seeing the Invisible Miracle Worker, and for each a miracle was wrought. This is The Eternal Science. The ways of the stars may alter, the calculations of mathematics may readjust but recognition of the Almighty Uncontaminate shall not fail of the miracle of saving, healing, restoring, reviving.

"Therefore," says Micah, 700 B.C., "I will look unto the Lord; I will wait for the God of salvation: my God will hear me." "Therefore I looked to the healing Lord standing before me, and the dying baby lived," whispered the mystically trained nurse, 1916 A.D. This Science of the watch Godward shines brighter and brighter and works stronger and stronger as time wheels forward, finding more and more obedients who do the will to prove the doctrine. "Sing unto the Lord a new song. Declare his glory."

Every invisible objective upon being acknowledged has its own modus operandi; its own steps toward manifestation; its own time of manifesting, and its own expressions upon arrival. "Therefore," said the Son of Sirach, "do thou thy work betimes; he shall reward thee in his time." "Ye believe in God, believe also in (the) Me," said the Greatest Expression.

As a right ministry we never forget that our neighbor has the Lord of his presence, his stately painless Soul, his Me, ever with him. We never forget that the Lord of our neighbor's presence is his rightful Self, which it is our ministry to bring forward. Our watch toward the High Deliverer wakes our awareness of the One Life ready to break forward in full shining as we face our neighbor. Therefore if we had not been told to reject man's false descriptions of himself we should find ourselves saying, "It is not so!" when we heard him telling of his losses or his pains.

"Remember only that He is looking toward you," said a certain Father Confessor to the Abbess of a convent. "Do not remember anything else. Exercise no self scrutiny." (See *Resume*.) So the Abbess remembered only that the Vast Vast Shining Countenance looked toward her. She ignored her mind's reminders of her troubles. She ignored everything but the Shining Countenance. She was a true Obedient, for a stranger suddenly appeared before her offering her a bag of gold, though the stranger had no knowledge whatsoever that the sole trouble of the Abbess was lack of money to buy food for her waiting nuns. Thus was the obedient Abbess a plain demonstration of the promise, Invisible Kindness she was visibly befriended.

"Holy Ann" of Canada spoke to Invisible Kindness on the subject of refreshment for the cattle, and suddenly a dry well was filled with water in time of great drought. A Jewish youth praised Invisible Goodness for making him a genius and much beloved. Genius began to wake in him and everybody began to love him.

A certain woman spoke praisefully to the Lord as Divine Beauty everywhere, and slowly beauty began to express in her own form and features. She praised Unexpressed Health, and bones and sinews, blood and nerves speedily began to express health. "Behold the beauty of the Lord," sang King David. "Oh that men would praise the Lord for his goodness, and for his wonderful works," sang Ezra, after keeping the same praises himself he had urged others to keep.

We are told to ignore untoward appearances. We are told to gather unto with undivided choice. For what we gather unto we express.

The Hindus call the ever-waiting Kindness, "Consciousness," or "Brahma" (from *brih*, to expand as Omnipresence); and they show that every particle of existence is a particle of Consciousness. Therefore we as consciousness gathering to Original Consciousness, express its Beauty and its Health if we gather to Consciousness as Beauty or as Health. We express it as Strength if we gather to it as Strength. We express it as Triumph if we gather to it as Triumph. We express nothing of Beauty, Strength, Triumph, if we do not choose Brahma—Supernal Consciousness, in Its native express-ion as Beauty, Health, Triumph. We must keep on devoid of health, triumph, strength, if we as consciousness gather not to Divine Consciousness. This is the genesis of rejection of the devoid states called disaster, weakness, failure. "Loose thyself from the bands of thy neck, O captive daughter of Zion." To us there must be no God sending tribulation. Only the God letting the oppressed go free and taking off every yoke is our God.

There are reservoirs of Good back of all appearances of sickness or unhappy circumstances. "The eye of Judah is red with wine" to discover the reservoirs of Good. Judah means praise. He who praises the Unseen Providence just above his head experiences the Providence. He who chooses

High Mysticism

Providence puts away contentious appearances, by firm rejections, like the Abbess of Port Royal, or he ignores them like Cosimo de Medici, in the rapt vision of Peace. His eye, inspired to right viewing ("red with wine"), is the eye of wisdom that Solomon says "seeth precious things."

The *guru* sees intelligence in his *chela* [beginning disciple]. He does not stop to criticise the *chela*'s stupidity. With steadfast gaze toward intelligence, like as Hufeland toward health, the guru enlarges the borders of intelligence. "Enlarge the place of thy tent," saith the voice of the Lord to Isaiah. "Salute no man (or claim) by the way," said Jesus. When the injured Chicago man talked to the strength back of his weak joints and muscles, he talked to the reservoir of good, the waiting Lord watching him. He saluted no claim of weakness hugging down over his bodily frame. And strength expressed itself so greatly that he who before could lift nothing, did suddenly lift heavy weights. "Ascribe ye strength unto God," sang David. And as we are always like the God we secretly describe, so David further sang, "God is the strength of my heart."

A boy in the cold is selling newspapers. Whose eye is "red with wine" to see the Lord strong and triumphant standing up tall and stately by or in the newsboy's presence, willfully rejecting his rags? Whoever opens eyes red thus with inspiration to see the precious Life, soon sees the newsboy in some great University teaching the music of the spheres. The ways of the Lord are always miracles.

There are reservoirs of gold back of all gold pieces. On behalf of the facing Unlimited, erase, reject the limitations hieroglyphed over the gold pieces. This throws them out to the Universal Unlimited. Simon Magus had his eye red with wine to see the levitating principle back of the attraction of gravitation. "Lift me up," he said, ignoring all pullings earthward. And the Responsive Centrifugal lifted him into the air.

"I make an everlasting covenant with you," saith the Lord. "Ask what ye will." And "concerning the work of my hands command ye me." This Covenanting Almighty faces us everywhere. Even Talleyrand, foreign minister for Napoleon, found that strength, success, and haughtiness stood forth in his colleagues if he recognized them as strong, successful, haughty; and that they drooped in weakness, failure and dejection if he neglected them. Rachel the actress, a contemporary of Talleyrand, could see a thousand people smile, and they would smile, or see them weep, and they would weep. Napoleon himself could vision men as victorious or defeated, and they would execute his views of them. He wrote to his unfortunate brother Henry: "I have seen with pain that you represent everything to yourself on the black side. Take a resolution and stand by it with your whole strength." In other words, face something worthwhile.

When Marcion of the second century advocated the ascetic life, he did so because he saw that success lies in being one-pointed, and in rejecting all that distracts from One Victorious Objective.

Jesus asked mankind to regard him as the great expression *in toto* [totally, the whole of] of the Victorious Unseen. Some said they must attend to their wives. Some said they must attend to their enterprises. Some said they must attend to their dead. They did not catch the mystic essential of his doctrine, that He that hath chosen Me, hath chosen the Finished Co-Efficient, touching all undertakings with flawless Finish. Touching all under-takings with supernal completeness. For "He that hath seen me hath seen The Father." And all things are right with him.

The Parsees of old declared that ninety-nine persons out of every hundred die by reason of the evil eye. They see their own spot of pain or illness so distinctly that it expands into a sum total of shadow for them; and the sum total of shadow is the full manifest of devoid, or death. A certain commissariat in the federal army could always foretell what soldier was to be killed in the impending battle. He told this by the shadowy haze that he saw clinging to the soldier's face. After the war he could by the same token select which of his parishioners was about to pass into devoid. When this commissariat-clergyman learned of the principle of rejection, putting away, refusing death, disease, failure, on behalf of God the "o'er all victorious" then present, he spoke with great firmness to the shadowy haze whenever it claimed his attention: "Go away! I'll have nothing to do with you! Leave this man to his Life! O Life! Stand forth! Stand forth Free Life, bold and joyous!" And the mysterious devoid would give way to Life and Health, the rightful manifest of all mankind. Who can deny that this clergyman did perform the noble Christian Ministry, set into the form of command, "Heal the sick, raise the dead."

It is told of Pope Pius IX that his vision worked ill luck with unfortunate speed. Doubtless he was clairvoyant to troubles about to come to pass according to the law of cause and effect; and probably he knew nothing of the Trismegistian law, "If thou wouldst accurately put away contentious words, thou wouldst find free Spirit, untrammelled Life dominating." And the pope did certainly ignore John's beautifully executive treatment— "That Thou mayest prosper and be in health, even as thy soul prospereth."

All people with the habit of looking for the Best have the good and the favoring eye. The good and the favoring eye coalesces with the Deific eye: "We cried unto the Lord God of our Fathers, and he looked on our labor, and our oppression, and our affliction, and he brought us forth out of Egypt."

Joash saw himself as Lord undefeatable. Amaziah looked him in the face on the plains of Beth Shemish hoping to defeat him. The lordly self-viewing of Joash won the day for him as lordly self-viewing always wins the day for any man. "Why criest thou out aloud? Is there no king in thee?"

Did not Hegel discover that "by oft recourse by inward viewing, the mind goes on to know and comprehend?" Mind is the ostensible and tangible nearest to ostensible and tangible outward activities. Hegel wrote his books about mind, because his inward viewing stayed not where his own words led him. Steadfastly maintaining his cause he would have written his books about the antecedent to mind, and so would have planted on earth the beautiful doctrine of viewing Godward, that the New Age might speedily usher in—

"When peace should over all the earth
Its final splendors fling,
And the whole world ring back the song
Which now the angels sing."

Pilate's wife urged him not to see Jesus crucified. But Pilate could not take his eye off the crucifixion. This premonitive viewing was suicidal for Pilate, as the vision of the crucifixion is always suicidal. "To the Christ that never was crucified! To the Christ that never was buried! To the Christ that never rose from the dead! To the Eternal Almighty Christ, I commend you!" cried Elias Hicks in one great moment of ecstatic vision. To endure as seeing the Triumphant Unkillable is to renew the life forces and catch the breath of Omnipotence. But Elias did not endure as seeing such Invisible. He altercated with sinful adversaries, fellowshipping with Chrysostom's fateful forgetfulness.

Somebody must maintain the doctrine, that He that beholdeth Me on high shall behold Me on all sides. He that beholdeth Me on all sides shall behold that I am watching him. Did not Hagar discover "Thou God seest me?"

"The fourth beast whose look was more stout than his fellows, made war against the saints of God, and prevailed against them, till the Ancient of Days came," wrote Darnel, seeing past, present and future beastly strong secret viewing toward devoids, as being some day defeated by enduring vision toward the Eternal Almighty.

Steadfast vision tangiblizes. "There are eight conditions to right living, and the first is right view," whispered the mystics of old India.[14] "With right glance and right speech man superintendeth the universe," insisted the far past Zoroastrian mystics.

Francis d'Assisi sat with closed eyes, inwardly beholding Jesus on the cross. With profound sympathy of feeling he entered into the pains of the wounded hands, feet and side of the image he thus vividly visualized. Suddenly he himself showed wounded hands and feet, and all the people cried, "Wonderful! Wonderful!" Can you not see that his only wonderfulness consisted in his persistence of view? Where would the world now be in demonstration if Francis d'Assisi had persisted in beholding the Unkillable Almighty, the High and Lofty One inhabitating eternity, "who healeth all our diseases, who redeemeth our life from destruction, who crowneth us with loving kindness and tender mercy?"

Doctors Bucknill and Tuke noted how a certain woman had a bruised foot from imaging the bruised foot of a child standing on the catch block of a swinging gate. As the gate struck the catch the woman fell with her own foot maimed, though the child was uninjured, its little foot not being in the clinch place where the woman had imaged. "That thou seest, that thou becomest." And that thou seest, that thou forcest on thy neighbor. Will the child ever have a mysteriously injured foot? Most assuredly; unless her upward cast of inward eye is toward Him who "redeem-eth the life from destruction."

Gregory the Great attested that St. Fridian changed the bed of a river by his strength of inward viewing, or one pointed gaze. Dr. Gentry tells of a man who caught eczema from a picture of eczema. Hot focus of inward viewing tangiblizes. This is the genesis of the axiom, "He that findeth me findeth life."

---

[14] This is the first step of the Buddha's "8-fold Noble path," established about 600 B.C.

"Turn ye even to me with fasting — and behold, the Lord will do great things for thee." Fasting and circumcision, and the sign of the cross and sacrificing have ever been the outward ceremonies of mankind intended to signify putting aside the rigors of the law of cause and effect. Mankind everywhere vaguely senses his sinfulness, or darkly surmises himself in the wrong somehow, and therefore bound for punishment for the same. Why not, if his God is a punishing God and not the God who blotteth out transgressions?

Mankind has tried fasting from food and other normal goods in the hope of mayhap squaring his account with the great Lawgiver. Mankind has tried sacrificing his treasures of flocks and gold in the same hope. He has tried circumcision to set himself aside from human hordes, and seal himself to the God of his own description, still groveling to placate the Lawgiver. Now and then one has boldly proclaimed that all these outward processes convey inward meanings, as that one should be circumcised from his heart's desires, or sacrifice himself for Principle, even to being burned at the stake or sawn asunder: "O ye stiff necked and un-circumcised of heart and of ear," cried Stephen, "ye do always resist the Holy Ghost. As your fathers did, so do ye." Stephen is going far towards true circumcision, for the High Deliverer is always speaking wonderful words to him who endures as seeing the Invisible.

How can the ears of the downward watcher, clogged with the stories of war and death, catch the voice of Him who saith, "I will instruct thee and teach thee?" "Walking in the comfort of the Holy Ghost."

Odilo of Cluny understood the sign of the cross as a blotting out and rejecting signal, and when he wet his fingers and made the sign of the cross, to indicate that he would have nothing to do with blindness chalk-marked across the shining God looking hitherward, blindness immediately disappeared from the eyes of the man born blind. By the same heavenly erasive signal he refused to see the ecclesiastic's great tumor; and it disappeared. The idiocy of

High Mysticism

a child was erased by this symbol of annulling, uttering forth from his inward viewing toward the Unspoilable Almighty looking straight into his eyes.

The priests of Plutonian Serapis made signs of the cross to signify their black handing with the evil on which their gaze was fastened. In this Christian day there are unwitting disciples of Serapis, first regarding the cross as sign of trouble, and second describing themselves on the devoid side. "I am all undone," says one. "I have been three days without food," says another. Both these are black handing their triumphing Lordship with de-voids. And we who say, "I am sorry for you," are doubling their black hand. We must silently stand by our true ministry.

"It is not so!" we silently declare, offering our sacrificings of denial with secret shoutings, like the priests of Judah. We give our best praises to the Angel of their presence, their Jesus Christ Self, with face shining as the sun, and raiment white as the light. "Thus have ye done it unto the Mysterious Me," and prosperity and joy gleam boldly forth.

All subjective or secret images come to the ostensible. William Blake, the poet, in his subjective or inward viewings, reveled in the hells as essentials of God; but when he outwardly beheld the suffering children, he flamed with indignation. He could not bear these tangible ostensibles of his own hidden limnings. He forgot his doctrine that hells are essentials. We must have a doctrine that we are glad never to forget—the doctrine that Invisible Kindness comes out to heal the starving children, rewarding our undiverted, right secret viewings with love hurrying into childhood's daily life. "This is the fast that I have chosen, to loose the bands of wickedness, to undo the heavy burdens, to let the oppressed go free, and take off every yoke." Fast ye from stories of pain, disappointment, poverty. They are only hieroglyphics painted across the joyous Presence. They represent looking away from the true God.

There is a force more mighty than mind, more potent than thought. It is the day spring from on high that falls down over the upward watch, giving light in darkness, and guiding into peace. It is the resistless Holy Ghost, waiting to be heard by the ears free from the hearing of evil. Micah heard it telling the Jews that the Lord was their Redeemer from the hand of their enemies. Zephan-iah heard it telling them that the Lord in the midst of them should cast away their enemies so that they should not see evil any more. Habakkuk heard it telling him to write his vision and make it plain.

Euripides wrote out descriptions of his visions of outwardly unseen men and women, gods and goddesses more powerful in battle and more daring and original in social encounter than any his outer eyes had beheld. So steadfast was his gaze toward these transcending images, that they made him know the words appropriate to their state and greatness. Then when Euripides the son of an herb seller, entered the theater, the Athenians rose as when their king appeared, and they cried that "the glory of the Athenian stage descended into the tomb," when Euripides ceased writing his immortal plays.

Whoever is one pointed to any objective begins to know its speech. Thus the eighth stone of character is the beryl stone, significant of one who hearkens to the teachings that wait at the silent heights. It stands for writing out the teachings. "What thou seest, write and send it unto the churches" said the voice of the Lord to John the Revelator. "Write thee all the words that I have spoken unto thee," is said to the man that heareth. "The Eighth was Simeon the hearkener."

Only one objective is worth our one pointed, undivided attention. Only one objective has healing on its returning beam. That objective is the Watcher hitherward, whose soundless call is, "Look unto me" — "Behold I bring thee health and cure."

Archimedes gave his undivided attention to mathematics. *"Noli turbare circulos meos"* ["nothing disturbs my circles"], he said to the soldiers driving their swords toward him. Could any attention be more undivided? But his beautiful mathematics did not save his life. For mathematics has never said, "I will contend with him that contendeth with thee." Beethoven with undivided attention to notes that burst forth into delectable sounds, was hard of hearing, for music has never agreed to unstop deaf ears, open the eyes of the blind and cause the lame to leap like harts. Only the Healing God has promised such lovely service. A deaf child prayed to God, and her ears were unstopped. A blind woman prayed to Him, and her eyes were opened. "Therefore I will lift up mine eyes unto Thee, O Thou that dwellest in the heavens." "He bindeth up their wounds."

We are all walled into chambers of imagery, taught Ezekiel. Of course! Why not, if our executive sense is drawing pictures from other objectives than the Free Universal? Why not, if our attention is drawing ideas from minds in all directions set toward us with their knowledges all foolishness to Original Wisdom? How unhappy was the little Dalai Lama of Lhasa, always phonographing the minds of those who came near him, even speaking the almost forgotten dialects of strangers, and reading their innermost thoughts! How could he help always dying young under the burden of so much imagery?

The greatest adept of time was Jesus of Nazareth, who drew his knowledges altogether from God. "What went ye out for to see?" he asked, "a reed shaken with the wind?" A being standing proud and glad at beholding your favorable opinions; drooping and ashamed at your disapprovals? Whoever stood so on his own feet, independent forever of the estimates of mankind! He ignored their estimates. What he was he was, and they could not kill him with secret hatred or with open castigation. "No man taketh my life from me—I lay it down of myself," he said. "What went ye out for to see, a prophet? Yea, I say unto you, more than a prophet." Samuel had been a great prophet. He was one who like

Talleyrand, and Rachel, and Napoleon, laid his views on mankind so thickly they could not hold their own. "'Thou art a victorious soldier," laid Samuel's silent estimate on young Saul. And Saul rose up a victorious soldier. "Thou art a king," pictured Samuel, and up went Saul to the throne of Israel.

"Thou art no king," imaged the same prophet, and down went Saul, mindless and throneless.

But Jesus never offered to paint men any different from their original estate. "Call no man upon the earth your father. One is your Father." "Ye are the light of the world." "Not of the world, even as I am not of the world." He put away from his Apostles the estimates of the whole world and their own estimates also. They were dull fishermen in the world's esteem, but he wrought forth their original light as the noon day, and their native radiance that height nor depth nor things present nor things to come can ever dim.

There is one Shining Me, the Unalterable Funda-mental, The High Reality of every son of man. This is the handwriting of God. All other sights and sounds of him are fictitious handwritings, as erasable by the right process as chalk marks on a blackboard.

It is the province of this eighth lesson in heavenly law to woo mankind to willing erasure of all fictitious estimates. "Man can never behold the face of the Father except in the eighth"—was an inspired utterance of Saint-Martin *"le philosophe inconnu"* ["the unknown (or hidden) philosopher"]. This was Saint-Martin's way of putting Isaiah's words, "He that is escaped shall come unto thee to cause thee to hear." One is escaped, or free to the view who has no imagery hieroglyphed across his presence. "Nay, not that!" says the Hindu, to all descriptions of the Lord of Life and Spirit.

"He is not Life, but Cause that Life is. He is not Spirit, but Cause that Spirit is. No descriptive fits the High Cause," wrote the Egyptian wise men as they laid the symbol of high denial on the shoulders of their sculptured gods.

"Blotting out the handwriting of ordinances against us — took it out of the way, nailing it to (signing it by) the cross," wrote Paul, learned in the significance of all symbols. "Beware lest any man spoil you through philosophy and vain deceit, after the traditions of men, after the rudiments of the world."

"The accuser of our brethen is cast down," said the voice of the Angel to John the Revelator. Accusation does fall down. It is the tongue silently or audibly detailing descriptives that do not apply to the Actual. "Then the ruffian looked at me, and wrought against me strange diseases," said the Parsee, speaking for mankind become self-accused, or neighbor-accused by lowly watching. "So mayest thou heal me thou glorious *Manthra Spenta*." *Manthra Spenta* is Lord, and lordly recognition of what lies back of the ruffianly accused heals. It is the Parsee way of urging the healing high watch.

Even objects of Nature, trees, plants, winds, waters, have been ruffianly accused of hurting powers they hold not in themselves. "The waters drown, the winds devastate, the plants poison," we are told. Not in themselves. Have they not all been pronounced good from the beginning? Did the waters drown Peter while his eye was on the Lord mighty to save? Did the winds overturn the ship while the sailors looked to the Master's face? Can tea make the Angel of God's presence nervous? Or coffee cause Divine Intelligence to degenerate? Can rum spoil the beauty of God? It is ruffianly to speak of man or item of Nature as having the power to hurt. Look at them as glowing with the face of One ever watching from every infinitesimal point of the universe. "Wheresoever thou lookest there I am." Take off the world's estimates from that Face, and lo, Beneficence only!

Do not go back on the knowledge that "Thou God seest me" from every direction. Thus are we dead to sin or aberrated viewings. Thus are we dead with the uncon-demning Christ, that we may live with him. Thus are we *tabula rasa* [blank slate] for truth from the circumambient kingdom in which we truly dwell.

"*Multum incola*" [much inside or alone], said the great [Sir Francis] Bacon. He was sensitive to world conditions. They made him ill and dulled his intelligence. He did not care what men called him so they kept out of his way and left him much alone to be sensitive to the wisdoms that fill the ethers. Thus being washed, set free from puny knowledges, he was taught new principles, which made him to be declared "wisest and brightest" of his generation.

Some way of getting *multum incola*, or much alone, has been the effort of all who would be powerful with Truth. Do not the Brahmins reject outward sounds and sights, and inward memories of sorrow and human vexations, until they are left alone with Brahma, or Universal Consciousness and its mysteries? Have the Brahmins not learned, by making themselves thus *multum incola*, many truths of the Universal with which they have practiced till their powers have astonished the world?

"Become relaxed," say certain practitioners among us. "Drop sights and sounds; drop thoughts; drop emotions; become blank for a few seconds; then allow one positive thought to take possession. Hold the thought firmly. It will demonstrate in time in outward conditions." This is their way of letting go, rejecting, on behalf of a thought. There is One above thought, above being, wrote the Seers of old Kabbalah philosophy. "It is The *Ain Soph*," they said. "Take no thought," said Jesus. "Look up to the fields white for the harvest."

Paul speaks of dropping the traditions and philosophies of men, that the life of Christ may take possession of us. Does not the magnet drop all sticks and stones and dust that its own may gather unto it? See the needles and the nails and the steel filings that the magnet loves, hurrying to gather to it!

"So runs the good with equal law Unto the Soul of pure delight."

High Mysticism

"Thy lot or portion in life is seeking after thee," — the Caliph Ali.

"Through the voice of the Lord shall the Assyrian be beaten down," wrote the prophet. "The Assyrian" is the power of darkness.

"The Messiah cometh to walk with men, when they hearken to the voice of the Lord," promises the Talmud.

How can men hearken to the voice of the Lord with its soundless wordings, if the sounded wordings of their neighbors are thick on their ears? How can we know the grand verity of our neighbor's Actual if we accept the outward shows and blatant estimates that make him cower and cringe to old age and death, disease and poverty?

This is a trumpet call that we take today, to accurately put away all contentious estimates and relate ourselves to the Right Estimate. It is the call of the Eight: "In the eighth month came the word of the Lord to Zechariah, the Son of Iddo the prophet, saying, Therefore say thou unto them, Thus sayeth the Lord of Hosts, Turn unto me, saith the Lord of Hosts and I will turn unto you, saith the Lord of Hosts."

How far reaching is the injunction, "Go, wash in the pool of Siloam" – the curative waters of erasure.

Go, gather unto the Unlimited. Erase age, destiny, inadequacy, disadvantage. On behalf of Divine Presence One and Uncontaminate reject its unlikeness.

Stand alone with Almighty Verity. Be one pointed to the Ever-Facing Lord Jehovah. Declare the Unburdening Free God. Be undimmed heralding Star of Messiah's Bright Morning.

9th Study

NOTE

The Italian Flagellants of the 13th century lashed themselves and gashed themselves with thongs and scissors but they felt no pain for the zeal which arose from some central flame within them permeated them through all their flesh and of itself neutralized flesh sensations. Even their minds were so alive with the central flame that they sprang the bounds of self pity in unconsciousness of personal hurts.

Some people explained that it was innate Will rising to new action with a new sense, as "I willed and new sense was given me."

The persecuted English Quakers of the 17th century declared that no blows or stones which their enemies administered upon them with ferocious energy were felt by them, for a central fire rose up in them neutralizing outward sensations by its ecstatic flame. They called it God Willing in them.

Martyrs of old sang hymns in the midst of their enemies' hot bonfires, and their faces were seen to shine with inward ecstasy even as Stephen's face shone while the hurling stones were cutting him. "They saw his face as it had been the face of an angel." (Acts 6-15). The martyrs, like the Quakers, called the mystery of supernal sensation, "God willing them to will and to do."

Some people have called that conquering central flame which can so overpower all human sensation and mental awareness the I AM of man. Some have called it The Spirit of man. This was Solomon's name for it. Some have called it The Spirit of God. Ezra called it The Spirit of God. So also did Ezekiel the prophet who was named The Strength of Jehovah.

Jesus, the All-overshining Jesus of Nazareth, declared, "The Spirit of God is upon me." He also said "I Am," and

High Mysticism

transcended all other martyrs in the risen splendor of the central flame common to but hidden deep in all mankind. He knew the risen vigor as Will. "Whosoever shall do the Will of God is my brother." He shouted of his glorification despite the wounds of the cross, and cried aloud of his almighty identification with Universal Spirit, "Into Thy hands I commit my Spirit."

Socrates hundreds of years before the time of Jesus felt himself outshining himself in the face of threatening martyrdom, and said to the judges, "I go about trying to persuade both young and old, not to busy yourself about your bodies or about money more than about your soul." "Manifestly it rules in us a King."

It is no wonder then that over the cross of him who picked himself up out of martyrdom and showed himself Indestructible Soul, they wrote, "This is Jesus the King of (the Soldiers of God, the Israelites) the Jews."

One historic life of this martyr-transcending King, lately written, lays such stress on the pains and torments of his martyrdom that people shudder and weep when they read it. And the supposedly greatest praise that has been lavished on an eloquent New York preacher reads: "We can almost feel the blood drip on our heads as we hear him preach the Cross."

But the true printed Life of Jesus should glory in telling of his sense of out-glowing all wounds on a still grander scale than the Flagellants and Quakers and noblest of earth's martyrs, because he knew himself with ecstatic zeal as God Himself proving the rightful status of all mankind. "Thou being a man makest thyself God" they said.

Mystical Science which shows how the Secret Flame can be wooed to rise superior to all human laws physical and mental, tells of an Over Splendor of attention toward us ever wooing our attention till its likeness in us rises into Oneness with its Splendor as Undefeatable Greatness. The greatness of Unconquerable Will.

"By so many roots as the marsh grass sends in the sod,

I will heartily lay me ahold of the greatness of God."

"He sent from above, he took me, he drew me out of many waters"—even the waters of humiliation.

It is not a matter of consciousness or unconsciousness of mind or body. It is not a matter of right or wrong of human calculation. It is the New Kingdom's Super Life.

This Ninth Lesson teaches to stand by our Super I with its high language, till its language fruitings lay out before us our true life field. It teaches to find that hidden Self! It teaches to speak from that! It teaches to choose what we truly will, and shows it as Universal Will as it was in the beginning, is now, and ever shall be, out of the reach of death and those shadows of death the hurts of flesh and of mind. E. C. H.

Numbers were alive to the ancients. Notice Parmenides facing The One till form and differentiations disappeared, the cosmic order let go and he was alone as if he were The Alone. There is but One SELF and Thou art That Self.

Five was a living number to the Hebrews. It signified The Representative, as Joseph for Pharaoh, as Jesus for Jehovah. Its symbol was the sardonyx, which held the engraving of the royal "I Depute."

Apollonius of Tyana would not allow his disciples to speak the number nine aloud, as it was to him the magician's number—the number of enchantment. If sounded it was likely to hit the super I having its location in a point back of the breast. To hit that I, or speak forth from that I, would be like "wishing" the words on somebody or something. Learn to wake the hidden I, but note the kindling mystery of it as the living black coal lingering in the breast waiting the bellows breath of right declaration.

To mankind the old I must aver according to appearance, as "I am sick," or, "I am overworked." This is its gospel truth. But the I, as kindling coal, avers, "I living vigor! I godly strength! I decree!"

High Mysticism

Ye shall eat of the old fruit—ye shall eat of the new fruit, according to kindling or non-kindling of the words by recognition of the I Spark. "My spirit shall not forever be humbled in man"—"I am the light. He that eateth me shall live by me."

"I" is a fodder. Man shall eat of the old fruit till the ninth, or till willing to take up the super I's great sayings, the "I decree!" At the ninth, man is willing to refuse the old fruitings. He declares as Christ in him, "I The Alive, I The Eternal, I the transfiguring and transforming all things by my 'I decree'."

The ancients cherished the scarab that drops its seed into a dirt ball for universal atmosphere to stir it to break its covering and fly as winged creature. They named it symbol of the resurrection of man as determining God Will from the encasement of shadow body formed of matter woven with mind threads, the stubborn web of hiding, "the shadow system gathered round the Me."

"Rise my soul, and stretch thy wings, Thy better portion trace."

Nine is the Assumption, the Joy of Mary, the taking for granted, the supposing of a thing without visible proof, the unwarrantable claim. The Great Assumption is the Great I Spark speaking its own joyous facts, which come forth glorifying the outer man with new fruitings.

Nine stands for the closing of an old cycle and the opening of a new cycle, the old touching the new and the new touching the old like beads on a rosary. The great mystics have prophesied that the Messiah appears at the beginning of some nine cycle as the old I giving way to the new I. The old I telling the truth of itself and others according to appearances, and the new I, or the awakening I, telling truth according to the kingdom of the super spark, till it flashes its dominion over animate and inanimate. It is the daring response of the Me, the I, praised, according to the fifth revelation, or the Fifth Study.

It is indeed the swift discovery with Hugo of St. Victor that the highest God and the inmost God is one God.

Acknowledge the Highest, The Great Countenance of the Absolute, and its I Seed awakes with the Assumption, the Unwarrantable Claim, the Word of the Lordship "very night unto thee, in thy mouth and in thy heart, that thou mayest do it," as Moses said to the children of Israel in the land of Moab. "I am as strong this day, as I was in the day that Moses sent me into Eshcol of Canaan. And now, Lo, I am this day four score and five years old," declared Caleb son of Jephunneh, who stood with good report from Eshcol as easily manageable by Israel, when others said there were unmanageable giants to meet.

The divine I that has its location in a point back of the breast, whose flame Apollonius asked his disciples to stir with good reports, is still alive in every breast on earth, and oft-time assumption of the things It sees, It feels, It knows, will cause them to show forth, brightening all the paths in which we daily move with the unprecedented, the unbelievable, the unexpected.

"Where is thy spark, Lanoo? Speak thou from that!"

The ministry of acknowledgment and recognition into which we are hurried, is wide and far reaching, or near and intimate in demonstration, according as our vision proceeds far or keeps close. "I fetch my knowledge from far," said young Elihu. "Remember that thou magnify his work, that men may behold it afar off."

The forty Christians enrolled in the twelfth Roman legion lifted up their hands to God in high heaven, when the *Quadi* seemed about to destroy the legion. And Marcus Aurelius Antoninus wrote it down for all ages to notice, that a Roman victory was wrested from the *Quadi* by the God of the forty Christians, and not by the swords and spears of the vaunted legion.

The original Francis Schlatter cured thousands of people by sensing that his God was near at hand, close and compassing, with only just one kind and merciful streak in his

High Mysticism

mighty composition, and that was his will to heal through the willing Francis Schlatter. His God would not let him be fed, or warmly clothed, or rested when weary, but he would touch Schlatter's hands with near curative balms for his neighbors.

The science of the recognition of the Presence of God in the Universe, by the uplift of the vision as to divine Beneficence, is the oldest science maintaining its stately march through the long non-acceptance of the human race. Abram, 1920 B.C. is told to lift up his eyes. Dante, 1265 A.D., declared that blessedness more depends upon vision than upon loving, for loving follows on after vision. It is told of a certain Bishop that his lofty character and great attainments were due to his oft-time gaze toward the glory of The Highest. We also may show forth lofty character and great attainments by oft-time gaze toward The Highest, the great countenance of The Absolute, ever facing us.

The Deity onlooketh thee, onlook thou the Deity.

The one mystery of man's accomplishing executive-ness is that whatever he persistently recognizes and acknowledges surely comes forward and deals with him.

Recognition and acknowledgment are the "two-law" from which something must come forth, worth while or not worth while. Man must woo and woo the Majestic and Responsive Beneficence ever facing him. His wooing will be astonishingly rewarded. "Go away," said the elder Gounod to his son; "burn your composition, the Muses have not called you." What did the elder Gounod know about wooing the Muses till they gladly come with their music, or their statuary, or their architecture, such as this present world has not set eyes upon? Even the Moekels' terrier disputes Gounod's position that the Muses neglect some people. The little dog did prove per contra that it is some people who neglect the Muses. By much wooing of the dog Rolf's intelligence Mrs. Moekel caused intelligence to speak forth through him with amazing answers to mathematical and philosophical questions. What wonderful music was closed down upon from expressing through young Gounod, when his father forbade his wooing the Muses! What enchanting singers have been silenced by teachers who did not help enlarge the smile of the song-muse the young voice was trying to woo — Voice that might have stayed the wars of empires!

"Muses" were ancient names for the Universal All-Power, demonstrating according to recognition and wooing.

Our eighth lesson urged recognition of the High and Lofty One as All-Power, and as The Universal, Rounded, Super Worthwhile, into whose glorious oblivion all limitations and false estimates may be thrown, by casting them away, having nothing to do with them. "It is not so!" is the eighth lesson's masterful shout to every word that disputes all Judah praise of the every-where watching Amen Ra, or Brahma, or God. Even the values of man as good in contradistinction to bad are to be circumcised, sacrificed, rejected, on behalf of the High First Estate above the pairs of opposites: good and bad, life and death, pleasure and pain. We must throw everything out to the ever present First Estate of The Universally Desir-able. This Ninth lesson calls attention to the Undifferentiated, Ever-facing Original, which the Egyptian priests called Soul, the Magi called Self, the Hebrews sometimes called God and sometimes called Angel of the Presence, and which truly is Free Spirit, Free Beneficence, Free Zeus, Free Giver. It is that Dominant of which the ancients were speaking when they promised that whosoever should put away all words contending against high praises, should find Free Spirit, Immortal Self, dominating.

Great promises have ever associated with the ministry of rejections, denials, sacrifices, fastings, circumcisions: "Grace, mercy and peace from God ...teach no other doctrine ...neither give heed to fables ...that thou mightest war a good warfare," wrote Paul to Timothy, the boy Bishop of Ephesus.

> "For God hath not given us the spirit of fear, but of love, and of power, and of a sound mind—circumcision without hands—putting

High Mysticism

off the body of the sins of the flesh by the circumcision of Christ—quickened together with him, having spoiled principalities and powers."

Did not Bhaskaranand of Benares find himself a powerful healer, after rejecting the influences of the world — "triumphing in himself," as Paul noted of Christ?

Coming thus to our own free Self, our own divinity Spark, our own I decree, clarifies the atmospheres of false instructions. Heretofore hidden truth comes boldly forth. I the mighty Truth. I the awakener to life eternal. "The Highest God and the inmost God is one God."

"Thy words were found, and I did eat them, and thy word was unto me the joy and rejoicing of my heart." So wrote Jeremiah in a moment of freedom from his own contentious complainings. He experienced the outward joys of Victorious Assumption, the living nine of Apollonius.

> There are promises with hearkening to the Heights:
>
> "He that hearkeneth unto me shall dwell safely, and be quiet from fear of evil"
>
> "The friend of the bridegroom which standeth and heareth him, rejoiceth greatly"
>
> "I will give you pastors according to mine heart, which shall feed you with knowledge."

Thus we are told how satisfying is I, Truth! We always feed on the super I's great claims. It affects our constitution much or little. As an eyelash falling into a pool affects it little, but a meteor falling in affects it greatly, so we are stirred greatly or slightly by the truths we hear and proclaim. Does it stir your life pool to be told that God is great and we know him not, as spoken through Elihu the Buzite? But if you should yourself hear one of the soundless truths that the great *Ain Soph* holds hidden in the etheric silence round about your head, especially waiting for your own ears only, promising that the desire of your heart is fulfilled this day, you would tremble from head to foot with joy. You would be found declaring, "Thy word in me is joy to mine own heart. I Joy, ray forth joy. I ray forth my own I Am, I Will, I Can."

Joy that inwardly stirs by truth from on high is a healing energy, or Savior, or Joshua. Joshua, or Joy, particularizes the spot or the scene of its triumphing "I decree." Joshua stretches forth the spear in his hand toward Ai, the mass or heap of spoiling principles as the I's old fruitings, according to its gospel truth speaking as things appear, that have gotten the better of man as sickness, sorrow, or despair; and Joshua, aware of the "I am Captain of the host of the Lord" facing him, taketh not back the hand wherewith he stretcheth out the spear, till all the inhabitants of Ai are utterly destroyed; or the spoiling principles annihilated; and in the precinct is no city save Bethel, House of the Lord Uncontaminate.

In ancient times the spear, the stick, the staff, the sword, the scepter, were used to knight the commoner, or to transform the sick man into the sound man, the timid man into the bold man, the common man into the titled peer. Elisha's staff was often used with this transforming effect. Kings to this day strike with sword or scepter the shoulders of certain subjects of their realm; and Mr. Henry becomes Sir Henry, and my friend becomes Your lordship. "Take thee one stick and write Judah (the unseen eternal and one stick and write Joseph (the manifest external), and they shall be one under thine hand," said the voice of the Lord to Ezekiel the most mystical minister among the ancient prophets.

Jesus did not take a visible stick or scepter to touch the beautiful Judah Self of the Joseph self of the corpse body of Nain, to make the Judah beauty glow and gleam and glorify through rosy lips and sparkling eyes and stirring blood as living widow's son at the city gates. He laid his hand on the Joseph self while steadfastly looking toward the ever waiting Angel of the Presence, flying swiftly, mighty in strength, ministering Spirit, doing wondrously; and he told his disciples to thus lay hands on the sick that they might recover

High Mysticism 457

their seemingly lost immortal Judah Self, the ever near Angel of the presence. He drew the waiting glow and glory of man's angel of life ever present, to gleam and gladden him as living strength, even when he seemed dead. "I drew them with cords, with bands, and I was unto them as he that taketh the yoke off the jaws."

"If I keep looking to a gazelle leaping from rock to rock, I dance the gazelle dance so that people clap their hands," says the child dancer of the New Age, harking back to the days of Aristoxanus, who taught to dance according to soul promptings and inward visioning.

"Keep your eye on the Eternal, and your intellect will grow." "Honor and fortune exist for him who remembers that he is in "the presence of the High Cause." Therefore, "Unto thee, O my Strength, will I sing, animating my particular Self with Thy Universal Energy! O Thou I, and I Thou!"

"Glance up often," writes Conan Doyle "to the spirits of the dead." Hosea the prophet would say that the great writer is calling attention high, but not to The Most High. Practice of the Presence of The Most High, The Great Countenance of The Absolute, the *Ain Soph,* caused Nahum the prophet to cry out, "Watch the way, make thy loins strong, fortify thy powers mightily!" For the loins do show strength by reason of high watch, and the "I Am Strength" is our giant truth.

> "And when he was in a certain city, behold a man full of leprosy, (spoiling principles), who seeing Jesus fell on his face, and besought him, saying, Lord, if thou wilt, thou canst make me clean. And he put forth his hand, and touched him, saying, I will; be thou clean; and immediately the leprosy departed from him."

It makes a difference who is reporting a miracle, as to whether the misery in its departure is mentioned, or the joyous state that remains is proclaimed. Luke the physician when reporting a case lays stress on the malady and its exorcise, as in the case of the "man full of leprosy," which "leprosy departed." So Joshua lays stress on the destruction of the spoiling principles massed as the old I's gospel truth.

Mark, the founder of the Alexandrine Church, writes with burning brevity of the happy estate of unmolested cure: "And he took the blind man by the hand; and when he had put his hands upon him, and spit upon his eyes, after that he put his hands again upon his eyes, and he was restored and saw every man clearly." Mark does not say the blindness departed.

Again, notice the unction with which the physician Luke details the distressing condition of the synagogue worshipper: "And, behold, there was a woman which had a spirit of infirmity eighteen years, and was bowed together, and could in no wise lift up herself. And when Jesus saw her, he called her to him, and said unto her, Woman, thou art loosed from thine infirmity. And he laid his hand upon her; and immediately she was made straight and glorified God." Notice how he threw the spoiling fruitings of the old I away into Universal Solvent!

So efficacious in drawing forth to visibility the Stainless Spark, or Judah Self of man, by the laying on of hands, was the Apostolic succession in Christian ministry, that for more than fifteen centuries the Christian minister laid with sacred tenderness his ordained hand upon the Joseph breast of his sick parishioner, whoever he might be, and repeated the accepted Christian formula for making the invisible Judah effulgence one with the outward body:

> "As with this visible oil thy body outwardly is anointed, so our heavenly Father, Almighty God, grant of his infinite goodness that thy soul, inwardly, may be anointed with the Holy Ghost, who is the Spirit of all strength, comfort, relief and gladness. And vouchsafe for his great mercy to restore unto thee thy bodily health, and strength, to serve him, and send thee release from all thy pains, troubles and diseases, both in body and mind—through Jesus Christ our Lord."

High Mysticism

And wonderful were the restorations of the Lord Self to the man or woman who had lost sense of vital oneness of Judah and Joseph in their own bodily form.

"Labor to keep alive in your breast the spark of celestial fire, the quenchless flame," said some of the mystics. Remember the smokeless fire, the effulgent centre capable of infinite procession *in extenso*, of far extending radiance — "The stainless Spark," of which Dante writes.

When Jesus touches the leper and says, "I will. Be thou clean," he is surely feeling the sweet fires running along from the God Self of himself through the palms of his hands and the tips of his fingers, as he sights with mystic energy the unseen Angel to wake joyous soundness where no waking seemed possible.

> "I drew them with the bands of love, and they knew not that I healed them."

> "Take thee one stick and write Judah, and one stick and write Joseph, and they shall be one under thine hand."

The Lord mighty to save stands stately and majestic everywhere facing us. "Two are ever in the field. One shall be taken, the other left." Call, "Stand forth, life! health! strength! Come ye blessed of my Father! It is God's will that you stand forth strong, and glad, and free! It is my will that you stand forth strong, and glad, and free! It is your will that you stand forth strong, and glad, and free!" This *memra*, or Will Word, is the one harmonic chord stretching its soundless note, world without end, through men and angels, from the just the mighty Will filling the universe.

Only he who has felt the blaze in his own breast can sense to the full the vital fire that burns in the breast of his neighbor, when his form seems lifeless, unconscious, past knighting with his own divinity. Therefore it is that all lessons of Ineffable Mysticism return again and again to the relation of one's own Lord Self to the High I AM, the experience it was death to go to the king; but Esther felt the celestial "I Go," in her breast, and faced the Invisible Lord standing masterful and majestic where other people saw only Xerxes the terrible. "Old born drunk" who had never had any will or mind, laid his hands on his breast, where the spark celestial glows in all men, and said, "I am determined to find God." And all the criminals and debauched of his part of London turned out with heads bowed and hats in hand, because "Old born drunk," blear-eyed, will-less sot, found God!

"I praise God that I am healed!" shouted one who felt his Spark Celestial stir to speak as truth speaks by inner Lord despite outer diseased contentions. And though all the people sided with his outer contention, or diseased form, he spoke again more loudly still of the Lord spark, burning truth in his breast, "Praise God! He has made me whole! I am healed!" And his truth of his own Lord Self transfused and uplifted and out-shone so that his outer frame glowed with the beauty of health, and all those who had sided with his previous showings were confounded. "Let them be confounded that are adversaries to my soul," cried king David, sensing the glow of the Christ spark in his bosom, the meeting place of the majestic Lord with every human form.

"I cannot retract—I am That!" exclaimed a young girl who had felt the glow of the stainless spark in her breast. And though she was held as untruthful, she fulfilled in herself all that she had said of herself "I am That!" She had spoken of the future as in the present tense, and that alone was her offense. Let us make no blunder here: The verities are in all tenses the same. The I am That belongs to us now as it was in the beginning, and always shall be, unabrogated forever. Whatever we will be we are, as Lord Self, ready to kindle the demonstration of "I am That," according to our acknowledgement. "Take thee one stick and write Judah, and one stick and write Joseph, and they shall be one in thine hand," is our privilege. For the great things of our Judah Self are the things our Joseph self can manifest.

High Mysticism

This has been called knowing the Self, or recognition of the pure Splendor inherent in all mankind as Omniscience, Omnipotence; Self Spark fearlessly waiting till I Am That be boldly spoken.

"Where is thy spark, Lanoo! Speak thou from That."

Joy follows hearkening to the voice of the ever-speaking Highest. "Thy word was unto me the joy and rejoicing of mine heart." And joy is strength: "The joy of the Lord is his strength." And strength is the bread of heaven: "Man shall feed in the strength of the Lord." And joy in the Lord as strength is a healing radiance. "The merry heart doeth good like a medicine." "The Lord loveth a cheerful giver," or a giver of cheer. For "they tread on serpents." That is, they bring forth health and strength and wise words from their neighbors as the sun draws forth the serpents of the stony fields. Serpents were in old days symbolic of health, strength, wisdom.

"Canst thou draw forth leviathan?" asks the great voice addressing Job. "Leviathan" is the strongest beast of the sea. The strongest constituent of man's constitution is his joy chord. Canst thou make thy neighbor joyous? He is surely cured of all his maladies if thou canst wake the joy that slumbers unstirred in his being. Jeremiah had three diseases from grieving: "Mine eyes do fail with tears—my liver is poured out—my bowels are troubled." No heart was ever stirred to healing joyousness in Jeremiah's atmosphere. But a man in the Himalaya mountains felt the smile of God so ardently, that people went from miles around to get kindled into health by the mysterious influence of the far extending radio-activity of his smile.

No condemnation abides with the awakened joy spark. "I came not to condemn," said the healing Jesus. "He that is of a merry heart hath a continual feast," said Solomon. "His barrel of meal," his barrel of healing power, "stayeth not." As the lily is not lessened in fragrance though a thousand people smell thereof, so the bottomless pit of the God spark stayeth not, is not lessened, by much procession *in extenso.* "There is that scattereth and yet increaseth" is true of the I am That of myself, and of the Thou art That which I ardently proclaim to my neighbor. There is no limit to his joy fountain, his I with its divine fruitings. "Go thy way," respondeth the Mighty Lord of my neighbor's presence; "eat thy bread with joy, and drink thy wine with a merry heart; for God now accept-eth thy words." "Ye shall be named the priests of the Lord. Men shall call you the ministers of God." "I make you a joy of many generations."

This Ninth tells of the joy that comes by communing with one stronger than Nature's forces and wiser than man's mind. "And your joy no man taketh away." "For he that communeth with me strengthened." Gideon communed with the Lord God Invisible. He endureth year after year as seeing Him. "And the Lord looked on Gideon, and said, 'Go in this thy might, and thou shalt save Israel from the Midianites and the Amelekites, and all the children of the east lying along in the valley like grasshoppers for multitude!'" And Gideon, who knew not the law that might is roused by communing with the Mighty, answered from his Joseph or human sense of himself, "Oh, my Lord! Wherewith shall I save Israel? Behold, my family is poor in Manasseh, and I am the least in my father's house." But suddenly Gideon rose up with a new sense of himself, kindled by communing with One to whom great works are easy, and masterful deeds simple; and he stood boldly forth before the haughty army of Israel and said, "Look on me!" And all the powerful soldiers of Israel acknowledged Gideon's right to untried martial leadership. He had touched the strength chord that stretches between universal Omnipotence and man's omnipotence. It is the joy chord also; and the love chord. It is the faith shout of "I Am Victory" in the hour of defeat.

The mystery of the victorious vision of Esther, and of David, and of Gideon, is our mystery of victorious vision by much communion with the same Victorious Lord.

High Mysticism

Scientifically speaking they all cognized from the God centre of their being, struck back to God centre by much association with the Unseen Worker, ever offering himself as Almighty Ally, without partiality to all, high or low, rich or poor, wise or foolish.

As the actinic ray in the sun is the secret of its life giving charm, so the joy of the Lord is his strength. And man may invigorate in that strength till he is royal magnet to the life of his neighbor, to the health of his neighbor, to the joyous smile of his neighbor, like Jesus to the ruler's child, Peter to Tabitha, Paul to Eutychus.

Mystic joy of heart that draws forth the Judah Self of the sick, is the magnetic mystery which no man on earth exhibits in the plenitude of its attractive energy, because no man puts forth from the magnetic I centre of his being, the I Jesus hand that came not to be ministered unto, but to minister.

At the magnetic spark centre of our being we are the Sun of Righteousness with healing in his beams.

As the sun draws the oak tree from out the acorn's stiff cortex, up through the hard mold, past the tough grass roots, to centuries of forest life, so the hand that taketh the yoke from off the Judah jaws of mankind must move out from a central magnet stronger than death, stronger than Satan, or the non-alliance of the sick themselves. (There is no Satan except such non-alliance.)

No accusation abides at the magnetic centre of our being. If it is love, it is love that ministers, asking nothing in return. It can wake to such might by our alliance with the Mighty that it draws forth the integrity that hides like a giant asleep in the hearts of all men. The recognition of giant integrity waiting to be awakened annuls the disposition to condemn. There is no time to parley with would-be hinderings. The main business engrosses: "It is your will — It is my will — It is God's will — Come forth!" And even Lazarus may not resist that king's command.

It is lode-star to the Logos of man. It draws forth the axiom of his Sonship to The Father. It wakes the key word to his diviner destiny:

"There is a message speaking within me from the heavens;
Whispering within me even in my sleep.
It stirs the victorious I am That!"

"I am a writer," said Balzac. Was not this word the chord to which his life vibrated? Did not that word act like a chain pump to the pool of genius hidden in his bosom? But there is a deeper and farther-reaching adequacy lying at the root of pure being than Balzac spoke.

There is an axiom that is bone of our bone and sinew of our sinew. It came with us when we hailed hither from our heavenly Father's bosom. If we speak it forth, word for word and letter for letter, we are the sunshine and gladness of every life with which we associate. No situation daunts us. It is the laughing topaz stone of fearlessness, because nothing hath power to hurt its self-existent verity.

No wonder that the true topaz stone, emblem of unkillable joyousness, is worth upwards of a million dollars in the gem markets of the world!

Inward buoyancy, kindling into speech, dissolves danger, animosity, failure. It puts them at disadvantage: "I have set the Lord always before my face, therefore my heart is glad and my flesh resteth in confidence," said David. He got his gladness of heart from setting the Lord always before his face. And the confidence of his flesh rose to such vigor that he set Goliath to one side, though a whole nation trembled at sight of him.

To this day the words, "I come unto thee in the name of the Lord of Hosts," which David used when he faced Goliath, have something of the victorious self-executive David energized into them, even when the genesis of their energy is not noted. There are living examples of people who, though they have not set the Lord always before their faces, and therefore have not stirred the joy spark of their being, yet have been made mysteriously triumphant by repeating

High Mysticism

David's words, "I come unto thee in the name of the Lord of Hosts."

The words turned their vision to the hard problems of their life as being met by that Unseen Ally who saith, "I will contend with him that contendeth with thee." It is a continuation of the shout of the Israelites following on after the Ark of the Lord, as it led forward into the ranks of their enemies: "Rise up, Lord! and let thine enemies be scattered; and let them that hate thee flee before thee!" Their vision toward an Unseen Ally moving with irresistible might before them, worked havoc among their enemies; took the yoke of enmity off the jaws of their rightful safety, drew glad security to their plain view. "I was unto them as he that taketh the yoke off the jaws."

Haggai promised that the "Desire of all nations shall come." He meant that the glorious Lord ever facing shall be acknowledged, recognized, sound, free, wherever we look. "Like attracts like." Magnetic gladness of heart attracts gladness of heart. This medicine divine stays waiting high watch, self recognition, joyous association with the Lord I Am of our neighbor, fearless of his hurting power fearless of all hurting powers, heavenly hosts for antiphons:

"Harvest from seed that was scattered
On the borders of blue Galilee."

"To him that overcometh will I give power over the nations." To overcome is to come over. To come over or above our circumstances and bodily feelings, by looking above to Him ever beholding hitherward, is to identify with power above the nations and combinations of delusions, as divine magnets to the strong, glad, free Self, even of multitudes: "Multitudes came unto him, and he healed them every one."

"From many an ancient river,
From many a palmy plain
They call us to deliver
    Their land from error's chain."

"Him that overcometh will I make a pillar." Pillar is strength. "The joy of the Lord is strength." Joy gives mysterious potency to the hands visible, and to the hands invisible. To stretch forth invisible hands and touch responsive strong Spirit, and say, "Come forth!" is to go into all the world and "lay hands on," that multitudes may come forward repossessing their own wholeness.

> "And they heard a great voice from heaven, saying unto them, Come up hither. And they ascended."
>
> "And Joshua was full of the spirit of wisdom, for Moses had laid his hands upon him."
>
> "And when Paul had laid his hands upon them, the Holy Ghost came on them, and they spake with tongues, and prophesied."

Though the Angel of man's presence has shown ages long renitency to wails of woe, it springs in full orbed splendor forth to greet the sceptred word of the joyous Shiloh spark of the New Healer — *Qui mittendus est* [who is sent].

With vision cast downward, Mary was accusing some gardener of hiding her Lord; with upward vision she beheld the Lord, and no guilty gardener. She brought forth the Angel out of the heavenly spaces, and forgot that the guilty gardener ever existed. "They shall forget misery as waters that pass away."

Thus with upward vision does the delusional age end, and the Reality age appear. Upward vision draws up from our native root of sincerity. By upward vision oft practiced every human being starts anew from his sincerity root, and drops the dry branches of lower attention, which have formulated into nervous prostration, decrepitude, poverty, discouragement, and apprehension, and flourishes forth from his Sincerity Root of Vigor Everlasting; his Bottomless Life-Pit; his Healing Joy-Fountain; his Winning Bosom-Spark; gathering the Angelhood of the universe to companionship. Is it not written, "Ruling all nations with rod of iron," or with the irresistible pulling strength of magnetic iron? "I, if I be lifted up, will draw all men unto Me."

So, with divine allurements, again at the alphabet of Mysticism, we are brought with David to "lift up our heart with our hands unto God in the heavens," with sweet commandment, praying, "Turn thou us unto thee, O Lord; renew our days as of old." This is the heavenly exhortation that makes our message as ointment poured forth. This causes the responsive nations to say with David's son, for the Great Ministry's sake, "Draw me, we will run after thee — Many waters cannot quench our love" of thy wondrous Word! — that *Memra* which created the world; which brought Israel out of Egypt; which wrought the miracles recorded in the deep book of Exodus!

"From the sixth hour there was darkness over all the land unto the ninth hour." Is it not always understood that darkness is ignorance? The sixth hour sets forth the law of spontaneous, or volitional calling after the Unknown and Invisible, to let It take possession of us after Its own fashion. The seventh and eighth tell of forging ahead for our neighbor's Unknown and universal Best Good to take possession of him, manifesting after Its own fashion. But the Ninth in all ages treats of the knowing, the cognizance, the independent awareness by our own apperception, of the reality of the High Best Self of our neighbor, the great Angel of his presence:

"What truth when number nine we see
Should we remember most?
The orders it should call to mind
Of all the heavenly host,"

says the child dancer of the New Age, harking back to the days of Aristoxanus, who taught to dance according to soul promptings and inward visioning.

"Keep your eye on the Eternal, and your intellect will grow."

"Honor and fortune exist for him who remembers that he is in 'the presence of the High Cause.' Therefore,

> "Unto thee, O my Strength, will I sing, animating my particular Self with Thy Universal Energy! O Thou I, and I Thou!"

"Glance up often," writes Conan Doyle "to the spirits of the dead." Hosea the prophet would say that the great writer is calling attention high, but not to The Most High. Practice of the Presence of The Most High, The Great Countenance of The Absolute, The *Ain Soph*, caused Nahum the prophet to cry out, "Watch the way, make thy loins strong, fortify thy powers mightily!" For the loins do show strength by reason of high watch, and the "I Am Strength" is our giant truth.

"And when he was in a certain city, behold a man full of leprosy (spoiling principles), who seeing Jesus fell on his face, and besought him, saying, Lord, if thou wilt, thou canst make me clean. And he put forth his hand, and touched him, saying, I will; be thou clean; and im-mediately the leprosy departed from him."

It makes a difference who is reporting a miracle, as to whether the misery in its departure is mentioned, or the joyous state that remains is proclaimed. Luke, the physician, when reporting a case lays stress on the malady and its exorcise, as in the case of the "man full of leprosy," which "leprosy departed." So Joshua lays stress on the destruction of the spoiling principles massed as the old I's gospel truth.

Mark, the founder of the Alexandrine Church, writes with burning brevity of the tantibility of the immortal and unspoilable Self, clothed, housed, fed, strong, glad, free, as the outward sign of our recognition of the oneness of his Judah and Joseph self. "Inasmuch as ye have done it unto one of the least of these, ye have done it unto me."

This closes the age of darkness, of the hiddenness of the Self, and gives tactile value to the Angel of God's presence speaking to us and dealing with us, whenever a human being speaks to us or faces us. We appreciate that as there is but One Supreme Self in the universe, ever inviting each self to transcend itself by recognition of its own One Supreme Self, we are all brethren, because our neighbor's One Supreme Self is our Supreme Self also. This is the genesis of the injunction to love the neighbor as the Self. It is the "Brahma Self, One Self, thou that Self," of most ancient teaching. Cornelius, a Centurion in the Roman Army, had lifted up his fearing vision Godward till the Angel of the High Supreme was tangibly present before him, conversing with him as man to man, lovely, masterful, wise.

"At the Ninth hour of the day" it was, as we read, Acts tenth chapter, "At the Ninth hour Jesus gave up the ghost." He dropped the sense of a body or mind differentiated from the Supreme Self. He sent forth his divine influence untrammeled by form, to be contagioned by all men world without end.

The Levitical law of Hebraism reads that man shall eat of the old fruits till the Ninth [month]. That is, we must stand by what we are taught as gospel truth of appearances, till we know to speak by our untaught Self. Peter is trying in his Second Epistle, to tell us that we have a native word of prophecy, "whereunto we do well that we take heed, until the day dawn and the day star arise in our hearts." Day star is lode star, magnetic centre, where the Original Knower in us waits our spoken I am That! and our neighbor waits our spoken Thou art That! And the very world waits our "I decree!" "Look upon Zion," says Isaiah, "there the glorious Lord shall be unto thee a place of rest. And the inhabitants shall not say, I am sick. The people that dwell therein shall be forgiven."

Surely this is a precious treasure, this topaz stone of independent recognition, and independent speech. What reactions of new wisdoms lie quiescent in us till our eyes do look on Zion, and the Lord Supreme be the place of our vision's glad rest! What consort with Angels our neighbors shall experience by our right view of them, as Mozart experienced new music by viewing angelic choirs!

Every other way of viewing our fellow-men exposes us to his shadow system's discordant traits. Jeremiah speaks of a whole nation as having eye failure because of "vain watching toward a people that could not save."

Balaam of Mesopotamia caught a cursing mind from associating with Balak, king of the Moabites, who was filled with the cursing mind. So Balaam was willing to curse the Israelites or any other people Balak might suggest. King Balak had a psychological influence over his associates, like many powerful people of our own time. And Midian, his envoy, who also was under his spell to defeat whomsoever might oppose him, right or wrong, added his vocal persuasions to the king's forceful psychology, and when Balaam got well into their swing he prayed God to make him strong to sweep the Israelites off the earth. After a night's communion with the I AM on high, he opened his mouth with sublime words of blessing and foretelling for the Israelites:

> "There shall come forth a star out of Jacob,
> and a scepter shall arise out of Israel."

Balak and the princes of Moab, with Midian, angrily reminded him that he had been hired and influenced to curse and not to bless; but Balaam, still under the bright sway of High Wisdom, caught by a night's communing with The Transcending One, could not enter again into their psychological aura, and despite their threats, being as it were in a trance, having his eyes still open, he pro-nounced the words of the High Deliverer:

> "How goodly are thy tents O Jacob, and thy tabernacles O Israel! Blessed shall he be that blesseth thee—How shall I curse whom God hath not cursed? or how shall I defy whom God hath not defied? For from the tops of the rocks I see him, and from the hills I behold him: Lo, the people shall dwell alone, and shall not be reckoned among the nations."

Balaam saw the life of the Jews on earth three thousand years ahead of him, even up to this day, when the Scepter of

High Mysticism

the Israelitish stock, the Star of the Son of Jacob is the morning magnet of the whole earth:

"The star that shone over the manger
Now covering the earth with its light."

"He that overcometh, and keepeth the word of my pa-tience, I also will keep him"

Come over the personal hardships by looking up. Did not the Great Prophet say: "In the days of world war and universal lamentation, Look up" (St. Luke, 21st chapter).

Keep the Great Name, or the Great Word, as set forth in First Study, and prove the promise, "I will keep thee from the hour of temptation."

A servant girl feeling the spark burning in her breast said, "I must be a missionary. With God all things are possible, and he has called me to be a missionary." When the mission board received her application they told her she had not the credentials for foreign missionary work. But nothing can down the flame of the I Am That when once uttered and kept as precious truth! Is it any surprise to be told that when delegates of different foreign mission stations were in the United States, and heard her sing:

"Waft, waft ye winds the story,
And you ye waters, roll,
Till like a sea of glory
It spreads from pole to pole"—

and

"Still, still with thee
When purple morning breaketh,
When the bird waketh
And the shadows flee,
Fairer than the morning,
Lovelier than daylight,
Dawns the sweet consciousness,
I am with thee,"

they invited her to go to foreign shores with them, telling her plainly she could win more hearts with her singing than they could win with their preaching?

Keep therefore the high watch and the wonder-working Name, till the spark

I Am That lets loose its executive splendor with its "I will and I decree."

> "Such are the Elect, Who seem not to compete or strive,
> Yet with the foremost still arrive,
> Prevailing still;
> Spirits with whom the stars connive
> To do their will."

Speak from the spark dominant and see its dominion! "So shall the word of the law go forth from Jerusalem," as Isaiah prophesied.

How reviving to mankind is the voice of the God-Will waking the silence of ages with the sceptered word addressed to the True Self of our neighbor:

> It is your will to be glad, and strong, and free! It is my will that you be strong, and glad, and free! It is the will of High God that you be strong, and glad, and free! Walk with me, acknowledging no other voice than the voice of The Supreme now chording all wills into Its One Will.

> I Am That will—Thou art That will—God is That will—There is but One Will!

10ᵗʰ Study

NOTE

"Man has become weary of his thoughts, and seeks for higher power to free him from his mental prison."—Corey.

"Look unto Me"—"I will show thee great and mighty things which thou knowest not." —Jeremiah.

Exaltation of the mystic Visional Sense wakes recognition of our own hidden God Seed; and inspiration fans our God Seed to full exhibition as children of the Promised Golden Age.

E. C. H.

Ten is the number of the light. It is the *Sephiroth* giving birth to everything. Ten is the number of the *memra,* the secret word of the Mystic Self, the hidden Knower in us all, waiting bold definite speech to coincide till the without shall be as the within. Then is the I Jehovah Self-Providing. I *Jehovah Jireh, Jehovah-nissi, Jehovah-tsid-kenu.*[15] "I the Sanctuary in the midst of thee in all places whithersoever thou goest. I the secret Word, the secret Warrior, the secret Music. I that Being declared and none else, "show thee hidden riches of secret places."

Aristotle, 384 B.C., found that there are but ten ideas in the world as there are but ten numbers. All the religions and philosophies and reasonings of the world but ring the changes on ten ideas, as all the mathematical calculations of the world ring the changes on ten numbers.

"With ten words was the world built," reads the Zend-Avesta. The ancient Hebrews declared that *Yod,* the tenth letter of the Hebrew alphabet, is key to the divine language

---

[15] Emma thought of Jehovah as something less than the Infinite, Omnipresent Beingness we call God. Jehovah, as presented in the Bible and some apocryphal, or "lost" books, is the ego's idea of God, with all the personality issues that the ego holds. So, Jehovah changes and has different aspects, while the Everlasting Unchanging is beyond all that.

some time to come forth from the I, hidden man of the heart; angels, authorities and powers then to exhibit themselves as forever subject unto that divine language.

Only one ten-character has ever yet appeared on this earth. Notice Him saying, "All power is given unto Me." "I have overcome the world." Ten is the Rose of the World coming into bloom. Ten is the Wonderful Mother, Desire of All Nations, Secret of Protecting Love. Ten is Symbol of Resurrection. "All the people came up out of the Jordan on the tenth day." "On the tenth day sound the trumpet of Jubilee."

Make note of the key speech of the hidden Light: I am the Lord, I change not. I give power; I take away power. I gave power to death; I take away the power of death. I gave power to defeat, danger, deafness, disease; I take away the power of defeat, danger, deafness, disease. "All power is given unto Me in heaven and in earth." Here I'll raise my Ebenezer, my Rock Eternal. I, the Lord that change not.

"I consulted with Myself," said Nehemiah. "And I rebuked the nobles and the elders; and I built the walls of Jerusalem." I had given power to nobles and elders. I took that power back to Myself, and the nobles and the elders obeyed Me. "I have overcome the world."

It is plain to be seen that all who are giving power to death, deficiency, debt, have not spoken from their *memra*, their Secret Lordword rebuking such nobles and elders. Notice that it is being declared and none else that take away the power of those elders on this earth—danger, defeat, death.

Everybody seems to be declaring for the powers given to these elders, that they may keep on with their powers, not denuded of their powers; but the promise is unto all mankind, "My spirit shall not forever be humbled in thee." "I will rise, I will be exalted."

This is the day of the Ten. It is the number of the Great Resurrection. "All the people came up out of the Jordan on the tenth day."

Number nine stands for joy in our own responsive God point, all peace and plenty.

The Jews of old had the joy of peace and plenty. They have it now. They offered it to the early Christians as the way of their God with all people according to the inspirations recorded in their Sacred Books. The inspired Jesus of the Jewish religion offered it to the Christians, saying, "Search the Scriptures." But they ran away from the inspirations of the Sacred Books and got up their own text, "Poverty and Penance." So the Christians have had to struggle with poverty, working themselves day and night, and practicing some way of penance for success in fighting poverty whenever success has crowned their strenuous-ness; or cowering under poverty or penance all the days of ignoring Peace and Plenty. They have rejected the generous beneficence of "Him Who giveth riches and addeth no sorrow," Whose "yoke is easy, and Whose burden is light."

Number Ten calling again our attention to our native majesty brings back to the joyous God-Self Its original "I The Lord give and I The Lord take away." This tenth lesson teaches us to start over again at our hidden *memra* and sound it forth till the earth shall hear and repeat the anthem, singing with the four and twenty elders of Revelations: "We give Thee thanks because Thou hast taken to Thyself Thy great power, and hast reigned."

The silent *memra* or *vach*[16] language of wordless knowing deep within us all is that language coming to speech soon after being noticed as incontrovertible verity. "Look to the Rock whence ye are hewn." Look to the hidden Center where the inmost Lord and the highest Lord is one Lord.

Victor Hugo found himself being taught by his hidden *memra* or original genius. If we go back far enough into our own crypt or hidden Superself, we find our own genius like Victor Hugo's waiting our bold expression. Victor Hugo wrote about the mysteries because his hidden Self knew the

---

[16] *Vach* is a Sanskrit term referring to the same state of being, or essence, or "I-Am-ness" that Emma has been describing all along. It is also the "word," the sound, out of which all things emerge.

mysteries as our hidden Self knows mysteries — Mysteries which we may tell forth, as new music or new life comes to register on our outer forms; as everything we declare soon registers on our outer forms.

How can it as yet be told so that the world will practice it, that we can willfully lift up ourself free from ourself, till lightness of weight and flawlessness of bodily condition are registered on the *locus standi,* the bodily self, we manifest to the world.

How can it be told so that people will practice inspiring those white breaths ever near us which contain the quickening of our vital interiors 'til

"Come Holy Spirit, heavenly dove
With all Thy quickening powers."

is to us no longer just a rhythmic figure of speech, but a white tonic to be inbreathed by the nostrils?

Who is there to make it a practical reality to us that we have given to disease, defeat, death, all the power they have, and that any time we choose we can take back to our self that power, till disease, defeat, death cannot be found?

When the cruelty that claims to be inherent in the breast of man gets roused, it runs away with him. Even when woman, the compassionate of human kind, lets slumbering cruelty get going, she laughs at the anguish of other human beings. So other slumbering traits within us being unleashed are sure to get the better of us and run us their way. We give them power to ruin our happiness or augment it.

Notice the power we give to people to hurt our feelings. Now we are taught to take back the power we have given them to hurt our feelings, and to start over again, putting something to work for us like as Nehemiah took away the power he had heretofore given the haughty nobles and elders of Jerusalem and started them to building for him the walls of the House of the Lord. When our secret eternal God Genius, the Nehemiah trait whom Jehovah comforts, starts over again with the nobles and the elders now denuded of their over-flowing power to hurt, we set them into their rightful business of forwarding our hidden lordship's great work of transfiguring the world.

"Be steadfast, unmovable, always abounding in the work of the Lord;" "He that standeth steadfast in his heart doeth well." Stand to the Nehemiah Lordship inherent in your breast till it gets going and denudes all cruelty of its seemingly well rooted nativity. "Every plant that my Father, (my original), hath not planted shall be rooted up."

Now we know to take back the power we have given to our emotions to capsize our peace of mind with grief or fear or joy, and to start them over again with new working efficiency as the Tishbite started three mighty kings in the Edomite valley centuries before our era. Now we know that the Tishbite thus ruling his special nobles and his elders was fore-type of our own giving unto and taking back emotions' power to hurt, and giving power only to the proper work of setting the miracles of God to showing forth wherever we walk.

"I have overcome the world" is our God-rooted plant, discovered upon taking back the power we once gave to hurt and emotion. It proclaims our secret right to rule, no matter how hidden by grief or anger, those terrible emotions winding always into disease and death wherever they are allowed to rule. Our Hidden Gnosis tells us that to sing as if we were the singer, while knowing that it is the Singer within who really sings, is to have the New Song put into our mouth according to ancient prophecy: "I will sing a New Song unto thee." Our Hidden Gnosis tells us that to fight on in life's battles as though we were the fighter, while knowing that it is the hidden Warrior who fights, is to have the New Warrior rise up with mystic overpowering so that nation shall never rise up against nation again forevermore. "A Warrior in white shall appear in the tenth Avatar" is the promise. The mystic warfare of the Warrior in white is already begun. "And they shall not hurt or kill in all My holy mountain"—in the Tenth Avatar. "I will work a work whereat all men shall marvel." This is the announcement of the Lord Integrity within me; my *Gnosis* [inner wisdom, inner knowing].

There is to be a New Doctrine revealed to man. It is to come shining forth like a new star in an early morning sky; like a view of the now unseen world that lies adjacent, exposed by some as yet undiscovered telescopic crystal.

There is a Throned One above the sheep and the goats; above the pairs of opposites, love and hate, peace and strife, truth and error. That Throned One hath promised, "I will show thee great and mighty things which thou knowest not." I have given thee an eye divine with which to look toward Me and then behold My works with thee.

All the doctrines that mankind have fought for and lived by, have been swirled around their views of good and evil, truth and error, spirit and matter — the differentiations of these as desirabilities and undesirabilities, blessings and menaces. With slight attention paid to the inspirations of the upward watchers, these views of the pairs of opposites have flung all people into the opposing currents of joy one moment and anguish the next moment; peace of body and mind one hour, and pain of body and mind the next hour: the choppy sea of human mutation.

The promises vouchsafed to the upward watchers have been enumerated: but upward watching toward the High Deliverer has slipped the practice of man. Therefore the most glorious doctrine is not yet expressed. We must do the mystical Will of the High Eternal "Look unto Me," an allotted term, to be sensitive to New Ineffable Mysteries.

And ye shall live, and know, and be strong, and nothing shall by any means hurt you, comes to pass by upward visioning. We must do the mystical Will its heaven allotted term, to experience immuneness from decay, weakness, ignorance, hurting power. There is to be a New Doctrine concerning Reality and Unreality: a doctrine that will hit the confidence of all mankind with the self evidence of the homely axiom, 'the whole is equal to the sum of all its parts."

High Mysticism

Is the doctrine of the unreality of matter as self-evident as "the whole is equal to the sum of all its parts?"

The Hindus have for centuries maintained the *non est* of all external things: "What seems external exists not at all," we read in their *Lanka Vatara*. "By such doctrine I am not in a pulpit preaching; there is no church, and no pulpit. Jesus never walked in Galilee; there never was any Galilee to walk in; this is a blasphemous belief!" said a great divine before a London congregation.

Coomra Sami of Tibet could make the trees and rocks and hills disappear from before the eyes of Hensoldt the level-headed German traveler.[17] This was evidence enough to Coomra Sami that the trees and rocks and hills were the insubstantial pageant of sense delusion. But when his hypnotic spell was off the German traveler's eyesight, the trees and rocks resumed their wonted appearance, and the centuries-old hills are still standing. (The endurance and substantiality of matter were more surely demonstrated by the operations of the sage of Tibet, than its non-existence.) And the mystery of hypnosis has never been fathomed. Only the promised New Doctrine can open the sealed books of many such mysteries of human encounter. "The mystery of God should be finished, as He hath declared to His servants the prophets."

Thus far we have arrived, namely, that with the baptism of the alkahest that falls from the Heights, matter and evil undo their laws of action. But it is only by exalting the visional sense that we the alkahest that looses matter's grip on the conditions of life and mind. It is therefore while "facing Thee," that our lips open to say with didactic firmness, "What seems external exists not at all."

By the subtle touch of grace descending, diseases unformulate. We are certain that "My grace is sufficient for thee." We see its sufficiency before the words have been uttered

---

[17] This is the same German who is depicted in the film *Seven Years in Tibet*.

forth. The genesis of all ideas is inward viewing, or percept. The greatest ideas are generated by highest viewing. This is not a new teaching. In scholastic metaphysics we read that "the existence of ideas is subsequent to that of perception — and even implies perceptual cognition."

So the doctrine of the formulative power of vision is not the New Doctrine foretold by the prophets, seers, and philosophers, but it closely precedes it, as the stiff insistence of the tremendous power of thought closely preceded the undownable insistence that inward vision gives mystical vitality to thought, and without inward vision the thought is sounding brass and tinkling cymbal.

The New Doctrine just at our gates, to follow close on the footsteps of the living veridity of attention upward, is not one that is now already declared. It is the "great and mighty thing which thou knowest not," as promised by the angel to Jeremiah six hundred years before Christ, and by the Angel of the Apocalypse one hundred years after Christ.

It is the hurrying of this New Doctrine hitherward that is sweeping such multitudes of downward watchers out of sight. Did not Jesus promise that in the day of nation against nation, only those who should be found upward watching should be manifestly blessed? And in ancient mythology do we not read that in the coming conflagration only he who sees is saved?

No insistence that I am strong and every whit whole can be found exhibiting strength and wholeness if the vision is still upon the body's misery-claims. Only vision above the body can bring back over the track or Tao of the vision the healing alkahests of the Heights. No insistence that I am victorious can bring victory, if the inward vision is still resting upon the misfortunes and evil liabilities of existing affairs. Only attention to the Highest Best can work the best into our life lot. "Man alone of all the animals knows enough to seek his highest good at the Highest Source, and he looks to his Maker," wrote the mystically wise Lactantius, tutor to the son of Constantine. The ninth chapter in Mysticism brings

High Mysticism

to speech the I Am God that glows with unquenchable might at the centre of every living being. It shows that the Highest Lord and the Inmost Lord is One Lord. It shows that visioning high we vision deep toward Christ in us the hope of glory, Whose is the power and the might forever.

This Tenth chapter in Mysticism drives to the sturdy Job declaration, "I will maintain my cause." So much has been written by the sages of the ages concerning this matter of maintaining a once expressed conviction, that we had better follow up to know the value of standing firm in the midst of the proud waters that sweep over the life of mankind, tempting to non-expression and forgetfulness.

"He that standeth steadfast in his heart doeth well," wrote Paul, as though some excellent work should outshow firm inward acknowledgment. "Beware lest ye fall from your own steadfastness," wrote Peter. "Thou shalt be steadfast and shalt not fear," said Zophar the Naamathite to the tormented Job, as though steadfastness to an inward believing spark would quench the smoke of fear.

This is, then, the genesis of the urge, *fear not*. That is, if we are steadfast to stand by the central spark *I am God* that never dies in our bosom, fear will take flight of itself. "Thou shalt not fear" is prophecy, not command.

David calls his inward spark, "mine integrity within me." Ezra calls it "his Sanctuary." Ezekiel calls it the Lord's "little Sanctuary." They all agree that it is the indestructible element, "the Rock of mine heart" in all mankind. And they all notice that it is the unworded *Logos* ever patiently waiting for the worded insistence of each of us, without respect of persons.

Any expression of the integrity Rock, the Believing Point at the silent depth of our being, acts exoneurally, or beyond the limits of the bodily presence, to affect the mind and nervous systems of our associates. Did not Dr. Mayo of King's College, London, feel the exoneural influence, or the influence beyond the limits of the bodily presence of certain people? Did not Pliny the elder notice that some people's bodies shed forth medicinal influence?

Inward God Believing stays unspoken through the lifetime if one does not choose with firm choice to speak it forth. With expression of the Integrity-Word "the Law goes forth from Zion, and the word of the Law from Jerusalem." Nothing resists firm inward maintenance of the Rock-Center-Truth that lies so still, native to us all, waiting and waiting bold, silent utterance. "All the people bless those who dwell in Jerusalem," wrote a Hebrew prophet. He knew that those who stand by their noble convictions exert far reaching influence.

"I believed, therefore have I spoken," said Paul, whose exoneural influence woke multitudes to new life in his generation; and whose influence proceeding forth to this day stirs the faith spark to shake the emotions, as Felix shook; or stirs a bold, responsive "I Believe," in others; strong in effect as was the convincing energy of the man at the Siloam pool.

Confession of faith is an invigorating practice. "I had fainted unless I had believed," said the king. "I consulted with Myself, and I built the walls of Jerusalem," reported the cup bearer of King Artaxerxes Longimanus, when surrounding enemies crowded him back to his Bedrock Executiveness.

The Throne Place in man is his Rock: "I Believe." It is strange that men have not noticed their own unbreakable original "I Believe, I the Lord," with its wonderful exoneural masterfulness! "Signs follow them that believe," said Jesus.

The faces of the golden Cherubim of the temple are always turned inward. Cherubim are emblems of thoughts and senses. The senses get their cues and clues from inward believing, either as clouds and darkness of false believings, or shining sparks of true believing. Is it not written that "thine own counsel shall cast thee down?" Do we not notice in life that the Napoleonic "I believe that God is on the side of the heaviest artillery," finally casts its Napoleons on the

High Mysticism

sands of defeat? Such a believing is a smoky believing, or a non declaration of Original Believing.

When Nehemiah consulted with Himself, he held his dialogue with the Throne Place of Himself, not with the clouds and darkness round about that Throne. He struck back to his Gnosis Rock, where Irresistible Rulership abides forever in all men alike. Thought and sensation are the cherubim of our sanctuary, our temple. They train together. They experience all things of existence according to the depth toward which the vision turns, from which depth they draw their conclusions. With faces turned inward to the Rock from which we are hewn, they draw from the Gnosis Throne, independent of outward encounters; or if self recognition is not to the Rock of I the Lord, they draw from the trembling cloud of unknowing round about the Throne of hidden Knowing.

At the Throne Place, the Zion Center, our Knowing and Believing are One. "I know Him in Whom I have believed," said Paul, "He is able." This was the Believing that Jesus meant; the Masterful Executiveness of mine integrity within me.

Wonderful things are spoken of the Indwelling Gnosis: "Thou fillest with hid treasure." "Let search be made for the king's treasure house." "He hath put wisdom in the inward parts."

With high instruction as to the training of our senses and our thoughts toward the treasure house of our kingship Isaiah enjoined, "Look to the Rock whence ye are hewn, the Hole of the pit whence ye are digged."

Thus without sequential presentation of that which builds thoughts and sensations, all the suddenly inspired of time have set their hand and seal to the precedence of the looking faculty in all accomplishings and all experiencings. And they show how the exaltation of the mystic sense to the heights is ever followed by its sure return to the Sonship Center, the Unlimited Executive throned in man himself.

"Did not He that made that which is without make that which is within also?"

Nehemiah reported that only one out of ten dwells at his own Center, even among those who have been told the Great Gospel. And he seems to know why all the people bless those who willingly offer themselves to look toward their own Jerusalem Centre. It is because they only of all the children of the gospel send exoneurally forth their integrity's resistless pulling power on waiting health, life, joy, wisdom. "Canst thou draw forth levia-than?"

It was Coomra Sami's firm believing that shed blanking over the German traveler's senses. He believed in his own power to give manifestation and his own power to take away manifestation. But his firm believing was not the Original Gnosis or Holder of his own power at his Throne Place, for the effects of his believing were transient, while rivers of the everlasting flow from the hidden place of our Original Knowing; our giving and taking Rock.

Behold, I will lay thy believings with fair radio-activity, is what Isaiah the prophet means by promising that our stones shall be laid with fair colors. When he writes of the sure Foundation, the tried Stone, he means the original Believer and Knower at our Centre, with its tremendous exoneural, far proceeding energies, world without end.

To look to the Rock whence we are hewn is to begin to say, "In mine integrity within me I Believe, I Know that I and the Father are One." This was the liver-forth point of the magi of old days; the lever-force, the Believer-executive never destroyed in any creature. Whoever has looked to this, his own Foundation Stone, and spoken according to its speech, has proved its working force.

"I Alfred Tennyson," said the young writer, when all the reviewers called his work "drivel and nonsense, and most dismal drivel at that." And he shut himself alone with his I Alfred Tennyson for ten years. At the end of that time I Alfred Tennyson was pronounced the prince of song from one part of the world to the other; in palace and hut, among the

High Mysticism

literati and the ignorant. For "he that standeth steadfast in his heart doeth well."

"I, I, I, Itself I, the whence and the whither, the what and the why, I, I, I, Itself I!" wrote forth one who had looked to the Original Rock—the pit of the unlimited Self. And such victories over the world's oppositions as this "I, I, I, Itself I," wrought forth, are the wonder of the New Age.

Mozart felt the music of the land adjacent, and with joyous confidence he offered his inspired pages to a publisher. "I will not pay you a penny for such music," said the publisher. "Then, my good sir, I must resign myself to die of starvation," answered young Mozart. And he did. Notice what power he gave the refusal of money! Notice what power he gave lack, deprivation! It has been pronounced a lasting disgrace to the land of Mozart's birth, that his death and burial were like a pauper's closing down. But were they? On the principle of the propulsive strength of inward believing, how could his contemporaries hold up against such positive steel needles of propulsion as his dangerous inward dialogue gendered? He did not remember that "We shall be made partakers with victorious Christ, if we hold the beginning of our confidence steadfast to the end."

Plato spoke of a handwriting on the liver in man. That was as near as he could express himself on what Job discovered as wisdom in the inward parts. By this we see that Job was nearer gathering his cherubim or senses and mind to the inward Knower than Plato.

Ezekiel the prophet tells how the King of Babylon consulted the livers of his responsive animals to read how it was proceeding with his own outward affairs. The death of Alexander the Great, and also of his general Hephastion, were foretold by the livers of their animals, acted upon exoneurally by these great men's inward dialoguings. How much they needed to know that they could take back the power they gave to the liver records and decree life renewing which the next animals would register!

Everything and everybody not braced to independence by looking to his own original Knowing and Believing Rock gets under the protective force of the inwardly stronger among the cloud-and-darkness believers; that is, under the exoneural power of his pro-pulsive neighbors. Much of the healing done in this age is accomplished by the strongest holder of a healing believing. When the man who believed himself aided by the great red dragon of Scriptures cured so many ailing people of England, was his believing based on the original Rock of Truth, or on a stiffly maintained conviction outside his Original Gnosis? Was it not from the cloud and darkness round about his deep I Know?

When a certain woman cured so many sick people by the influence of an invisible Indian attendant, was she strong in Original Truth, or sturdily believing outside its Inward Throne?[18] That is, outside her "I gave power to the Indian; I can take back the power to myself and need nothing but my own far extending right decree to cure my neighbors."

"There is a Light that lighteth every man that cometh into the world." Nobody doubts Its word when It expresses Itself. From deep to deep the world around each answers "I Know That!" This Tenth chapter urges the finding of the I Know.

George Eliot declared that she was possessed by an inward demon of despair when she wrote the book, *Romola*. This was her dangerous consultation with cloud and darkness believing, held firmly till its exoneural affected all the people who read the book. They caught a touch of her inward despair.

Napoleon's false believing worked with strong influence on his responsive soldiers, till at Waterloo, in Belgium, 1815, his believing that God was "on the side of the heaviest artillery" broke down. For, "Every plant that my Father hath not planted shall be rooted up." Napoleon's plant was never

---

[18] Possibly a reference to Madame Blavatsky, or even Alice Bailey...

planted of our Father. Our Father's Plant reads, "Not by might and not by army, but by My Spirit, saith the Lord."

The Holy Spirit is the *radio-in-extenso* [radiating outward; extending arms] of God. The Holy Spirit revives, instructs, empowers, defends. It is the *radio-in-extenso* of all who look to their own Inward Integrity Root, and rest on its victory-shedding "I Believe! I Know!"

And believing is stirred by seeing. Dr. Evans the great healer, could with inner vision see so plainly the action of the *vis medicatrix naturae* [natural healing power] in sick people, that he could say with bold confidence, "You are being healed." And they would hurry into health. He began to see in himself the action toward him of the exoneural energy of some who conceived of him as a menace to their own precedence. Having no vision toward the Unhurtable Me at his inward Foundation, he perished. The far-reaching influence of the mistaken conceptions of his persistent enemies found workable soil in Evans. See how great a defense from damage it is to have a boldly declared inward conviction of the undestroyable Me: "He that believeth on Me shall never die."

Let us take today to 'look to the Rock whence we are hewn, the Hole of the pit whence we are digged." Let it be nothing to us how badly or how goodly human activities are secretly or openly dealing with us. The more executiveness they show, the stronger the call for our looking to the Rock where I Believe in Myself as Undefeatable Lord of the harvest.

When Paul discovered that Timothy at Ephesus was always breaking down under the secret criticisms of the Ephesian Christians, he wrote to him urging him to take heed unto himself, and to continue in his doctrine; "for in doing this, thou shalt both save thyself, and them that hear thee." And obedient Timothy looked to the Rock whence he was hewn, and strengthened up by re-stating his original Believing and his original Knowing, to such a degree that he ceased from oft-time falling into sickness and tears of discouragement, and drew the Ephesian Church with him into an invigorating Centre of Divine Ministry.

Paul wrote to little Titus, the terrified preacher to the Cretans, those celebrated liars of Homer's time and of Paul's time: "Speak thou the things which become sound doctrine — sound speech that cannot be condemned, that he that is of the contrary part may be ashamed — that they which have believed in God might be careful to maintain good works."

And Titus maintained his Rock Integrity so robustly that he stopped the lying of the Cretan Christians; made his own instructions their guide, and his name their watchword for more than a hundred years.

"Like attracts like." "No man cometh unto Me, except the Father that is within Me draw him." Father is sometimes mentioned as Faither — The Integrity Rock of my God Faith, my Believing Centre, my inward Knowing-Point. The artist draws artists around him. The musician draws players upon instruments and singers of sweet tunes. The sound in doctrine draw around them lovers of sound doctrine.

The great draw the great. The greatly true draw lovers of truth. The Integrity-healed strike forth Integrity-Health as flint and steel strike forth sparks.

By the practice enjoined by the ninth chapter, we pay attention to the Judah Angel of Man's presence; and the Judah Angel of his presence glows and invigorates the Joseph human of his presence, till only the sound, sane, powerful Son of the Everlasting Father stands visibly before us! It is magian ministry to use our power to draw forth the Judah Self of man.

Often the Joseph self, the external mind and bodily frame, show forth the perturbations of readjustment. As the sun breaking through the clouds causes a hurrying and scurrying of the clouds, but the sun wins hitherward its shining face, so the disorders of flesh and mind hurry and

High Mysticism

scurry for the Sun of Righteousness with healing in His beams to glow in face and form of neighbor.

When the sun has won its glorious way the clouds cannot be found. They have been lost in sunshine. Thus all excitements of mind and body disappear. The emotions of fear and anger, grief and distrust, jealousy and greed subside. The pains and sicknesses of the body rage and hurt anew, then disappear.

Whatever of Bedrock Truth is real to us is soon real to our neighbors. Though their dissensions rage, they are sure to show forth health and strength as signals of agreement. Is it not written that Michael and his angels fought against the dragon and his angels, but the dragon and his angels fought among themselves, till they could not be found? So do the clouds hurry and scurry among themselves till they cannot be found. As nothing of cloud has hurt the sun, so nothing of dissension has hurt the shining Me of our neighbor. He feels our recognition of the immortal and victorious Spirit of God glowing through him, and straightway he forgets his old sensations.

To obey the command Look unto Me, is to be a stirrer-up of seditions among the sensations and thoughts of our associates, like Paul among the men of Jerusalem, when by carrying the victorious Name in his heart he caused a great uproar among them.

Paul was not found disputing with any man, yet they called him a "pestilent fellow." He did not try to set the people to quarreling, yet he was arrested as a "stirrer-up of seditions." Ezra the reformer, nearly seven hundred years before Paul's time, wrote, "I am a man of peace; but when I speak, they are for war." Ezra could not even speak peace in his secret heart without setting his neighbors to wrangling.

The secret heart set for shining peace stirs up the cloud thoughts of men. But peace is a ruler as the sun is a ruler. "My peace give I unto you," said Jesus. And families shall become excited, and friends shall argue, as their former thoughts begin to let go; but I will not cease calling, "Come, ye blessed of my Father!"

Let him that standeth for the might of peace ever abiding as the Masterful at his Secret Throne not give way to the turmoils of mind or matter. Let there be firmness in the heart. Keep to the Key Science, as the true singer in a choir of voices keeps the keynote regardless of the voices out of tune. If the true singer loses the key the choir is not choir, but dissonance. If the true singer maintains the key all the other voices come to accord. It is inexorable truth that maintaining the Throne Science is standing at the Success Point of our being.

Standing on our original conviction that God reigns, we find that what seems to be punishment for sins is unformulation of the framework of false notions. Is it not a false notion that Peace is only victorious by killing those who offend against Peace? Yet this is the position taken century after century by the teachers and leaders of the easily beguiled children of earth.

At the siege of Leyden, was the little handful of helpless people obliged to slay the crews of the Spanish battle ships in order to be victorious? No. The people of Leyden prayed till they struck back to the Rock Place of their own original confidence in Victorious Peace, and the menacing Spanish fleet disappeared.

Is the law of the Rulership of our Throne Place abrogated? No. "If My kingdom were of this world, then would My servants fight" is everlastingly true of the Throned Christ in men. The time is ripe to stand for the I Christ in you the hope of glory; the mystical mastery of Mine integrity within me, taking back the power we gave to fighting for peace, and giving forth peace for fighting. "If thou wouldst believe, thou shouldst see the glory of God."

In the presence of Death, the supposed world conqueror, there was a greater Master feeling the far radiance of the Living Father, His own Original Self. And Death let go its clutches. And the soldiers of the Roman legions fell on

High Mysticism

their faces before Him. "Watch ye, stand fast in the faith, quit ye like men, be strong" — for "the angel of the Lord doeth wondrously."

We all believe in this divine law of action at our own original Believing Point. Let us inwardly say so! And let us maintain the secret word of our own Original Knowing till it demonstrates beyond ourselves by its own exo-neural or far-reaching Energy.

When the head of a nation declares that the only pillar upon which his nation rests is his army, can he expect his pillar to endure? Must he not eventually feel the army-pillar cracking under the weight of a nation's leaning?

The leader of a nation has a great opportunity. The more he is revered the more gladly his people believe as he believes. Let him declare with the Original Believing common to himself and his people, as the King of Judah declared before his army, leading them to incredible victory, "Believe in the Lord your God, so shall ye be established; believe His prophets, so shall ye prosper."

If the whole world is hide bound in its cloud and darkness believing, the whole world will be in hurrying and scurrying of unformulation when the silent few shed forth the mastering beams of their firm confidence in the Lord as the Only Defense of the world. They know their kingship because they know that the Highest Lord and the Inmost Lord is one Lord.

"Call to remembrance that after ye were illuminated ye endured a great fight of affliction," wrote Paul to the Hebrew Christians hide bound in their old believings. Felix trembled at the preaching of Paul, but did not tremble hard enough to unformulate defeat and death. The Swami Vivekananda trembled in the silent presence of a believing Guru, till he unformulated all the false notions that hugged him down. The notions made him sick in body and hysterical in mind as they hurried to disband. But the Sun of the Guru's knowing that I in you Almighty, won Its way, and made a shining light of the youthful Hindu.

"The hand of God hath touched me," said Job, when the perturbations of his mind and body and affairs of life threatened his utter destruction. But he came out as Job the triumphant Lord of Ur.

"I Daniel fainted, and was sick certain days." What made Daniel tremble thus into sickness and unconsciousness? An angel had touched him, reaching to the integrity within him. And Daniel rose up greater than the mind and body of his former self, and stood forth as revered head of the astonished magi of Babylon.

Balaam's body pained him and his mind was angry and argumentative. What had stirred the thoughts of Balaam's mind to fury and the state of his body to pain? The presence of a shining angel standing in the way. Balaam calmed down upon agreeing with the angel's message, and lost himself and his pains in tranced sight of the Star of Jacob, the Bright Messiah of time to come.

Many a sickness and many a mental resentment would subside, leaving a Believer with wholesome health, if the pangs of their unformulation had not frightened the preacher of the truth. See how much more *radio-in-extenso* the stiff believer in his troubles exercises than the gentle Timothy-like preacher of the Truth sometimes brings to bear. Let the Timothy type retire him to his closet, and looking to the Rock, whence he is hewn, the original I Believe and I Know in himself, let him state again silently and firmly: "I gave power to opposition. I take back to myself the power I gave to opposition."

"Could we but stand where Moses stood,
And view the prospect o'er,
Not Jordan's stream, nor death's cold flood
Could fright us from the shore."

The rough River Jordan was the dividing line between the Hebrews as slaves in a foreign land, and their establishment in their own country as a free nation. There is a

High Mysticism

dividing line between being caught in the machinery of the terrifying non-statement of inward knowing, and standing free born and masterful on the silent Insistence of What I Inwardly Believe and Know!

This is our Jordan Tenth. Notice how "all the people came up out of the Jordan on the Tenth." Notice how the firm Joshua told the people to sound the trumpet of jubilee on the Tenth.

All people with some inward believing from which they never swerve find things of nature and affairs of life entering into league with them. Peter was told that heaven would stand by his bindings and his loosings, making his speech to work miracles, because his original Believing had expressed Itself. Peter sensed his own I gave power and I take away power. He felt what Jesus had announced: "I have overcome the world."

Elijah the prophet astonished the Zarephath woman by the miracles his speech effected. Others had spoken the same words but they had accomplished nothing. Elijah had held the divine dialogue unswervingly: "I, the man of God."

The wife of Manoah was not overthrown by her husband's declaration that they had seen God and therefore they must die. She stood sturdily by the plant of our Father's planting, that to see Him is to live. And she brought forth Samson, the strongest man Israel ever produced. He had the sternest legislative ability and the boldest executiveness Israel had ever confronted. The anarchistic majority were held in awed subjection by his masculine masterfulness. And the marauding nearby tribes fled at sight of him.

Something Samson-great is always the outcome of boldly maintaining the Gnosis or Deeper Wisdom born with us. Job accomplished great things by steadfastly beholding toward the face of the Transcending Almighty and daringly proclaiming, "Thy hands fashioned me—Is not the root of the matter in me?"[1]

I in you is the Plant Indestructible. It is the Rock of Refuge in the day of calamity. It waits the Moses-smiting of my oft-time stem insistence, till what I am in mine integrity within me masters for me wherever I walk.

Our own secret text gives its color, clue, and climax to our life affairs. "I believe God reigns," said a young man, with his heart in his voice. Every business he undertook failed under his hands without his once flinching from his rooted conviction. At last one failure more disastrous than the preceding nearly choked off his "I believe!" But he rallied, and uttered it forth again. A miracle suddenly turned the scales. Suddenly he was as victorious as David of Judah. If he had neglected that last utterance of his believing he could not have entered into the miracle, for it was by looking up and protesting, "I still believe God reigns," that he was suddenly given the miracle of new heaven-prospered conditions.

"In the morning sow they seed," said Solomon, "and at evening withhold not thine hand; for thou knowest not whether shall prosper, either this or that."

Unswerving maintenance of inwardly planted Truth to the time of its outer demonstration, is symbolized by the chrysoprasus stone—the apple green stone of a fresh new earth; or new outward conditions among our associates and their affairs: the invariable resultants of our silent dialogue, "I the Lord."

No matter what adversities face us, they are breakable under the ministry of Inward Truth invariably stated in trouble or in peace. "If thou faint in the day of adversity, thy strength is small." That is, great strength will not show forth by standing to and practicing flinching.

"By the rivers of Babylon there we sat down
we hanged out harps on the willows
for there they that wasted us required of us singing but,
If I forget thee, O Jerusalem,
let my tongue cleave to the roof of my mouth."

Though savage enmity and perpetual misfortunes seem our portion, let us not forget the Jerusalem Rock Self whence we are hewn, with its gushing waters of goodly miracles, our rightful portions forever.

We must not forget our Zion Lawgiver though our emotions seem nearly to wreck us. "Get thee to the prophets of thy father, and to the prophets of thy mother," cried angry Elisha to the King of Israel who had insulted him. But suddenly Elisha remembered that his mission was to bless; and he blessed King Jehoram and his two friends with heavenly victories.

There is a Voice within us inaudible till made audible by our definite insistence. And "It shaketh not only earth but heaven," said Paul, "that those things which may be shaken may be removed; that those things which cannot be shaken may remain."

"And they said unto him, Master, where dwellest Thou? And He said unto them, Come and see. And they came and saw where He dwelt, and abode with Him that day; for it was about the tenth hour:" "I in you."

From the beginning it has been written that the priests of Integrity shall wear clothing (or aura) of salvation, till all flesh shall transform and all mind shall renew as heavenly exoneural of their definitely stated inward conviction, not of sin but of The Mighty-Believer in each man, Lord of Its own environments, Knower of the Final Doctrine; Seer of Itself as Self-Existent Deity, giving life to the faint by taking away the downward crowding power of faintness and decreeing strength; inaugurating Peace by withdrawing the power of war and decreeing Peace.

These signs shall follow him that consulteth with Himself, taking to himself his scattered power to reign as A New Worker in A New Dispensation. "Take heed therefore unto yourselves, and to all the flock, over which the Holy Ghost hath made you overseers."

11th Study

NOTE

The Eleventh and Twelfth Lessons constitute a science by themselves; a science for the most part unintelligible save to the awakened practitioners of the directions of the First Ten Lessons.

The Eleventh and Twelfth Lessons are the Eschatology of The Mystical Science. E C H

Keep hard to one science till you master it. Light flashes on any subject or object by much attention to it. The disciples of the Christ preached One Name only till it flashed into magian effulgence through them and they founded that mighty league the world has since acknowledged as destined to endure forever. They believed that "He that is faithful over a few things, I will make him ruler over many."

King Solomon stood to the building of one house till in the eleventh year it shed abroad such an influence from the unseen world to which it was pointed that all who looked to it were set at liberty. Jonah in the darkness of his dreadful prison, looking often and often to the temple's distant dome glistening under a noon-day sun his outer eyes saw not, left his dark prison, hurled suddenly toward the Heaven-charmed house of Solomon.

David knew that whoever would look straight to the Unseen Highest would be set at liberty from his weight of flesh and his weight of foolishness. "They looked unto Him, and were lightened," he declared. So true has this ever been that people have actually found themselves dropping corpulence by seeking *Ain Soph* the Beautiful Countenance of the Absolute, above thinking and above being. They have also found themselves lightened of their cap of ignorance, knowing wonderful and happifying laws by oft-time and

High Mysticism 497

oft-time answering back the wooing Supernal with wooing responses. "Thou hast made me wiser than mine enemies," cried David, after daringly announcing that his "eyes were ever toward the Lord."

Looking toward a sky beyond our visible sky, the ancient Norsemen saw the Adam and Eve of the new world which should once more arise after the twilight and destruction of the gods. They caught Norse names for the Adam and Eve of the world to be — Lif and Lifthrasir,

Looking to the sky above the sky, the Mayans of ancient days found the origin of mind. It was a goddess. They named her by a Mayan name signifying, Mother of The Nature-Mind.

Gazing high, Hesiod the Greek saw rushing spirits scattering gifts among the sons of men, which the sons of men took no notice of except when the gifts rushed into them here and there, as stars sometimes collide with each other. Hesiod did not seem to discover that the sons of men may woo the rushing gods to grant each its own kind of gift to the wooing one. Other Greeks tell us that as the worshippers of Mercury wooed Mercury to grant unto them prosperity, and the worshippers of Morpheus cried unto him for sleep, lifting up their hands with their eyes, beckoning and beckoning Morpheus till in his whiteness he folded them in sleep, so every nineteen years the hither-wooed Apollo came into sight to grant happy harvests and beautiful offspring.

Some oft-time watcher toward the Heights above the skies, to what a great king once called "the glory above the heavens," is to catch a new language. It is not to come to the greatest linguist among us for he has had his gaze on men to catch their intonations and accents; or on books to teach him grammatics and word derivations. The new *lingua* [language, tongue] shall be the speech of right judgment to some second Abraham facing Unspeakable Judgeship, baring his head to The Inscrutable Unseen, meekly declaring, "Shall not the judge of all the earth do right!" And a great multitude shall speak his language; a great multitude whom no man can number; for it shall be the speech of heaven and earth as one speech, whose words shall instantly accomplish that whereunto they are sent.

If Apollonius could speak six languages he had never studied, because of his much talking to invisible gods, how wonderful must be the discourse of "the great the mighty God, great in counsel and mighty to work" for that new Abraham who much and often notices that the judge of all the earth is speaking divinely executive words never before heard on this planet!

The very name Abraham means a great multitude. What a wide swath shall the new Abram or Abraham cut, he who holds his conversation high!

Notice how broken up and wildly dissatisfied people are if events and circumstances run into unwanted cosmic currents which no human being seems to be able to stem! They are no Abram or Abraham of the New Dispensation. Only the old language of grieving and rebellion advances forth from them toward us. The psychometry of them is old "Ephraim like a silly dove, without heart," as Hosea the prophet explained.

Let us notice the comrade Abram drew toward himself by agreeing that a Wonderful Judge is handling the universe: Melchisedek visited him! Origen said Melchi-sedek was an angel. Martin Luther and Melanchthon said he was Shem, a Survivor of the Deluge. Epiphanius said he was the Son of God appearing in human form. The Jews said he was the Messiah made visible. He brought out bread and wine to Abram, and blessed him!

So he who holds his conversation high shall comrade with noble visitants, and cause their inspiring instructions through his speech to ray forth New Truth throughout the earth. "Is it well with thee?" sayeth the High Judge. "According to Thy judgment it is well with me, therefore it is well" he shall answer. Thus he grants the judgment of The Great

Judge to strike fire with his own judgment, as bamboo stick striking bamboo stick sparks fire, sparking him into new life conditions. So, and only so responding, can man swing in with the advancing New Order, rejoicing with New Rejoicings, shedding across the earth morning beams of The New Age. Let us isolate with the Heights that our ministry be of the Heights, new, far reaching, irresistible, after the order of Melchisedek!

Attention to The Overlooking Vast Highest wakes Self recognition; calls attention to hidden Self; what Novalis the poet friend of Schiller, called our transcendental ego. Some other long-ago mystic Germans noticed that as they were glancing upward they found The Heights gazing toward them. Then they declared, "God's sight with which he sees me is the same sight with which I see Him."

As all invisible operations clashing together form visibles, so right judgment is made visible in speech and action by looking toward the Judge "that shall be in those days," as Moses foresaw for us. "He shall bring forth thy judgment as the noonday."

We have certain invisibles to glance toward which cause undesirable speech and action to formulate. Notice John Calvin upward watching toward his own dying imaginations, and seeing them smiling on his actions as he burned the good Servetus[19] for disagreeing with him! Beza, an adorer of Calvin's imaginations, declared that all who opposed Calvin ought to be hanged.

But "When Thy judgments are in the earth, the inhabitants of the world will learn righteousness." "Thy judgment was unto me a robe and a diadem."

"'Thy speech betrayeth thee,' the officers said to Peter, who had been with Jesus the New Teacher in Jerusalem.

---

[19] Michael Servetus came to Calvin looking for refuge from the Roman Church's inquisition, which had sentenced him to burning for believing what is now called Unitarianism: that God is One, not three persons in one.

Doubtless when Peter spoke of high watch they knew he was a Christian and could probably raise the dead.

Only attention to the Highest wakes Self recognition that rises to cross the bar above prejudices and false judgments. Across that bar Truth is the only language. Truth according to that language has promised to stop the discords of human mind and its angry sensations. We are all candidates for that victorious truth not yet spoken.

There is a Health zone facing us. Notice that the sick who have not crossed the Health zone have to spring above the bar, laying hold of Health, or they must stay under, this side the Health zone. David lifted up his hands with his eyes and caught on to the Hands of Health stretching toward him. "I cried to Thee and Thou hast healed me," he acknowledged. So also Peter laying hold of The Hands beyond the bar stretching toward him, crossed above into Health, taking many people along with him.

There is originality beyond the bar. Let us lay hold of Original Knowledge stretching hitherward and be drawn up into new quickening doctrines. Let us speak with New Tongues. The quickening wisdom hither streaming shall cause those people who like Sisera are planning to do the world mischief, to suddenly forget their plans, and themselves be 'drawn high across the bar into Wise Peace.

Let us acknowledge High Judgment. Let us cross the bar into that state where we are not afraid. Judging this side the judgment bar we are often afraid; but "he that harkeneth unto me shall dwell safely, and be quiet from fear of evil."

Come, O people! Let us all together cross the upper bar, laying hard hold of The Hands that stretching toward us draw us into fearless wholeness!

> "I went through fire and water, but Thou broughtest me out into a wealthy place."
>
> "He sent from above; he took me; he drew me out of many waters."

High Mysticism

Let us all together be born into The Above! The Apostles called high in their iay. led off by Peter the ardent: "Stretching forth thine hand to heal," he cried, "signs and wonders may be done by The Name. "In strength of hand the Lord spake thus unto me," reported the son of Amoz, brother of the king: "The people that walked in darkness have seen a great light."

The executive faculty in man is his inner visional sense. Wherever this visional sense looks other senses are pointed and insist likewise with it. Looking upward to a sun it cannot see the oak tree rises into a higher country all sunshine, wind, and rain to nurture its awakening greatness of body, limb, and leaf. Enduring as seeing the Sun of Righteousness with healing in his beams, man enters the country above where visible angels and their judgments comrade with him. A new sunshine gives him new views of his fellow man. No longer can he see the precious sons of Zion any other than the fine gold Jeremiah declared them to be. As the morning sun shows off the roses in the garden to be altogether different from what they looked to be in moonless night time, so people everywhere are judged differently by all who have crossed the bar into the bright upper country. Let us not look back to Chaldea, or Egypt, or India, for the great secret of miracle-working life. Let us look to the upper country close at hand. "By Stength of hand the Lord brought us out from this place," shall say the New Leaders heavenward. Let us spring past the bar of bondage into the free country of Health and Right Judgment. "Now is the accepted time. Now is the day of salvation."

Caliph Ali was called the lion of God because high vision had taught him that man's own lot or portion in life is seeking after him.

"When ye pray, believe that ye have, and ye shall have," said Jesus. They all say the same things when they look to the upper kingdom.

"Far through the misty future,

> Like an arrow of golden light,
> An hour of joy ye know not
> Is winging its silent flight."

But how can we enter the joyous realm while we are bemoaning our lower lot? Even Dante saw that we must take heads. He agreed with the son of Amoz: "When ye see this your heart shall rejoice, and your bones shall flourish like an herb."

The Moslem knows that knowing that his own is this minute looking toward him is a drawstring on its hurrying toward him. Knowing is a drawstring:

> "Deep in the heart of thee,
> Soundlessly low—
> The Vach language wordless—
> Thy Soul pointeth, Lo!"

The *gnomon* [the part of us that knows, without thought or perception (Greek)] in the heart is ever tending toward the upper country. "Homeward is the Tao's course." By the law of Number ten we learn to take back to our self the lordship we gave to defeat, deafness, death. We take back to our self the power we gave to people to hurt our feelings. We take back to our self the power we gave to poverty, inconsequence, ignorance. We learn that the four and twenty elders of Paradise are gratified at our temerity, and shout, "We give thee thanks because thou hast taken to thyself thy great power, and hast reigned."

By the law of Number eleven we learn to use our hither drawn plenteousness of power to spring upward into our native and rightful New Wisdom, New Health, New Views of Life. The Egyptians saw in us, so re-empowered, a likeness to the Scarab drawing sustenance from the very dirt ball that humiliated it, and using that sustenance so drawn, to strengthen its n pressed wings to fly into free sunshine, free airs, free rains; free denizens of higher life.

This is not only euphony, sweet wordings; it is humanly practical. Immediately people do stop hurting our filings and sink into flatness when we take back to our self the power we gave them to hurt us. Immediately ignorance lets go and genius of a new order is ours when we take back to our self the harming power we gave to ignorance. So our genius for rising as Fore-Helpers to the discouraged and defeated in the battles of human beings with their human dirt fulfills the prophecies of three thousand years ago: "I will lead them in paths they have not known." "They shall mount up with wings, as eagles." They shall be an angelic ministry.

It is no wonder that Jesus of Nazareth could go in and out of the kingdom at his will, seeing that he had taken back to himself the crushing power he had given to earth, and the hiding power he had given to heaven! How triumphant his voice: "All power is given unto Me, in heaven and in earth." "Where I am, there ye may be also."

Was not Paul wonderful to say, "I live; yet not I, but Christ liveth in me"? Were not the Brahmins wonderful to discover, "Brahma is you yourself"? Was not Jesus wonderful to explain, " Did not he that made that which is without, make that which is within also?" himself always crossing the bar beyond the shadow system, forever finding that the Highest Self and the inmost self is one Self?

Men act foolishly by reason of judging from the evidence of the shadow system this side The Highest. As, if our money is snatched away we judge that we are deprived and humiliated. That is judging within the shadow system this side the High Rich Zone. Looking up and crossing the judgment line we lay hold of The Hand that stretching hitherward giveth liberally. Miracles of unexpected combinations, shadows of Finished Splendors from across the Bar do surely then transact in our behalf! So we judge another way and word concerning life. We judge with Abraham that truly "the Judge of all the earth doeth right." We jubilantly talk face to face, "In thine hand it is to make great and to give strength." "Riches and honor come of Thee."

Wise Hebrews of old were watching for the power of the Highest to overshadow some divinity-sensitive human and drop a Messiah into the world. It is declared by certain

Hebrews that many Jews have really believed that Jesus and Mary fulfilled the prophecy, though they were pledged to act against their own believing. As there is an exoneural influence from secret believing, we now see over six hundred million declared Christians as outward marks of the secretly held believing of the Hebrews.

For unexpressed believings come to outward showings. They are the idle words that burst forth into active exhibitions. They are still believings that find their way into loud results.

> "For every idle word thou shalt give account."
>
> "Now is come the time of the dead (the still) that they should be judged."

An Emir of Kashmir had an occult reader of secret, unexpressed believings. It was his genius to lay his finger on the unconsciously held believings of the high court officials and prophesy exactly how they would actualize. Many an important personage was astonished at being removed from office. Many a lesser personage was amazed at being promoted.

The Emir sent the occultist to England to put his finger on the subsecret of England's greatness. "Britannia rules the waves, and the sun never sets on her dominions." This for the outward grandeur of a little island people must be explained to the Emir. He waited three years while the occultist watched for the hidden springs. Finally the occultist found the deepmost national secret of England's greatness. It was I. H. S: *Jesu Hominem Salvator,* or *In Hoc Signo* ["Jesus the Savior of mankind", or, "In this sign," usually followed by "we conquer"].

The Emir ordered the mystical formula I. H. S. to be inscribed on all his own possessions; curtains, rugs, gold and silver plate. "Go to, now, I also will be a great power," he said.

The Hebrews of old had an almost forgotten formula of faith. It was, "There shall no man be able to stand against thee"—"I will contend with him that contendeth with thee."

On this account the Jews were not allowed to number their army. They might have an army; but small or great in number, the Augment thereof should always be the Unseen Almighty, in whose victorious alliance they firmly believed.

They just as firmly believed that if they numbered their army it would be defeated.

David had always conquered all foes with his invincible soldiery. He had become proud and hard-headed as victorious kings always become, and numbered his forces, though Joab his leading general implored him not to number them, saying "The Lord makes his people an hundred times so many more as they be." But David made out the tally of his ranks, oblivious of Joab's protests.

Then Gad, who was David's occult reader of the outrushings of secretly held unspoken believings, told King David of the opening he had made for the outrush of the sub-reservoir of universal Hebrew certainty that numbering the army was disastrous. He showed David that numbering the army was doubting the Ally.

Within three days 70,000 of David's most stalwart warriors had fallen dead from pestilence. The king had made an opportunity for subbelieving to come forth with unrestrainable energy into nation-wide manifestation.

Jerusalem (the self) is besieged to the eleventh year of Zedekiah, or Justice of Jehovah. Until the only secret believing is the boldly declared original truth of my Father's planting—the gnosis not subject to defeat, there is ever the menace of some idle word. " What a man soweth, that shall he also reap." "There shall not a jot or tittle[20] pass from the law, till all be fulfilled."

---

[20] Jots and tittles are the marks added to Hebrew letters to indicate vowel sounds, tense, and case.

There have been two grandly uttered great believings in the history of man. They have sprung boldly forth from the divinely planted deep wisdoms of the inward parts. High Watch has struck back to them, and great have been the outward demonstrations of these two believings. Mankind has lately crossed them over with disbelievings, and sodded them down with refusings, till they are lost to view as original truth capable of mighty executiveness. They are sung and recited now long since as beautiful figures of speech, symbolics of unknown laws; but when God put wisdom in the inward parts, and showed the deep findings of upward look toward His Vast, Vast Countenance, He made these believings the energy of executiveness to save from war, pestilence, disease, death.

The first, is believing in the power of His Revealed Name. "For this cause have I raised thee up, that my name may be declared throughout all the earth."

The name of the God of Jacob defend thee." "And this is His commandment: that we should believe on the name."

Whosoever shall call on the name of the Lord shall be delivered." "Our Redeemer from everlasting is Thy Name."

The second deeply planted *gnosis* [inner knowing], is that mankind does not fight for the Almighty; the Almighty fights for mankind: "Set yourselves, stand ye still, and see the salvation which the Lord will work for you; for the Lord shall fight for you, and ye shall hold your peace." "My kingdom is not of this world. If my kingdom were of this world, then would my servants fight." "Fear not, I will help thee thou Jacob, and ye few men of Israel." "Not by might, nor by power, but by my spirit, saith the Lord."

One attempted believing there has been, over which mankind has stumbled and fallen and quarreled much. Nobody has given mankind the clue, for nothing of it is to be revealed till the fulfilled moment of steadfast obedience to the ever-uttering mandate, "Seek ye my face evermore."

This attempted believing has been as to the substance and nature of the Presence of Deity in the universe. Mankind has partly believed in the Being of Deity as Principle, and partly believed in the Being of Deity as Person.

As "Principle" demands reasoning, it follows that the ill made or weak brained are left out of the scheme of salvation. The weak brained can hardly come at the algebra of "One Presence in the Universe; therefore as I AM, I am that ONE." To the very cleverest brained Jesus said, "Why reason ye?" as though the reasoning of the reasoners was not the light of salvation. "What I say unto you, I say unto all, Watch," he said; and he repeated the injunction.

There is no child so stupid but can be made to look up to One ever beholding him, till gleams of intelligence steal down the track of his upward looking.

As "Person" intimates form and collect of parts, the term Person applied to Deity has stirred wide human resentment. "Who is like unto thee, glorious, fearful, doing wonders?" sang the children of Israel. "Touching the Almighty, we cannot find Him out — with Him is terrible majesty," cried Elihu the Buzite. Yet the children of Israel and Elihu the Buzite had come nearer to knowing Deity than any on earth before them, or, saving the Apostolic hierarchy, even since their inspirations. "The nature of Deity is undetermined," reads the most modern of Cyclopedias.

By the instruction of the Tenth Study in Divine Law we find that lower attentions strike back no farther than the shadow system gathered round the throne place of our inward being, while attention toward the countenance of the High Redeemer inhabiting eternity strikes back to the original Believer, the divine *Gnosis*, the throne place of our own being, where the knowing of the Lord Self lies deep.

Daniel got caught in a lions' den by much knowledge of cause and effect in wickedness. He was in the teeth of the law of what a man soweth that shall he also reap. Had he not aforetime thrown other men to the lions? But he had never let go the bold statement of his inward certainty that God should send his angels to keep him. "O King, live forever/' he said, "My God hath sent his angel, and hath shut the lions' mouths, that they have not hurt me."

Likewise also Paul got caught by stones till he died of stones. Had he not in times past stoned other men to death? But his inward certainty that "He that believeth in me, though he were dead, yet shall he live," waked him from death. Thus mighty is an inward certainty firmly maintained, never ignored, never forgotten!

Nations with nation-wide certainties should remember them often, keep them flaming by bold oft time expression. If there is certainty of conquering and salvation in *Jesu Hominem Salvator*, a nation should never talk or write of sacrificings of its men, but only of conquerings and victories by its men daringly going forth in the power of Jesu.

If it has once stated its trust in the Almighty to deliver with bloodless victory, it should never let the trust get cooled over by fear of armed foe or dread of failure of its Backer and Ally. On account of not fearing, wrote Isaiah, "Thou shalt be far from oppression."

"The eleven stars did obeisance to Joseph." All the stars and the laws of the stars give way to the miraculous touch of the Supernal. "Joseph" means, He will add. He the Supernal Unseen will add to life as it now stands, life by the miracle. He will add to powers as they now show forth, powers unaccountable. Every attempt was made to slay Joseph, but the Unslayable Supernal was his shield. Poverty and slavery tried to crush him, but the Unseen Lord Un-crushable folded him as a buoying sheath. He was not afraid because he had made the Fearless One his high watch tower. Is not fearlessness a defense? But how does a coward generate fearlessness? By no process we may be sure except by much attention to the Author of fearlessness. Do we not show forth that which constantly attracts our inward gaze? Consider how the sight of the angels of *Mons* [mountains] altered the looks and the conduct of the soldiers who beheld them!

"In the eleventh year was the house finished," and Solomon said that all who looked to the house should feel its Mystical Rulership for miraculous liberty.

"House" signifies character. "Finished house" is character at its eleventh state, with all its mystical powers in full action. To look at the light burning in the upper chamber of the house of Rai Shalligram, postmaster general of North Western India, was to sense the effect of Rai Shalligram's mystical rulership. He had faced the splendor of invisible Brahma till his whole being was infused with the miracle of Brahma. He was certain that if he were naked and alone in a desert, Almighty Brahma would feed him, clothe him, shelter him, protect him from ravenous beasts. The rulership of his unshakable certainty was like far gleaming points irresistible to the men who caught sight even of his house. They all felt like throwing aside their families, their business, their clothes, their previous minds, and fleeing to trackless desert places to be alone with Great Brahma.

The "house" of Gideon had reached its eleventh stage. "Look on me" was all he had to say to cause Israel's armies to wake victorious liberty for all Israel.

Peter and John had touched the eleventh stage of character. "Look on us" was all they had to say for natural laws to unclamp.

Character is judgment, and judgment is character. We are known to our neighbors according to our judgment.

If we judge according to Universal Protection, seeing all mankind embraced in Its mighty arms, upbearing, defending, as wings of eagle mothers under untried eaglet pinions we give all who look toward our house new emotions, new judgments concerning Universal Allah, Brahma, God, as though for them a new light had broken on life and its mysteries. They catch bold assurance of Omnipotent Augment. "Their judgment and dignity proceed of themselves," wrote the scientific prophet Habakkuk. Did not Socrates say that right judgment straightens out conduct, and wrong judgment deflects it? Did he not urge people to get right judgment by some attention to that which would eventuate in right judgment?

The establishment of the Jesus Christ judgment in man is the fruition toward which all religious and mystical laws are bent. "The Father hath committed all judgment unto the Son," he said. "My judgment is right." The judgment day is come when all men judge the Jesus Christ judgment. It is the day of fire and brimstone to all other judgments. Appearances count for nothing. What stands back of appearances in its unalterable excellence holds undiverted attention. Is not man, back of his appearance of folly and decay an immortal being, stately, wise, flawless?

Ezekiel says we have been in Eden the Garden of God, when we have looked toward our own deep rock integrity, our hidden God Self: "Thou hast been in Eden, the Garden of God, and the ruby is thy covering." Taking Martin Luther's advice to let the Scriptures interpret themselves, we let Job interpret "covering" or robe. "My judgment was unto me a robe and a diadem," he declared. Bo the ruby signifies right judgment and kingship. "A king that sitteth in the throne of judgment, scattereth away all evil with his eyes."

No mistake is made by one who looks straight forth from his integrity centre. He sees a full barrel of meal where the widow sees bare boards. He sees genius where others are seeing failure, or death, or insanity. He is the judge who sees the way to raise the dead as the mathematician sees the way to cube the fraction. He sees the right relation of man to man, and his word is the expression of his sight. Did not the word of the Lord in Elijah's mouth raise the Zarephath child? How had his word caught the spark of such executiveness? By his recognition of his own "I the man of God." How had he come to such high estimate of his own "I"? By much attention to the Lord God of Israel, before whom he declared himself as forever standing.

The Eleventh Lesson in Divine Law tells of the integrity within as right judgment resident in all men alike; covered

High Mysticism

in all men by flesh and its mind as in a crypt of darkness. As silent is right judgment as if dead. It is called the mountain of Zion by Jeremiah, who wails that the "mountain of Zion is desolate, the foxes walk upon it." He means that small, low, mean, myopic judgments run ahead and formulate our speech: "The precious sons of Zion," he said, "comparable to fine gold, how are they esteemed as earthen pitchers."

As Elijah's recognition of his "I" as the word nigh him, even in his heart and in his mouth, came from much recognition of the High Redeemer inhabiting eternity, and this looked forth from him as right estimates, so other men catch their self recognitions from associating with other stronger men, and pass on their judgments wherever they go.

"Many seek the ruler's face, but every man's (final) judgment cometh from the Lord."

The Ganges mother loved her baby. She hugged it to her with passionate devotion. But she threw it to the crocodiles, because her husband's judgment was the ruler's face that she was daily seeking. So her judgment catching fire with her ruler's judgment struck forth into action against her beloved baby.

As bamboo stick striking bamboo stick sparks fire, so judgment sharpeneth judgment.

Notice the difference between the prophet Elisha's judgment striking against the Shunammite's inner chords, and the judgment of the Ganges husband on the Ganges mother's chords. Elisha was judging always the judgment of life, joy, victory. "Is it well with thee?" he asked the Shunammite, whose heart was breaking. So strong was Elisha's living agreement with life and joy that she answered, "It is well." "Is it well with thy husband?" asked Elisha. "It is well," she answered. "Is it well with the child?" "It is well," was still her word. The smite of Elisha's judgment on the waiting chords of her being struck forth the spark speech that waked life in the dead child, joy in the husband, the day of judgment in the mother.

Saul caught fire with the judgments of the prophet Samuel by constant association, till the men of Israel were astonished at Saul's prophecies.

There is One with whom we can associate till our "speech betrayeth us." His Vast, Vast Countenance shining as the sun, now beams upon our heads divine wisdoms, and glows life giving actions in our undertakings. He is the Great Ruler whose judgments strike fire with our waiting chords, till the Lost Word sparks again on earth, with its instantaneous miracle working energy. The life coal lingering in the faint must fan to flaming fires of undying Omnipotence at the smite of the Lost Word on the ethers. The joy chord mute in the breast of humanity must tremble with good news as from a far country at the Lost Word's sweet import.

The judgment of the Great Ruler is on the Finished Estate that faces us from every infinitesimal point in the universe. All things and all people are adjustable at every instant to their own finished estate of flawless excellence as judged by the Great Ruler's judgment. They all wait the promised New Speech to show their own finished fact.

"Give ye ear, my judgment is toward you," saith the Great Judge. "I come near to you to judgment."

"Pray as if you had already received," taught the Master. Of course we have already received, if it is already finished and near at hand. Is it not waiting the lighted eye to make the prayer of acknowledgment a simple truth?

The angle of repose in physics is that angle at which one body may rest upon another without falling. The angle of repose between God and man is where man's judgment and the judgment of God agree. "I have put my judgment in thee for a light—Here is my rest forever; here will I dwell," saith the Judge of all the earth.

"They neither marry nor are given in marriage," said Jesus. Of course not. They are already married from all eternity under the eye of Allah. What is all this marrying and giving in marriage but trying to adjust to the Finished Marriage? This great truth was visible enough to "Baal Shem" so that he could sometimes see which people were married, and he led them across the breadth of the land to meet each other.

He knew, like all advanced Moslems, that What Ought to be Is. "If we ought to be there, then we are there; let us sleep." And a week's journey was performed in one night, while they slept, because the great Moslem rested on the Ought to be that Is!

Solomon was the forerunner of the resters in the Ought to be that Is. He knew that according to the judgment of Jehovah God he already knew, therefore he knew. And though he had not studied them he told of the stars and the stones, and of the growing things, from the cedars of Lebanon to the hyssop that springeth on the wall. Jesus knew that according to God the Father he already knew all things, therefore he needed not that any man should teach him. "Is it not written in your law, ye are gods," he asked the people.

As there is no respect of persons with the Highest I AM, he told his disciples to call no man upon the earth their Father, regardless of appearances, that the straight line of healing energy from their Father might run through them, to the revealing of what verily Is, everywhere they walked. Thus to them the apparently dead were as alive as the apparently living. To them the sick were only as straight sticks deflected in water. So they took the sick by the hand, and pulled them standing. "Rise and walk," they said.

They were hard masters, reaping where they had not sown, for they had not to sow the seeds of good instruction and see them spring up where the sick or dead were concerned. They saw that what already Is was under everybody's feet, and all anybody had to do was to stand on it!

Right Place. Right People. Right Powers. Right Possessions.

This is the High Science of Jesus Christ: "Go thy way, thy son liveth."

Anthony of Padua suddenly saw into the kingdom. From his pulpit in Padua he heard them telling the woman that her son was dead. " He is alive!" shouted Anthony. And to the astonishment of all Padua, not one of whom had any knowledge of the Unalterable, Finished Fact, the boy they had seen dead was found to be alive.

The Finnish woman subconsciously knew that according to the judgment of the Lord Inexorable she could not be in debt, for what was hers was hers unalterably, and what was the other's was his from the beginning, and nothing could take from or add to the original endowment. With some awe but not with any astonishment, she saw sixty dollars multiply to one hundred and sixty on the table under her fingers. As she was only reputed to be in debt one hundred and fifty, she wondered for a moment what the extra ten might be there for, when she suddenly remembered that she had always believed the till would never be empty. Her forgotten believing had come to open showing. The word idle even as the dead had come to expression. "Now is come the time of the dead," when some heaven-born recognition of the Eternal Actual wakes in mankind!

"And the Eleventh was the jacinth." Pushing the red of the jacinth to its highest value we have the ruby, symbol of beauty and symbol of judgment. Beauty and judgment present the same credentials for our favor. They represent the proper adjustment of part to part, man to man. A good judge is more sought after than a king. He puts man into right relation with his fellow man.

Beauty is the proper adjustment of part to part. "How beautiful—how beautiful!" we exclaim of the Taj Mahal of Agra, India, and of the Mosque of Omar at Jerusalem. Yet each part of each temple is no more beautiful by itself than the similar parts of millions of other buildings. It is the proportion, the balance, the inimitable adjustment of part to part of the Taj Mahal and the Mosque of Omar which satisfies our secret Zion standard.

"The Lord shall send down judgment with fire." "Thou shalt not pervert the judgment of the stranger." The greatest stranger to man is God the Lord. Some heard the sound of his voice and said, "It thundered." Others said, "An Angel spake." But Jesus heard the voice of God in coherent speech: "I have glorified my name, and will glorify it again." The judgment of the Stranger was perverted by the people, but Jesus received it as the mystery of that Name which when called upon saves from sword, famine and defeat. He sealed to mankind the foretellings of the great prophets, that his Ineffable Name, key to the mysteries of the universe, should part the ages old silence with the promised new language, hastening over the Tao or Track of High Recognition.

"And the Eleventh lot cometh forth to Eliashib" — whom God restores. "I will restore unto thee all the years that the caterpillar hath wasted." "If any man sue thee at the law, and take away thy coat, let him have thy cloak also." For what is the man suing? Surely he is violently striking out for adjustment to his own lot or portion in life. He strikes for judgment. He must not mistake his man. Meet him with the judgment firing one who has companioned with the Owner of the spheres. Give him the goods he strikes for, till by thee he also companions with the Original Giver and Divine Restorer to each man of all his inalienable rights. "With what measure ye mete, it shall be measured to you again." There are coats and cloaks of greater value, to take the places of the coats and cloaks wrested from man by the other man on his rough way to his own goods.

"Whosoever shall smite thee on thy right cheek, turn to him the other also." He, as before, is on his violent, mistaken strike for his own good. Let him not mistake his man. Nothing shall by any means hurt thee as the man strikes fire with thy right judgment: "No man taketh my life from me." So estimating the blows of human encounter, we cross the bar between earth and heaven, and the ruby blood in our veins is the morning glow of the New Kingdom. "I saw the city," said John; and boiling oil and slander felt the estimates of the John Supernal. They had no power to hurt.

"Thou shalt not steal." Is this a commandment or a promise? This must be according to your ruler's face, lawmaker of the Ganges, or Lord Jehovah of the Fixed Estate. One veils the sight of the Inalienable Undiminish-able that faces us. One exposes the Self Existent rounded Good not to be added to by action or non-action forever.

One whose judgment has been the strike on our secret chords causes us to shut our neighbor away as a diminisher. One causes us to see him driving for our judgment's bamboo smite, passed on from the Lord of the Inexorably Undivided, who sees the everywhere fixed lot awaiting its owner's acknowledgment. Your speech "betrayeth" your class.

"Thou shalt not take the name of the Lord thy God in vain." Have we not discovered that the name of the High Redeemer is the Lost Word, the Apocalyptic trumpet, which causes the shadows to flee away from the dead, the sick, the unhappy, the earth hindered, the instant it is spoken? It cannot be taken in vain! It is instantaneous in its rending of the curtains of hiding. Has the name God this instantaneous sign of its executive-ness? What name can we not take vainly? We have learned that as the language of our lips "betrays" our associations, either with the learning of the schools, or the Knower to the schools unknown, so our answer to the Mosaic decalogue "betrays" our God.

And our acquaintance with Jesus Christ, Holder of the New Name that cannot be taken in vain, tells whether we are nearing the speaking of the Name that cannot be taken in vain, or driving round about to find it. For the Lord Christ only hath daringly declared, "I will give a New Name, which no man knoweth, save he that receiveth it."

"Of all that thou hast given me," said Jesus, "I have lost not one, save the son of perdition." "Son" is idea, and "perdition" is loss. I have lost only the idea of loss, he said. The idea of loss is Judas. He is lost; and in the place of Judas is Matthias, the gift of God.

"And Matthias is numbered with the eleven." He is the value of all the eleven in one, as the gift of Elohim compasses all the good mankind could ask for, or even think, as good.

Is there not one sense of loss that haunts the best of the sons of earth? The death of that one sense of loss is the death by which he must glorify the Great Restorer. In the river Euphrates, or the river of human life that flows through mankind, we dam the onflow of original goods as they drive from the banks of the Land Beautiful to the Port Supernal. We dam by hugging hard to goods that harbor the Judas miasma of loss.

Approbativeness is hugged with its Judas miasma of loss. The dog whines under the table when its neighbor dog is praised. Yet no praises bestowed on the neighbor dog detract from the whining dog's standing. It is only the idea or sense of detraction that hurts. Could the unhappy beast know the truth he would be free from his miserable Judas.

This is the death by which many, even great people, might glorify their Heavenly Giver's impartial munificence: namely, by letting others be praised to high water mark for what they themselves, the great people, feel they deserve all recognition. They must stand to the truth which the dog cannot appreciate. They must know that the praises belonging to them are theirs, and are near at hand; nearer for the spaces made by the departing encomiums. "I will also glorify them, and they shall not be few," saith their Judge, their Great Original.

Affection is hugged with its Judas sting of the possibility of loss. What a log it is among the goods driving down the human life river! Somebody wins away our beloved in whom we have delighted. No hope remains. Philosophy may declare that when half gods go the gods arrive, but neither philosophy nor good will can help the heart to let go its one only among all others.

But why should we not trust to the Voice of the Highest? We are not dogs that cannot listen to the voice of Revelation. If the beloved is ours, none can remove the beloved! "I will restore," saith the miracle working Restorer. Confidence in the miracle of Jehovah is the ruby stone among the gems of character. It colors the blood with living fire. Let go, for the miracle of Jehovah! Make way for the miracle!

Ambition is charged with the miasma of humiliating Judas. How many of mankind have dropped out of sight, because their high seats have failed them that others might succeed in their places. It is the agony of kings, emperors, presidents, officials all along the lines of human emulation. Who has had voice to reach them with the divine verily, verily, that seats, thrones, honors, let go when they go, make way for the Restorer's miracle of honors? Age nor sex nor handicap can hinder the coming of the miracle of the Unseen Giver. The high seat belonging to each of earth's millions on millions must see the old ambition log in the Euphrates life river give way, before it can come into place. "Sit thou in that seat, and none can make thee rise," declareth Allah the Inexorable.[21]

Acquisitiveness is another sign of Judas. The fear of loss of possessions goes ever with the acquisition of possessions. Nothing can neutralize the secret fear of loss in the breast of the owner of goods, save attention toward the mystic light of the Inexorably Determined that shines unnoticed over his head. What Allah has given cannot be diminished. And Allah has given more than man has amassed or ever shall amass!

Man's face turning toward destruction, how can man help judging according to destruction? We judge according to our attentions.

The watcher toward Unlimited Ownership in the Upper Realm so near, has inward assurance of security.

---

[21] Allah is the Arabic word that would be translated as "God." It is not another entity, different from the Judeo-Christian Creator, just another language referring to the same being—drawing from the same root as the Hebrew word *El* and *Elohim*.

Why do men build battleships, or lock their doors? Surely it is because of fear of loss of some sort. Nothing voids of the Judas fear of loss till high watch teaches free letting go of fleeing goods for the coming of Matthias, the gift of the Father Munificent.

Letting go, letting go! How free may be the life river when we know the wherefores of our denudings! "Which he spake, signifying what death he should die."

"Wheresoever thou lookest, there is Allah."

From every point in the universe the question faces us, "Is it well with thee?" And to every point in the universe the question-smitten chords of our being answer, "According to Thy judgment it is well with me; therefore it is well." By so agreeing, man strikes beyond the pairs of opposites, success and ill success, honor and dishonor, and is he of whom the Apocalyptic seer writes, "To him that overcometh, will I grant to sit with me in my throne."

The vision of the Universal Judge ever toward the sons of men, being met by the return gaze of the sons of men, drops into the beautiful speech of the New Age just at our gates.

The Beatitudes of The Great Judge are all uttered as invigorating high science to the initiated. Notice how the non initiate stumbles at the blessedness of being reviled and persecuted and spoken evil against falsely. But the Initiate is no crying saint or rebellious Nietzsche. He knows that the persecutor by evil speakings and hateful revilings is knocking at the right gates. The Initiate at his judgment seat stands to it that the reviler is only violently taking the kingdom of his own heaven. The evil speaker is striking for right judgment. He is the Shunammite over again, meeting his Elisha the Tishbite, who does not flinch from yielding the basic good that the reviler is earning by hard labor, though he knows that the reviler might have had his good by an easier and quicker method.

Elisha did not quail at the signs of weeping. He held his own. Let us never flinch at what is happening around us. What is transpiring above us is our concern. And this wins all battles; for the kingdom across the bar is the ruling kingdom. It is the high watcher's business to get all the world to be interested in The Ruling Kingdom for which its heart is truly yearning.

The Judge that standeth up in the universe facing us, saith, as if testing us, "Is it well with thee?" We answer, "According to Thy judgment, it is well with me; therefore it is well." We find that this bold communion accomplishes a strange victoriousness over all our undertakings. Being well with us according to high judgment, we see that it is well with all others. Over all habitations we see the Other Kingdom glowing. We hail complaining speech as divine challenge; our great opportunity. Under all feet we are aware a finished globe rolls with wonderful offerings. Let us salute the ever waiting answers to our prayers. Is it not declared, "Believe that ye have, and ye shall have"? Is it not declared, "Thy lot or portion in life is seeking after thee?" I counsel you to heed no contrary clamorings. "Who is deaf as the messenger I sent," saith *Jehovah-Nissi*. "Salute no man (or opposition to The Judge) by the way." The long looked for Judgment Day is within our gates. Let us joy in the fire of its purifying. Let us catch its brimstone Truth, the mysterious great and mighty things not yet known to this world, which the prophets all heard announced as coming in with High Watch and glad accord with High Judgment.

12th Study

NOTE

The Sacred Books of all ages mention three sciences: Material, Mental, Mystical. Material Science declares laws that are sure; as that iron sharpeneth iron, and hydrogen and oxygen clashing together fall into thirst quenching waters.

The Sacred Books proclaim a Mental Science to which the world can subscribe, as, "All that we are is made up of our thought."

Mystical Science announces the miracles of "Predicateless Being," setting the ways of matter at naught, and nullifying the thoughts of mind:

"The flesh profiteth nothing."

"Take no thought."

"In such an hour as ye think not."

Mystical Science is a chalice of golden wine passed along to the sons of men by John's angels of the Apocalypse,

It is a new song for the hearts of the Children of the New Age. E. C. H.

The twelve gods of the Egyptians were twelve rulers of this world declaring twelve obligations for this world to fulfill. The astronomically prophetic Pyramid of Gizeh was built by the duo-decimal system which finally arrived as the twelve inches of the English foot, every inch alive with its own god law. Twelve is the number of Mount Zion: the number of the Heavenly Jerusalem.

The twelfth stone is the amethyst, symbolic of Revelation of the Mysteries; discovery of secret values; the hitherto valueless coming to light as long hidden Royal Passports.

Do we highly value idleness? Yet the idle hold the key to the city of the Great King. "Labor not," said Jesus. "Your heavenly Father worketh." Therefore, why should they work? And the careless also, whom we hold in light esteem; yet the high law reads, "Cast all your care" — "Your heavenly Father careth" — Why should you care? The thoughtless, the thinkless, we will not praise them, but they hold the heavenly key of "Take no thought" — "In such an hour as ye think not" — "Your heavenly Father knoweth." You do not need to think.

A new accomplishment, a new protection, a new knowing, shall come to the user of this hidden key that opens golden gates to walls of Zion all jubilant with song.

Another feared and half despised condition is old age. How afraid people are of old age, covering all its symptoms with powders and paints and dyes to show how they hate it as an undesirable! Who has told the aged that the secret of a forgotten science hides under faltering brain and stiffening limbs? Who has told them to cease from noticing the faltering and the stiffening and regard with new regarding the science of sparkling re-living hiding under these, ready to break forth with power of youth such as no youth has ever known?

Now and then along the centuries some old, some very old, person has stirred with the hidden science and has done what no young person on all the earth could do, or seeing it done could duplicate.

Joshua at 85 years of age quickens with a mystic tone that throws down the walls of Jericho and starts the Boaz family of forebears of royal David, forefather of *Jesus Nazarenus Rex Judaeorum* ["Jesus the Nazarene, King of the Jews"(the title Pontius Pilate had put on Jesus' cross)].

Moses at 120 years of age inspires with heavenly fervor that shakes the still Jehovah wisdom in Joshua as he lays his hands alive with power upon him. No younger man than Moses at 120 could wake the Spirit of wisdom in old Joshua so that he had almost risen into the heavenly Jerusalem in Supernal manifestation among the great ones of Israel.

High Mysticism

John at Rome in the cauldron of Domitianus, at 80 years of age sets the boiling oil at naught by some mystic atmospheric so generated by the Sacred Name that the Apostles at Ephesus carried him into church with a plate of gold on his brow on which was inscribed the Name of majesty he had so proved as able to save to the uttermost. No young man had come out of boiling oils alive. Only John at 80. And at 89 he, still holding his mystic atmosphere, was most honored among the Christians of that New Age just sending its first golden beams over this dark earth.

Massini in *Firenze* [Florence, Italy] singing Gounod's Sanctus at 70 years of age so entranced the people that some felt themselves transported as to a Paradise they had left behind them or a Paradise they were moving toward. No young singer in all the choirs of Italy could touch the still chords of love, rest, and home like old Massini.

It is for us of the age just shedding its promised daylight over our earth to wake again the slumbering science of reliving so that something diviner than youth may fling its celestial signals forth from behind the falterings of ages-old human processes.

— a —

Man miraculously victorious shall stop his persistent reiterations of descriptions of Deity and His One Idea Man, and urge face to face recognition of Deity as Responsive Servitor.

"To him that ordereth his conversation aright will I show salvation."

Learn to converse face to face with The Ever Facing All-Knowing.

"Therefore, behold, I will proceed to do a marvelous work among this people. I will do a new thing; now it shall spring forth!"

"And there is no discharge in that war," spake Solomon, catching in one of his high moments, the mystery of the amethyst stone holding mystic signification as endless inspirings from endless Wisdom.

Mary of Bethany caught the light of The Endless and started the Christian Church numbering millions on millions of people, and endlessly increasing millions.

"Other foundation can no man lay." These are wonderful words. They stand for the power of a Name. They stand for the mystical influence that wakes the heavenly power called Inspiration, Holy Ghost, working miracles upon this earth, making new conditions like in beauty and joyousness to that other realm called by the Brahmins The Perfect Land.

Daniel, royal captive to the King of Babylon, 500 b. c, felt the Spirit, or inspiration of "the holy gods," and three kings set him into high authority as wiser than all the wonderful wise men of old Babylonia. They found him charged to the brim with mystical knowledge. Daniel knew a name which woke inspiration: "Blessed be the name of God forever and ever, for wisdom and might are his," he said. "He revealeth the deep and secret things."

So today we come again upon the heavenly mysteries all known to Jesus of Nazareth, royal world captive, who offers to the world at large what Daniel offered to the three dynasties Chaldean, Median, Persian, more than two thousand years ago:

"In my Name the Holy Ghost shall teach you." The Holy Ghost hath a voice. John turned to see the wooing Voice. Now and then one of us hears the same Voice. Sometimes it is a soundless chord in music, like what Ole Bull caused whole audiences to be stirred by, after he had roused their inner ears beyond the power of his bow across the strings.

Whoever shall continue to hear the unrecorded strain shall fetch forth the prophesied New Music. Sometimes it is in apperception, as great teachings smite our heart chords. Whoever keeps the apperception shall give us The Vision of The Presence that sweeps this world aside for The New Kingdom to be our dwelling place.

High Mysticism

The teaching and miracle working Holy Ghost saved Daniel in the midst of the starving lions. It saved the three wise men in the midst of the fiery furnace. It saved Paul stoned to death at Lystra.

Daniel was in the teeth of the law of cause and effect by reason of having thrown other men to the lions. He was in the law of "What a man soweth, that shall he also reap." But he having touched a law above human cause and effect came forth unharmed.

The three wise men were in the teeth of the law of cause and effect by reason of having thrown other men into fiery furnaces. They, scenting the winds of the other world, set aside the law of cause and effect and stood forth unharmed.

Paul, who by the law of sowing what we reap was stoned to death as he had stoned others to death, having acknowledged the New King, rose up alive, happy in The Living Kingdom as the sibyls had foretold. Death lifted its cloud and passed away as the sibyls had foreseen; the Cumaean Sibyl, the Erythraic, the Samian — did they not all a thousand years before Paul's time declare that to acknowledge him who should come as king was to rise free and happy in his kingdom, though "hostile men should spit upon that king, and on his sacred back they should strike"?

All the Mystical Laws declare Christ Jesus of prophecy, history, and the Undescribable New Age — this very age swept clean of delusions by the breath of *Atman*, showing our feet standing not on old earth but on a New Earth forgetting the former things as if they had never existed.

— b —

Great events of history, striking to the heart's core of mankind, are heralded by signs in the sky, and earthly eccentricities.

Was it not recorded that at the birth of Jesus of Nazareth the pole of the heaven stood motionless, while everything on earth which was propelled forward was intercepted, workmen with upturned faces and hands mysteriously suspended in air, and cattle strangely pausing at their fodder? Did not even the far away Chinese post it in their astronomical tables that a new star burst into the heavens at that date?

Has not the earth lately slowed up on its axis, the sun shaded its face with new dark spots of mystery, and a more splendid sun come gleaming forth in far distant night skies? Are we oblivious to the fact that these all have presaged the unexplained Armageddon of old Biblical prophecy?

Our globe has crossed a bar, and no prophecy based on previous astrological data can set us straight as to our status in our own constellation. We are driven to the visions of Daniel, Malachi and John the Revelator for sole comfort and edification as to the finals of the vast Apocalyptic combat in this twilight of the gods.

This is the time of which Joel and Paul were foretelling, when only those that call on the name of the High Deliverer shall be delivered from identification with the conflict in which all others on earth are occupied.

Mystical Science, top-currenting the material and mental sciences that run through the prophetic sacred books, lays large stress on the hurrying assistance of the divine Name, whose sounded syllables catch up the flakes of living ether that lie in the common airs softly awaiting inbreathing recognition.

Mystical Science lays large stress on noticing the surrounding ether's soft healing flakes. It teaches to practice inbreathing the waiting Christ breath with its vivific stimulus. It urges to bide the time of the healing elixir's kindling all our flesh with the freshness of its own eternal fires. "For is he not *Atman*, the breath and the life of the universe?"

There is a vital difference between talking about the inspirations that wake the waiting God seed in the breast, and practicing healing inspirations as daily breath.

There is a vital difference between talking about the Judge of all the earth, and answering face to face the Judge's unceasing decision as questioning, "Is it well with thee?"

High Mysticism

Answering face to face according to the Great Judge's inexorable decision is the mystical recognition that personifies. One comes into our life judging us according to our best only, as the great Judge judges, and so judging he warms forth our best into flowering beauty. One comes causing our hidden genius to bloom. One comes shoving us into our rightful environment and delivering to us our rightful possessions. One loves us for our native, original excellence.

And if one thus loves us and judges us, another comes thus loving and judging, and still another, and another, till we are surrounded by the personifications of our acknowledgments of the decisions of the ever Facing Judge of purer eyes than to behold iniquity.

If we have spoken face to face with the Invisible Highest as Wise Counselor, we shall find the personification of our acknowledgment in some new friend's arrival all alive with high counsel.

If we have spoken face to face with the Invisible Highest as Powerful Champion, some unexpectedly greatly powerful champion of our cause hails into comradeship.

For each acknowledgment face to face with the ever facing Mighty Judge personifies. Is it not promised, "Act as though I were, and thou shalt know I Am"? And every personification multiplies, till our whole field of life is dotted with champions and counselors and wise judges. Therefore, "Endure as seeing Him who is invisible."

Endure to the personifyings. Catch the love fire of the sun of recognition on the stalk and bud of hidden possibility everywhere facing us. "Wheresoever thou lookest, there is Allah."

The sun flower endures as seeing the sun though the sun's glowing face is nightly obscured by a dark globe's eight thousand miles of thickness. It squeezes in the sun's hot beams with ecstatic adoration, till living seeds fall from its yellow bosom and other sun flowers spring up and fill the garden patch with sun flowers.

So did Gideon find his senses enthralled by the angel of peace, Jehovah Shalom, till all the Ophrah field was peace for forty years. So did Cosimo see peace, with all his senses enthralled, till *Firenze* was at peace throughout her borders. So shall "all thy land be Beulah, married to the Lord, and great shall be the peace of thy children" — sweet, effortless propagations!

In whatever time of mankind's history we read of his steadfast attention toward the Vast, Vast Countenance of the High Redeemer inhabiting eternity, we find him personifying his high descriptions with people like unto his descriptions. "Thou art my light and my salvation," sang the Hebrew captives in Babylon. Then came great Cyrus lighting up their half forgotten religion, and his Persian army with him, to hew for the singers their lost way back to Jerusalem their half forgotten home.

In our own time, by practicing the same law in lesser fashion, the young Dorman declared himself so identified with Omnipresent Spirit all health, that like the ardent Sufi he felt "O Thou I and I Thou!" This made him as the Sun of righteousness with healing in his beams. All who came near him sensed healing elixirs stirring in their veins, and blessed his miracle working sunshine.

Dorman did not notice the people's wailings. He did not grieve for their misfortunes. He was deaf and dumb to all save the healing "Thou I and I Thou." "Who is blind, but my servant? or deaf, as my messenger that I sent? Who is blind as he that is perfect, and blind as the Lord's servant? Seeing many things, but thou observest not; opening the ears but. he heareth not." Thus the blind and the deaf like the idle and the aged hold the mystic key to another world's wonderful gates. Are we not all of us open-eyed and open-eared to signs and cries of distress? But the truly open-eyed see the heavenly host free, wise, immortal.

The twelfth stone of character is the amethyst, significant of divine deafness and blindness. As the ruby is the most precious of all the precious stones, in the estimation of man, being significant of judgment, so the amethyst is least precious among men, being significant of Dorman deafness and blindness, two terrifying conditions in the estimation of man, depending for their supernal transactions upon face to face recognition of the transmuting God. "Though they cry in mine ears with a loud voice, yet will I not hear them," saith the Lord. Yet "I am the Lord that healeth thee."

Is the Sun mindful whether it warms the rock or freezes the water? So on my hot hate the healing heights let fall a cooling silence, and on my cold despair they drop a loving warmth. Notice how the Great Unnoticing heals its opposites!

> "Now last of all comes number twelve,
> And what should that recall?
> The Apostolic college
> When completed by Saint Paul."

Paul was the College, or collect, of the marriage of all the twelve Apostles to the Risen Christ Jesus, Victorious, Almighty. Never such lovers on earth! They were so in love with their Risen Lord that boiling oil had no terrors for them, lions' jaws no hurting menace.

Paul was the transmuted of the Apostolic lovers. He was transubstantiated from Saul the persecutor of the Christians into Paul chief star in the Christian firmament, founder of the Protestant Church, the most stalwart and vigorous religious body on earth. "I am least of the Apostles," Paul said, "because I persecuted the Christians": "But God hath chosen the weak things of the world to confound the things which are mighty."

Thus was the beautiful dogma of transubstantiation, believed in by the steadfast Roman Catholics, demonstrated beyond cavil by Saul-Paul, and set in the earth as the mystic amethyst of Christianity.

The twelfth lot cometh forth to Hashabiah, twelfth leader of the twelfth course of Levitical Singers. "Hashabiah" signifies such as "Jehovah esteems." "Hashabiah" is he who is set as a precious stone when the Lord maketh up his jewels. For the Hashabiah type sings in the night time of adversity and in the day time of prosperity; in the prisons of enemies and in the castles of friends.

Songs of the heart's Hashabiah well-springs bubble up through external affairs send shrapnel of tribulation or thunders of applause. Paul and Silas in the dark Macedonian prison are singing with their feet in the stocks,

> "Send down thy Spirit free,
> 'Til wilderness and town
> One temple for thy worship be,
> Thy Spirit,
> Oh, send down."

And the inbreathing Free Spirit fills their prison house to bursting, breaking apart the binding stocks, and transmuting prisoners and prison keepers to worship of the Sender-down of Omnipotent Free Spirit.

"Thrice was I beaten with rods," said Paul; "once was I stoned; thrice I suffered shipwreck; once was I picked up for dead." "But I glory." And thus glorying, even Paul's hands had transubstantiating effects; for it came to pass that "when Paul had laid his hands upon them, the Holy Ghost came on them and they spake with tongues, and prophesied."

In the alchemist's crucible the precious metal was separated from the vile amid chemical violence. Thus was Elisha's anguish at the departure of his beloved Elijah turned into transmuting beams that cured brackish Jericho waters, by his crying out, not for departed Elijah, but for the God of Elijah: "Where is the God of Elijah?"

The sand grain or the insect's torture in the amethystine shell wakes the sleeping nacre in the oyster's cold bosom, and the priceless pearl is created. So "surely the wrath of man shall praise thee," sang the "Hashabiah" singers. Was not Jesus angry and grieved? Who is there among us quick-witted enough to transmute his rage into some glowing tribute to Jehovah's healing responsiveness by shouting to Him, "Stretch forth thy hand!" in imitation of the prompt speaking

High Mysticism

Christ Jesus? Jesus thereby used the philosopher's transforming stone for which the magi vainly sought. He stirred the fabled health fountain lying deep in him as in all men. He struck forth the elixir vitae of the God Presence, by shouting aloud his praiseful transmuting recognition, in the midst of his anger and grief.

Who uses the hot words that exactly express his anger or grief, and then is shocked at their reactions? Who gives excuses for terribly efficient exclamations that close the portals to miracle working? As well give excuses for angrily thrusting hands into molten metal!

Take lesson of Jesus of Nazareth, and in hot anger or violent grief use the portal opening words, "Because of Thee I am greater than whatever can happen to me! Because of Thee I am richer than any riches that can fall to my lot! Because of Thee I am more befriended than by the great friends that come to me!" Even on the cross, the Hebrew translation translates, "How thou hast glorified me!"

And the twelfth lot cometh forth to Jakim, "whom God sets up." Whom doth God set up? "I will set him on high because he hath known my name."

Jakim and Jacob being the same consonantally, and holding the same relation to names as mysterious energizings, we see how Jacob was the cord of his own inheritance, by the use of some name of that High Redeemer to whom in his lowly estate of timidity and sin he continually looked for miraculous helping.

The greatest blessing David could think of to confer upon his people, was "The name of the God of Jacob defend thee."

Jacob conferred names on his sons which had in the mystic potency of their sounded syllables the power to compel victorious outcomes. When he told Asher that he should dip his foot in oil, he meant that Asher by holding fast to the secret name of God folded within the syllables of his outer name, all his happy truths should prosper. Was it not a happy truth that the Sufi sang, "O Thou I and I Thou"?

Was it not a happy truth that the captive Hebrews sang, "Thou art my salvation"? Was it not a happy truth that Dorman sang, "O Thou Free Spirit"?

They must have dropped down the line from Asher, the steadfast-to-the-secret-doctrine held fast in some name they used, till it unlocked the mystery of quick successes.

When Jacob told Reuben that "unstable as water, thou shalt not excel," he meant that Reuben's secret name of the Highest Helper would hold him forever steady in the midst of his unstable tendencies, if he would steadfastly declare, "I Reuben the steadfast!" Down Reuben's line, by his fidelity to the whispered secret name folded forever in his outer name Reuben son and friend of God, should spring forth a new order of great men to bless the world.

But Reuben never could remember, except here and there and now and then at odd intervals, to declare "I Reuben the steadfast," till the secret saving name given him by his father Jacob, the name within the name enlarged him beyond his temper and his talents. Reuben neglected the mystic principle as moderns have neglected the mystic possibilities in the Jesus Christ syllables. For the name Jesus Christ holds within its claspings the Lost Word with its power to open the gates of heaven and breathe through our human frames mysterious wafts of immortality. Those who neglect or reject its offers are those dropped down the line of Reuben first born of Jacob and Leah, by inheritance not over handicapped, but by reason of downward viewings out-stripped and out-done.

When the birthright of Reuben was taken from him and passed on to Judah the ever praiseful, the ever-rejoicing seer of pillars of excellence standing up in hardships and handicaps, Jacob handed out to us one of the mystical lessons for which he is now honored: "I Judah, recognizing the precious fire charging my own name as precious fire charges all names, ready to spring forth with new powers by recognition..."

Jacob was teaching the terrible alternative of moral and mental and material life activities: if we stand on our feet we can walk. If we do not stand on our feet we cannot walk. If we know that our thoughts come from our inward viewings we oft-time view Godward; if we do not know this origin of thoughts we oft-time view down and perforce must oft-time think low.

Was not this the ever-presenting bar of "terrible alternative" mentioned by the ancients? Jacob showed it by human beings, giving each son a name with functions for triumph if held heavenward, but closing down in unmiracled warfare and labor if held as man to man or man to dust.

"For this cause have I made thee stand," said the voice of Jehovah to Moses; "that my name may be declared throughout all the earth." "From the rising of the sun shall he call upon my name," seeking my face evermore.

Attention to any objective makes duplicate, replica, in achieving powers as in character. "By me kings reign," saith the King of kings and Lord of lords, Ruler in the heavens and the earth.

Attention to the manner in which kings receive homage would result in kingly manners commanding homage. But only in king's houses are children taught to receive homage as kings. To be a noble courtier is the height of even the titled subject's ambition.

It was only as scion of the king's house that the little dauphin six years of age was seated on the French throne, with scepter in hand and crown on head, that all the magnificent people of the court might pay him homage, that he might early learn to receive homage in kingly fashion.

At a certain point of attention to mathematics the origin of reckoning is touched, and man can perform any given calculation with numbers. At this height he spills over with mathematics. The very airs around him are instinct with his science. Omar Khayyam was one of the greatest of mathematicians, and one of the greatest of observers of transactions by visioning; he wrote,

"As when the tulip for its morning sup
Of heavenly vintage from the ground looks up,
Do thou devoutly do the same,
Till heaven to earth invert you."

Kings of old sought such as could spill over or distil their knowledges into the atmospheres, to associate with the royal infants, that by psychometric encounter, or unconscious suggestion, the children of the royal house might learn easily, and thus easily outstrip all the children of the subjects of the realm.

Masters of art along any line affect the mystic brain films of those with whom they associate. How stimulating to the brain film is the aural spilling over of one who has been taught by Him of the Heavenly Heights, who saith, "Look unto me," "I will instruct thee and teach thee," "I will show thee great and mighty things."

What healing peace may circumadjacently radiate from one who has acquainted himself with Him of the Heavenly Heights ever inviting, "Acquaint now thyself with me, and be at peace."

What rest to the weary may radiate from one who has come into identification with the Heavenly Presence ever calling, "Come unto me, and I will give you rest."

Is not Rest the greatest achieving power mentioned in the books of inspiration? "They rest from their labors; and their works do follow them." God is Rest. "Return unto me," He saith. "Returning unto the Root is rest," wrote the Chinese sages.

Should a man be as rested as God he would do the works of God. The twelve labors of Hercules would be his daily accomplishment. Mythology veils these mystic lessons in story form. Whoever should rightly read mythology would find each god a noble lesson in Mystical Science. He would find the history of man and the cosmos lined out from start to finish.

Notice how Atalanta lost the race by saluting one little temptation *en route*. "Salute no man by the way," said Jesus. Notice how Thor is first among the gods to be destroyed in the twilight of the gods, the Armageddon of the last age. Thor of the ruthless hammer! Then the other gods also to be annihilated, step by step, till there be left only One God and His Name One, the New Name which no man knoweth save he that receiveth it. Is it not easy to pick out the god of each nation in this twilight of time?

Who is obeying the single edict of the high and lofty One inhabiting eternity,

> "Look unto me and be ye saved"
>
> "And I will give you rest."
>
> "There remaineth therefore a rest to the people of God. For he that is entered into his rest, he also hath ceased from his own works, as God did from his. Let us labor therefore to enter into that rest."

The only labor for mankind is oft-time glancing up to the Lover ever with him, the Lord of Hosts his name. "Zeus," said the Greeks, "Zeus is his name. He was, and is and ever shall be, the glorious of man and of the fruitful earth; therefore call upon Zeus."

Rest is relatedness to the Lord of effortless achievement. Its symbolic stone is amethyst. Rest that heals the sick and strengthens the weak is the happy arrival of one that hath chosen the God of Jacob for his strength, by choosing his name of achieving Rest—"Name above principalities and powers, and above every name that can be named."

The twelfth stone stands for happiness. The happy do not care what happens to them. They are the care free; the truly care-less. They have cast all their care on the Author of omnipotent energy. Men wot not what Zeus glory hides its beams in carelessness, the outer significant husk of flawless, unweighted executiveness.

The symbolic stone of the happy carefree is the amethyst, least precious hiding the most precious, the Benjamin stone among the jewels: "The Lord shall cover him all the day long," said Jacob. It is the Joseph stone: Blessed is he, for his are the "chief things of the ancient mountains." It is the Gad stone, signifying one who executeth the justice of great Zeus, enlarging himself by recognizing his own centre as the glorious I AM: Highest God and inmost God — one I AM.

The happy are the hopeless. Over the gates of Dante's Inferno it was written, "Abandon hope." Over the gates of his Paradiso it is also written, "They hope not." For do they hope in heaven? How can they hope when the hoped-for is come? Does the bridegroom hope for his bride when she is already his love, rest and home? Does the mother hope that she shall have a son, when it is already born and nursing at her breast? No, it is come. "Ye are come unto Mount Zion, to the heavenly Jerusalem, and unto the city of the living God, and to an innumerable company of angels; to the general assembly and church of the first born." "We are saved by hope," said Paul, "but hope that is seen is not hope. For when a man seeth, why doth he yet hope for?"

The symbolic stone of hopelessness, advance signal of hidden love, rest, and home, is the amethyst. The amethyst serpent in the diadem of every Pharaoh was symbolic of a secret royal and divine power. It often turned out to be rod of wretchedness for the weak as occult power exercised by kings of dark old Egypt. But the amethyst is now symbol only of the as-yet-unworded wisdom, true waiting rod of the energizing Christ Jesus Name, filled with deliverance for the soldiers of the Armageddon in the twilight of the gods. "For the name of the Lord is a strong tower; the righteous runneth into it, and is safe."

The amethyst stone is symbol of health-giving indifference. Indifference is a state hiding the potent scepter of Almighty Zeus. God is the Great Indifferent leaving the world to lay hold of the beams and ethers of mystic healing, or let them go by. Our sun is the great indifferent, not caring whether it is ripening the grape or rotting the apple. Dorman was the great indifferent, unmindful of cries of pain, yet calming them by his marriage to the regulating Sunshine, glorious, peace-giving *Amen Ra*.

Indifference that achieves is the child of upward gazing. "And the government shall be upon his shoulder," wrote the prophet Isaiah. In the Kabbalah, the intellectually mystical book of ancient Jewish lore and law, the child of the heavenly Dominant is born last in mankind; the crucifixion is first. If the honoring praise of our neighbors sets us up, the government is on the shoulders of praise and honor. If the hostility or hatred of our neighbors depresses us, the government is on the shoulders of hostility and hatred, two crucifying energies overpowering our powers. But if neither praise nor hostility obscures our sense of our I AM dominance, the government is on our shoulders, and by us our neighbors are set into their rightful relations with us, catching our principles of life and arriving side by side with us, neither condemning nor praising, but fellowshipping with us in glad hurrying toward the discovery of the New Science just at our gates, yet now hiding its splendid face from even the most advanced of mankind.

Virgil declared that the discoverers of new principles wear white chaplets on their heads in the Elysian fields, to distinguish them from the common shades who never discovered a single one of the uncountable new laws that press against our mystic brain films.

There is a discovery for every mystic brain. There is a discovery for our fellowshipping brain; the crowning science, held in renitent hiding, till unwarring fellowship makes all mankind as one.

The amethyst signifies originality. It signifies the coming unity of mankind, that can by united drawing charm, raised to Nth power, pull hitherward the New Science that ushers in the millennium.

All who have discovered new principles have acknowledged that it was more as if they remembered the principles than as if they had never known them. Archimedes, Pythagoras, Euclid, remembered. "If they had only been mindful," said Paul; (or remembered) "whence they came out."

Remembering is returning. And returning is repenting. Mary of Bethlehem remembered, returned, repented; the power of the Highest overshadowed her, and she brought forth Jesus, the only un-hypnotized man that ever walked the planet. He was not hypnotized by the world belief in the drowning power of water, the incurableness of leprosy, blindness, deafness, death. He was not caught in the limitations of bread or water or gold. He set the Christian Religion in the earth nearly a billion strong today, equal to victorious grappling with the powers and claims of all who oppose his love and peace doctrine, or forget his vicarious finished work.

We are all fated to remember, return. repent, and bring forth some mighty sign of our recognition of the overshadowing God. This is high light thrown on the doctrine of fate. Did not the ancient Romans declare,

"None could breake ye chaine of forged destinie,
that firme is tyde to Jove's eternal throne"?

Did not the Chinese of dim antiquity proclaim that each man is chained by a single golden thread to the flowery upper land of bliss? Did not they all declare that holding fast by our own upward drawing cord is clue to our own self-transcending, like to Jacob's holding fast the cord of his self-transcendence?

The sages of old India announced that memory is the thread that draws us upward to love, rest, and home. They remembered and remembered their sacred writings tome on tome. The early Christians insisted that by good works should man attain to heaven his longed-for home. But Jesus said love, rest, and home, should be ours by repentance in

High Mysticism

his name, beginning at Jerusalem, or each self. As in the days of Augustus all roads led to Rome, even so do all the mystical lessons lead back again to repentance by Upward Glancing, and fidelity to the Revealing Name.

The Ophites and Nazarenes of old prophesied a wisdom religion to come to the world, having an ineffable name for the secret of its triumphs. Tacitus and Seutonius declared that a man from Judea should subjugate the nations. Who hath transcended Jesus of Nazareth, baptized with Christ the Victorious God, till death and hell and warfare can be glorified out of existence by the influence of his secret name ever breaking through his common name?

Who hath so transcended all laws of nature, rising from the dark tomb by identification with Christ the unburiable? Who being thus risen hath led his Apostolic worshippers as far as Bethany, and lifting up his hands hath blessed them as a heavenly host on high, unnoting of their estate as earth born mankind?

Bethany means house of dates, or house of misery, according as the vision is God ward or earth bound. Here again is the terrible alternative as led off by the mystic sense of inward viewing.

Note how the Apostles being blessed as heavenly host by the Risen Christ Jesus, returned to Jerusalem, or began at their Jerusalem self, shouting to the Most High, "Blessing, and glory, and wisdom, and thanksgiving, and honor, and power, and might, be unto our God!"

Note how they preached union with the Highest and communion with the sons of light. They had been taught that two are ever in the field, man and super-man; one should be taken, the other left. Their address was thus ever to the super-man, the angel of man's presence.

To the angel of the amusement bound, to them of the church of Ephesus let us write as to Risen Christ. To the angel of the beauty bound, to them of the Church of Smyrna, let us write as to God, Origin of Beauty. To the angel of each church, let us write the great things of The Highest.

To the Pergamos angel let us write; to them of the grandeurs of wealth, statecraft, learning; to the lovers of art, architecture, music, war. To them let us write as to One who transcends all grandeurs.

The Apostles wrote to the Pergamos type concerning the true Healing God whom the Pergamites were worshipping in the temple as Aesculapius, the key god invisibly filling his outer temple, urging his own worship with promises of health auras if mankind would only marry unto him, the god of healing, radiating his sunshine through his temple's ivory walls, to envelop his devotees with resistless magistrum.

The Apostle wrote to the Angel of the Church of Pergamos, mentioning the truly victorious God, whom the Pergamites were adoring in the golden temple as Jupiter the Mighty. They wrote to the Angel in the Church of Pergamos, the Joyous God, whom the Pergamites were wooing in the shining temple as Bacchus the delectable. To the Angel of Pergamos, the city of splendid temples built of *shittim* wood and ivory, sandal wood and ebony, the Apostles of the Lord Christ of the one God wrote glowing letters.

Not to the people did they write, but to the Angel of the people. Herein is great light on the mystical ministry of the Messiah Christ. As he blessed his disciples as an angelic host, and thus made of them the transcendent among mankind, so all those who regard their neighbors as angelic host, above their seeming selves, imbue their neighbors with immuneness to disease, and hurting powers, and death, turning them to adoration of The High Redeemer.

The mystical books of the oracles could be found in Pergamos of old. To this day the subtle aromas of the books of the oracles are sending athwart receptive brain films their New Age wisdoms. For though the scrolls of high teaching be outwardly burned, their secret messages go ever stealing forth.

High Mysticism

Though the Caliph Omar destroyed the scrolls of Pergamos and Alexandria, yet the writings on the scrolls are still whispering across our mystic brain films. Let us hearken for the high teachings with which the inner airs are charged. "The value of all the scrolls is in the Koran," shouted the Caliph Omar. And so it is. Does not the Koran declare "Most Highest Allah", who teacheth what before mankind hath not known? Shall not the Master and the scholar who teacheth less than "Most Highest Allah" be cut off out of the tabernacles of Jacob? Is not our prophet Malachi inspired, when with foresight like to the makers of cosmic myths, sighting the end of the world's beloved gods, he sees that all of low viewings must be ended with their gods' great twilight?

When the Christian Theophilus, hurrying with his mob through Pergamos to burn the Sibylline prophetics, shouted that all books were as nothing in the light of Christian Scripture, was he not shouting better than we have credited to him? For what is the point of Christian Scripture now breaking in upon us, save, "Seek ye my face evermore" — "And every eye shall see, and every tongue confess." Did the Sibylline books go so straight to the saving instruction, though their secret doctrines read that Hecate, man's own I AM, shares equal honors with Zeus, the One I AM, because as there is but one I AM in the universe, I AM that I AM ?

When Mark Anthony gave to Cleopatra 200,000 precious volumes from the library of Pergamos, was he not corralling heathen knowledge and mythological significants into one spot of old Africa, to silver the Christian gospel yet to be, with the wise secret potencies of hoary antiquity?

Shall not the Original Christian Gospel reach us in its own appointed time? Shall not the foretold Messenger arrive to whom even the Jews shall shout Hosannas? The Christ of the New Christian Gospel is not crucified, not buried, not risen. The Christ of the New Christian Gospel is the Able-to-save-from-falling, by the mighty power of the

Name within the name of that Wholly Christ imbued One, bloom in the Garden of Time.

"Great is Diana of the Ephesians!" they shouted. But Diana gave way to Mary. "Great is Mary!" they shouted. But Mary gives way to the Holy Ghost. "Great is Jesus the Crucified!" they shouted. But Jesus the Crucified gives way to Uncrucified Free Christ.

Christ was never crucified. Christ is the uncrucifiable, unburied and unrisen— the Eternal and Changeless Self Existent High Redeemer—The Awakener of New Powers and New Knowledges. Let the Name that hides The Name of the Uncrucifiable Self Existent ascend, till its hidden manna nourishes our mystical bodies into joyous prominence! Till the Holy Ghost that teaches all things is our daily breath.

Breath of heaven all truth revealing.

Kindling in us life divine!

Only he of the mystical Christ Body Dominant can be the writer of the New Book that is promised to expound the fundamentals of the New Dispensation and explain the starry signs no other science seems to get right—signs declaring that new heaven and new earth now hurrying through the thundering Armageddon gates.

"The Stars in their Courses fought against Sisera," because Sisera fought against the stars.

For the stars in their courses are a framework inevitable. They go according to Peace, and Order, and the way of Kindness. Whatever opposes the purpose ox the order the stars do serve, must take the reactions of defiance to their stately signalings.

For many years Sisera's kingdom had been working' to overthrow the Jehovah Inexorable, as set forth by the Israelitish prophecies. His king Jabin had harassed Israel secretly and openly, and with stored munitions of iron chariots, nine hundred strong, had suddenly met outwardly unprepared Israel in battle array on the great plain of Esdraelon.

The Framework of heaven gives to each star its path whereon not only to shine, but in its visible integrity to figure forth the Invisible integrity of a Finished Prototype.

Whatever people, or tribe, or country, or globe shall stand up for the Integrity that swings the stars, as according to loving kindness, and peace giving, and life-and-joy-defending, shall be, by so far as he thus stands up, in league with The Undefeatable.

How then could Deborah the prophetess, with upward vision, find any other prophecy for Barak of Israel, called the thunderbolt of the Framework, than that Barak defense should stand in better with the stars than Jabin-Sisera onslaught?

"On earth peace, good will toward men," sang the angels, heralding One who never stepped out of league with the stars in their courses.

Then, if there is any nation or globe in the spaces that is preparing to molest the peace of its neighbor, it is out of step with the heavenly legions, visible and invisible, and can not win its iron-charioted way, even though all its munitions and plannings have risen to the Nth power of antagonism. Let not any such Sisera expect to triumph against the stars that wheel only Good Will.

Glance up, glance up often, O Man! So shalt thou find thyself in unhinderable step with the Victorious Highest, Author of the Integrity that sends the stars on their sublime marches; Father of him who gave his life to set mankind into rhythm with life everlasting; who gave his life to quicken our recognition of the Responsive Divinity overlooking the stars above the signal stars; the Responsive Divinity quiescent like a sleeping giant in the breast of every one of us; who gave his life to call our own attention to our own deeply held Acquaintance with the Secrets of the Finished Universe, to the "light that lighteth every man that cometh into the world."

Let us write to the Angel of our neighbor's presence: Ye are above the wheel of matter and the network of mind. Ye are light of the world — free, flawless, immortal.

— ∞ —

Resumé

Practice Book for the 12 Lessons

NOTA BENÉ

"He that would perfect himself in any art whatsoever, let him betake himself to the reading of some sure and certain work upon his art many times over; for to read many books upon your art produceth confusion rather than learning." ~ Old Saying.

"*Cave ab hominem unius libri...*" (Beware the man of one book - he knows) ~ Roman Proverb.

"Yea, even a single person occupying with the Thora is sure of reward." ~ *Thora*.

"And a book of remembrance was written." ~ *Malachi 3:16*.

"Seek ye out of the book of the Lord, and read: no one of these shall fail." ~ *Isaiah 3:16*.

"And I wept much because no man was found worthy (willing to persist) to open and to read the book." ~ *Revelation 5:4*.

CONTENTS

NOTA BENE	549
I. REPENTANCE	554
II. REMISSION	558
III. FORGIVENESS	561
IV. FAITH	567
V. WORKS	573
VI. ILLUMINATION -UNDERSTANDING	573
VII. MINISTRY	577
VIII. MINISTRY	581
IX. MINISTRY	581
X. MINISTRY	585
XI. MINISTRY	594
XII. MINISTRY	59804

To Remember:

Commit to memory this page of Bible texts on the first Study:

"The Lord looketh upon all the inhabitants of the earth." ~ *Psalm 33:14*

"Look unto me and be ye saved, all the ends of the earth, for I am God and there is none *else*. " ~ *Isaiah 45:22.*

"Repent and turn away your faces from all your abominations." ~ *Ezekiel 14:6.*

"Behold, he cometh with clouds, and every eye shall see him."~ *Revelation 1:7.*

"They sing the song of Moses, and the song of the Lamb." ~ *Revelation 15:3.*

"That led them by the right hand of Moses with his glorious arm, dividing the waters before them, to make himself an everlasting name." ~ *Isaiah 63:12.*

"That repentance should be preached in his name, beginning at Jerusalem." ~ *Luke 24:47.*

I REPENTANCE

The High and Lofty One inhabiting Eternity has been understood by His lovers to be forever inviting mankind to look unto His Countenance shining as the sun with healing strength.

The Deity looketh upon us; let us look to the Deity. This is the way of salvation from sin, sickness, misfortune and death.

Isaiah understood it as a Soundless Mandate: "Look unto me and be ye saved, all the ends of the earth" *(Is. 45:22)*. Ezekiel understood it as the law of repentance, or returning: "Repent, and turn away your faces from all your abominations" *(Ezek. 14:6)*. Jesus called it The Watch: "What I say unto you, I say unto all, Watch" *(Mark 13:37)*. Plato understood the Watch as a privilege: "It is time to lift the eye of the soul above the outlandish slough in which it is buried, and set it toward the Elysian Fields."

It has been found that what we vision steadily causes our thinking. Even Hegel noticed this law in his *Introduction to Logic,* where he avers that we secretly perceive toward an object before thinking it.

If we exhibit in this posit we call our "me" according to the direction we oftenest set this visional sense, which can see toward God or toward the workings of our own brain, it is high time we set the important and all-achieving sense definitely toward that objective calculated to build us to the best advantage.

If back over the Tao, or Track, of this wonderful sense can come infinitesimal pictures of the objective it views toward, we will choose the "Great, the Mighty God, great in counsel and mighty in work" *(Jer. 32:19),* for our objective. This is the way of being God-taught. "I will instruct thee and teach thee" *(Ps. 32:8)*. It is the way of being divinely guided. "I will guide thee with mine eye" *(Ps. 32:8)*.

John the Revelator was God-taught. He saw all truth in symbols, or pictures. He called the great lessons he learned, "Angels," or messages. He divided them into seven. The seventh he repeats over and over, like Joshua sounding one tone with rams' horns on the seventh day of his circling of Jericho. The tone John sounds is, "I looked, " and, "I beheld."

With obedience to the mandate, "Look unto me," John saw hail and fire mingled with blood falling upon the earth *(Rev. 8)*. "Hail" is new fresh truth. How can we help having new truth if we set our eye in a new direction? It is the resistless truth of the eternal Heights. "Fire" is the emblem of heavenly fervor. The heart flames up with new zeal, new ardor, new love, if the vision is upward.

"Blood" is the emblem of new life. Men can appear who were not born of the will of man but of the will of God. Such an one walked along with Tobias. Such an one appeared to Jacob. Such an one sometimes appears in our own age. Two were seen by a highway robber to be walking along with a missionary at midnight when the missionary supposed himself to be alone. The robber hurried away from the three of them.

This is the new life we cannot help encountering as we seek our highest Good at the highest Source. The disciples felt their hearts burn while such an one talked with them as they walked toward Emmaus. Their oftime gaze had been heavenward where on the right hand of God Omnipotent they had visioned their Lord and Master, Jesus the Christ.

As a result of their upward watch, the empowering Angel of God's presence was tangible to them. Such appearances are the blood of obedience.

John the Revelator sees a third of the trees disappear. He sees all the green grass burn up *(Rev. 8)*. "Trees" are the emblems of flourishing practices. One third of these practices cease, even in the life of the individual, as the flaming zeal for God kindles.

Competitive examinations competitive trades, competitive platforms, which constitute the ginger and glow of

Resumé 551

unvisioning life, cease for such as know that their true provisions and their true positions come straight from above, and nothing and nobody can take them from them.

All strenuousness on every line must cease. The laborers and anarchists, the pole hunters and the gold grabbers must calm down, for the Countenance that shineth hot with healing tenderness and rich giving is of more value than all that can possibly come by the clash of endeavor.

"Grass" is emblem of the seasons of human life, childhood, youth, middle age, old age, such as the new people know not. Did the Son of God, seen in the fiery furnace by the King of Babylon, know anything of childhood and old age? *(Dan. 3)*. The upward watch of the King must once have been true and steady to have found in the fiery furnace the man with eternity stamped upon his brow. The robber who beheld the two guardsmen of the missionary must have at some moment of his life looked upward, whence the daysprings fall, and some of the prisons where he was shut in must have sometimes been unaccountably opened for him. For the High and Lofty Majesty inhabiting Eternity is the "bad man's deliverer," said Lao-tze the God-taught.

The visional sense that seeks the Vast Countenance ever shining hitherward, can bring back news of any objective it sets itself toward, from the rocks of the gorges to the midnight stars. Did not untaught Bramahaupto find out the names and the motions of the suns and constellations by gazing toward them even in his dreams? Can you not feel that a starry radiance must have shone forth from Bramahaupto's eyes, since, "that thou seest man that too become thou must?"

Obeying the sublime mandate, "Look unto me," we sense the mystery of redemptive energy. John tells us that the Redeemed are given two songs *(Rev. 15)*. Perpetually recurring names are songs. Job was the song of his scornful neighbors. "*I AM that I AM*" was the song of Moses. "*Jesus Christ*" was the song of the first Christians. These names are full of the meaning of life and the transports of Eternal Truth.

Zoroaster was told that the name "*I AM that I AM*" is the name of kingly might and majesty. He repeated it often and stepped out of the rank and file of men into rulership of the nation.

> "The Lord is high above all nations and his glory above the heavens.
>
> "Who is like unto the Lord our God who exalteth himself to dwell on high?
>
> "He raiseth the poor up out of the dust that He may set him with princes" *(Ps. 113)*.

With that Name, which means that no one knows the nature and character of Him that bears it, Moses led two million slaves to triumphant liberty: "That led them by the right hand of Moses with his glorious arm, dividing the waters before them, to make himself an everlasting name" *(Is. 63)*.

With the Song of the Lamb in his heart, Peter converted three thousand people to Christianity by one transcendent sermon. "There is none other name under heaven given among men, whereby we must be saved," he said *(Acts 4:12)*.

Let us take Monday to repent, or turn away our faces from all the things, events and people that call our attention. Let us often look upward toward the Deity ever beholding us. Let us tell that "*Ain Soph*, Great Countenance of the Absolute above thinking and above being," as the Kabala avers, that we know His Name of up lifting might; His Name of majesty and grandeur. It is *I AM that I AM*. Let us tell Him that we know His Name of manifestation in the flesh; His embodying Name, His Name of our own manifested health and undefeatable free Spirit. It is *Jesus Christ*.

It is on the principle of doing things in order, as Paul enjoined. *(1 Cor. 14:40)*, that we begin the week days with obedience to the heavenly ordinance, "Look unto Me," which is preaching repentance, beginning at Jerusalem, or the Self *(Luke 24:47)*.

To Remember:

Commit to memory this page of Bible texts on the second Study:

"That remission should be preached in all nations beginning at Jerusalem." ~ *Luke 24:47.*

"Then Peter said unto them, Repent, and be baptized every one of you in the name of Jesus Christ for the remission of sins, and ye shall receive the gift of the Holy Ghost." ~ *Acts 2:38.*

"Looking diligently lest any man fail of the grace of God." ~ *Hebrews 12:15.*

"Nothing shall by any means hurt you." ~ *Luke 10:19.*

"Thou dissolvest my substance." ~ *Job 30:22.*

"The earth and all the inhabitants thereof are dissolved." ~ *Psalms 75:3.*

"If any man will come after me, let him deny himself." ~ *Matthew 16:24.*

II REMISSION[22]

On the Principle that what we oftenest view with the inner eye, that we show forth outwardly, we can easily understand why the poor cripple near the temple gate *(Acts 3)*, with vision in the dust, had never felt the dissolving of the manacles of impotence till Peter and John bade him look up.

Something then fell down over his upward visioning and undid his chains of mind and body. "Preach remission," said Jesus. "Preach the dissolving Grace."

"When men are cast down thou shalt say, 'There is lifting up,' and God shall save the humble person," said Eliphaz *(Job 22:29)*. There are shouts of freedom handed down from antiquity that represent the experiences of remission, or liberation of the upward watchers throughout the ages. They declare the disappearings of foolishness and ignorance. They are recognitions that foolish virgins or objectives, with no oil of healing and no oil of illuminating in their sayings, are shut out.

There is no oil of healing and no oil of illuminating in descriptions of evil in any way. Description of evil is a foolish virgin. The description of evil doubles evil. It does not lessen it. See then how foolish to describe evil and thereby double it. If we see an army of locusts alighting on the green vegetation we mourn because the people must starve. This is our foolishness. We increase starvation by such mourning. According to Jesus the risen and triumphant man of God, we are to look up to the shining face of our Father looking tenderly down upon us, and declare, "Steadfastly facing Thee, there is no evil on my pathway." For only abundance and gentle kindness fall from the Vast Countenance shining hitherward.

---

[22] This is Tuesday morning's study.

Resumé

According to the experiences of the men of light, the locusts must vanish in all directions if we exalt our vision above them — dissolved like the Ammonites, Moabites, and Seirs, from Jehoshaphat's pathway, when he said, "Oh, our God, our eyes are upon Thee" (2 *Chron.* 20).

St. Augustine found that God sees no evil. So also did Habakkuk *(1:13)*. We catch the viewpoint of those with whom we associate. Let us catch the High God's viewpoint and go free from sight of evil. Zephaniah cried, "Shout, O Zion: thou shalt not see evil any more!" *(Zeph. 8)*. He saw for a short period as his God was seeing.

Matter also has been found to have no health in its operations. No descriptions of matter quicken the pulses with healing blood, or fill the stomach with strengthening energy. No study of matter illuminates the spiritual wisdoms that wait like unlighted candles just above our heads. Only the kindling fires of God's hot glance can illuminate our waiting intelligence. And we must recognize the glance, acting under obedience to the order, "Behold Me" *(Is. 65)*.

Matter moves aside for indestructible free grace to act, when by upward viewing we shout, "Facing Thee, there is no matter with its laws."

Neither is there any oil of healing in descriptions of lack and deprivation. This is the foolish virgin that woman is said to hug to herself. "No wine," she says. "Not enough — not enough of this, or of that good thing." She must let go that foolish saying, and look up to him who saith, "They shall want for no good thing" *(Ps. 34:10)*. She must preach to the heavens that facing the Father there is neither lack nor deprivation.

There is no acting free grace visible to one who describes hurts and pains. Peter sank into the raging waters when he took his gaze off the powerful Jesus *(Matt. 14)*. But with his eye uplifted he walked above the waves, side by side with Omnipotence. There is a shout of liberty anyone can give when hurts come grinding and burning upon him:

·

"Facing Thee, there is nothing to fear, for nothing shall by any means hurt me" *(Luke 10:19)*. All hurting power is darkness. The dayspring from on high gives light to them that sit in darkness, to guide their feet into the way of peace *(Luke 1:79)*.

Sinfulness with its sickness and death is only the description of what is encountered by men with aberrated vision, or downward gaze. It is downward gazing to describe a child's bad temper or a friend's unkindness. Not only they, but we who describe, must get warped and ill by reason of the excitement their ill behavior causes us. It is the one foolish virgin that works with surprising haste. See how quickly you have cramps, or influenza, or something else, when you are excited by the willfulness or deception of your wife, or husband, or friend.

The shout of the free must be given before we feel the freedom, as the Sons of Judah at the watchtower in the wilderness shouted liberty before they came into it *(2 Chron. 20)*. Did not Jesus shout, "It is finished," before it was finished? But see how quickly the anguish left him when he shouted with a loud voice, "It is finished" *(John 19:30)*.

Let us take Tuesday to shout liberty, free grace — remission — unburdening, as we look upward. Free grace comes softly stealing over the Tao, or Track, of the upward watch. Take the shouts in order. Look up to the Vast Countenance with its beaming and kindling free grace, its dissolving alkahest, ever hitherward streaming, and with joyous heart proclaim:

> Facing Thee, there is no evil on my pathway;
>
> There is no matter with its laws;
>
> There is no loss, no lack, no deprivation;
>
> There is nothing to fear for there shall be no power to hurt;
>
> There is neither sin, nor sickness, nor death.
>
> Because Thou Art The Unconditioned and The Absolute, I also am Unconditioned and Absolute.

Because Thou Art Omnipotent Free Spirit, I also am Omnipotent Free Spirit.

To Remember:

Commit to memory this page of Bible texts on the third Study:

"There is forgiveness with Thee." ~ *Psalm 130:4*.

"To the Lord our God belong forgivenesses." ~ *Daniel 9:9*.

"If my people, upon whom my name is called, shall humble themselves, and seek my face, and turn from their wicked ways; then will I hear from heaven, and will forgive all their land." ~ *2 Chronicles 7:14*.

"He that humbleth himself shall be exalted." ~ *Luke 14:11*.

"Put on humbleness of mind, and meekness." ~ *Colossians 3:12*.

"Because thine heart was tender, and thou didst humble thyself before God — I have even heard thee also, saith the Lord " ~ *2 Chronicles 34:27*.

"Behold, my servant shall prosper, he shall be exalted and extolled, and be very high." ~ *Isaiah 52:13*.

"Who forgiveth all thine iniquities, who healeth all thy diseases." ~ *Psalm 103:3*.

III FORGIVENESS

If nothing hurts Free Spirit and I am Free Spirit, unhurt forever, I have something given *for* the imagination of hurting which has now slipped away from me. This that takes the place of hurts is Beauty, Joy, Praise, Wholeness. The Hindus stay enchained in devotion to removals, dissolvings, non-estness. They bury themselves in the ground to show that nothing can by any means hurt them. They transform material things out of sight by denial of materiality. They call the body the dark shadow of the Soul. They teach to regard the body as of no concern to the True Self. "To know this disregard as righteousness is true liberation, the highest state the sage can attain" (*Zend-Avesta,* Fluegel's translation, p. 94). The Hebrews touch lightly upon what disappears. They describe with flourishing of banners the splendors seen when the shadows pass: "My servant shall be exalted, he shall deal prudently, and be very high" *(Is. 52).* "The Lord God hath given me the tongue of the learned" *(Is. 50).* It was Hebrew before it was Christian to preach forgiveness, or the given-for; as: "the garment of praise for the spirit of heaviness;" and "the plantings that glorify God, *for* desolation" *(Is: 61).* "The Lord shall forgive" *(Num. 30).*

As the needle can become a magnet by rubbing against a magnet, so we can do God-works by closely relating ourselves to the Healer of all diseases, the Redeemer from destruction, the Great in Counsel. As the needle must utterly yield herself so must we utterly yield our selves. We must have our eye single to One Only to be full of that One Only. Utter yielding is called "meekness," in the Scriptures.

There is a Divine Fiat ever going forth. There is a Divine Providence always acting. If we hold the magnetic needle still it is restless till it is free to point north. So we are restless under the cramps formulated by our own visioning toward evil, or the body of matter, of pain and decay. These slough off with the high watch and the shouts of the free. We sense the Divine Providence — the Heavenly Fiat. The sense of the kind and good and joy-giving Providence upbearing us forever, has been called the "Cosmic Consciousness." Its ecstasy of rest in the Lord has been called "forgiveness."

Great Proclamations have issued forth from those who have experienced the cosmic consciousness, or forgiveness. These proclamations have been called "Affirmations of Eternal Truth." They have been called "Hymns to the Eternal." They have been figuratively spoken of as "Wise Virgins," with oil of healing and oil of illuminating in their influence. As the needle cannot attract like a magnet if it does not yield itself *in toto* to the magnet, so no man can be the embodiment of the five eternal proclamations who has not let his mind, his life, his heart, his body go free to the winds of the Divine Fiat, looking up often to the Sun of Righteousness with healing in his wings.

Professor William James tells of an Oxford graduate who volitionally offered himself to the Stream of Divine Order, letting go of himself like a reed in the wind, fully expecting annihilation. To his surprise he found his bad habits gone, his despair dissolved, his character and body strengthened and his whole being infused with radiance. Hannah let herself go into the Divine Order, through self-abnegating prayer, till she staggered. Eli the prophet thought she was drunken with wine. But she was like the needle just ready to rise into powerful repute. Suddenly, Eli prophesies for her, and she shouts the gist of the five great affirmations of truth:

> "There is none beside Thee. The Lord shall judge the ends of the earth; and he shall give strength unto the king, and exalt the horn of his Anointed" (*I Sam. 2*).

The risen Christ taught volitional meekness, volitional offering: "He that humbleth himself shall be exalted" *(Luke 14:11).*

Let us take Wednesday to voluntarily offer our self to the King of Kings and Lord of Lords. They that worship in meekness are the ready harp strings for the divine melodies of the five hymns of praise, the five proclamations of truth. They are the voicing instruments of Health and quickening life.

Here is a form for voluntary surrender of self in meekness, and the, full text of all the illuminative sayings for centuries, whenever men have found themselves yielding in humility and rising up for given:

> Here is my mind. I spread it out before Thee. Forgive Thou its foolishness and ignorance with Thy bright wisdom. Here is my life. I offer it to Thee. Forgive Thou its contrariness to Thee. Here is my heart. It is Thine only. Forgive Thou its restlessness and dissatisfaction. Forgive its discouragements. Forgive its resentments. Forgive its loves and its hates, its hopes and its fears. Here is my body. I cast it down before Thee. Forgive Thou its imperfection with Thy perfection. Forgive me altogether with Thyself. Give for myself Thyself. So only can I know that:
>
> Thou art, and there is none beside Thee, in Thine own Omnipresence, Omnipotence, Omniscience—
>
> I am Thine only and in Thee I live, move, and have being—
>
> I am Thine own substance, power, and light, and I shed abroad wisdom, strength, holiness, from Thee—
>
> Thou art now working through me to will and to do that which ought to be done by me—
>
> I am forgiven and governed by Thee alone, and I cannot sin, I cannot suffer for sin, nor fear sin, sickness or death.

"Bow down thyself to me and thou shalt come even to me. Take sanctuary with me alone and I shall liberate thee from all sin, by the resplendent Lamp of Wisdom" *(Vedic Hymn).*

Resumé

With the experience of forgiveness, or the *Hestia Vestia* of bold Truth, John foresees a star called, "Wormwood," falling to the earth *(Rev. 8:10)*. A "star" is a great character. And "wormwood" is mind preserver, or mind cure. One shall be the embodiment of Truth so inspiringly that he shall cure the world mind of its earth-drowse.

When a man is sick or in pain, he is in telluric slumber or earth-drowse. He is magnetized by foolishness and ignorance. His mind is thralled by foolishness and ignorance: the earth-sleep. John the Revelator sees one to arise all awake. His vivid sense of Living Spirit shall kindle in men now asleep the vivid sense of Living Spirit, of the giving for matter's laws the law of the Spirit of life in Christ Jesus.

To Remember:

Commit to memory this page of Bible texts on the fourth Study:

"Let us therefore come boldly unto the throne of grace." ~ *Hebrews 4:16.*

"Faith is the confidence of things hoped for." ~ *Hebrews 11:1.*

"In whom we have boldness and access with confidence by the faith of him." ~ *Ephesians 3:12.*

"The revelation of the mystery, which was kept secret since the world began, but now is made manifest, according to the commandment of the everlasting God — for the obedience of faith." ~ *Romans 16:25, 26.*

"Concerning the work of my hands command ye me." ~ *Isaiah 45:11.*

"Here are they that keep the commandments of God and the faith of Jesus." ~ *Revelation 14:12.*

IV FAITH

That nature rises up in us before which we have worshipped. The meek Jesus was worshipper before the King of Kings and Lord of Lords, therefore he must at some moment proclaim. "All power is given unto me in heaven and in earth" *(Matt 28:18).* "I have overcome the world" *(John 16:83).* "He that hath seen me hath seen the father" *(John 14:9).*

Napoleon was meek before the generals of the French army and rose up head of the army. Joan of Arc was meek before the angels who had accompanied her all her life, and she rose up with supernatural powers, Both Napoleon and Joan of Arc fell, because there is no nature worth practicing subservience unto except the Ruler in the heavens and the earth, "Let the Lord be thy confidence, he will not suffer thy foot to be taken" *(Prov. 3:26)* "Hast thou faith? Have it to thyself before God" *(Rom. 14:22).*

God is the Author of faith, as Paul wrote to the Ephesians *(3:12),* which Jesus of Nazareth caught so completely that the whole creation was subject to his strong word of authority. Faith is always associated with authority. Faith is confidence to command. One little spark of it no larger than a mustard seed, would cause authority enough to move a mountain *(Matt 17:20),* Moses caused two million people to obey his lightest command after the spark of authority flamed up in him. He had been meek and lowly to the loss of his self-consciousness, while kneeling before God on the mountains of Midian. Self-consciousness is a poor stuff to present before men or nature if we want to command them even for their good. Is if not Self-consciousness that makes a person appear poorly before his neighbors? It is the wiping out of this tough integument that lowliness before The King of Kings accomplishes. Self-consciousness is sometimes called self-will because it is a perversity of the whole constitution, and because the divine authority that rises out of its demolition is a new will.

Elisha had all his life been lowly before God. He bathed the hands and feet of Elijah while yet his eyes were heavenward. Suddenly, no man in Israel had so much authority over men and nature as the hitherto meek Elisha,

The exercise of authority is good exercise. It gets its kindling from practicing upon the most obedient servant first. The Supreme God is the most docile and obedient Servant. David commanded the High God: "Show me a token for good that they which hate me may see it" *(Ps. 86)* He was astonished at the results of his firm authority: "Thou through thy commandments hast made me wiser than mine enemies" *(Ps. 119),*

Isaiah understood that we must practice commanding the Supreme Presence in the Universe. While listening in lowly humility before Him he heard these words, "Concerning the work of my hands command ye me" *(Is. 45).*

Jesus commanded the Supreme Servant, "Glorify Thou me." On the cross he cried, "How Thou hast glorified me!" This is one of two translations of the words reported in *Mark 14* as "Why hast Thou forsaken me?" Jacob commanded the angel of God's presence, whom he called God himself, "I will not let thee go except thou bless me" *(Gen. 32:26).* Job said, "I will demand of thee, and declare thou unto me" *(Job 42).* Jesus commanded the God of Lazarus, He commanded the God of the withered arm. Always lowly meekness rises to confidence to command. Napoleon could never really understand how he came by such commanding confidence, but we can see that it was by reason of his prompt obedience to the authority he recognized vested in his superior officers.

Jesus told his disciples to speak to the Supreme Servant in the terms of the Lord's Prayer as the firm insistence of their own lordship or hidden man of the heart whom all authorities obey. It is a formula full of short commands to the

Resumé

Great Servant who asks, "Is anything too hard for me?" *(Jer. 32:27)*.

We will take Thursday to practice speaking to the Great Servant with firm command, in the words of the hidden Lord's Formula. We will speak it over and over fifteen times, as the sick people do at the Waters of Lourdes when they are urging God to heal them by way of the Waters, "Fifteen" is the number where the waters of misfortune cease to prevail against us, as *Gen, 7:20,* It is the number of using to walk above hardship.

Notice that Marcella of the Roman Catholic Church, taught her nuns the inner meaning of "Give us this day our daily bread." She said it ought to be, "Give me this day my super-substantial bread." Our secret ego, our God-spark, our "hidden man of the heart," as Peter called it *(1 Peter 3:4),* must have the bread of heaven.

Notice how "Lead us not into temptation" has lately been translated as. "Let us not into temptation," or, "Let me not into temptation," meaning, "Warn me when I turn away from Thee." Notice how "Forgive us our debts" is now understood to be, "Give for our emptiness Thy Substance." Paul called faith a substance. There is a great mystery about "faith" which, as Paul's word "substance", is rendered as "confidence," in the margin of Hebrews eleventh chapter, first verse: "Faith is the confidence of things hoped for."

Grow more and more urgent, insistent, commanding, as you go on repeating the Great Formula to the Greatest Servant amongst us. Let confidence solidify. Let the God-spark speak. "The gods love courage armed with confidence" *(Bonduca,* translated by Beaumont and Fletcher).

To Remember:

Commit to memory this page of Bible texts on the fifth Study:

"And the word was made flesh, and dwelt among us, (and we beheld his glory, the glory as of the only begotten of the Father,) full of grace and truth." ~ *John 1:14.*

"Behold, my sheaf stood upright." ~ *Genesis 37:7.*

"He that ruleth his spirit is better than he that taketh a city." ~ *Proverbs 16:32.*

"Pleasant words are sweet to the soul." ~ *Proverbs 16:24.*

"When thou shalt make his soul an offering..." ~ *Isaiah 53:10.*

"I have finished the work Thou gavest me to do." ~ *John 17:4.*

"As far is the east is from the west, so far hath he removed our transgressions from us." ~ *Psalm 103:12.*

"That he might deliver us from this present evil world..." ~ *Galatians 1:4.*

V WORKS

Faith without works does not exist. Faith always works. It stirs boldness, confidence, to dare the seemingly impossible. Notice Elisha's bold faith when he ordered the widow to borrow vessels and pour oil, seemingly from nowhere, into them *(2 Kings 4)*. Command of the Great Servant is a practice that changes the nature from timidity and doubt to commanding boldness, from timid following to daring leadership, from obedience to authority. So was Jacob's name changed to "Israel" when he fought with the angel till daybreak, and won in the battle *(Gen. 32)*.

Authority with God discloses authority with the Self. The divine Self, the *esse,* lies quiescent, still, waiting in all men to be stirred into action by the outer self. Two kinds of address stir the still *esse* to action, viz., command and praise.

Solomon lauded the ruling of the Spirit *(Prov. 16:32)*. Recognize the Spirit and it acts. Recognition has a subtle law of its own. Body, and its speech are woven into relationship with the Soul, or Self, or *esse,* by recognition. Walt Whitman said, "I believe in you, my Soul." He said, "Loose the throttle of my throat." So did Isaiah say, "Loose thy self from the bands of thy neck, O captive daughter of Zion!" *(Is. 52).*

The Hindus explain this for us by telling us to turn and speak to the divine Self back of us. As our speech has hitherto been all shot forward, speaking to our neighbor, so now at the turn of the tongue, we speak backward to upraise our outer self by our hidden Self. This Self back of us, like a Shekinah pillar of cloud by day and of fire by night, is the friend of our outer self, or outer life. It can make the outer life whole and strong, and sane.

Man is not really sane while his body is ill. For he that is truly sane knows the health he can waken outwardly by recognizing his Soul's free, flawless, immortal excellence.

"The Spirit of a man is the candle of the Lord", said Solomon *(Prov. 20:27)*. And by recognizing this candle sound health is established in the outer man. "Awake up, my glory!" shouted David *(Ps. 57:8)*. "Awake thou that sleepest!" cried Paul *(Eph. 5:14)*. They are addressing, with strong command, the ever-present glorious Soul. And both David and Paul thereby awoke divine chords of being in themselves for all ages to wonder at.

He whose Soul glows and flames through all he does and thinks, has discovered a bottomless well of living refreshment to draw from. Everything he does has the touch of spiritual charm about it. For the Soul is the everlasting reservoir of enchantment. "The fifth angel sounded," said John the Revelator *(Rev. 9)*, and a star-like character appeared upon the earth, teaching men to draw from the depths of their own Soul, or the bottomless well of power and glory. And John saw that the man of Soul showed men how to put their consciousness of flesh limitation and common sensations of pain and pleasure into trance, or sleep, for the sense of God's presence to be most real. And thereby should men know new laws of life, having in them as much strength as the scorpion law of labor, law of lucre, law of learning, law of loving have strength. This is the stone of the New Law that filled all the earth in Daniel's vision *(Dan. 2)*.

For centuries on centuries we have been urged by Hebrew and Hindu to praise and command the hidden limitless Self of us. Let us begin now, this night, to praise and command the Self: "Oh, Wonderful Me! Oh, strong and unspoilable Me! Beautiful Me! Influential Me, Enchanting and Immortal Wisdom!" It answers, "I am all that and more." For "It hath not entered into the heart of man to conceive," said Paul *(I Cor. 2)*, what is in the storehouse laid up.

Let us continue with strong commands to our great Self: Rise up, my Soul, and heal the sick wherever I walk! Show people how to be strong! Make people love God! Quicken me with heavenly fervor! Show me the finished kingdom through which I walk! Show me the words that make the world glad and sane!

The Soul, or Free Spirit, answers, "I can all that and more." We must never give over commanding the Soul Self every night of the life before we sleep. Some day, like Jesus of Nazareth, we shall sense our ever-present abilities. It was by the sense of his masterful Soul that he saw he could take all the sin and all the consequences of the sins of the world, into himself, and because he was full of the Godhead bodily, he could utterly annihilate sin, sickness and death.

There is a strange and very little observed law ever operative among us. It is the law of vicarious or transferred suffering. Jesus saw this law and entered into it, and for all who would accept his great offer there is freedom from unconscious or mechanical guilt. If a mother shuts her child into a dark closet to discipline it, thinking that she is doing right, how does she know that the shock of the closeness and the darkness causes arrested brain development in the child, and, under the action of natural law, he can never rise to his proper intelligence? Jesus offered to take her guilt and the child's bearing of the consequences of the same, into his own self, and thereby lift from both mother and child the weight of the law. "God sent forth his son to redeem them that were under the law" *(Gal. 4:5)*. He offered to do this for all unwitting sinners upon the earth. "He is the propitiation for our sins, and not for ours only but also for the sins of the whole world," said John *(I John 2:2)*.

Philip preached this great doctrine to the eunuch *(Acts 8)*. The eunuch asked if possibly it might not be each man's soul taking the consequences of his own unconscious guiltiness. Then Philip preached the opus of Jesus. Let us acknowledge the great and unprecedented and uncopy-able achievement of Jesus of Nazareth, who, by recognition of his own Soul, did the humanly impossible. He is the pivotal man. He is the Soul-bloom in the garden of man, the first fruits of them that slept *(I Cor. 15:20)*.

The stillness of our nonrecognition is called sleep. "It is high time that we awake out of sleep," said Paul to the Romans.

We will take Friday to acknowledge before High God the surpassing accomplishment of Jesus of Nazareth. "When thou shalt make his soul the offering for sin, the pleasure of the Lord shall prosper" *(Is. 58).*

The fifty-third chapter of Isaiah contains the full text of his coming accomplishment. Peter, John, Paul and Philip reaffirm the report as contemporary witnesses of the finished fact. Every one of them tells us to acknowledge before God that we walk through a redeemed healed, unpunishable world, because of the vicarious suffering of Jesus of Nazareth, who, being all Godhood, was and is forever, Christ Jesus — or God Jesus — the living manifestation of what man can do and be by recognition of his own sonship to Omnipotence. "That God the Father may give you the spirit of Wisdom and revelation for the acknowledgment of him" *(Eph. 1:17, margin).*

He found that death is the result of mechanical or mathematical guiltiness. And he took unto himself death, that might deliver them who through the fear — or expectation — of death were all their life-time drawn toward death *(Heb. 2:15).* "He hath abolished death," said Paul *(2 Tim. 1:10).*

Let us accept our liberty. Let us accept our health, let us accept our redemption, by stating what hath been done. So shall we by sighting one completed work enter upon our own ordained opus. "God is not unrighteous that he will forget our work" *(Heb. 6).*

As there is but one unit *one,* but as many expressions of the unit one as we please, each occupying an independent and differentiated position, so there is but one Supreme Self in the universe, manifesting as the Self of Jesus, or yourself, or myself.

And there is one work for each of us. As Jesus did his work, so we are to do our work. His work was to show the law of vicarious suffering. It is the natural religion of

Resumé

natural man having in it an action not much recognized on earth. The Hindu native women gash their flesh to draw the sufferings of their children to themselves. Catherine of Siena took several sicknesses into herself, and her neighbors were relieved.

We will accept the Scriptural doctrine that "Himself took our infirmities, and bare our sicknesses" (that we might go free) *(Matt. 8)*. We will believe the report, and to us shall the "Arm of the Lord," the finished work of Christ, "be revealed" *(Is. 53)*.

Every, Friday, let us lift up our voices to acknowledge, "Jesus Christ as Emmanuel (which being interpreted is, God with us), hath borne my griefs and carried my sorrows. He was wounded for my transgressions. He was bruised for my iniquities, the chastisement of my peace was upon him, and by his stripes I am healed. Himself took my infirmities and bare my sicknesses. He is the propitiation for my sins and not for mine only but for the sins of the world."

This acknowledgment is promised to send an ether balm across the heart and brain.

To Remember:

Commit to memory this page of Bible texts on the sixth Study:

"In him was life; and the life was the light of men." ~ *John 1:4.*

"All things are delivered unto me of my Father." ~ *Matthew 11:27.*

"And whatsoever ye shall ask in my name, that will I do." ~ *John 14:13.*

"That whatsoever ye shall ask of the Father in my name, he may give it you " ~ *John 15:16.*

"I press toward the mark for the prize of the high calling of God in Christ Jesus -- if in anything ye be otherwise minded God shall reveal, even this unto you." ~ *Paul to the Philippians 3:14, 15.*

"Call unto me, and I will answer thee, and show thee great and mighty things which thou knowest not " ~ *Jeremiah 33:3.*

"The Holy Ghost, whom the Father will send in my name, shall teach you all things." ~ *John 14:26.*

VI ILLUMINATION - UNDERSTANDING

When the disciples had associated with the Risen Christ long enough to sense that he had been wounded for the transgressions of a world, and that by acknowledgment of the same the world might go free -- "then opened he their understanding that they might understand the Scriptures" *(Luke 24:25)*. And the "Scriptures" he gave them was his own name: "The Holy Ghost whom the Father will send in my name shall teach you all things" *(John 14:26)*.

This name constitutes the most remarkable book ever mentioned on earth, for the Spirit of Truth it wakens shall guide into all truth, and show mankind of things to come *(John 16:13)*.

Every man's name conveys his qualities. If he is a strong intellect, the repetition of his name, especially the calling of his name earnestly, imbues the caller with new intellectual strength. If he is heroic in battle, a certain accession of heroism stirs the caller. Cruden, in his immortal Concordance, under the head of "Call," declares that things which had no existence may come into sight by strong words of calling, as *Rom. 4:17*:

> "I have made thee like unto Him, even God, who quickeneth the dead, and calleth those things which be not as though they were." And, "Who hath God so nigh unto them as the Lord our God is in all things that we call unto Him for?" *(Deut. 4:7)*.

Isaiah lamented that no man called for justice *(Is. 59:4)*.

The Gnostics of old proclaimed that the word *Abraxas* was a sacred *pleroma*-name, or word: that is, a sacred word full of blessings, to fall upon whomsoever strongly called it. The Hebrews at one time believed that the fullness of blessing was in the name "Habrakah." Thomas Carlyle called, "O Fortune! Grant me literary distinction!" The giving-forth power of some names has been known for centuries. Canon

Farrar, in his *Life of Christ*, says it would be well for us if we were to pick up that old well-known law and practice it.

Surely, by this law, the man who has shown the most superhuman power must confer the most superhuman powers through his name. Therefore the disciples of Jesus Christ became the most wonderful Apostles of doctrine that the world has ever known; for no man's name ever named stands for such colossal achievements as the Christ Jesus they spent so many weeks calling upon.

John the Revelator had been among these callers, and he knew that the little book in the right hand of him that sat upon the throne *(Rev. 5)* was the name, *Jesus Christ.*

"The throne had six steps" (*1 Kings 10:19*). "Six" is the number of attainment to spiritual insight, or illumination above the brain. It is often rendered "understanding." We can know a great deal, be mathematicians, linguists, dialecticians, without this brightness of the Over-Soul shining upon our words and deeds. Man can be so full of mathematics that other men will round the globe to sit at his feet for instruction. This is the meaning of "six"–*i.e.,* throneship.

Man can be so full of epidemic that whosoever, but touches the hem of his garment may be cast down into a bed of sickness. Has anyone seen a man so full of the contagion of God that whosoever touched his raiment was instantly healed, and himself shed abroad health like a contagion?

Saul was told to call upon the name Jesus Christ *(Acts 22)*. His name was changed to "Paul", and his aprons and handkerchiefs were full of the contagion of God *(Acts 19)*. As many as touched Jesus were made whole *(Matt. 14:36)*. Whoever stepped into the shadow of Peter, calling on Jesus Christ, was healed *(Acts 5:15)*.

Whosoever called on Minerva the goddess of wisdom, was, in the days of Aristides, the Minerva-imbued Archon of Athens, believed to inhale wisdom.

Resumé

There was a contagion ready to burst forth in the name of Jesus Christ in old days. That contagion still exists, but there is either curiosity mixed with doubt, or pure doubt without curiosity, in the minds of all who are now told to call upon it, to cry sharply upon it, as Clovis, King of the Franks, cried at the battle of Tolbiac, through and above his doubt, to answering victory.

The name is like an alabaster box that has to be sharply broken open in order that the precious ointment may be obtained. Is it not written, "Thy name is as ointment poured forth?" *(Cant. 1:3)* Nebuchadnezzar called Shadrach, Meshach and Abednego to come forth, and they came forth out of the fiery furnace *(Dan. 3)*. Aristides at one time called both Minerva and Aesculapius so sharply and inhaled their influence so thoroughly that they came from the skies and stood plainly in his room.

We will choose the name of the one who wrought forth power over earth and heaven, and in whose name is folded the new name with new powers in it *(Rev. 2:17)*. We will choose the name of him who hath redeemed us out of every nation *(Rev. 5)*. To sight toward an object and call its name is to finally be related to it. Pope Sixtus V stretched out his hands toward Rome when he was a mere lad and said, "I will be pope of Rome." Then every event and circumstance moved him to the papal seat.

"We can always see how the ideal of a man started with some fixed attention. Abbot Lawrence Lowell, President of Harvard University, had all his life studied principles of government. His steady attention thereto placed him at the head of the College of Governors. We must give our strict attention to something supernally worthwhile. Let us take Saturday and Sunday to call upon the name *Jesus Christ*. As the Jews gathered the same portion of manna for Saturday and Sunday so we will gather the manna promised to fall in the calling of that name *(Rev. 2)*.

"It is the name above every name," said Paul *(Eph. 1)*.

We will stretch our hands and cry to that name. "Doth not Wisdom cry?" *(Prov. 8)*. Let us declare our great need, for he answers, "What wilt thou?" And he has promised, "Whatsoever ye shall ask in my name, that will I do" *(John 14:13)*.

The Zoroastrians believed that the *Ardai Viraf* name reveals the mystic doctrine. Pythagoras believed that there is an ineffable name that is key to the mysteries of the universe. According to the Christian Scriptures the name Jesus Christ is that revealing name, key to all understanding.

To Remember:

Commit to memory this page of Bible texts on the seventh Study:

"But in the days of the voice of the seventh angel, when he shall begin to sound, the mystery of God should be finished.

"And the voice which I heard from heaven spake unto me again and said, Go and take the little book which is open in the hand of the angel. . . .

"And I took the little book out of the angel's hand, and ate it up, and it was in my mouth sweet as honey: and as soon as I had eaten it my belly was bitter" (mind cure or wormwood).

"And he said unto me, Thou must prophesy again, before many peoples, and nations, and tongues and kings." ~ *Revelation 10:7-11.*

"And the seventh angel poured out his vial into the air; and there came a great voice out of the temple of heaven, from the throne, saying, It is done." ~ *Revelation 16:17.*

"The, tongue of the wise is health." ~ *Proverbs 12:18.*

VII MINISTRY

> And if men slight thee take no heed, And if they hate thee have no care. Sing thou thy song and do thy deed. Hope thou thy hope and pray thy prayer. And claim no crown this does not give. *-Beatty.*

David feels the Spirit of the Lord speaking by him *(2 Sam. 23:2)*. He has caught the tongue of praise. To speak silently the spiritual truth to our neighbor and never to agree with his physical descriptions, is to live by the word of the Spirit, or the Soul's law. It is speaking the truth. "Let every man speak truth to his neighbor, and let none of you imagine evil against him," was the great doctrine of Zechariah *(8:16, 17)*.

It is the day of the new tongue when the true description is perpetually in our heart, and in our thought, and in our speech. This new tongue toward our neighbor is the new preaching, or the new prophesying, which John heard the angel telling him to go forth with to the people and to the nations *(Rev. 10)*.

Always "seven" is identified with heavenly speech, or description of the free Spirit. "And when he had opened the seventh seal there was silence in heaven" *(Rev. 8)*. "Heaven" means harmony. "In the seventh place the Lord imparted them speech" *(Apocrypha)*.

To see the free Self is to speak words that harmonize with it. "Beautiful, Strong, Joyous, Flawless," we say silently. We have come to the seventh stone of character, when we see the beautiful, the strong, the flawless namely, the chrysolite stone *(Rev. 21)*. Chrysolite means, "touch of gold."

Nobody is poor or old or sick who comes near the man of right speech; for his tongue is health whether he speaks silently or audibly *(Prov. 12: 18)*. Pliny wrote that some people carry health by their presence. No one can fail to carry health if his secret tongue is all praise, never yielding to condemnation, no matter what the claim or temptation.

"At the seventh hour Jesus said, 'Go thy way, thy son liveth'" *(John 4)*. It is the seventh praise repeated over and over that the Seventh Angel starts. Joshua sounded the horns over and over on the seventh day.

All the rest of our life we are to praise the free Self of our neighbor. No man so mistaken, but we are to praise his wise free Spirit only. No man so negligent or reprehensible, but we are to praise silently his integrity and righteousness. No man so old, but we are to praise his beautiful free Self. No man so sick or lame, but we are to praise his flawless divinity.

On Monday we must choose some sick or palsied or wicked person, as he appears outwardly, and praise his divine Self. Speak silently to his Omnipotent God-self. No matter how long it takes, keep on, Monday, after Monday.

"The Lord turned the captivity of Job when he prayed for his friends" *(Job 42:10)*. Something falls away from us as we pray in the words of praise and command to the Free Omnipotence, or the Jesus Christ of our Neighbor.

Pantaleon, in days of Maximian, took a palsied and dying man by the hand and spoke to his Jesus Christ free Self, and the man was instantly healed.

There is no set formula for praising the transcending Self. Joseph kept on sighting peace and silently speaking peace to his eleven brethren, exactly as his father Jacob had commanded him, for twenty years. At last the brethren were all healed, even of wickedness.

Here is a silent description with great awakening in it. Make it the key speech or your opinion of your neighbor every time you see him outwardly as sick, or poor or unhappy. Let no such images keep before your eye. Remember the Real Self. Describe it. And on Monday remember the particular case you are to bring forth out of the darkness, as:

> I see you, John Marston, above, transcending your past. I see you unweighted, free; I see you as complete Spirit.

Nothing can be added to you; nothing can be taken from you. I see you as Health. You are one with Universal Health. Nothing can spoil Universal Health. It is God putting away disease. I see you as Omnipotence. Nothing can defeat Omnipotence. It puts aside weakness and shows me God working before me for you, and through you, and by you, forever and ever. You face me up as God, unweighted, unattached, unspoiled forever and ever. I see you as Wisdom looking toward me to speak by you of your heavenly wholeness and peace. I *see* you as Peace. I see you facing me as Peace that the world cannot take away. I see you as Peace putting aside discord. God is showing Peace now with its touch on your outer life at every point. You are free God becoming visible for my sake, that truth may prevail.

By the grace of God Almighty—the grace of the Holy Ghost—by the grace of Jesus Christ now falling upon you and working in you, I command you to show yourself to all the world as untainted Health and free Omnipotence from this day forth.

To Remember:

Commit to memory this page of Bible texts on the eighth Study:

"Circumcised on the eighth day." ~ *Philippians 3:5.*

"Ye stiff-necked and uncircumcised in heart and ears, ye do always resist the Holy Ghost: as your fathers did, so *do ye.*" ~ *Acts 7:51.*

"He that escapeth shall come unto thee to cause thee to hear it with thine ears." ~ *Ezekiel 24:26.*

"The ears, of them that hear shall hearken." ~ *Isaiah 32:3.*

"For through the voice of the Lord shall the Assyrian be beaten down..." ~ *Isaiah 30:81*

"Thine ears shall hear a word behind thee saying, this is the way." ~ *Isaiah 30:21.*

"The accuser of our brethren is cast down." ~ *Revelation 12:10.*

"Every tongue that shall rise against thee in judgment, thou shalt condemn." ~ *Isaiah 54:17.*

"Now go, write it before them in a book." ~ *Isaiah 30:8.*

"Blotting out the handwriting of ordinances against us nailing it to his cross..." ~ *Colossians 2:14.*

"The eighth, a beryl..." ~ *Revelation 21:20.*

"The eighth was Shimeon" (hearkening) ~ *Ezra 10:31.*

VIII MINISTRY

"The eighth lot came forth to Abijah" *(1 Chron. 24).* "Abijah" is the son of the speaker, Aaron. A "son" is an idea. The order is very direct. An idea always comes to us at some point in our description of the Real Self of our neighbor. This idea tells us what to add to our previous phrases and commands. Each neighbor needs some special message. When an idea comes we can speak it audibly to the neighbor, if we like. Its effect is almost always instantaneous. If it is the message his whole being craves, his disease will soon drop off and his smile break forth.

King Bruce watched a spider, and a sudden courage and valor flamed up in him. He had stopped his own thinking for a few seconds, and what he watched affected his whole constitution. St. Cyran, Father Confessor at the Port Royal Nunnery, instructed the nuns to look toward God in a listening attitude. "He has something to tell you," said St. Cyran.

In the Talmud it is written that the Messiah will come when the people hearken to the voice of God. In the Old Testament, we are told that the escaped or the free Spirit, will cause us to hear, or to have the right idea *(Ez. 24:26).* After eight days, Jesus the Risen came visibly present to the waiting disciples, and said, "Peace be unto you." *(John 20).*

Peter and James and John heard Moses and Elias speaking of the future of Jesus, after about eight days *(Luke 9).* Aeneas had kept his bed eight years waiting for the right word, which Peter then gave him *(Acts 9:33).*

There is the word of punishment if the eye is downward toward the sinfulness of the people. Ezekiel was a great hearkener for the punishments that are exactly meted out to different sins. So did the Zoroastrians hearken for the different kinds of results of different wickednesses: "If crime is not punished, there shall be pestilence." "If justice is not done to the innocent, war shall follow." "When some pay tithes, and some do not, drought is the punishment."

It is only the upward watcher who hears the promise of peace and health and forgiveness. Ben Soma, the Jew, hears the words, "Despise no person and no thing for everyone and each thing have their appointed hour." That which is told from above is always of universal application and universal worth and is therefore worth writing, as we have been taught by Jeremiah *(30:2)*, "Write thee all the words that I have spoken unto thee in a book."

We may spend a while in a listening attitude before one whose Free Omnipotence we have praised. The air has been spiritualized by describing silently the Free Spirit. We are ready, like Hannah *(1 Sam.)*, to hear the words which strike into view the answer to our prayer. "He shall come unto thee to cause thee to hear" *(Ez. 24)*.

We must repeat the idea firmly, as if it were the final word. Zechariah repeated it three times: "Thus saith the Lord of hosts, Turn ye unto me" *(Zech. 1)*.

The "eighth" is circumcision *(Phil. 3:5)*. "Circumcised on the eighth day" means that we are cut off from the stories of pain, disease, poverty, death. We are hearkening intently to the heavenly speech. "O ye uncircumcised of heart and of ear!" cried Stephen, "Ye do always resist the Holy Ghost" *(Acts 7)*. The Holy Ghost is the teacher. The harvest of sayings from the Holy Ghost above causes the end of the world *(Matt. 13)*.

The sign of the cross is the sign of the undoing of the past by the sight and hearing of the New. It is the sign of the blotting out of ordinances against us, as Paul discovered *(Col 2)*. The Egyptians and the Chaldeans made the sign of the cross to signify that the present state of affairs is blotted out. The priests of Isis blotted out the evil. The priests of Serapis blotted out the good, "I can make wiles in battle; I can make corn and cattle; that they shall never thrive," was their chant.

Resumé

The Christian St. Felix spat upon the metal image of Serapis in the time of Diocletian, and it fell down from its pedestal and was literally broken to powder. Spittle was in old times regarded as a charm by Jews, Greeks and Romans. When they made the sign of the cross they wet the finger with spittle. It is the symbol of erasure.

As soon as Odilo of Cluny met sickness or blindness he wet his finger and made the sign of the cross, to signify that what was presenting itself was nothing at all: the unseen Christ was all.

How can the ears hear the truth regarding a blind man while the blindness seems so real and sad? No wonder that we need to have some sign that the flesh profiteth nothing, as Jesus said *(John 6)*. Only the words of the Healing Spirit are life and healing strength.

Take Tuesday to blot out all the words of sickness, pain and death. Take Tuesday to erase the pain, poverty and disease, from over the free Spirit of some one person. Take Tuesday to hearken to the particular message that belongs to Monday's case. Hearken all day Tuesday to the voice of the Lord whispering behind thee, as Isaiah said *(Isaiah 30)*. It comes as an idea. It is undeniably true. Remember that the truth makes free *(John 8)*.

All sick, or lame, or unhappy people would spring suddenly into freedom if some one would speak to them the truth belonging to them. "A right word, how good it is; who can measure the force of a right word?" "He sent forth his word and healed them" *(Ps. 107:20)*. "He wakeneth thine ear to hear as the learned" *(Is. 50:4)*. "The tongue of the wise is health" *(Prov. 12:18)*. "A good word maketh the heart glad" *(Prov. 12:25)*. "The Lord God hath opened mine ear and I was not rebellious, neither turned away back" *(Is. 50:5)*.

They that can hear the word of healing have touched the beryl stone of character. They are of value on land and sea as the beryl stone is the color of both land and sea. Their written words convey health to all who read them.

To Remember:

Commit to memory this page of Bible texts on the ninth Study:

"The ninth a topaz." ~ *Revelation 21:20,*

"The topaz was in the breastplate, and had the name of Simeon upon it." ~ Cruden's *Concordance, p. 687.*

"Thy words were found and I did eat them, and thy word was unto me the joy and rejoicing of my heart." ~ *Jeremiah 15:16.*

"The joy of the Lord is your strength." ~ *Nehemiah 8:10.*

"The friend of the bridegroom, which standeth and heareth, rejoiceth greatly." ~ *John 3:29.*

"He that is of a merry heart hath a continual feast." ~ *Proverbs 16:15.*

"A merry heart doeth good like a medicine." ~ *Proverbs 17:22*

"They shall lay hands on the sick, and they shall recover." ~ *Mark 16:18.*

"Ye shall eat of old fruit till the ninth year." ~ *Leviticus 25:22.*

IX MINISTRY

The law of listening is the law of joy. "The friend of the bridegroom, which standeth and heareth, rejoiceth greatly" *(John 3:29)*. The upward watcher gets his inner ear opened to know how matters and things are progressing.

Isaiah tells Hezekiah: "Thou shalt die." He is judging by the law of impetus downward. He does not see that Hezekiah has obeyed his prophets' injunction to lift up his eyes and behold who is the Creator *(Is. 40:26)*. King Hezekiah had a strong moral vitality and could lift up his eyes out of the depths of pain and death, and proclaim with all his heart, that the upward watch was life, even though his eyes were failing *(Is. 38)*.

Isaiah did not have very cheerful views of his neighbors. This was the rock on which he split.

The mystics have always failed in proportion as they have insisted on the wickedness and failings of their neighbors. Even Zechariah, who proclaimed that we must never imagine evil of or against anybody, was so under the spell of the prophets before him that he heard the voice of the howling of the wicked shepherds *(Zech. 11:3)*, and not the chants of the forgiven.

But even at the cross Jesus saw the forgiven world. It is a matter of strong fixed sight that gives the ideas that show in conduct and flesh.

If you forget a name look steadily toward the person who bears it and the name will come to you. If you do not get it promptly it is evident that your vision does not stay fixed. The photographic plate has to be exposed to the object long enough to catch its impress distinctly or the configuration is indistinct. Try again and look longer. Looking toward God on high, Moses caught laws just suited to people of his age. Looking toward God on high, Mohammed caught laws just suited to people of his age. Looking toward God on high we can catch the law just suited to the person who seems to be unhappy. If we do not catch the law at first we must look again.

The words caught from above have always uplifting and healing potency in them. "Thy word was unto me the joy and rejoicing of my heart" *(Jer. 15:16)*.

The description of the strong and beautiful Self localizes the universal truth. This localizing is called healing. "I will give you pastors that shall feed you with knowledge," said the Lord to Jeremiah, *(Jer.* 3), and all the people shall be new and glad. How can pastors feed with the joy of right if they have not themselves been fed?

The Hindus have taught that we must animate the particular from the universal. The "Particular" is the man or object. There is a root of strength and vitality about everybody and everything that the right speech with the right tonic in it would animate into astonishing virility. Even an apparently dead tree is reachable by one with this mystery of vitalizing tone in his secret speech.

It is an unkillable quality resident at the roots of life, as the actinic ray that sweetens the grape is an unquenchable constituent of the sunshine.

Joy must be quickened from somewhere. The Scriptures declare that it is quickened from hearing vitalizing truth. "Thy words were found and I did eat them; and thy word was unto me the joy and rejoicing of my heart" *(Jer. 15: 16)*.

This joy that comes of being in direct communication with the I AM is an increasable product. Gideon got such a new estimate of himself by coming into speaking relationship with the Supernal Original, that he rose from being of no consequence among the Jews to bold leadership. Abraham talked with angels, and transcended his neighbors.

We speak to the Soul, the Jesus Christ of man, and we are comrading with the Supernal neighbor. We are keeping high company. God hath set us on high because we have

Resumé 587

first known his name *(Ps. 91:14)*, and at every turn we behold Divinity manifesting as beauty, health, joy, the outward signs of the Universal Highest. Joy is the leviathan power resident in man. Whoever can wake God joy in his neighbor brings forth the most powerful principle he covers.

It is a secret charm which people covet and follow after and get comfort from. Haggai says that it is the real desire of all nations *(Hag. 2:7)*. He is told three times in the ninth month that the heavens shall shake and the desire of the nations shall come *(Hag. 2)*. Its symbol is the topaz stone. The true topaz is so valuable that it is worth a million dollars. It signifies that the triumph of steadfast vision has come in the words which set nobility where wickedness had hitherto been visible, as Joseph's long vision and unvarying speech, under the direction of his father Jacob *(Gen. 37)*, finally transformed his murderous brethren into lovers; as Peter and John transformed the impotent man at the gate of the Temple called Beautiful *(Acts 3)*, and in these days certain people among us can transform cramps and deformity into beauty.

Ofttime glancing to the Heights brings back transforming words that stir the joy chords. For it is a joy to tell the words that transform pain into peace, and disease into health. It awakens youth to feel the joy currents leap within us. It makes the hand magnetic to the angel, so that it pulls the angel of man's presence forward when we stretch forth the hand.

Jesus touched the free Spirit of the leper *(Matt. 8)*, and the angel of the child of Nain *(Luke 7)*. He said we ought to lay hands on the sick to make them recover *(Mark 10:18)*.

He means that we have come to the ninth stone of character, where the angel is tangible to us. The early Roman Catholics called the tangibility of the angels the real meaning of the number nine.

Let us practice touching the invisible yet tangibly present angel of some sick person. Let us take Wednesday to stretch forth invisible bands and urge the angel to make himself manifest. This urge is our will. It is the man's will. It is God's will. This is the song of the topaz, viz., the universal will to be well.

There is a pulling power in the hand as we say to the Angel of the presence, "Come forth! It is God's will, it is your will, it is my will that you be well and strong and glad. Come forth!" Tell him your most joyous text. Repeat it over and over as a song is "I drew them with cords, with bands of love — and they knew not that I healed them" *(Hosea 11:4, 3).*

To Remember:

Commit to memory this page of Bible texts on the tenth Study:

"The tenth shall be holy to the Lord." ~ *Leviticus 27:32.*

"And the people blessed all the men that willingly offered themselves to dwell in Jerusalem." ~ *Nehemiah 11:1, 2.*

"And the people came up out of Jordan on the tenth day." ~ *Joshua, 4:19.*

"Then shalt thou cause the trumpet of the jubilee to sound on the tenth day." ~ *Leviticus 25:9.*

"I will put my law in their inward parts." ~ *Jeremiah 31:33.*

"They said unto him, Master, where dwellest thou? He saith unto them, 'Come and see.' They came and saw where he dwelt, and abode with him that day, for it was about the tenth hour." ~ *John 1:38, 39.*

"I in you..." ~ *John 14:20*.

"Go stand and speak to the people in the temple." ~ *Acts 5:20*.

X MINISTRY

The tenth stone of character is the chrysoprasus *(Rev. 21)*. This signifies that no situation daunts us. The people came up out of the raging waters of Jordan on the tenth day *(Josh. 4)*, but they had not noticed the raging waters, their vision was so glued to liberty. To them the water had parted *(Josh. 3)*.

When we mean to heal our neighbor we sometimes find that his whole secret mind opposes the healing truth we so ardently tell him. His mind and body get excited with pain or sickness. All his old diseases show forth. Dysentery, influenza, fever, rheumatism, disturb him. He is irritable, confused, weepy.

To be phased by such a showing forth is to prove that we have not come to the tenth stone of character. "If thou faint in the day of adversity, thy strength is small," said Solomon *(Prov. 24:10)*.

To stand on our stone of confidence, assurance, certainty, with respect to a man who is very sick, is to reach the everlasting health which shines like a sun back of his sickness. That sun with its healing beams can brush aside his sickness as the sun in the skies brushes aside the clouds. The clouds may hurry and scurry and glower darkly, but they have nothing to do with altering the sun. The sun is the same it was before the clouds gathered.

When the Sun of health back of sickness is once seen, the sickness is not recognized. It is a great day when nothing moves us, either pain, or disease, or crying, because we are sighting the reality of peace. It brings forth a happy neighbor. He feels the apple green of a new base. He suddenly shines forth saying, "I see that my life is God, to whom I am looking for life."

After years of looking upward to God as his Sovereign, a man, passing through many vicissitudes, was suddenly set into prosperity beyond his expectations. This gave him great leverage with his neighbors, and his doctrine that "God reigns," was hastened to. He was not looking for money; he was looking for the Great Fiat, "Look unto me," and the Divine Providence, the Countenance that shineth was his goal, but the effect was a dominant relationship with his fellow men.

The adversities that shrouded his path had been the opposing activities that would have shrouded through his whole lifetime had not his high statement and his high watch held out to the end, finally parting the waters of his Jordan.

To yield to doubt and fear because conditions are gloomy is not to hold out to the end of the clouds. Some people let go of God and the great truth that they started forth with. So they never see their victory in this life. It is pretty certain they will have to try again somewhere, but how much better to settle the question of the high watch and the truth of the Soul right here, now!

Our neighbor is Free Spirit. No pain, no disease, can be added to the free Spirit, or taken from it. Our neighbor is not flesh and blood, quaking and crying. We touch him as the angel of God's presence. We speak to him as Omnipotent Soul. This is truth, whether he shows it outwardly today or not. If he does not show it outwardly, but instead he complains and has more trouble than ever, the truth is true all the same.

"Mine integrity within me," said David *(Ps. 1:8)*. Job's wife asked him if he still held to his integrity while he was still in his misery *(Job 2:9)*.

At our interior God-point we see as God sees and know as God knows. In the midst of affliction we must speak forth this secret knowing and seeing. It is the heavenly fact told us in secret to be proclaimed upon the housetops *(Matt. 10).*

Whenever anyone to whom we have whispered the praises of Soul begins to act quite wretched in his body, let us look to our temple place, our sanctuary within, where we know as God and see as God. Let us "look to the rock whence we are hewn" *(Is. 51).* Let us read from the law as it is in our inward parts *(Jer. 31:33).*

We will take Thursday to regard our neighbor as within, at our hidden meeting place with God. Also on Thursday we will speak to the one that we love best, at our meeting place with God.

> In mine integrity within me, where I see as God and know as God, I know you, John Child, as free Spirit. I know you as alive with life that death cannot touch. I know you as strong with Omnipotence, whole and complete as Son of God, wise to know yourself as unhurt by matter or mind. Show yourself to all the world as I know you at my integrity point. Acknowledge with boldness and confidence that you are free, strong, glad Spirit, without pain or disease.

This is a good treatment to give concerning one who has had an accident or who has been taken suddenly ill. It takes him past the chemical change, or Jordan River he is passing through. There was an angel near Daniel when he fainted and was sick certain days.

There is an angel always standing near one in trouble. Let us agree with the angel and see health and strength made visible by our firm secret insistence.

"He hath put wisdom in the inward parts" *(Job 38:36).* There is no healing that we can trust like the healing that comes from recognizing from own unshakable centre just how it is forever with our neighbor.

"Go stand and speak to the people in the temple," said the angel to the apostles *(Acts 5:20).*

"Ye are the temple" *(I Cor. 3).* "I in you" *(John 14:20).*

This practice disciplines for new and impromptu treatments unsuggested by previous experiences. "Now therefore go, and I will be with thy mouth, and teach thee what thou shalt say" *(Ex. 4:12).*

To Remember:

Commit to memory this page of Bible texts on the eleventh Study:

"And they took knowledge of them that they had been with Jesus." ~ *Acts 4:13.*

"Thou hast been in Eden, the Garden of God; and the ruby was thy covering." ~ *Ezekiel 28.*

"My judgment was unto me a robe." ~ *Job 29:14.*

"A king that sitteth in the throne of judgment, scattereth away all evil with his eyes." ~ *Proverbs 20:8.*

"God is judge himself." ~ *Psalm 50:6.*

"Their judgment shall proceed of themselves." ~ *Habakkuk 1:7.*

"I will make my judgment to rest for a light." ~ *Isaiah 51:4.*

"All the heathen shall see my judgment." ~ *Ezekiel 39:21.*

"In the eleventh year was the house finished." ~ *I Kings 6:38.*

XI MINISTRY

"In the eleventh year was the house finished," and Solomon said that whosoever should look to the house would be set at liberty (*I Kings 6*).

"House" signifies character. A man's judgment constitutes the sum total of his character. A good judge is more sought unto than a king, for he establishes right relations, man with man. Something about right appeals. Even an infant weeps at injustice and stops weeping when justice is rendered.

One with right judgment according to the Jesus Christ of himself knows instantly what to do to heal the sick man, or raise the dead man, or help the disheartened.

All the voluntary practices of the presence of God which we are making have been the inspirations of such as have beheld their Heavenly Father's countenance till they knew that whatever they themselves did was right, and they could see that whatever was happening outwardly had back of it and over it some wonderful blessing. They did not have to scramble and pull things and events into order. By sighting the Trend, or the Providence, or the Fiat, and seeing the finished fact, they accomplished mighty things.

St. John of the Cross ploughed twice as many furrows as any other of the monks, because his eye was on the finished land of God. The whole creation is finished, complete, now, in the eyes of God. To see for three seconds a thing in its completeness, as it truly is, is to find the thing acting of its own weight to exhibit itself to everybody as complete.

Dr. Gordon of Boston wrote about the new healing as a process of seeing a strong arm where a withered one claimed to exist, as Jesus cried with a loud voice to the living Lazarus.

Resumé

Whatever we see with the inner eye comes by and by to the outer eye. Everywhere we look a finished objective faces us. It is the thing as God sees it. "Why dost thou show me iniquity?" cried Habakkuk, "therefore doth judgment never go forth from me" *(Hab. 1)*. It is the angel of repose between God and man to see as God sees. "Is he not too pure to behold iniquity?" *(Hab. 1:13)*.

The Mohammedan Caliph Ali found that every man's lot or portion in life is seeking him, or looking toward him. He called upon us to be at rest from seeking our good. It is in straight line with us. We can pray as if we had received, for here it is, no matter what it is we have asked for. "Pray as if ye had received ~ believe that ye receive," said Jesus *(Mark 11)*. "Ask what ye will," he said *(John 15)*.

Judgment is communicable. Rai Shalligram, a postmaster in Northwestern India, saw that Divine Providence was under his feet and moving along with him. It was so real to him that he concluded to go away from his good business and let himself be fed without doing anything at all. Providence would always take good care of him, he said. No one could look at the light burning in the upper chamber of his house without feeling that he also could give up his business and be a wanderer, fed by Universal Good.

Notice how the mothers of India threw their babies into the Ganges, because their dervishes held the fixed judgment that it was pleasing to God to drown infants. Notice how the Shunammite woman said her child was well, because she saw Elisha's face, and his judgment laid its steadying words of life on her heart *(2 Kings 4)*.

So we catch God-judgment from the face of God. "Many seek the ruler's face, but every man's judgment cometh from the Lord," said Solomon *(Prov. 29:26)*. We have generally caught only prejudices, notions, what Jeremiah called "foxes across Mount Zion" *(Lam. 5)*.

We will take Friday to stop throwing any estimates out over people. We will let the finished good of them declare itself to us.

By this stopping of thoughts engendered by associating with downward watching men, the Son of God faces us in all men, and his judgment and our judgment is one judgment.

"The eleven stars did obeisance to Joseph" *(Gen. 37)*. This means that every estimate falls down into nothingness before the God-estimate. "Joseph" means, "he will add." That is, he will add to life as it now stands, a life by a miracle of God. He will add to gold as it now stands riches by the miracle of God.

Joab told David not to count his army. "God shall add unto the people an hundred-fold how many soever they may be," he said. But David's own judgment was hot within him, and Joab's words were unheeded. So there was disaster in Jerusalem *(2 Sam. 24)*.

To let the ark move forward is to let the great Trend alone, to rest, because it is finished. "In earing time and harvest thou shalt rest," for, "God shall bring forth thy judgment as the noon-day" *(Ps. 37:6)*.

"The eleventh was the jacinth" — the red rubelite. Pushing red to its acme of perfection it is the priceless ruby, emblem of priceless judgment.

Beauty is another word for judgment. Beauty is poise, balance, as judgment is balance. "Out of Zion, the perfection of beauty, God hath shined" *(Ps. 50:2)*.

According to Thy judgment it is well with me, therefore it is well. According to Thy judgment it is well with all men, therefore it is well.

To Remember:

Commit to memory this page of Bible texts on the twelfth Study:

"And the twelfth lot came forth to Jakim" (whom God sets up). ~ *I Chronicles 24:12.*

"And the twelfth lot came forth to Hashabiah" (leader of the hosts of song). ~ *I Chronicles 25:19.*

"The twelfth foundation was an amethyst." ~ *Revelations 21:20.*

"Canst thou bring forth the twelve signs" ~ *Job 38:32 (margin).*

"Then two shall be in the field; the one shall be taken, the other left." ~ *Luke 17:36.*

"To the angel of the church in Pergamos, write..." ~ *Revelations 2:12*

To your Angel, Greeting: ~

You are Spirit of Life, making hardy the flesh and inspiring the perceptions ~

You quicken the whole being with genius ~

You fix the heart with divine purpose ~

You write your name with the Saints of Light ~

Your new powers are to-day manifest.

XII MINISTRY

"The twelfth lot came forth to Jakim" - whom God sets up (*I Chron. 24:12*). "He is set on high because he hath known my name" *(Ps. 91:14)*. Jakim is head of the twelfth course of priests. Jakim, the true high priest, is not man-taught. He is taught from above. Elisha was such a priest and this put him at the head of the schools of the prophets at Jericho and Gilgal.

He had poured water on the hands of Elijah and otherwise waited upon him like a menial, because he had seen that Elijah communed face to face with Jehovah. This gave a quality to the association. "Where is the God of Elijah?" was his cry when Elijah flew upward *(2 Kings 2:14)*. He did not mourn Elijah's departure. His secret quest was God.

Tesla's secret vigils with electricity have set him in the forefront of electricians. Napoleon's secret watch toward high seats gave him the crown.

"And the twelfth lot came forth to Hashabiah," head of the twelfth course of Levitical singers *(I Chron. 6)*. The Levitical singers cause men to forget trouble and anger as Elisha forgot his animosity toward King Jehoram, when he heard the musical instruments playing dulcet melodies *(2 Kings 3)*, as Paul and Silas forgot they were in prison while singing of the free Spirit *(Acts 16)*.

When curses can be turned into blessings we have touched the divine alchemy. The oyster that turns the anguish-giving sand grain into a pearl with the lustre of the skies in its whiteness, is emblem of man glorying in the midst of affliction. "We glory in tribulations," said Paul *(Rom. 5:3)*. Paul was the collect of all the Apostolic virtues in the earth. It took all the twelve Apostles to strike his curses into blessings. He was the convert from animosity to identification. "Canst thou bring forth the twelve signs?" asks God of Job *(38:32)*.

Any moment our obedient watch may turn Saul into a Paul among those unto whom we are ministering. The practice of looking toward the Judge of all earth who doeth right *(Gen. 18:25)*, causes us to recognize the right judgment native to every man, woman, child, on earth.

As what we recognize comes to the surface in its own good time, our neighbor's outward actions and speech must soon be according to our recognition.

Men catch our prejudices as they catch our measles. They catch our right judgment as they catch our smallpox. Notice how soon our family stops drinking tea if we have a prejudice against tea. Notice how soon they look up if we look up.

"By me kings reign," saith the Lord of Hosts *(Prov. 8:15)*. This means that we have kingship by associating with the king. We have wisdom by associating with the Author of Wisdom. "I will instruct thee and teach thee," he saith *(Ps. 32:8)*.

At a certain point of attention to mathematics the student touches the origin of reckoning and can perform any given calculation with numbers. Then he is master of his art. He radiates reckoning. It is the same with the musician. Zangwill's Baal Shem was Master of the Holy Name and could work miracles by it. But he had had to give strict attention to it for a lifetime before its magic mysteries were his own. At the point of their radiating mathematics, the Oriental monarchs sought the Masters of the science of mathematics to associate with royal children, that they might easily outstrip other children.

At the point of identification with the King of Kings and Lord of Lords, the world seeks the men and women so identified, to snatch health and vigor from their bright flying sparks of secret God-quality. They rest from their efforts but their works are effectual, as it is written, "They rest from their labors, and their works do follow them" *(Rev. 14:13)*.

God gives us this rest, and our works go forth.

"I will give you rest," he saith *(Matt. 11:28)*. Did not Paul's clothing radiate his secret relationship with Him who healeth all our diseases?

It is the highest state of ministry possible when without thinking anything or trying in any way to help our neighbors we are yet their health and their joy. "Let us labor therefore to enter into that rest," said Paul *(Heb. 4:11)*.

The twelfth symbolic stone of character is the amethyst *(Rev. 21)*. It is the emblem of rest, of arrival. The harness is put off; we, passing through the valley of Baca (weeping), make it a well of refreshment *(Ps. 84:6)*.

As the ruby is most precious of all the precious stones, so the amethyst is least precious, in the estimation of man. It is the emblem of taking the weak things of this world to confound the mighty and the prudent *(1 Cor. 1:27)*. He who touches the twelfth characteristic has no hope. What shall one hope for who hath attained all? Does the bridegroom hope for his bride when she is already the mother of his children? The amethyst symbolizes one without expectation. This is a state held in low esteem on earth, but in heaven it is the state of the angels. He who touches the twelfth characteristic is indifferent to sickness and crying. Does the sun regard whether it is ripening the apple or rotting the pear?

He is the greatest healer who is so identified with Health that even his outer ears cannot hear complaints of sickness. "Who is deaf as my messenger that I sent?" saith the Lord *(Is. 42:19)*. The Lord's messenger sees only the Lord's finished work. He hears only the talk of wholeness. To him there is neither male nor female *(Gal. 8:28)*. To him it is easy to eat what is set before him, and ask no questions *(1 Cor. 10)*.

Paul did not go between them. He did not go on to the language beyond eating and not eating, though he had risen to say that neither if we eat are we the better, nor if we eat not are we the worse *(1 Cor. 8:8)*. We must go on to the next language. We must not stop to discuss what is right or wrong to eat, or what is the difference between the sexes.

The two that are in the field are, Soul unmolested, and flesh in mental turmoil. "Two shall be in the field," said Jesus the Master of the Unspoken Name; "the one shall be taken, the other left" *(Matt. 24:40)*.

John the Revelator told us to write to the Soul, whenever the mind and body present intellect, vanity or emotion, like a church wall of hiding to our doctrine.

There are seven types to whose angel we must write *(Rev. 2)*. First, there is the Ephesus type. They are the emotional, the excitement lovers. Then the Smyrnans. They are the lovers of adornment. Then there are the Pergamites. These are the lovers of art, literature, science and statecraft. Pergamos had temples dedicated to the gods of science, art, and government of life. The one to Science, whose keynote is healing was called *Aesculapius*. Out of the Pergamos type is to come the writer of the little book which is to alter the life of the world and usher in a new dispensation. Then there is the Sardis type. These are body devotees. They are afraid of draughts. They are afraid of what they eat. They are always seeking the comfortable, the soft, the pleasant things of bodily life. Then there are the Thyatirans. These are the easily offended. And the Philadelphians, who are the philanthropists of human existence, who seem so worthwhile yet whose vision is glued to human woe; we must write to their angel, otherwise their mind will never agree with the doctrine of unmolested Sonship to Jehovah. We must write to the angel of the Laodiceans also. These are the people who are always changing their religion.

We need not show these people the letters we have written to them. We can burn the letters. All addresses to the angel have subtle flavors that can penetrate through the strong walls of unlikeness to the meanings, without the necessity for acknowledged communion. Kings shall know that which they have not been taught, said Isaiah, in his fifty-second chapter.

"Now ye are come to an innumerable company of angels, written in heaven," said Paul to the Hebrews.

We must take Saturday and Sunday[23] of each week to write to the angel of some otherwise unreachable neighbor. We must keep high company. We are on a great ministry. It is no less than showing men their Sonship to God and their inheritance of the Jesus Christ character, free from the law of matter.

SUGGESTION

Fill the blank spaces with quotations from philosophers, poets, mystics, on the foregoing twelve points.

Put with them your own original inspirations as they come to you. So will you write your name with the stars, and make the foundation of an original book.

It has been prophesied that a little book is to come to the world, altering its life and ushering in a new dispensation.

No station in life, no age, no sex, no color, no previous acquirements, shall indicate the writer of the book.

Only the Keeper of the Name and the High Watch can write it. Should your hand pen the revolutionizing doctrine, no heart so praiseful as mine.   E. C. H.

---

[23] In later versions, Lesson XII is assigned to Saturday midday and letter writing is assigned to Sundays.

Afterword

The material in this book is as close as possible to the actual words that Emma Hopkins spoke and wrote during the period between 1889 and 1918. During that period, she is documented as having worked with 11,000 students, helping them overcome their own symptoms and learn how to treat others. When many of those students asked to become ordained into the ministry, she herself was ordained (by a former Methodist minister, a member of the board of her Seminary) and went on to ordain 110 ministers in the tradition that she came to call High Mysticism.

She closed her Seminary in 1906 and traveled, lecturing and working with individuals, until 1923, when a heart condition that she said "was not so much an illness, but rather God calling an end to a career" caused her to restrict her activities to the area around her family home outside of Killingly, Connecticut, for a year. She returned to her New York hotel room for one last season in fall and winter of 1924-1925, then made one last trip back to the farm, where she passed from this earth in April of 1925.

Her many followers treasured every word, and kept their notes and transcripts of her lectures, later publishing them as books "authored" by her. As a result, there are many versions of Emma Hopkins' 12 lessons in print. Some of them have been thoroughly edited; some were incomplete transcriptions to begin with.

The books on which this volume is based were all published within a few years of her passing, by her closest associates, so we have reason to believe that they are accurate renditions of her teachings.

At WiseWoman/Portal Center Press, it's our hope that you will find inspiration and a deeper understanding of this remarkable woman's teachings as you peruse the material in this volume. However, if you, like many before you, find her prose sometimes almost impenetrable, we offer the book *Unveiling Your Hidden Power* as a modern-language interpretation of the ideas and lessons that are offered here. For most, working through the *Unveiling* material makes it much easier to absorb the essence of what Emma called her "complicated way of explaining myself."

Bibliography

Emma Curtis Hopkins Materials published by WiseWoman Press

- First Lessons, from her journals, 1887
- Class Lessons Of 1888
- Scientific Christian Mental Practice
- Judgment Series In Spiritual Science
- Bible Interpretations, 1891 - 1893
- Genesis Series, 1894
- Drops Of Gold (A Quotidian)
- The Gospel Series In Spiritual Science
- High Mysticism, Studies In The Wisdom Of The Sages Of The Ages, 1918
- Resume, Practice Book For The Twelve Lessons In High Mysticism
- Esoteric Philosophy, Advanced Study

- Self-Treatments, Including The Radiant I Am (selected from her lessons and journals)

WISEWOMAN PRESS

An Imprint of

Portal Center Press

www.portalcenterpress.com

www.ingramcontent.com/pod-product-compliance
Lightning Source LLC
Chambersburg PA
CBHW030507080526
44586CB00011B/96